The Presocratics after Heidegger

SUNY Series in
Contemporary Continental Philosophy

Dennis J. Schmidt, Editor

The Presocratics after Heidegger

Edited By
David C. Jacobs

STATE UNIVERSITY OF NEW YORK PRESS

Production by Ruth Fisher
Marketing by Nancy Farrell

Published by
State University of New York Press, Albany

For information, address the State University of New York Press,
State University Plaza, Albany, NY 12246

Library of Congress Cataloging-in-Publication Data

The presocratics after Heidegger   /   edited by David C. Jacobs.
    p.   cm. — (SUNY series in contemporary continental
philosophy)
    Includes bibliographical references and index.
    ISBN 0-7914-4199-7 (hardcover   :   alk. paper). — ISBN 0-7914-4200-4
(pbk.   :   alk. paper)
    1. Pre-Socratic philosophers. 2. Heidegger, Martin, 1889–1976.
I. Jacobs, David C., 1962– . II. Series.
B187.5.P745 1999
182—dc21   98-47345
                                                                              CIP

10 9 8 7 6 5 4 3 2 1

In Memoriam

Reiner Schürmann
Teacher, Scholar, Thinker

Contents

vii

Acknowledgments

I gratefully appreciate the permission from Hermann Heidegger and Bouvier Verlag to publish a translation of Martin Heidegger's "Letzte, nicht vorgetragene Vorlesung (XII) aus dem Sommersemester 1952," *Hegel-Studien* (Bonn: Bouvier Verlag), Band 25 (1990), 23–34; from J. C. B. Mohr (Paul Siebeck) to publish a translation of Hans-Georg Gadamer's "Heraklit-Studien," in *Gesammelte Werke*, Band 7 (Tübingen: J. C. B. Mohr (Paul Siebeck), 1991), 43–82; from the editors at *SubStance* to publish Michel Serres' "Anaximander: A Founding Name in History," *SubStance*, vols. 71/72 (1993); and from David Smith, ed., *The Silverman Lectures* (Pittsburgh: Duquesne University Press, forthcoming) to publish Dennis J. Schmidt's "What We Didn't See."

Dennis Schmidt, Series Editor of Contemporary Continental Philosophy at SUNY Press, and John Sallis must be acknowledged for their initial and continual support for this collection from its inception. Without them, this project may never have begun and have come to its completion. Also, gratitude goes to the Editors and Staff at SUNY Press for their sponsorship of this book.

I express a deep thanks to the authors and the translators for their enthusiastic participation in the development and realization of this collection. Dr. Kristin Switala stands out as my chief source of inspiration; she has offered magnanimous support for this and all of my projects.

Abbreviations

GA 29–30   Die Grundbegriffe der Metaphysik—Welt, Endlichkeit, Einsamkeit (Frankfurt am Main: Vittorio Klostermann, 1983).

GA 33   Aristoteles: Metaphysik Θ 1–3 (Frankfurt am Main: Vittorio Klostermann, 1981).

GA 34   Vom Wesen der Wahrheit. Zu Platons Höhlengleichnis und Theätet (Frankfurt am Main: Vittorio Klostermann, 1988).

GA 39   Hölderlins Hymnen "Germanien" und "Der Rhein" (Frankfurt am Main: Vittorio Klostermann, 1980).

GA 40   Einführung in die Metaphysik (Frankfurt am Main: Vittorio Klostermann, 1983).

GA 45   Grundfragen der Philosophie. Ausgewahlt "Probleme" der "Logik" (Frankfurt am Main: Vittorio Klostermann, 1984).

GA 51   Grundbegriffe (Frankfurt am Main: Vittorio Klostermann, 1981).

GA 53   Hölderlins Hymne "Der Ister" (Frankfurt am Main: Vittorio Klostermann, 1984).

GA 54   Parmenides (Frankfurt am Main: Vittorio Klostermann, 1982).

GA 55   Heraklit (Frankfurt am Main: Vittorio Klostermann, 1979).

GA 65   Beiträge zur Philosophie (Vom Ereignis) (Frankfurt am Main: Vittorio Klostermann, 1989).

H   Heraklit (Frankfurt am Main: Vittorio Klostermann, 1970).

HW   Holzwege (Frankfurt am Main: Vittorio Klostermann, 1972).

N 1–2   Nietzsche, 2 vols. (Pfullingen: Günther Neske, 1961).

SD   Zur Sache des Denkens (Tübingen: Max Niemeyer, 1969).

SZ   Sein und Zeit (Tübingen: Max Niemeyer, 1956).

US   Unterwegs zur Sprache (Pfullingen: Günther Neske, 1965).

VA   Vorträge und Aufsätze (Pfullingen: Günther Neske, 1954).

W   Wegmarken (Frankfurt am Main: Vittorio Klostermann, 1978).

WD   Was Heisst Denken? (Tübingen: Max Niemeyer, 1961).

English Translations of Martin Heidegger's Texts

BC   *Basic Concepts*, trans. G. E. Aylesworth (Bloomington, IN: Indiana University Press, 1993).

BQ   *Basic Questions of Philosophy: Selected "Problems" of "Logic,"* trans. Richard Rojcewicz and André Schuwer (Bloomington, IN: Indiana University Press, 1994).

BT   *Being and Time*, trans. Joan Stambaugh (Albany, NY: SUNY Press, 1996)

BW   *Basic Writings*, Second Edition, ed. David Farrell Krell (New York: HarperCollins Publishers, 1993).

EB   "Hölderlin and the Essence of Poetry," trans. Douglas Scott, in *Existence and Being* (Chicago: Henry Regnery Company, 1949).

EGT   *Early Greek Thinking*, trans. David Farrell Krell and Frank A. Capuzzi (San Francisco: Harper & Row, 1975).

FCM   *Fundamental Concepts of Metaphysics: World, Finitude, Solitude*, trans. William McNeill and Nicholas Walker (Bloomington, IN: Indiana University Press, 1995).

HS   *Heraclitus Seminar*, trans. Charles H. Seibert (Evanston, IL: Northwestern University Press, 1979).

IM   *An Introduction to Metaphysics*, trans. Ralph Manheim (New Haven: Yale University Press, 1959).

NE 1–4   *Nietzsche*, 4 vols., trans. David Farrell Krell (San Francisco: Harper & Row, 1979).

OTB   *On Time and Being*, trans. Joan Stambaugh (New York: Harper & Row, 1972).

OWL   *On the Way to Language*, trans. P.D. Hertz (New York: Harper & Row, 1982).

P   *Parmenides*, trans. André Schuwer and Richard Rojcewicz (Bloomington, IN: Indiana University Press, 1992).

PLT   *Poetry, Language, Thought*, trans. Albert Hofstadter (New York: Harper & Row, 1971).

PR   *The Principle of Reason*, trans. Reginald Lilly (Bloomington, IN: Indiana University Press, 1991).

WGM   "The Way Back Into the Ground of Metaphysics," in *Existentialism from Dostoevsky to Sartre*, ed. and trans. Walter Kaufmann (New York: Meridian Books, 1966).

WCT   *What is Called Thinking?*, trans. Fred D. Wieck and J. Glenn Gray (New York: Harper & Row, 1968).

WP   *What is Philosophy?*, trans. Jean T. Wilde and William Kluback (Schenectady, NY: The New College and University Press, 1958); bi-lingual text.

Presocratic Greek Resource

DK   Hermann Diels and Walther Kranz, *Die Fragmente der Vorsokratiker*, sixth edition (Berlin: Weidmann, 1951). Diels and Kranz designate testimonial fragments about the Presocratics by other thinkers with the letter **A** and fragment number, and they indicate the direct citations of the Presocratics with the letter **B** and fragment number. All Presocratic fragments conform to the numbering of this edition of the text, unless otherwise noted.

Introduction

Heidegger, the History of Being, the Presocratics

David C. Jacobs

This collection of essays is devoted to thinking through Heidegger's reading of and relation to the Presocratics. For the articles written specifically for this collection, there was no attempt in the solicitation of authors to restrict their readings to a set viewpoint; instead, each author was given a topic and plenty of latitude. In this way, what we have is a wide array of approaches to Heidegger and the Presocratics. This collection is meant for those philosophically involved either in Presocratic scholarship, the works of Heidegger, or both. What I propose to do here in this introduction is to lay out Heidegger's approach to the history of philosophy so that an understanding of the Presocratics can be developed from this. Thus, for many who already have sufficient knowledge of Heidegger's relation with other philosophical thinkers this introduction will be unnecessary, and they can proceed directly to the articles. However, for those with philosophical training who lack an intimate knowledge of Heidegger's work, this introduction will prove to be useful, since the attempt is made to explicate Heidegger's engagement with our tradition.

Heidegger's innovation in his reading of the Presocratics stems from his awareness of the philological and philosophical debates surrounding how to interpret Presocratic thinkers *and* from his willingness to carry interpretation beyond the limits of these debates. Employing his often cited statement about the activity of phenomenology, Heidegger's reading and interpretation of the Presocratics remains open to possibility and is not restrained by the actuality of the current generation's scholarly debate.[1] Much criticism of his reading comes from the assumption that Heidegger is ignorant of or merely rejects the previous and current discussions of Presocratic interpretation.

1

This criticism, however, misunderstands Heidegger's aims and lacks an awareness of the tradition from which he thinks. Heidegger's reading of any thinker or philosopher[2] in the history of philosophy is not for him a place to rehearse all available interpretations and then to criticize a given thinker along with the interpretations themselves. From his early engagement with other philosophical figures within our history to his last works, Heidegger's project is to think in relation to these thinkers and philosophers. In order to understand his project, we need to speak briefly of two of his predecessors who shed light on how Heidegger understands the history of philosophy. Both Hegel and Nietzsche approach the history of philosophers not in order to add to the current debate over interpreting the arguments of the philosophers; they have another plan in their readings of others—*to think, to philosophize.* They both engage in a relationship with the history of philosophy in order to have an impact upon that history, not merely to sit near by speaking *about* philosophy but, rather, to be engaged in it. We shall see with both of these thinkers, as we shall witness with Heidegger, that they are not primarily concerned with a "correct representation" of prior philosophers but are philosophically engaged in the matter at hand. For both Hegel and Nietzsche, we do not historically return to the beginning of the history of philosophy in Greece, but we do return to the "soil" from which all philosophy grows, by engaging with prior philosophers in order to enter into the philosophical matter at hand, that is, what needs to be thought. For both, the matter to be thought is precisely that which we are entangled in without our explicit awareness: for Hegel, the dialectical process of the absolute spirit coming to have self-consciousness; for Nietzsche, the eternal return of the will to power.

In the first section, we will briefly examine Hegel's view of the history of philosophy as it relates to his metaphysical system, presented in his *Science of Logic*, and we will elucidate Nietzsche's view of the role of history with regard to the will to power and the eternal return. In the second section, with these views laid out, we will explain Heidegger's view of thinking within the history of being in light of these two views and his reading of the Presocratics. Finally, in the third section, we will propose a few directives on how we can think about the Presocratics and the history of philosophy *after* we have engaged in Heidegger's thinking.

Hegel and Nietzsche

Although the relationship between Hegel, Nietzsche, and Heidegger is extremely complicated, for our purposes here what is significant for all three is a need to have their thinking involved in the matter of the history of philosophy itself, that is, they attempt to take part in the movement of history itself by philosophizing. Although the three differ on what the matter of this history is, there are striking similarities in their approach: all three do not wish to rehearse the current debates surrounding the interpretations of philosophers; all three are not concerned with correct representations of previous philosophers; all three attempt to expose the "ground" of the history of philosophizing itself and thereby further what is necessary in this ground.

Hegel's great ingenuity is to detail the philosophers' principles, explaining the context of each, illustrating how and why the history of philosophy unfolds the way it does, and defending how his own philosophical view fits into this history (i.e., he attempts to think his own philosophy as historical). Because of this, Heidegger states, "Hegel is the only Western thinker who has thoughtfully experienced the history of thought" (EGT, 14). Moreover, Hegel does not separate the history of philosophy and his philosophical and metaphysical views. For this reason, the dialectical process of beginning can negate the indeterminate idea of being and proceed to the absolute idea, whereby absolute spirit comes to know itself, as presented in his *Science of Logic*. The pure "scientific" and dialectical unfolding of his philosophical view occurs in the specific stages in the history of philosophy. Hegel writes, "I maintain that the succession of philosophical systems in history is the same as their succession in the logical derivation of the categories of the idea."[3] Thus, Hegel interprets the history of philosophy as the same unfolding as his own metaphysical system, that is, as absolute spirit coming to know itself. What is significant for Hegel is that his own philosophical age in the history of the West is the culminating stage where absolute spirit attains self-consciousness. Like all stages in this history except the first, his stage is essentially connected to all prior stages that have preceded it and have determined it (ILHP, 11). Hegel reads the history of philosophy to be a progressive development from the first beginning of the Presocratic Greeks to the apex of the Enlightenment. Driving the history of philosophy is what all philosophers have attempted to explicate in their philosophical systems—the philosophical idea itself. Thus, Hegel does not hold that there are separate philosophical systems but one single, universal idea that is developing, or self-actualizing. He writes, "There is *one* idea, in the whole and in all its members, just as in a living individual *one* life, one pulse beats in all its limbs" (ILHP, 20). The one single idea that remains the center of philosophical systems is what develops in the history of philosophy because, Hegel says, it has the urge to develop; its nature is to develop itself (ILHP, 20, 67).

The dialectical process is the methodology that unfolds this development. This formal process of positing a thesis, contradicting with an antithesis, and uniting into a synthesis is at the root of all progressive development in Hegel's philosophical view; it is, however, differently expressed in the various regions of philosophical activity. The dialectical development of the philosophical idea in the history of philosophy is similar to its development in the *Science of Logic*. The development of the idea *in* the history of philosophy is of course *historical* or *in time* (and, because of this, the idea itself appears as tainted by the opinions of individual humans). The main thought or philosophical view of an age permeates all aspects of the age, culturally, artistically, religiously, philosophically, and so on (ILHP, 26, 88). Although the idea at its beginning is indeterminate and immediate, it must withdraw from its immediacy and become external by permeating the human world. The idea or spirit "externalizes" itself in order to be other to itself so that it can come to grasp itself. Since it is eternal, it becomes temporal in a world historical moment in order to conceive of itself other than it is. Hegel writes, "the spirit has to advance in the consciousness of itself, and this advance is the development of its whole mass, its concrete totality, which is externalized and so *falls into time*" (ILHP, 88; emphasis added). This falling into time allows for the externalization and for the grasping of itself; the content of the idea itself is not essentially affected by time.[4] This grasping progresses because in the subsequent stage the idea or spirit will externalize and grasp itself again but only to come to know itself better in a more explicit way. In each specific age, it grasps itself *and* all prior stages that have led up to it—and it continues until full self-grasping occurs.[5]

The Greek inception receives a significant place in Hegel's interpretation because it marks the emergence of self-consciousness, which in his account concerns the whole history of humanity. The Greeks free themselves from religious pictorial representations of the divine absolute and think on the level of pure thinking. That is, through the Greeks, absolute spirit first "descends into itself" and grasps its inner content and recognizes itself in this content (ILHP, 140, 171). This great inception which frees thinking into a pure realm of thought allows the absolute spirit to begin the twenty-five hundred year journey to self-consciousness that unfolds dialectically as the history of the West. The Presocratic Greeks receive distinction because "the starting-point of the Logic is the same as the starting-point of the history of philosophy" (EL, §86). In the abstract grasping of being by Parmenides, philosophy proper begins because pure thinking was first "objective," that is, it had the elements of universality and necessity (cf. EL, §41).

What remains significant in Hegel's philosophical endeavors for both Nietzsche and Heidegger to follow is that one does philosophy only when one is engaged with the matter at hand; for Hegel, this occurs through the historical/dialectical development of the absolute idea. In viewing his own philosophy as part of the historical and dialectical movement from abstract awareness to the full self-consciousness of absolute spirit, Hegel philosophizes about the major figures in the history of philosophy not in order to depict their principles and arguments *accurately* but in order to further the dialectical movement itself.[6] In other words, Hegel philosophizes about the Western philosophical tradition as historical in order *to philosophize*, to engage with the philosophical matter at hand—the absolute idea. As we will see, for both Nietzsche and Heidegger following Hegel on this point, to think then is to be engaged *with* the history that precedes one's own thinking and is the condition for one's own thinking.

Nietzsche's early view of history, expressed in "On the Uses and Disadvantages of History for Life," advance the position that humans need the activity of history not for the truth but for the sake of life and action.[7] In order to use history for the advancement of life, Nietzsche holds, one must both live historically (i.e., recall certain historical events) and unhistorically (i.e., forget certain historical events).[8] The historical and the unhistorical are necessary for the health of an individual, of a people, and of a culture (UM, II, §1). The health stated here is dependent upon the soil on which it thrives. This soil which allows the condition of health is life itself, which Nietzsche cryptically defines here as "that dark, driving power that insatiably thirsts for itself" (UM, II, §3). Each individual, community, and culture must determine how it is to be historical and unhistorical, how it is to do history, and how it is to thrive. Although Nietzsche lays out different possibilities of how one can do history (i.e., monumental, antiquarian, and critical), when we think of how he approaches the history of philosophy later in his thinking, we see how his general conception of history becomes an enactment of critical history. In other words, Nietzsche's own view becomes a re-thinking of how history must be done in order to aid life itself, and he brings current ways of doing history, philosophy, and morality before a tribunal to examine them and finally condemn them (UM, II, §3). In this form of history and Nietzsche's philosophizing, one forgets all that might be beneficial to life but concentrates on the fact that life is somehow dying from its own past. Here, one "takes the knife to one's roots" severing oneself from the past in order to live in the future (UM, II, §3), that is, in order to let life thrive once again. One must kill that "nature" in us that is destroying us and replace it with a "nature" that benefits life. Nietzsche writes,

> The best we can do is to confront our inherited and hereditary nature with our knowledge of it, and through a new, stern discipline combat our inborn heritage and implant in ourselves a new habit, a new instinct, a second nature, so that our first nature withers away (UM, II, §3).

Nietzsche's own approach to history is not to have "a consuming fever of history" (i.e., to excavate every minute detail of history and express it), but to remember only what aids life itself. Although this can be done in a variety of ways, Nietzsche's re-thinking of the historical practice is itself critical, severing itself away from the historical fever.

In the first, quite significant turn in his thinking, Nietzsche lays out not a new understanding of history but a fuller one in relation to life itself. In *Human, All Too Human*, he proclaims, "what is needed from now on is *historical philosophizing*."[9] This new type of philosophy is concerned with the history of the genesis of thought by tracing terms and concepts back to their *historical* origin and their *physiological* origin without an attempt to find a pure metaphysical starting place (see HATH, §§ 10, 18). Thus, Nietzsche, like Hegel, attempts to think and philosophize about philosophy in its historical contexts and dimensions; however, he differs from Hegel in that he wants to relate philosophy more intimately to its historical contexts.

This turn that takes place in Nietzsche's thought in the late 1870s does not form a philosophy that is distinct from his later genealogy, but is does express a view that flourishes in his later work. After the ideas of the will to power and the eternal return have been thought and added to his thinking, his genealogical philosophy becomes more complete. In his later thinking, Nietzsche's experiences his own ideas as "intertwined and interlaced;"[10] each performs its task or tasks in the battle against the Platonic and idealistic tradition. Nietzsche still maintains that our "nature" must be replaced with a second "nature." He enacts this replacement with his genealogical thinking which does not attempt to find a pure origin by maintaining a faith in opposite values—that is, in pure/impure, good/evil, eternal/temporal, etc.[11] On the contrary, Nietzsche continually attempts to disrupt the construction and continuance of these metaphysical dichotomies by tracing the "eternal" ideas and values back to very "temporal" conditions. Thus, he shows that philosophies, ideas, and moralities do not have a pure origin and what is maintained within them are not pure, good, and eternal, but rather mixed with their opposites (see BGE, §2).

At the heart of his genealogical thinking is the dual role of interpretation and evaluation. Each living entity interprets according to force that it is in relation to other forces. Thus, his perspectivism surely falls into a relativism if one still maintains the standard of an absolute, objective viewpoint. However, Nietzsche continually disrupts our tendency to accept such a viewpoint by asking—from where does the need for this viewpoint come? He writes in his notes, "not 'to know' but to schematize—to impose upon chaos as much regularity and form as our practical needs require."[12] This imposition of regularity and form takes place and must take place in order for the living entity, the human being, to live. Humans schematize by subsuming the particulars of experience according to general ideas and concepts. Nietzsche maintains that the heart of human experience is given over to an artistic enterprise; his sword, however, is double-edged—all of humanity has this creative ability to invent by schematizing, but its views are not and cannot be eternally true, because they are necessary fictions that are life-enhancing. By re-orienting us toward the conditions of our ideas, philosophical thinking and thus all generalizing becomes interpretation that is carried out for one's own life or for the rationalization of a way of life. What in life is driving one to do this? For Nietzsche, it is not merely self-preservation, but the will to power—which includes the venting of one's strength (BGE, §13). This venting involves "appropriation, injury, overpowering of what is alien and weaker, suppression, hardness, imposition of one's own forms, incorporation. . . . " (BGE, §259). By introducing the will to power as the driving force of all living things, including human beings, Nietzsche can revaluate the philosophical tradition which attempts to remain pure, good, and eternal. Instead, he thinks the philosophical tradition in its historical conditions—that is, how each philosopher comes to think from out of a historical context.[13] One's theories, ideas, and moralities were attempts to schematize the chaos in order to vent its strength, and this tradition cannot own up to its deeds. Thus, Nietzsche holds that even though philosophers do attempt to vent their strength and the strength of their way of life upon the world and others, they are also slandering of life itself because they cannot view the mixture of their pure philosophical actions with the drives that compel them to philosophize.

Instead of the pure origin of all things from a godhead, Nietzsche strategically places the will to power and the eternal return at the center of this thinking. The world as we know it, our values as we revere them, and our souls as we attempt to maintain an ideal state—all are not from a pure, metaphysical source. They are part of the world of the will to power. Nietzsche writes:

> This world: a monster of energy, without beginning, without end; a firm, iron magnitude of force that does not grow bigger or smaller, that does not expend itself but only transforms itself [. . . .] *This world is the will to power—and nothing besides!* And you yourselves are this will to power—and nothing else! (WTP, §1067)

Although the eternal return receives psychological interpretations from what is said in *The Gay Science* (§341) and physical interpretations from his comments in *The Will to Power* (§§ 1053–67, *et passim*), Nietzsche's use of the idea, like all of his ideas, attempts to battle the traditional drive of philosophy toward another world which thereby devalues this world and life. This world, the only world we know, is for Nietzsche the will to power transforming itself continually, and it will eventually transform itself back into its previous shape. This idea, however, is not expressed to characterize a general law about nature, but to challenge the idea of a metaphysical origin of all things that has become our "nature"—since, it has become innate to believe that there must be a pure origin. Nietzsche employs the will to power and the eternal return as strategies to impede what he calls the "orbit" of philosophical thinking. These ideas are presented to "break open" (WTP, §1057) the possibilities in our thinking, or, better stated, allows us to re-acquaint ourselves with the conditions for the possibility of thinking at all—forces, drives, creativity, invention, etc. Thus, Nietzsche's re-thinking of philosophy is an attempt to transform philosophy itself by returning to its historical context. He re-thinks how philosophy takes place by finding a hidden ground for thinking, but this ground is not a pure, metaphysical origin; it is only the place from which one person thinks which remains connected to other people, places, forces, and so on.

Nietzsche's re-thinking of our tradition does not demand that he correctly represent the thinkers before his own time. He lays out another's ideas merely to prompt his own thinking so that he can put forth the strategies needed to battle the tradition. This does not mean that he attempts an easy way out, because he takes on the whole tradition, battling the chief metaphysical ideas. In thinking this way, then, Nietzsche is not simply escaping the tradition but transforming it by re-thinking what is necessary for the tradition to live.[14] In other words, he is attempting to replace the first "nature" with a "second" that affirms the conditions of its possibilities, and thereby upholds the historicality of philosophy and thinking.

Both Hegel and Nietzsche surely impose their own philosophical viewpoints upon the historical figures they interpret. However, they do this in order to be engaged with the philosophical matter at hand—for Hegel, in order to advance the development of absolute spirit; for Nietzsche, in order to return thinking *affirmatively* to the historical context by invoking the eternal return of the will to power. Both have a philosophical and historical relation to the philosophical tradition; they both maintain that one cannot merely repeat what one has said prior to one's own thinking. Rather, one must philosophize in relation to others in order to do one's own philosophy. In this way, they do not attempt comprehensive and correct representations of the other philosophers' views, but they remain involved with what propels their own thinking.

This argument may appear to relieve both thinkers of any responsibility for philosophical scholarship, but the demand for correct representations is based on an a-historical conception of philosophy which is assumed to be the true way of philosophizing. One assumes in this case that we can easily extract the philosophical arguments from a prior historical period without losing their historical meaning. The hermeneutical issue of traveling to another historical horizon with different values, linguistic meanings, and philosophical truths is left aside in the "correct representation" of another's thought. What one is doing, however, is interpreting from one's own historical position with the priority of *its* values, linguistic meanings, and philosophical truths. In other words, when one attempts a "correct representation" one is still imposing one's view upon another as Hegel and Nietzsche do; the philosopher is merely extricating philosophical bits and pieces from another's thought and then fits these parts into a contemporary schema. This view does not attempt to think the prior view and especially its own view as part of a history; one attempts to interpret the predecessor and keep one's own thinking *a-historical*. This presupposition of the "correct representation" of earlier thinkers warrants some deeper thought about historical philosophizing and about one's own philosophical and historical purpose in philosophy itself.

Heidegger's History of Being and His Reading of the Presocratics

Heidegger draws essential aspects from both Hegel and Nietzsche's philosophical views of history and especially the history of philosophy, but transforms these aspects as he appropriates them for his own thinking. From Hegel, Heidegger reads the history of philosophy as falling into epochal periods, where all aspects of the culture are governed by an essential principle. For Heidegger, the question of history will be how the determination of epoch periods occurs and how human thinking is involved in this determination. From Nietzsche, Heidegger maintains that a transformation took place in classical Greece that changed the West and that the metaphysical thinking inaugurated there has resulted in nihilism. For Nietzsche and Heidegger, a thoughtful relation to history can transplant us out of this nihilism; thus, both offer a philosophy *for* the future. Nietzsche offers a destructive upheaval severing us from the life-denying past and returning us to an affirmation of the forces of life. Heidegger puts forth a preparatory thinking that returns us to metaphysics, that steps back into metaphysics so that we "enter into a questioning that experiences" (BW, 246)—that is, the originary experience that prompts all thinking, what Plato and Aristotle call wonder (Θαυμάζειν).[15] By this stepping back, we are placed into a new relation with what should be thought—that is, we raise the question of being anew (see BT and SZ, §1). Just as the will to power is the ground of history but not independent of history, Heidegger's understanding of being is also the ground of and grounded in history; it should not be thought of as outside of history. As is the case for both Hegel and Nietzsche, Heidegger's connection to the history of philosophy is not about duplicating what has been said prior to his own thinking; his concern is to have a philosophical connection with prior philosophers in their thinking *in order to think* on his own. Thus, Heidegger heeds both Hegel and Nietzsche's approaches on this point; philosophical activity should not remain at a safe distance from what is to be thought, by accurately depicting the principles and logical arguments, but instead should and must make a thoughtful connection to the matter of philosophy itself. What must be spelled out then is what the matter of philosophy is in the history of being, how Heidegger develops a relationship with the matter of philosophy, how Heidegger approaches philosophers and thinkers within the history of philosophy, and how he reads the Presocratics.

Heidegger reads the history of Western philosophy as the response on the part of the philosopher to heed the call of being, to respond to what calls thinking to think—being itself (PLT, 183). Being for Heidegger is not a particular being, the highest being, or the most general being, but, thought in a verbal sense, being is the event that dispenses, gives over, and allows for the unconcealment of beings to human thinking. Heidegger calls this the dispensation and giving of *presencing*, that is, beings come to show themselves in their presence to human thinking (OTB, 5).[16] Being for Heidegger is the event of this presencing, this giving over of beings to thinking. Why does Heidegger characterize being as *presencing*? In the 1962 lecture, "Time and Being," Heidegger answers this question:

This question comes too late. For this character of being has long since been decided without our contribution, let alone our merit. Thus we are bound to the characterization of being as presencing. It derives its binding force from the beginning of the unconcealment of being as something that can be said, that is, can be thought. Ever since the beginning of Western thinking with the Greeks, all saying of 'being' and 'is' held in remembrance of the determination of being as presencing which is binding for thinking (OTB, 6–7).

In other words, characterizing being as the presencing of beings is not Heidegger's interpretation, but has already occurred in our tradition; philosophers have thought of beings in their presence and their coming to presence (i.e., their presencing, their dispensation to human thought) according a basic principle of presence. What has allowed this basic principle to guide human thinking according to presence, for Heidegger, is being itself thought here as the historical event that determines the meaning of beings. Thus, for Heidegger, being lets or allows for presence. "To let presence means: to unconceal, to bring to openness" (OTB, 5). How beings appear to human awareness is governed by the historical event that delivers or unconceals beings over to thinking.

Philosophers respond to how being dispenses beings, i.e., how beings come to show themselves to the thinking of philosophers. Heidegger writes, "to think 'being' means to respond to the appeal of its presencing. The response stems from the appeal and releases itself toward that appeal" (OTB, 183). This appeal or call by being is not some mystical revelation that appears only to asocial thinkers, but is the appeal or call that occurs in the showing of all beings to thinking—what Aristotle calls φαινομένον, what appears or shows itself. In explaining how Parmenides came to his statements about being and non-being, Aristotle states that Parmenides "was compelled to follow the phenomenon" (ἀναγκαζόμενος δ' ἀκολουθεῖν τοῖς φαινομένοις, *Metaphysics*, 986b31).[17] In a very basic way, humans in philosophical reflection come to think about what appears to them—beings. In philosophical reflection, Heidegger maintains that thinking can get caught up in beings *or* think about what allows for this showing of beings. Thus, Heidegger wants to exploit the dual sense of the Greek φαινομένον—it is the appearing or showing *of* the things that appear. What we receive in the appearing of things to our awareness is on the one hand the things as they appear, but on the other hand the appearing, the showing of things to us. The dual aspect of showing has prompted philosophers to distinguish ordinary beings and the highest being (forms, substance, God), but for Heidegger the understanding of the highest being is still ontic—that is, a thinking determined by a thinking of beings.[18] The showing of beings cannot be understood according to an understanding of beings. This showing must be understood as that which determines the meaning of beings presented. In Heidegger's thinking, one must think the ontological difference between beings and being (BW, 226), that is, the beings presented to thinking and the showing of these beings.

From a realist perspective, we might want to say that things just appear as they are and that there is no appearing or showing in itself. The realist, however, cannot account for the extreme diversity in fundamental interpretations of what it means *to be* in our history. Heidegger does not want to follow the arrogance of the realist who claims that the world is and appears (and has been and has appeared) exactly as it does to this human subject, nor in contrast does he want to follow the idealist who claims that the world is as it is due to this human subjectivity. Heidegger here falls outside the traditional dichotomy. In different historical periods, what it means *to be* has been thought differently because being has dispensed beings *to be* in a unique way for each epoch. Although thinkers have thought beings according to presence, how beings appeared or showed themselves to thinking occurred in their own unique way for different epochs of Western history. The realist merely responds and says that humans did not depict these things as accurately *as we do today*, and the Hegelian idealist would respond by saying that beings appeared differently because of the development of absolute spirit (which our consciousness aids in thinking). Heidegger sidesteps the arrogance of the realist who believes that we, in a contemporary setting, view the world correctly and can condemn the entire tradition for viewing it incorrectly. Also, he does not affirm the role of consciousness that is crucial to the idealist—that is, Heidegger dismisses the interpretation that our consciousness (aiding the absolute spirit) is *determining* what it means to be for beings. We will have to spell out below the role of human thinking, its relation to being, and how thinking and beings are connected.

Heidegger reads the history of the West as the history of being where different epochs have expressed a distinct thinking and living; what it means *to be* is unique for each epoch of history. The question then is how being is related to history by dispensing or showing beings to human thinking. Heidegger does not want to split up reality with the temporal and sensible on one side and the atemporal and supersensible on the other. For Heidegger, there are not two different realms—on the contrary, since the unfolding of history and the thoughts about beings are inseparable from the being within history, both are *within history* (in this way, he is following Nietzsche and not Hegel; the latter still maintains a realm independent of historical movements, while the former affirms only the realm of history). Always attentive to the etymology of words, Heidegger understands history (*Geschichte*) and destiny (*Geschick*) in the verbal sense of sending (*schicken*). Thus, what is presented to human thinking within a historical epoch is sent or offered to it by the epochal event itself, what Heidegger calls being. Being for him is not a being outside of time and history determining what it means to be for beings and humans (for this would be being as the highest being), but being is the dispensing or sending of the event of history itself. Being dispenses beings to human thinking, but does not show itself separately from this showing or appearing of beings. Heidegger writes, "the history of being is the '*Geschick*' of being that offers itself to us in withdrawing its essence" (PR, 61). Being offers itself to us in the showing or dispensing of beings, but it does not, over and above this showing of beings, show itself as separate from beings. Being in its showing of being withdraws, Heidegger says, in favor of giving or dispensing beings over to thinking (OTB, 8). How can we understand this withdrawing or holding back of being showing itself in the showing or dispensing of beings? Heidegger attempts to connect the withholding of being in its showing of beings and the history of being, for it is precisely the withholding that allows for the sending of beings and the sending of history. The sending or showing of beings that being enacts allows for the historical epoch, in the way that Heidegger reorients our thinking to an historical period. This sending of beings by being itself holds back or withdraws; it does not have a self-manifestation, only the manifestation of beings. Heidegger writes:

> To hold back is, in Greek, ἐποχή. Hence we speak of the epochs of the destiny of being. Epoch does not mean here a span of time in occurrence, but rather the fundamental characteristic of sending, the actual holding-back of itself in favor of the discernibility of the gift, that is, of being with regard to the grounding of beings (OTB, 9).

Thus, each historical epoch, in which beings appear to human thinking differently according to the sending or showing of being, has the dispensation of beings because of the withholding of being. What else do different epochs have in common? In each, philosophers have been claimed in their thinking by the dispensation of being and have *expressed* the fundamental meaning and truth of beings in their writings; the history of being, for Heidegger, "comes to language in the words of essential thinkers" (BW, 238). Humans, therefore, have a significant role to play in the dispensation and showing of beings.

There is not a dialectical, progressive process occurring in the history of philosophy as Hegel thinks, and although Heidegger calls attention to an oblivion of being (i.e., being remains basically unthought in our contemporary epoch) there is not a regressive process as Nietzsche contends. For Heidegger, there is a free succession[19] between historical epochs, because the historical periods are not dependent upon their prior epochs to determine how thinking and living are to occur. How one comes to think is dependent upon how being dispenses beings to thinking—although within the context of how being dispenses beings to human thinking there is a fundamental decision humans can make: to think being in its dispensing and showing of beings *or* to think being according to beings, that is, to think metaphysically.

In Heidegger's reading of previous philosophers and thinkers, his concern in following Hegel and Nietzsche is not to depict their arguments and main principles (for this would not be philosophizing), but his interest lies in determining how their thinking was claimed by being in the dispensation of beings. Why, however, *engage with* previous philosophers? We already witnessed that Hegel does this in order to advance the self-consciousness of absolute spirit, and Nietzsche does this to battle the tradition by affirming the historical contexts of philosophy and thinking. Why does Heidegger involve himself with other thinkers? He does this not in order to criticize previous philosophers nor to accurately present and argue about their positions, but in order to establish a dialogue with them. For Heidegger, to criticize or to accurately present earlier philosophical positions amounts to keeping a distance from the thinking that has occurred—or, more importantly, to remain distant from one's own possibility of thinking. Heidegger writes:

> Philosophy demands that we do not look *away* from it, but apprehend it from out of itself. Philosophy itself—what do we know of it, and what and how is it? It itself *is* only whenever we are philosophizing. *Philosophy is philosophizing* (FCM, 4).

Thus, Heidegger's approach to philosophy and to previous philosophers is to be involved with philosophy, i.e., to philosophize, to think the philosophical matter that demands to be thought. Heidegger enacts dialogues with philosophers in our tradition in order to make a connection with what they spoke, what they philosophized about; he does this in order to think, in order to philosophize himself. Heidegger writes in *What is Philosophy?*:

> When do we philosophize? Obviously when we enter into a dialogue (*Gespräch*) with philosophers. This implies that we talk through (*durchsprechen*) with them that about which they speak (WP, 66–7).

If philosophers are responding to the dispensation of being, that is, how being presents beings to thinking, then Heidegger's concern in dialogues is to think how philosophers have been claimed in their thinking by being so that one's own philosophizing thinks how one is claimed in *this* historical epoch. The concern has to be then what happens to one's own thinking while partaking in such a dialogue. He continues:

> If we assume that the being of beings addresses itself to philosophers to the extent that they state what beings are, insofar as they are, then our dialogue with philosophers must also be addressed by the being of beings (WP, 66–9).

Many critics have asserted that Heidegger does not portray the philosophers in our tradition with accuracy. His concern, however, is to read them as they respond to the claim of being, that is, how being dispenses beings to their thinking and how they respond by thinking and writing. Following Hegel and Nietzsche, he wants to be engaged with the matter of philosophy and history itself. Heidegger re-reads a philosopher's main principles in light of how they are a response to being's claim. Does this mean then, as critics claim, that Heidegger merely ends up doing his own philosophy when interpreting our tradition? Following Hegel and Nietzsche on this point, Heidegger always stays within the thinking that is first and foremost concerned with thinking what should be thought—that is, he responds to the claim that being itself makes upon his thinking. To answer the question, then, we might say that he is doing his own thinking, the thinking that is called upon to think.

Heidegger understand this re-thinking of our tradition as *Destruktion*. In *Being and Time*, though he is not primarily concerned with a dialogue with other philosophers, the problem arises as to how we are to think the question of being regarding its own history in our tradition. Heidegger does not want to read philosophers according to the traditional answers to the question of being (i.e., to depict their systems accurately), but to raise the question of being itself. Similar to the dynamic of the dialogue mentioned above, Heidegger sees *Destruktion* as a "loosening of the sclerotic tradition and a dissolving of the concealments" (BT, 20). A *Destruktion* is carried out not to reconnect with our past by returning to it, but "to come into full possession of the most proper possibilities of inquiry" (BT, 18; SZ, 21). Years later, in 1955, Heidegger still thinks of his approach to the tradition according to the idea of a *Destruktion* of the history of philosophy. He writes:

> *Destruktion* does not mean destroying, but dismantling, excavating, putting to one side the merely historiographical assertions about the history of philosophy. *Destruktion* means to open our ears, to make ourselves free for what speaks to us in the tradition as the being of beings (WP, 70–3).

The *Destruktion* that occurs does not merely dismantle the tradition but alters our relationship to our tradition, enabling us to think *how* metaphysical thinkers come to think, that is, what calls them to think, to question, and to put forth metaphysical systems. What are these "most proper possibilities of inquiry" that can be awakened in our dialogue with previous philosophers and thinkers? Heidegger answers this question in "Moira (Parmenides VIII, 34–41)":

> Proper inquiry must be a dialogue in which the ways of hearing and points of view of ancient thinking are thought according to their essential origin, so that the claim (under which past, present, and future thinking—each in its own way—all stand) might begin to announce itself (EGT, 86).

Thus, in entering a dialogue with previous philosophers and thinkers, that is, in employing a *Destruktion* of the obscuring layers that cover

over our tradition, Heidegger attempts to be addressed and claimed by what addresses and claims all thinking—being in its dispensation and sending of beings and the sending of the contemporary epoch. In other words, Heidegger's interpretation of philosophy and thinking is done in order to think, in order to philosophize, because *"philosophy is philosophizing"* (FCM, 4). All the criticisms of Heidegger's questionable interpretations of previous philosophers come down to this question: What does it mean to philosophize and think in our contemporary epoch? This question Heidegger takes seriously and continually thinks through. To philosophize and think is to think the claim that being makes upon us in the dispensation of beings and the historical sending of our epoch.

If Heidegger is determined to bring about a dismantling of and hence re-connection with our tradition by having a dialogue with philosophers and thinkers in order to think and be claimed by being, why does he then have a preoccupation with the Presocratics? Granted that Plato and Aristotle represent the beginning of philosophy and the center of re-thinking for him during the stage of "fundamental ontology" (as manifested in the thematic of *Being and Time*), the Presocratics here still play a part, and they take on a significant role after this stage. In his middle and later thinking, the Presocratics are the continual touchstone for his re-thinking of the tradition. What must be kept in mind is that Heidegger does not read these thinkers in order to lay out their principles for inspection, but in order to re-connect with what they thought. The Presocratic thinkers remain crucial for Heidegger because they are *pre*-metaphysical—what they think gets covered over in later metaphysical thinking. Plato's and especially Aristotle's metaphysical interpretations of their predecessors get handed down in our tradition, and the predominate view of the Presocratics becomes that they are naive metaphysicians. This view takes hold because Plato and Aristotle become the benchmark for metaphysical philosophy, and any view not up to this standard is labeled inferior to their great systems. Heidegger's dialogue with the Presocratics is an attempt to think along with them without the Platonic and Aristotelian framework draped over their thinking, and it is here that Heidegger's *Destruktion* comes into full force. By not continuing the naive metaphysical labeling of the Presocratics and by not becoming caught up in the current interpretative debates (a continuance of the Platonic and Aristotelian heritage, for Heidegger), he can attempt to dismantle the interpretive layers that obscure Presocratic thinking and "to open our ears, to make ourselves free for what speaks to us in the tradition as the being of beings" (WP, 72–73). To what do we open our ears? What is uncovered in the Presocratics? With this *Destruktion* or dialogue with the Presocratics, Heidegger underscores for us time and again—this is done "to make ourselves free for what speaks to us in the tradition"; this is done to affect us, to change how we think, and to think about our own historical context that brings about our own thinking. This is not done so that Presocratic scholarship will get to the *real* Presocratic philosophy. The attempt on Heidegger's part is to construct a dialogical relationship with the Presocratics *so that* he (and we) can come to think that which called them to think and *so that* we can come to be called by this.

Although Heidegger does some exegesis of Pindar, Homer, and other ancient poets, his reading of the Presocratics generally centers around Anaximander, Parmenides, and Heraclitus. Since extensive interpretations of Heidegger's reading of these Presocratic thinkers have been published for decades now, what needs to be done here is to express why Heidegger goes to these thinkers for a thoughtful dialogue. In regards to these three thinkers, Heidegger writes:

> Anaximander, Parmenides, and Heraclitus are the only inceptional thinkers. They are this, however not because they open up Western thought and initiate it. Already before them there were thinkers. They are inceptional thinkers (*anfängliche Denker*) because they think the inception (*den Anfang*). The inception is what is sought in their thinking. [. . .] The inception is that which begins (*anfängt*) something with these thinkers—by laying claim on them in such a way that from them is demanded an extreme retreating before being. These thinkers are the *in-cepted* by the *in-ception* (*die vom An-fang An-gefangenen*); they are taken up by it and are gathered into it (P, 7–8; GA 54, 10–11).

Heidegger examines Anaximander's saying in order to see how he thought the coming to presence, lingering, and passing away of beings. From his reading of Parmenides, he can view how the Eleatic experienced but did not fully think the duality of τὸ ἐόν (i.e., the presencing of beings) and how thinking and saying are intimately connected in the meaning of being. For Heraclitus, he thinks not only the role of λόγος as the gathering and letting lie of the epochal event of being but also

how ἀλήθεια as unconcealment and concealment govern his thinking
of nature (φύσις) as what reveals itself and hides along with this re-
vealment (cf. Heraclitus, Fragment B16).

Heidegger reads the extant works of these Presocratic thinkers as
they were drawn to think what called or laid claim upon them to think.
Heidegger labels this the "first inception." Heidegger performs these
readings not to uncover the hidden history of our tradition (although
something like this does occur); he does this to affect us in our thinking—that is, in order to "retrieve (wieder-holen) the inception of our his-
torical-spiritual existence, in order to transform it into the other
inception (anderen Anfang)" (IM, 39; EM, 29).[20] Although Heidegger
maintains that these Presocratic thinkers experienced the inception and
attempted to think it and bring it to language in their writings, they
do not fully think the inception. Their thinking is still fundamentally
caught up with beings (GA 65, 179). He constructs his dialogue with
the Presocratic thinkers in their first inception so that we can come to
be thoughtfully involved in the "other inception" that can occur in the
present age. What Heidegger is preparing in his dialogue with the
Presocratics then is a "transition from metaphysics to another thinking
(andere Denken)" (WGM, 220) In other words, Heidegger attempts a
dialogue with the Presocratics, not to add to the scholarship of authors
who dispute the "arguments" of their fragments, but to think what
prompted the Greeks to think in this way in the first place. What occurs
in this other thinking, in this other inception? We experience and think
explicitly the truth of how being calls us to think (GA 65, 179), how we
come to think because of the dispensation and showing of beings, and
how our thinking is historically bound to our epoch.

Concluding Questions after Heidegger

Heidegger gives us no set methodology that we can follow in our
thinking in order to be thinking correctly. He offers paths of thought
that he has ventured in order to think, in a preliminary way, the truth
of being and how we come to think within our historical context.
However, these paths are not a meta-level narrative (a prolegomena)
to direct our future endeavors in philosophical reflection. I think that
he does present to us two main directives that can be followed up in
our own thinking. After engaging one's thinking within the Heideggerian corpus, one cannot dismiss the need and urgency when discussing

philosophy and philosophical figures *to philosophize* and the need to think about one's own *historical context of thinking*. Both of these elements Heidegger shares with Hegel and Nietzsche, but he alters them to provide us with that which is thought-provoking. As Nietzsche might ask: How now for us? We must engage with the Presocratics, with Heidegger, with our tradition, in order to philosophize, in order to determine and to think about the matter of thought—not merely to argue with other scholars about the correct interpretations of the main principles of others.

If we take seriously the historical nature of thinking as presented in Heidegger's works, then we must come to think not only the historical contexts of previous philosophers, but our own as well. What is it that calls us to think in our own contemporary epoch? Is it the call of being, the loss of eternal values, the suspicion of grand narratives, the consequences of practical matters, the transformation into an information age? What we must determined is not whether Heidegger is correct with this interpretation or that, but why *we* come to philosophize at all. What is it about our own historical epoch that conditions us to think in the way we do and to have these ontological commitments that we do? Following *after* Heidegger, not merely chronologically but philosophically, prompts us to *re-think* Heidegger's works, the Presocratic fragments, and the traditional philosophical problems so that we can come to think our historical and philosophical matter at hand. That is, why is it that after twenty-five hundred years of philosophical reflection we are still compelled to ponder the *why* of this activity? This is not a useless, academic question proposed so that we can turn in continuous reflective circles; it is a question to be asked and answered so that we can determine what it means to be, to think, and to be historical. In other words, it is the question that we must face philosophically before all others. Again, why do we philosophize? Following Heidegger, we should not ask this because we are concerned with what philosophy can do for us. Heidegger writes, "might not philosophy, if we concern ourselves with it, do something *with us*? (IM, 12; EM, 10).

NOTES

1. Heidegger's statement about phenomenology reads, "higher than actuality stands *possibility*" (BT, 34; SZ, 38).

2. Although Heidegger usually distinguishes between thinkers and philosophers by maintaining that thinkers think and say being as it is and philosophers think being metaphysically (to be defined later), for the purposes of this introduction I will conflate the terms.

3. G. W. F. Hegel, *Introduction to the Lectures on the History of Philosophy*, trans. T. M. Knox and A. V. Miller (Oxford: Clarendon Press, 1987), 22; henceforth, this text is cited as ILHP with pagination.

4. Cf. G. W. F. Hegel, *The Encyclopaedia Logic*, trans. T. F. Geraets, W. A. Suchting, H. S. Harris (Indianapolis, IN: Hackett Publishing, 1991), §20; henceforth, this text is cited as EL with section number.

5. Hegel's dialectical thinking also presents the entire history of Western philosophy in three main stages. The Greek beginning of philosophy occurs when the "essence of things comes into consciousness in the form of pure thinking" (ILHP, 165). This awareness of the essence of things comes about by grasping the metaphysical principle of all things—what Hegel calls the beginning of all things. This grasping of the essence of all things marks the beginning of pure thinking producing itself. In this way, philosophical freedom occurs when thought rises above mere pictorial representation and "apprehends the idea of the absolute" (ILHP, 164); in this beginning, Hegel holds, the spirit thinks itself and constitutes its being (ILHP, 172). Following Greek philosophy is the philosophy of the middle ages which Hegel calls either Roman and Christian philosophy (ILHP, 175) or Scholasticism (EN, §31); this period did not grasp its philosophical content but presupposes it as given—specifically, in Christian theological philosophy the content was *given* by the Church (EN, §31). In Hegel's reading, however, this lengthy period of theological philosophy was the "externalization" of the spirit. Consciousness did not grasp its content because it was not apprehended as posited by itself but externally, i.e., from religious authorities. Modernity, or what Hegel calls "Germanic philosophy," begins with Descartes conceptually returning home to the spirit (dramatically depicted when Hegel places the famous "Land Ho!" in Descartes's mouth, as if philosophically thinking had been out to sea and has finally achieved its destination—the self-conscious awareness of the conceptual). This arrival or return occurs when consciousness comes to grasp the spirit again and becomes aware that the subject and object are but the same; Hegel writes, "this is the Germanic principle, this unification of subject and object" (ILHP, 179). This awareness is based on the self-producing absolute; when pure thought occurs the subject produces the object at the same time. The dialectic plays itself out in each specific stage of philosophy but also in history as a whole. The three main stages are unfolded dialectically as the self-productive beginning of consciousness grasping the essence of all things; although still abstract, this beginning requires further dialectical development. In the second stage, the absolute appears as other to consciousness as an absolute content only to be perceived pictorially. In the last stage, consciousness comes to grasp the absolute and apprehends that it is that which grasps and that which is grasped.

6. An "accurate" portrayal of a philosopher's view would include aspects of this philosophy that were merely temporal (i.e., connected to the personal opinion of the philosopher) and not eternal. Hegel's project is to interpret what is eternal in each philosophy; in this way, he must overlook certain details that do not pertain to the dialectical process itself.

7. Friedrich Nietzsche, "On the Uses and Disadvantages of History for Life," in *Untimely Meditations*, trans. R.J. Hollingdale (Cambridge: Cambridge University Press, 1996), Foreword; henceforth, this text is cited as UM with essay and section numbers.

8. Nietzsche is undermining the drive toward "correct representations" here by equating the historical endeavor with the correct representation of all prior historical events and by equating the unhistorical with forgetting or with the creative interpretation of prior historical events.

9. Friedrich Nietzsche, *Human, All Too Human, Vol. One*, trans. R. J. Hollingdale (Cambridge: Cambridge University Press, 1994), §2; henceforth, this text is cited as HATH with section number.

10. Friedrich Nietzsche, *On the Genealogy of Morals*, Preface, §2, in *Basic Writings of Nietzsche*, trans. and ed. Walter Kaufmann (New York: Modern Library, 1992).

11. Friedrich Nietzsche, *Beyond Good and Evil*, §2, in *Basic Writings of Nietzsche*; henceforth, this text cited as BGE with section number.

12. Friedrich Nietzsche, *The Will to Power*, ed. Walter Kaufmann, trans. Walter Kaufmann and R. J. Hollingdale (New York: Vintage Books, 1968), §515; henceforth, this text is cited as WTP with section number.

13. An example of this is from the Preface for the Second Edition of *The Gay Science*: "All those bold insanities of metaphysics, especially answers to the question about the *value* of existence, may be considered first of all as the symptoms of certain bodies," Friedrich Nietzsche, *The Gay Science*, trans. Walter Kaufmann (New York: Vintage Books, 1974) Second Preface, §2.

14. In fact, in words similar to Heidegger's, Nietzsche writes the following about overcoming the metaphysical tradition: "if he [the human who has rejected superstition and religion] is at this level of liberation he now has, with the greatest exertion of mind, to overcome metaphysics. *Then*, however, he needs to make a *recoiling movement* (rückläufige Bewegung): he has to grasp the historical justification that resides in such ideas" (HATH, §20). This recoiling movement is the movement back into and through metaphysics which enables one to determine its historical contexts and dimensions.

15. Cf. Heidegger's remarks on Plato and Aristotle's understanding of the beginning of philosophizing in wonder, in BQ, §36, pp. 133–136.

16. Heidegger interprets the common phrase, *es gibt*, which we would translate in our colloquial phrase, 'there is', literally as 'it gives', similar to the phrase 'it rains'. In both, there is not literally a being, 'it', that does both actions—

one that gives and one that rains—because this is a middle-voice activity, which would read as 'the giving gives of itself' or 'the rain rains from itself'. These odd phrases attempt to express how activities can take place without a subject-agent (and without, as Nietzsche holds, imposing on nature or reality a subject-agent model). For Heidegger, then, the 'it' that gives is being, and the giving that is done is the dispensation of beings. He writes, "for the 'it' that here 'gives' is being itself. The 'gives' names the essence of being that is giving, granting its truth" (BW, 238).

17. Cited by Heidegger, in *Being and Time* (BT, 197; SZ, 213).

18. This thinking which is determined and directed primarily toward *beings* brings about metaphysical thinking; it attempts to think the conditions of beings, but since it is determined by beings it pursues the conditions of beings as if these conditions were founded or grounded by a being also. Thus, this metaphysical thinking attempts to find the highest being, the most general being, etc., in order to give the metaphysical ground of all beings. For Heidegger, even though it separates itself from ordinary physical objects, metaphysical thinking is still determined by a focus upon beings and not on the showing of beings.

19. *Eine freie Folge*, WP, 62–3, and OTB, 52.

20. See GA 65, §91, "From the First to the Other Inception," for Heidegger's distinction and relation between the "first inception" and the "other inception."

One

The Destruction of Logic:
From Λόγος to Language

Jean-François Courtine

Translated by Kristin Switala and Rebekah Sterling

It is generally agreed that three different periods can be distinguished when one attempts to characterize the relation that Heidegger's thought maintains with Greek philosophy[1]: the first period corresponds essentially to his years at Marburg; it is the period of the drafting of an *Aristotelesbuch* that emerged as *Sein und Zeit*.[2] This period is primarily aimed at reviving the γιγαντομαχία περὶ τῆς οὐσίας, or in other words, at *re-posing* anew the question of the sense of being. This question, echoing the Platonic question of *The Sophist*, is put into practice by Heidegger in *Sein und Zeit*.[3] The method—phenomenological destruction—employed here tends at first to undo the overlappings and the stratifications of the tradition, in order to reach, at a new cost, the heart of the questions initially elaborated by Plato and Aristotle. In this perspective, it is clear that the Presocratic thinkers, as such, do not play any fixed role in the economy of the destruction: it is always Aristotle who constitutes the interlocutor and privileged guide.[4] The second period, upon which we want to focus in what follows, is precisely when Heidegger invents the Presocratics as a radically critical entreaty with regard to the Platonic–Aristotelian inception of metaphysics. This corresponds roughly to the courses in the 1930s and 1940s, and it is marked by Heidegger abandoning his plan of "refounding" (*Grundlegung*) metaphysics, taking fundamental ontology as a conducting-wire (*fil conducteur*). No doubt, it would be useful here to define finally a third period whose chronology is, as a matter of fact, more difficult to establish precisely: the period where the very idea of an "other beginning," in its strict correlation with the repetition commemorating the grandeur of the first pre-Platonic and pre-Aristotelian beginning, gives

25

precedence to a thought more liberally centered on words and their immanent play, even if, as we will try to show, the thought experiments of this final period[5] still presuppose the gains of the second great debate with the Greeks before Socrates, and notably the idea of "tautology."

We have given this very schematic overview in order to indicate from the outset that our present aim does not at all intend to put forth something like a general assessment of the Heideggerian interpretation of the Presocratics, and even less to restore the rights of philology against this or that particularly risky exegesis of a fragment of Heraclitus or of Parmenides. What we would like to help elucidate is rather the position of the Presocratic moment in the general economy of Heidegger's thought. In order to do this, the question of logic or of the "logical" appears at first to furnish a privileged conducting-wire, insofar as it allows us to follow through the passage from the historico-critical destruction to the shaking or dismantling of the reign of logic—the emergence of a meditation about λόγος opening onto the essence of the word. "What is logic? With this question, we are already placed before a problem whose solution is reserved for the future."[6] The question, formulated in this way by Heidegger from 1912, can be considered in fact as one of those principial (*principielle*) questions, capable of integrating the principal stages of a long path of thought, while restoring in them the most rigorous coherence.

In the introduction which he drafted, in 1972, on the occasion of the first re-issuing of his *Frühe Schriften*, Heidegger himself emphasized the intimate correlation between the question of logic, the question of being, and what would become the question of language and of its essence, bearing in mind the collations of 1912, also the dissertation of 1913 (*Die Lehre vom Urteil im Psychologismus. Ein kritisch-positiver Beitrag zur Logik*), and above all the habilitation thesis of 1915 (*Die Kategorien- und Bedeutungslehre des Duns Scotus*):

> These first works announce already a *"Wegbeginn,"* the beginning [the first clearing] of a still-obstructed road. What is announced is the *Seinsfrage* under the figure of the problem of categories, the question of *language* under the form of a doctrine of signification.[7]

In this path which leads from logic to language, we can once again distinguish at least three stages: the stage of the works of his youth still marked by the problematic of validity as the first elucidation of being in judgment; the second step is that of the phenomenological "destruction," a process which essentially consists of returning from the "academic" or "academicized" interpretation of Aristotelian logic to a more original problematic of λόγος intended as a mode of disclosure of, among others things, being and of its truth. This step corresponds roughly to the Marburg period and to the elaboration of *Sein und Zeit*, its ultimate point being perhaps the 1929–30 course (*Die Grundbegriffe der Metaphysik*),[8] of which the final exam summarized, in the horizon of the problem of the world, the critical analysis of the enunciative proposition and of its alleged foundation in the Aristotelian doctrine of λόγος as λόγος ἀποφαντικὸς.

The third stage is no longer a stage of "destruction," if at least we always mean "destruction" in the sense of phenomenological "deconstruction."[9] Rather, by destruction we mean it, hereafter, in the sense of shaking (*erschüttern*), "dismantling" or "disorientation," according to the strong image of a gesture consisting of taking something off its hinges (*faire sortir des ses gonds*)—an image that one finds in particular in the *Einführung in die Metaphysik*.[10] This last stage (the last in any case in which we will be interested[11]) corresponds to the establishment of a new partition which occurs henceforth, inside ancient philosophy, between Plato and Aristotle on one hand—the inception of metaphysics conceived as γιγαντομαχία τερὶ τῆς οὐσίας—and an earlier thought, that of the Presocratics. In this way, the "beginning" is in some way split in two and in a sense the *Zweideutigkeit* emerges, which had been affecting, up until then, the teaching of Plato and Aristotle. In other words, we can consider that the Presocratic "moment" emerges as such in the internal economy of Heidegger's thought from the moment when, in Greek philosophy itself, a rift is revealed, which gives his thought its peculiar and vivid rhythm, between a first beginning and an end whose grandeur is placed under the sign of Plato and Aristotle.[12] And it is this "end," taken as a beginning, which subsequently will not cease to "degenerate," until its Hegelian summation.[13]

In the present state of the publication of these seminars, it is again relatively difficult to mark with precision the exact date of this deliberate return to the Presocratics, on this side of Plato and Aristotle, which is also a return to the foundation of metaphysics with a view to its overtaking. We can clearly see when looking back what makes a system by means of such a "return": the idea of an end of metaphysics by exhausting its initial possibilities, the abandoning of the project—

which found its highest expression in 1929 in the *Kantbuch*—of a re-
foundation (*Grundlegung*) of metaphysics, and correlatively the renunciation of the task of fundamental ontology articulated from the
(phenomenological) destruction of the history of classical ontology. In
this large sweeping motion, the principal pivoting axis is attached, no
doubt, to a radically new understanding of the forgetting of being. If
in the perspective of *Sein und Zeit*, the express repetition of the question of being was aiming at first to rescue the question from the forgetfulness into which it had sunk, since its first elaboration by Plato
and Aristotle, then, soon after, the teaching of Plato, with that of
Aristotle, would be envisaged as forming the major documents of a
bend, turning, or metamorphosis which affects the very notion and,
beyond, the Greek experience of truth as ἀ-λήϑεια Moreover, everything occurs as if Greek philosophy itself, in the extraordinarily short
sequence that Heidegger always kept in mind, was henceforth becoming hollow from the inside in order to force the appearance of its background, premetaphysics, of which the trace has been conserved for us
in the fragmentary words of a few rare thinkers. And it is very much
a matter of "words" (*paroles, Worte*[14]), indeed quite few in number and
for which it is important at first to recover the force of nomination:
φύσις, λόγος, ἀλήϑεια, whose constellation delineates the general horizon of an experience not thematized as such nor investigated by the
first philosophers.

Upon this internal curve which is formed by the Greek moment
overall—from "Anaximander to Aristotle"—and of which the central
element is certainly the very concept of λόγος in the differentiating multiplicity of its meaning and of its status—it is no doubt necessary to
reserve a privileged place for the first courses from the beginning of
the 1930s. In particular the Summer 1931 course (*Aristoteles: Metaphysik
Θ 1–3*) brought about for the first time a significant displacement of the
investigation, still ontological, concerning οὐσία toward the task and
the implementation, in particular by means of the pair δύναμις—
ἐνεργεία, quite like the course of the following Winter semester (1931–
32), dedicated this time to Plato: *Vom Wesen der Wahrheit. Zu Platons
Höhlengleichis und Theätet.*[15] At the same time, we will be careful not to
appeal too much to these two courses which are situated still quite
clearly in the continuation of the Marburg courses, and in particular
the Winter 1925–26 course (*Logik. Die Frage nach der Wahrheit*[16]), since
for Heidegger it has always been a matter of recovering, beyond the

academic and traditional sedimentation, the access to a Greek experience of the truth as a revealing, a yet-to-be-discovered, an extracting
from the dissimulation.

In the present absence of the publication of these two courses,
which could well have marked the veritable caesura in the evolution
of the Heideggerian interpretation of the Greek beginning, which had
at first been identified with the inception of metaphysics by Plato and
Aristotle,[17] namely the Summer 1932 course (to appear as volume 35
of the *Gesamtausgabe*): *Der Anfang der abendländischen Philosophie*
(*Anaximander und Parmenides*) and the Summer 1933 and Winter 1933–
34 courses (to appear as volume 36/37): *Die Grundfrage der Philosophie,
Vom Wesen der Warheit*,[18] it seems to us more illuminating to emphasize in the perspective we are taking here—by following the conducting-wire of the question of logic—the rupture which the Inaugural
Lecture has introduced in regard to the perspective of phenomenological destruction, even if this rupture is still awaiting its definitive
determination: it would take place in 1935, at the beginning of the
Einführung in die Metaphysik. It is in any case a new form of the
"destruction" of logic which is at work in the Inaugural Lecture of
Freiburg: *Was ist Metaphysik?*

Let us quickly recall in this perspective the trend of the lecture:
nothingness (*das Nichts*) is what runs counter to anguish in fundamental experience, but it does not allow itself to be spoken of without
violating the elementary rules of logic. Why this logical impossibility
to talk about nothingness? Because "nothingness" is neither an object
(*Gegenstand*), nor a "state of being" (*Seiendes*), but neither is it, as the
experience of the *Grundstimmung* of anguish is sufficient to attest,
nothing whatsoever; it is no longer a matter of some "phenomenon"
inferable from something else, for example from language, from a
proposition, from negation, from negative judgments of the type: "this
is not that. . . ." The *Verneinung*, the negation, must then be considered
here as what gives evidence of the continuous and diffuse, even though
deceitful, appetization (*aperite*) of the Nothingness in our existence.[19] It
is necessary, therefore, to conclude from this that the "not" could not
be produced by the negation (*die Verneinung*), but that it is on the other
hand the negation which is "founded" upon the "not" (the *Nicht*), which

in turn finds its origin in the being-nothing of nothingness (*das Nichten des Nichts*).[20]

We recognize, thus, in the Inaugural Lecture a classically Heideggerian gesture: to lead back to the *Verhalten* and to its multiple ways, beyond the statement and of every purely theoretical attitude. Such an attitude is very much, moreover, the central thesis of the lecture, against which Carnap, in particular, would react.[21]

> Nothingness is the origin of negation and not the inverse.
> Das Nichts ist der Ursprung der Verneinung, nich umgekehrt (GA 9, 117).

And its corollary which interests us in the highest degree:

> If thus the power of the understanding in the field of questions concerning nothing and being is broken, then the fate of the sovereignty of "logic" within philosophy is thereby decided as well. *The very idea of "logic" dissolves in the whirl of a more basic questioning* (GA 9, 117; emphasis added).

Heidegger would add in a marginal note on his copy: *Logik, d.h. die überlieferte Auslegung des Denkens*—"logic, that is to say, the *traditional* interpretation, received from thought."[22] It is understood that the question which emerges from then on would be expressed soon after as: *Was heißt Denken?* and that this question would seek to be stated in a form worthy of its appropriately revolutionary stake.[23]

Let us recall further this other formulation of the fundamental thesis of the lecture, which is of direct interest here to our aims:

> The question concerning the nothing crosses at the same time the whole of metaphysics, insofar as it forces us to place ourselves in front of the problem of the origin of negation, that is to say at the ground before the decision touching the *legitimate sovereignty* of "logic" in metaphysics.[24]

It is once more this question of the sovereignty or domination (*Herrschaft*) of logic which would be examined in the *Einführung in die Metaphysik*, according to a sense of destruction more and more resolutely polemical. In fact, it is a matter from then on of thwarting a domination, of overthrowing a "sovereignty," whose empire is such that it is allowed to neglect all of the secondary differences and in particular those which would mark something like a progress of logic. "Logic" is completed, sealed in its fundamental traits, Heidegger stresses, referring to Kant's famous verdict: "Logic has not made, it seemed to him, one step forward since Aristotle." And Heidegger (not in 1787 either, but in 1935) confirmed:

> This not only seems to be so. It is so. For despite Kant and Hegel, logic has not made a single advance in the essential and initial questions. The only possible step that remains is to stand on the very ground from which logic rose and to overturn it as the dominant perspective for the interpretation of being.[25]

A formula whose violence echoes that of the preceding year, when Heidegger alluded to the necessity of shaking (*ershüttern*) logic[26] by opening it up to the question of essence speaking of the word. But it is assuredly, even today, the great course of 1935 (*Einführung in die Metaphysik*) which constitutes the clearest testimony to this new interpretation which all at once concerns metaphysics, its directive question, its Platonic–Aristotelian inception, also its background, and at the same time concerns its necessary overtaking. In the *Einführung in die Metaphysik*, Heidegger would once again evoke "the power of logic which constantly increases,"[27] this "force" of which he finds the most clear-cut formulation in the *Encyclopedia* of Hegel (§19): "Logic is the absolute form of truth, and even more, pure truth itself." (Das Logische ist die absolute Form der Wahrheit und, noch merh als dies, die reine Wahrheit selbst.)

And in this same course which constitutes the first great evidence of the movement which leads back, beyond the Greece of the Platonic-Aristotelian inception of metaphysics, to an earlier beginning, Heidegger summarizes the group of questions which would henceforth direct him:

> Wie geschieht das ursprüngliche Auseinandertreten von λόγος und φύσις?
> Wie kommt es zum Heraustreten und Auftreten des λόγος?
> Wie wird der λόγος (das "Logische") zum Wesen des Denkens?

Wie kommt dieses λόγος als Vernunft und Verstand zur Herrschaft über das Sein im Anfang der griechischen Philosophie?[28]

It is in fact these questions, rigorously formulated from 1935, which still order the 1940s courses (Winter 1942–1943 and Summers 1943 and 1944), dedicated respectively to Parmenides and to Heraclitus. But these great "canonical" moments of exposition, the essential points of which his last contributions of *Vorträge und Aufsätze* would take up several years later, refer to a new approach concerning the first Greek thinking before Socrates, well before the 1940s. This approach which clears a path for itself through his reading of Hölderlin—absolutely decisive in this perspective—undertaken from the Winter of 1934–1935, and his reading of Nietzsche, undertaken in 1936–1937. This supports the hypothesis that we are formulating here, namely, that if the *Einführung* in 1935 clearly marks a first moment of balance in the new configuration of Greek philosophy, we may nevertheless trace the inquiry back to the beginning of the 1930s and precisely to the Inaugural Lecture of 1929 which this time expressly concerns metaphysics with a view to its over-taking, at the price of a radicalization of the critique of logic.

This last sense of destruction—to make logic come off its hinges or, perhaps, disorient itself, in view of a meditation concerning the word as a reply to the call of being—had manifested itself, as we have seen, for the first time in the Summer 1934 course: *Logic-Language. Über Logik als Frage nach der Sprache*, through the programmatic declaration: Wir wollen die Logik *erschüttern*.[29]

We want to shake logic, to shake it until its collapse, to dismantle it. The metaphor here is clearly one of "demolition." In the somber context of the epoch, Heidegger begins by evoking the general critique of intellectualism, but it is in order to put into effect immediately, according to a gesture familiar to him, a significant step backwards: It is no use, he remarks, wielding the term "intellectualism" as an insult, what is necessary is first to measure the *"Macht der überlieferten Logik,"* if at least one wants to actually break it. This implies first that logic must be taken seriously!

We renounce the cheap presumption that sees in logic only "red tape" (*Formelkram*)—hollow formulas. . . . Logic is for us . . . the place where humans come into question (*die Stätte der Fragwürdigkeit des Menschen*).[30]

With logic what is ultimately put back into question is in fact the determination of the essence of humans, for example (!) as ζῷον λόγον ἔχον, if it is true, as Heidegger emphasizes again here, that the question of "the essence of language (*Sprache*) is the fundamental directive question of logic." What it is necessary then to ask is this henceforth: "Does language constitute a private sector?—Preliminary question: What is language's mode of being?"

The question of "language's mode of being" refers to the *Sprechen*, to "speaking," and by that to the mode of being of humans.[31] In this way, the preliminary question is transformed into these underlying questions on the way back to the first beginning: the question of the essence of humans, the question "who?" and "who are we?"

The *Einführung in die Metaphysik*—which is everything except an introduction to metaphysics[32]—is also the text where the violent identification (metaphysics/Platonism/nihilism) falls into place, which would find its canonical formulation in the course on Nietzsche. The 1935 course in fact opens—as everyone knows—with the distinction of two absolutely heterogeneous questions, the directive question and the fundamental question (*Leit- und Grundfrage*), and with the accentuation of two contrasted senses of "nothing" or of "nothingness" (*Nichts*), such as emerge from the differentiated understanding of "the" metaphysical question, in its classical Leibnizian stamp: Why is there something and not rather nothing? By thus stressing the *Zusatz* of the Leibnizian question ("and not rather nothing"), the course is directly linked to the finale of the Inaugural Lecture and takes up again, while radicalizing, the critique of "logic" which already underlies the lecture:

> Wer vom Nichts redet, weiß nicht, was er tut. Wer vom Nichts redet, macht es durch solches Tun zu einem Etwas. Sprechend spricht er so gegen das, was er meint. Er wider-spricht sich selbst. Ein sich widersprechendes Sagen verstößt aber gegen die Grundregel vom Sagen (λόγος), gegen die "Logik." Das Reden vom Nichts ist unlogisch. [. . . .] Wer das Nichts ernst nimmt, stellt sich auf die Seite des Nichtigen. Er fördert offenkundig den Geist der Verneinung und dient der Zersetzung. Was sowohl das Denken in seinem Grundgesetz mißachtet, als auch den Aufbauwillen und Glauben zerstört, ist reiner Nihilismus (EM, 18).[33]

To this logical prohibition Heidegger opposes, in referring implicitly no longer to Plato's *Sophist*, but to Parmenides' *Poem*, the essential
and original correlation of the question of the state of being and of the
question of non-being, nothing or nothingness. Thus, what is indicated
through the Leibnizian *Zusatz* is not only simply a *"Begleiterscheinung,"*
a closely related phenomenon, but rather what inexorably assesses the
radicality of the questioning concerning the state of being in its being.
From then on the charge of nihilism made against the *"Grundfrage"* and
its characteristic destruction bears witness to the lack of understanding of the question of being, signifying even the most profound
Seinsvergessenheit:

> So rundweg ist nämlich noch gar nicht entschieden, ob die Logik
> und ihre Grundregeln überhaupt den maßstab bei der Frage nach
> dem Seienden als solchem abgeben können. Es könnte umgekehrt
> sein, daß die gesamte uns bekannte und wie ein Himmelgeschenk
> behandelte Logik in einer ganz bestimmten Antwort auf die Frage
> nach dem Seienden gründet, daß mithin alles Denken, das
> lediglich die Denkgesetze der herkömmlichen Logik befolgt, von
> vornherein außerstande ist, von sich aus überhaupt die Frage nach
> dem Seienden auch nur zu verstehen, geschweige denn wirklich
> zu entfalten und einer Antwort entgegenzuführen . . . (EM, 19).[34]

The counter-attack here is aimed, most likely, at Carnap. However,
henceforth, it shares as well in a fight against "science" in general.[35]
From this dissociation (*"Philosophie—Wissenschaft"*), still not completed
in the Rectorate Address,[36] it releases a new constellation which remains
dominant in the new "appropriation" of the Presocratics: that of
"Dichten—Denken," to which we will return. The emergence of this
configuration marks also the first elaboration, in the 1935 course, of the
question to which Heidegger will apply himself to exploring all its
defenders, the question: *Was heißt Denken?*[37]

The 1940s were the years of the great courses dedicated to the
Presocratics.[38]
The central question is, henceforth, on the conducting-wire of an
inquiry concerning logic, aiming to recover its original, pre-Platonic[39]

determination, the question: *Was heißt Denken?* What is called thinking? A formula that it is necessary to intend or mean at present as that of a search for what directs thought, for what offers itself to thinking, making to it the gift of thought, thus is required by the call. The Heraclitus course is indeed subtended by a principial opposition between logic, traditionally defined as *"Lehre vom richtigen Denken"*[40] (a study of the rules of thought), and logic in its original sense as an opening attentive to the matter in question (the *Sache*)—its requirements, its proper development. But what is the *Sache*, when it is no longer anything but a question of thinking? The response at first will seem necessarily "poor" and disappointing. What calls for thought is the "before-being-thought": the *Zudenkendes*. Thought is only truly itself, to the depth of its essence, when it responds to what is bestowed or destined to it, worthy of a history conceived, henceforth, as the unity of a "sending" (*Geschick*). We will be careful not, however, to oppose here the task thus formally defined—thought as a commemoration of what offers itself to thinking since the origin of a first beginning never yet truly occurred as such—to the demand to think what is. The commemorating thought does not intend in fact to make itself historical in recapitulating by memory (*Erinnerung*) a past thus ensured of its relief, but it applies itself rather to extricating the fundamental traits from what is and what Heidegger names, after Nietzsche, nihilism or the dominant figure of inspection, the *Machenschaft*, and then the *Gestell*.

It is by this, likewise, that thinking emerges as a task, that it becomes *for us*—when a first destinal sending finally lets itself be seized again as such—necessary, indeed the most necessary:

> Denken ist not, damit wir dadurch einer wohl noch verborgenen Bestimmung des geschichtlichen Menschen entsprechen. [. . . .] Richtig denken, aus der Sache denken, überhaupt denken, ist not, ja allerzeit denken lernen—ist das Nötigste.[41]

We see here that this new determination of thinking attuned to the λόγος[42] engages nothing less than a new determination of the essence of humans as historical. That is to say, precisely as that singular state of being (*Da-Sein*) demanded by an address, a destinal sending: "'der geschichtliche Mensch'—dies meint dasjenige Menschentum, dem ein Geschick zugedacht ist und zwar als das Zu-denkende."

Just as in the era of *Sein und Zeit*, it was possible to extricate a structure of anticipation (the *Vorstruktur*), as a directive structure in the interpretation of understanding, likewise, we now are permitted to emphasize the import of a structure which lets itself be characterized as a structure of the address (*Zu-Struktur*).[43] This structure becomes directive concerning the central question of the Heideggerian meditation which henceforth takes into sight the Presocratic moment, namely, the question, "what is thinking?" when thought no longer lets itself be determined either as representative, or as objectifying, or above all and principially in the horizon of λόγος ἀποφαντικὸs (according to the structure of a λέγειν τι κατά τινοs) understood as the cornerstone of the reign or empire of "logic."[44] What are the consequences of this concerning thought and its object, or better, its task (*Aufgabe*)? The "object" of thought is henceforth and unambiguously thinking (*cum emphasi*), or if we must further "specify"—the thinking of thinkers. It is necessary (χρή) (but what exactly is compelling here? what is the origin of the law, of the command?) to think thought or to think thinking, certainly not in the sense of the νόησιs νοήσεωs, a characteristic trait of an Aristotelian self-sufficient and self-pleasing god, nor in the Hegelian (speculative–dialectical) horizon of a *Wissenschaft der Logik*, even if the debate with Hegel remains in a sense always subjacent in the relation of Heidegger to Greece, this debate whose stakes would be also or initially to extract the Presocratics from the dialectic logic of the Hegelian relief.[45]

Is that to say that thinking, emphatically understood here, gives itself over to being, to being as what properly gives to thinking, what calls to thinking? No doubt, but how does it stand with being? One thing is clear in any case, it is a question less and less of being of the state of being, and more and more that of the attempt to think being without the state of being, the attempt which is indicated orthographically from the first courses on Hölderlin by the usage of the archaic term: *das Seyn*. And here to think being is similar to thinking the internal object of thinking, that is, to think what is meant by thinking, what calls to thinking— "abstract," "absolute," or "intransitive" thinking, as the Heraclitus course indicates in a particularly striking manner.

But neither does that signify, for Heidegger as the "inventor" of the Presocratics, that the task is to think what *is*, the *esse*, existence, the "what," indeed the world as such, according to a perspective still phenomeno–logical, liable to return to some of the thoughts concerning existence (Schelling, Coleridge, Wittgenstein). For with respect to the emphatic thinking, it would be rather more appropriate to speak of logo-logy, according to a structure of tautological reflexivity, to which we will return.

In the critical mode we are nevertheless allowed to ask ourselves in order to know whether and to what extent the Heideggerian meditation, when it is overcome by the non-dialectical "reflexivity" of *Denken*, does it not risk, at the same time, losing the phenomenality in its specificity and its regional diversity,[46] that is, the very dimension of "φαίνεσθαι"? One can even be tempted to see there something like a fatal form of the error of Parmenides to which Heidegger would have yielded, in refusing to repeat for his benefit the Platonic gesture of parricide!

Χρή τὸ λέγειν τε νοεῖν τ᾿ἐόν ἔμμεναι· μηδὲν δ᾿ οὐκ ἔστιν.

It must be that what is there for speaking and thinking that it is. Whereas there is not being for being, and it is nothing which is not (Parmenides, Fragment B6.1-2).

Therefore, thinking or, absolutely expressed thinking what is to be thought is, from now on, taking the measure of "λέγειν," in the horizon of what Heidegger, referring to Novalis, would finally call logology. We can recognize in fact in that emphatic sense of "*Denken*"— thinking what is to be thought, thinking thinking, thinking about "*Zu-denkendes*"—as the original principle of what would become soon after, with the later Heidegger, the "tautological" structure of the "word."[47] As we have already emphasized in fact, the principal stakes of the destruction of logic—radicalized by means of the return upstream to the original words of the first thinkers[48]—are to open a new access to language and its proper essential deployment: the *Wesen der Sprache* as *Sage*, μῦθος. At least since the Summer 1934 *Logik* course,[49] the question of logic is expressly engaged "on the way to language"—*Unterwegs zur Sprache*: if logic must be dismantled, it is precisely because it bars access to a renewed understanding of λόγος,[50] the misreading of which constitutes perhaps the fundamental trait of the destiny of the West.[51]

What is, furthermore, absolutely remarkable in this return to a renewed understanding of λόγος out of the first Greek thinkers is that this understanding is attached exclusively to "words" (*Worte*) to the detriment of all dialectic discursivity. The destruction of logic in fact always implies that of grammar—philosophical and propositional; it intends to go back up this side of the syntactic and thus to reach a more original figure of language, in its parataxic structure, and alone to be able to leave to words (*mots*) (which are no longer only terms in a proposition, were it to be speculative) their whole power of disclosure and of nomination, according to the first and unshakable unity of "*Sagen*"— "*Zeigen*" and of the "*Sache*"—of the very unity which Heidegger would thematize a little later in an exemplary manner in his commentary on the poem of Stefan George: *Das Wort* (US, 220; OWL, 140):

> Das Walten des Wortes blitz auf als die Bedingnis des Dinges zum Ding. [. . . .] Das älteste Wort für das so gedachte Walten des Wortes, für das Sagen, heißt Λóγος: die Sage, die zeigend Seiendes in sein *es ist* erscheinen läßt (US, 237).[52]

But this new relation to language, which the frequentation of the Presocratics opens, in making itself attentive once more to the "words" (*mots*) or to words (*paroles*)[53] resulted from an experiment all at once of "thinking" and of "language," and is already what underlies the whole approach of the 1935 course:

> Wir überspringen . . . diesen ganzen Verlauf der Verunstaltung und des Verfalls und suchen die unzerstörte Nennkraft der Sprache und Worte wieder zu erobern; denn die Worte und die Sprache sind keine Hülsen, worin die Dinge nur für den redenden und schreibenden Verkehr verpackt werden. Im Wort, in der Sprache werden und sind erst die Dinge (EM, 11).[54]

It is certainly difficult, if not impossible, to distinguish, within the extraordinary conjunction that is elaborated in the middle of the 1930s, between the principle motives and the related or secondary motives. No doubt, it is necessary to try to think together: the new determination of nihilism and of the forgetting of being apprehended henceforth in its destinal dimensions; the return to the Presocratic beginning; the opening of a new and other beginning, at first understood as a beginning-again, recommencing (*wiederanfangen*), according to a more original modality, from the first Greek beginning. What emerges in any case, is the extraordinary historial-destinal (*historiale-destinale*) "dramatization" of the question of being, according to its new accentuation,[55] in the sense of the question: *Wie steht es um das Sein?* How does it stand with being for us today?

> Ist das 'Sein' ein bloßes Wort und seine Bedeutung ein Dunst oder das geistige Schicksal des Abendlandes? Fragen: Wie steht es um das Sein?—das besagt nichts Geringeres als den Anfang unseres geschichtlichen-geistigen Dasein *wieder-holen*, um ihn in den Anderen Anfang zu verwandeln (EM, 28-9).[56]

The necessity of this re-petition of the first beginning emerges, just like the *Rückgang in den Grund der Metaphysik*, from the moment that the latter, associated with nihilism, is inscribed and circumscribed in the history of the truth of being, by way of a figure of erring (*Irre*). The repetition appeals to our decision and is by that able to open a future anew. The new thematization of the beginning, that we find in the *Beiträge zur Philosophie*, but also in the Summer 1941 course,[57] envisaged this beginning not as what would be far behind us, deep in the past, in that case, an object of an antiquarian curiosity, but more so as what, never having taken place *as such*, remains essentially to come.[58]

In one sense, it could seem legitimate to compare such a thematic of the beginning to the Husserlian approach aiming at a return, beyond the sedimentations and overlayings which debase the original sense and disfigure the initial intention, to the proto-foundation (*Urstiftung*). Heidegger himself emphasizes moreover the decisive dimension of any true beginning: "By beginning, we mean the original decisions which carry and support in advance Western history in its essentiality" (GA 51, 15; BC, 13).

On account of this, the meditation concerning beginning depends in turn on a reflection newly-centered on freedom. There is in fact a true beginning and a beginning freedom only "where humanity demonstrates decision in its relation to the state of being and to truth" (GA 51, 16; BC, 13)

Of course, it remains to be specified that such an inaugural decision is all but arbitrary or fortuitous: it does not start from nothing, reveals no such voluntative (*voluntatif*) or voluntaristic trait, since it is defined more in terms of listening, of response to the address, the call, the promise (*Zu-spruch*). It is also by this—let us repeat—that the meditation concerning beginning in view of an "other" beginning is still closely linked to the question of language and of thought in language:

Was heißt Denken? "Wir stehen vor der *Entscheidung zwischen dem Ende und seinem vielleicht noch Jahrhunderte füllenden Auslauf—und dem Anderen Anfang.* . . ."[59]

In this way, Heidegger expresses himself in the Winter 1937-38 course, more or less contemporary to the *Beiträge*. It is in any case the experience of the end of metaphysics, linked to a determined regime of λόγος, as "logic" and as language, which opens the meditation concerning a new beginning and which by that calls for inquiry about the inaugural words of the Presocratic thinkers. The return upstream on this side of Plato, on this side of metaphysics as a unitarily Platonic-Aristotelian determination, makes a system with a double decision, relative to the "truth" and to the "word."

What awaits our decision is indeed at first the "question" of truth, whether it is true that there it concerns a question not elaborated nor explored thoroughly by the Greeks, even the Greeks before Socrates. It would be necessary here to want to be able to follow in detail, stage by stage, the development of Heidegger's position in his attempt to establish the status of truth understood as *Unverborgenheit* in the horizon or rather as the horizon of Presocratic thought. In the Summer 1931 course, *Vom Wesen der Wahrheit*, where it is a matter at first of characterizing in its historial import the mutation which is fulfilled with Plato and the resulting subjugation of truth to exactitude,[60] the first Greeks are credited, through Heraclitus, with an essential glance into the structure of truth. The fragment of Heraclitus (B123) is then assigned a central function:

φύσις κρύπτεσθαι φιλεῖ

in diesem Spruch des Heraklit ist *die* Grunderfahrung ausgesprochen, *mit* der, *in* der und *aus* der ein Blick in das Wesen der Wahrheit als Un-verborgenheit des Seienden erwachte. [. . . .] Dieser Spruch spricht *die* Grunderfahrung und Grundstellung des antiken Menschen aus, mit der allererst und gerade das Philosophieren beginnt. . . .[61]

And even if the first thinkers, as Heidegger emphasizes a bit later, did not *pose* the question of truth as ἀ-λήθεια, *Unverborgenheit*, that does not simply authorize us to maintain that they would have neglected it (*Versäumnis*).[62] The Greeks did not neglect anything at all, nor "forget" anything; they unfolded their thought on the ground of "*Grund-*

erfahrung" or of *"Grundstimmung,"* and it comes back to us finally, after the event, to pose the question of the epochal essence of truth as withdrawal:

> für die Griechen, die ἀλήθεια das Anfängliche und Fraglose blieb. . . . Die ἀλήθεια bliebt im *Dasein* der Griechen das Mächtigste zugleich und das Verborgenste . . . (GA 45, 205).[63]

However—and this is the point which here interests us in the highest degree—the first thinkers, upon the ground of this non-thematic experience of truth as ἀ-λήθεια, are also those who let appear, in its flashing light and its power of nomination, language in its essence. Let us recall here simply these two passages from *Vorträge und Aufsätze* where the Greek inception of thought and the apprehension of the essence of language are found intimately associated:

> Once, however, in the beginning of Western thinking, the essence of language flashed in the light of being. . . . But the lightning abruptly vanished.[64]

> "[T]hat first illumination of the essence of language as saying disappears immediately into a veiling darkness. . . ."[65]

If therefore it is to *us* that it returns historically and historially (*historialement*) to elaborate the still reserved question of truth, and if with this question the question of knowing "who we are ourselves" can finally be decided, we understand how the question of truth is articulated strictly with that of language. To which it is undoubtedly necessary to add also that the opening of the inquiry in the direction of language allows us to remove the difficulties or the dead-ends which are linked to the problematic of thinking, taken absolutely. That the question of language or better of poetic speech is henceforth intrinsically linked, in the Heideggerian meditation, to the radicalization of the destruction of logic and to the thematic elaboration of truth as ἀ-λήθεια, we find its most striking indication in the fact that it is the dialogue with Hölderlin which, prior to the "discovery" of the Presocratics, constitutes the true horizon of the meditation opened in the 1930s. The self-explanatory evidence, transmitted by O. Pöggeler, assuredly deserves to be taken seriously and it allows us above all to understand what are the stakes invested at the outset in the interpretation of the Presocratics:

> Im Augenblick des Abwerfens der letzten Mißdeutungen durch die Metaphysik, d.h. in dem Augenblick der ersten äußersten Fragwürdigkeit des Seyns selbst und seiner Wahrheit (Wahrheitsvortrag 1929–1930) wurde Hölderlins Wort, zuvor schon wie andere Dichter zunächst bekannt, zum Geschick.[66]

What is this destinal figure worth to the speech of Hölderlin and why was it able to play an absolutely decisive role in the reading of the Presocratics? The first course dedicated to Hölderlin, during the Winter of 1934–1935, by endeavoring to examine the hymns, "Germanien" and "Der Rhein," supplies us, no doubt, with the beginning of a response. Right away, the course takes for its conducting-wire the last line of the hymn, "Andenken":

> Was bleibt aber, stiften die Dichter.

A line which Heidegger immediately "ontologizes" in making of the "*Dichtung*," which becomes henceforth the paradigmatic figure of language, the "*Stiftung des Seyns*."[67] If poetry is thus assigned a decisive import in the inception of being and the world, it is not because it would permit us to go back up to an entreaty of subjective brilliance, but it is more so because the poet finds himself immediately placed in the position of mediator between the gods and humans, or between god and the people.[68] It is to him that it returns in fact to capture in his speech the signs (*Winke*) of the gods, and he can thus represent in an exemplary manner human existence as much as it is "ecstatic entreaty," and exposure all at once to being, to truth, to the injunction of the telling:

> The poet encloses and averts the lightning of the god in the word, he makes this word enter, charged with lightnings in the language of his people . . . he stands "under the storms of god . . . his head bare," left defenseless and dispossessed of himself. Dasein *is* nothing else but the *exposure to the overpowering nature of Being*.[69]

If the meditation concerning poetic speech of Hölderlin plays such a role in the destruction of logic and of the propositional regime elaborated upon the model of λέγειν τι κατά, it is at first because the poetic speech does not let itself be interpreted as an expression of the states of the soul, nor any longer as "objectivation." The only "object" of the *Dichtung*, is the poetical (*Das Gedichtete*). The *Dichten* is himself *"Sagen in der Art des weisenden Offenbarmachen."*[70] Poetry is to tell, and telling, worthy of its essence, is to tell of being. Concerning the hymn, "The Rhein," Heidegger writes in this sense:

> The first stanza of our poetry, and even this poetry, is not a picture of nature, and not a simile either. In a word, there is not here some enunciation which says something about something else. The telling of this poetry is in itself the jubilation of being. [. . . .] This telling is not the covering in words for some meaning hidden behind the surface; it is on the contrary itself, just as it is said, the reign of being.[71]

The "*Dichtung*" finds itself thus performing a quasi-speculative or specular function opposite being: it is in and through poetic speech that it establishes its reign. It is still within the framework of the exegesis of Hölderlin that Heidegger redefines in turn the being of humans—they who "live poetically"—as a dialogue (*Gespräch*), to be understood at first as a dialogue between gods and humans for which the poet exercises his function of mediator. Through the dialogue humans are in language; better, we are a language-event, come to the word from what claims it:

> We are a dialogue. What is the relation of dialogue to language? In dialogue, language happens, and this happening is properly its being. We are a happening of language (*Sprachgeschehnis*), and this happening is temporal, not only in the superficial sense where it unfolds in time, where one can measure in time its beginning and end; but above all because the happening of language is the beginning and the ground of proper historical time to humans. [. . . .] Our being happens as dialogue, when it happens that the gods summon us, and place us under their summons, *brings us to language*, that which asks whether and how we are. [. . . .] Only where the word of language happens does being and non-being open up.[72]

It is no doubt from this understanding of the dialogue, within the Hölderlinian context, that Heidegger thematizes the word as a response or a co-respondence (*Entsprechung*) to a call or an address (*Anspruch*), by extending to thought what emerges first in the poetic telling. The poetic character (*Dichtungscharakter*) of thinking remains still veiled, Heidegger noted in an aphorism.[73]

The Hölderlinian poetic, by its insistence upon the "word" (*mot*, *Wort*), in its dimensions of nomination and its function of commemoration, could well be thus what commands in depth the discovery of the Presocratics: to name, is to call by name, that is to say, to tell the truth, to respond to the entreaty of what offers itself to telling and to thinking. It is always a "gift" which calls to thinking, Heidegger will repeat in his last great course: *Was heißt Denken*? However, the gift which gives to thinking is also precisely the gift of thought: thought is not here a gift in return (a counter-gift in exchange for an initial gift), but thought is itself the gift and the acknowledgement or the thanks. The gift of the word or better of that "speaking which language speaks through man."[74]

If then the thinking and telling, in response to the gift, or better as that response through which the gift is attested as such, must tell and think being:

χρὴ τὸ λέγειν τε νοεῖν τ᾽ἐόν ἔμμεναι,

if the authentic thinker is always necessarily identical to that to which he gives himself:

ταὐτὸν δ᾽ἐστὶ νοεῖν τε καὶ ὅυνεκεν ἔστι νόημα,

then it is important to define in its ground thinking as commemorating or giving thanks (*Gedanc*, *Dank*), then it is also important to reflect telling upon itself, according to the determining figure of tautology or of logology, dear to Novalis.

Meanwhile, we may ponder, asking incidentally if the Novalisian logology does not open up the space of play of a less sacred (*sacrale*) word, more playful, attentive in any case to the mixture (*bigarure*) of what is always phenomenally specified; asking above all if the Hölderlinian poetic, as powerful as it is, is alone in a position to open the ear to the word of the first thinker-poets of Greece. The concern of language and what is said in and through it is unfolded no doubt in multiple modes, without having necessarily to favor that of the agreement taken as essential or destinal: Hölderlin-Heraclitus, Germanien.

NOTES

1. Cf. Marlène Zarader's study, "Le miroir aux trois reflets," in *Revue de Philosophie Ancienne*, 1986, 5–32.

2. Cf. Theodore Kisiel, *The Genesis of Being and Time* (Berkeley: University of California Press, 1993), 248 sq.

3. Cf. John Sallis, "Where Does *Being and Time* Begin?," in *Delimitations: Phenomenology and the End of Metaphysics* (Bloomington, IN: Indiana University Press, 1986), 98–118.

4. Cf. in particular the opening of the course on *The Sophist*, GA 19, *Platon: Sophistes*, 10 sq.: "Historische-hermeneutische Vorbereitung. Der Grundsatz der Hermeneutik: Vom Hellen ins Dunkle. Von Aristoteles zu Plato."

5. Cf. *Unterwegs zur Sprache*: "Die folgenden drei Vörtrage . . . möchten uns vor eine Möglichkeit bringen, mit der Sprache eine Erfahrung zu machen" (US, 159). "The three lectures . . . are intended to bring us face to face with a possibility of undergoing an experience with language" (OWL, 57). (Translators' note: English translations of Heidegger's German are given when available.)

6. "Neure Forschungen über Logik," in GA 1, 18: "Was ist Logik? Schon hier stehen wir vor einem Problem, dessen Lösung der Zukunft vorbehalten bleibt."

7. "Vorwort zur ersten Ausgabe der 'Frühen Schriften'," in GA 1, 55: "Gleichwohl zeigen sie einen mir damals noch verschlossenen Wegbeginn: in der Gestalt des Kategorienproblems die *Seins*frage, die Frage nach der *Sprache* in der Form der Bedeutungslehre."

8. GA 29–30, *Die Grundbegriffe der Metaphysik—Welt, Endlichkeit, Einsamkeit*.

9. "Historical critical destruction," according to the formulation in the 1925–1926 course, *Logik. Die Frage nach der Wahrheit*, GA 21.

10. EM, 144; IM, 188–89.

11. It would be indeed another question to know if the new division operated in the very womb of ancient philosophy, the division with which we will be concerned in what follows is, in turn and radically, put back into question by the different "retractions" which concern in particular the interpretation of ἀλήθεια. Cf. in particular in "The End of Philosophy and the Task of Thinking" (SD, 76 sq.), the "debate" with Paul Friedländer, well documented by Robert Bernasconi, *The Question of Language in Heidegger's History of Being*, ch. 2 (Atlantic Highlands, NJ: Humanities Press, 1985), and by John Sallis, "A Threshold of Metaphysics," in *Delimitations*, 176 sq.

12. Cf. *Einführung in die Metaphysik*: "Dieses Heraustreten des λόγος und die Vorbereitung desselben zum Gerichtshof über das Sein geschieht noch

innerhalb der griechischen Philosophie. Es bestimmt sogar das Ende derselben. Wir bewältigen die griechische Philosophie als den Anfang der abendländischen Philosophie erst dann, wenn wir diesen Anfang zugleich in seinem anfänglichen Ende begreifen; denn erst dieses und nur dieses wurde für die Folgezeit zum 'Anfang' und zwar derart, daß er den anfänglichen Anfang zugleich verdeckte. Aber dieses anfängliche Ende des großen Anfangs, die Philosophie *Platons* und die des *Aristoteles*, bleibt groß, auch wenn wir die Größe ihrer abendländischen Auswirkung noch ganz abrechnen" (EM, 137). "This secession of the λόγος which started λόγος on its way to becoming a court of justice over being occurred in Greek philosophy itself. Indeed, it brought about the end of Greek philosophy. We shall only master Greek philosophy as the beginning of Western philosophy if we also understand this beginning in the beginning of its end. For the ensuing period it was only this end that became the 'beginning', so much so that it concealed the original beginning. But this beginning of the end of the great beginning, the philosophy of Plato and Aristotle, remains great even if we totally discount the greatness of its Western consequences" (IM, 179).

13. Cf. *Einführung in die Metaphysik*: "Die Philosophie der Griechen gelangt zur abendländischen Herrschaft nicht aus ihrem ursprünglichen Anfang, sondern aus dem anfänglichen Ende, das in Hegel groß und endgültig zur Vollendung gestaltet wird" (EM, 144). "The philosophy of the Greeks conquered the Western world not in its original beginning but in the incipient end, which in Hegel assumed great and definitive form" (IM, 189).

14. Translators' note: We have translated both "*paroles*" and "*mots*" as "words" throughout the text; due to the infrequency of the author's use of "*mots*" we have indicated this by following the translation with this French term in parenthesis in each instance.

15. GA 34.

16. GA 21.

17. We will note in this perspective the "genealogy" of the questioning beyond the "physics" established by the exegesis of the allegory of the cave in the "Platons Lehre vom Wahrheit," GA 9, 235. "Plato's Doctrine of Truth," trans. J. Barlow, in *Philosophy in the Twentieth Century, Vol. Two*, eds. W. Barrett and H. D. Aiken (New York: Random House, 1962) 251–270.

18. Recalling these dates is already sufficient to program the study yet to be conducted of the possible intimate connection among the opening of a new relation to Presocratic Greece, attentive to its inaugural words, the thematization of the first great beginning, whose repetition imposes itself upon us today, in view of an other and new beginning, and Heidegger's political engagement, at least as much as it is declared in the *Rektoratsrede*.

19. Cf. "ständige und ausgebreitete, obzwar verstellte Offenbarkeit des Nichts in unserem Dasein . . ." (GA 9, 116). ". . . [T]he constant and widespread though distorted revelation of the nothing in our existence . . ." (BW, 104).

20. "Die Verneinung ist aber auch nur eine Weise des nichtenden, d.h. auf das Nichten des Nichts vorgängig gegründeten Verhalten" (GA 9, 117). "But negation is also only one way of nihilating, that is, only one sort of behavior that has been grounded beforehand in the nihilation of the nothing" (BW, 105).

21. R. Carnap, "Überwindung der Metaphysik durch logische Analyse der Sprache," *Erkenntnis* II, 1931. French translation in *Manifeste du Cercle de Vienne et autres écrits*, ed. Antonia Soulez (Paris: Puf, 1985), 153–179. "The Overcoming of Metaphysics through Logical Analysis of Language," in *Heidegger and Modern Philosophy*, ed. M. Murray (New Haven: Yale University Press, 1978).

22. GA 9, 117. Unfortunately it is impossible today, as we know, to date these "marginalia."

23. EM, 90; IM, 118.

24. GA 9, 120: "Die Frage nach dem Nichts durchgreift aber zugleich das Ganze der Metaphysik, sofern sie uns vor das Problem der Ursprungs der Vereinung zwingt, d.h. im Grunde vor die Entscheidung über die rechtmäßige Herrschaft der 'Logik' in der Metaphysik."

25. "Es scheint nicht nur so. Es ist so. Denn die Logik hat trotz Kant und Hegel im Wesentlichen und Anfänglichen keinen Schritt mehr getan. Der einzig mögliche Schritt ist nur noch der, sie (nämlich als die maßgebende Blickbahn der Auslegung des Seins) von ihrem Grund her aus der Angeln zu heben" (GA 40, 197). Cf. also, GA 40, 128 sq.; IM, 188.

26. *Logica. Lecciones de M. Heidegger (semestre verano 1934) en el lagado de Helene Weiss*, bilingual edition, ed. V. Farias (Madrid: MEC, 1991), 2.

27. "[D]ie sich ständig steigernde Machtstellung des Logischen" (GA 40, 130; cf. IM, 121–122).

28. GA 40, 131. "How did the original separation between λόγος and φύσις come about? How did a separate and distinct λόγος come to appear on the scene? How did the λόγος (the 'logical') become the essence of thinking? How did this λόγος in the sense of reason and understanding achieve domination over being in the beginning of Greek philosophy?" (IM, 123).

29. Nachschrift to *Logica* by H. Weiss. Which the resumption echoes, a little later, in the 1943 Postface to the lecture (*Was ist Metaphysik?*), marking that "logic" (the term is henceforth always used with quotation marks) is only *one* interpretation of truth: "the barely formulated question makes it necessary now to know whether or if this thought takes place well within the law of its truth, when it follows only the thought which 'logic' confines within its forms and rules. Why does the lecture put the term in quotation marks? In order to indicate that 'logic' is only *one* interpretation of the essence of thought, precisely that one which rests, as the word indicates, on the proof of being reached in Greek thought. The mistrust towards 'logic', of which logistics

can be considered today as the natural degeneration, arises from the knowledge of this thought which finds its source in the proof of the truth of being and not in the consideration of the objectivity of the state of being. . . . The original thought is the echo of the favor of being, in which the only reality—that the state of being is—lights up and lets itself happen. This echo is the human response to the silent voice of being. The response of thought is the origin of the human word (*parole*), a word which alone gives birth to language as disclosure of the word (*parole*) in words (*mots*) . . ." (GA 9, 308, 310).

30. *Logica*, 2.

31. Cf. *Einführung in die Metaphysik*: "Denn Menschsein hießt: ein Sagender sein. Der Mensch ist nur deshalb ein Ja- und Neinsager, weil er im Grunde seines Wesens ein Sager, *der* Sager ist" (EM, 62). "For to be a man is to speak. Man says yes and no only because in his profound essence he is a speaker, *the* speaker" (IM, 82).

32. Heidegger expressly indicates, in *Einführung in die Metaphysik*: "'Einführung in die Metaphysik' heißt demnach: hineinführen in das Fragen der Grundfrage" (EM, 15). "'Introduction to metaphysics' means accordingly: an introduction to the asking of the fundamental question" (IM, 19).

33. "He who speaks of nothing does not know what he is doing. In speaking of nothing he makes it into a something. In speaking he speaks against what he intended. He contradicts himself. But discourse that contradicts itself offends against the fundamental rule of discourse (λόγος), against 'logic'. To speak of nothing is illogical. . . . He who takes the nothing seriously is allying himself with nothingness. He is patently promoting the spirit of negation and serving the cause of disintegration. Not only is speaking of nothing utterly repellent to thought; it also undermines all culture and all faith. What disregards the fundamental law of thought and also destroys faith and the will to build is pure nihilism" (IM, 23).

34. "For it cannot be decided out of hand whether logic and its fundamental rules can, altogether, provide a standard for dealing with the question about beings as such. It might be the other way around. Perhaps the whole body of logic as it is known to us, perhaps all the logic that we treat as a gift from heaven, is grounded in a very definite answer to the question about beings; perhaps in consequence, all thinking which solely follows the laws of thought prescribed by traditional logic is incapable from the very start of even understanding the question about beings by its own resources, let alone actually unfolding the question and guiding it toward an answer" (IM, 25).

35. "Das Nichts bleibt grundsätzlich aller Wissenschaft unzugänglich" (EM, 19). "In principle, nothingness remains inaccessible to science" (IM, 25).

36. Cf. J.-F. Courtine, "Phénomnénologie et science de l'être," in *Heidegger et la phénoménologie* (Paris: Vrin, 1990), 187–205.

37. EM, 90; IM, 118.

38. GA 51, *Grundbegriffe* (Summer semester 1941); GA 54, *Parmenides* (Winter semester 1942–1943); GA 55, *Heraklit* (Summer semester 1943 and Summer semester 1944). An abstraction made once again of the Summer 1932 course (to appear): *Der Anfang der abendländischen Philosophie (Anaximander und Parmenides)*. We must also note that the Summer 1942 course on Hölderlin, *Der Ister* (GA 53), is occupied, in its central part (63–152), by the interpretation of humans in Greek (Sophoclean) tragedy.

39. GA 55, 185: "Die einfache Absicht dieser Vorlesung geht darauf, in die ursprüngliche 'Logik' zu gelangen."

40. GA 55, 189.

41. GA 55, 189.

42. Heraclitus, Fragment B50: οὐκ ἐμοῦ ἀλλὰ τοῦ λόγου ἀκούσαντας ὁμολογεῖν σόφον ἐστιν ἓν πάντα εἶναι. Heidegger's translation reads: "Habt ihr nicht bloß mich angehört, sondern habt ihr (ihm gehorsam, horchsam) auf den λόγος gehört, dann ist Wissen (das darin besteht), mit dem λόγος das Gleiche sagend zu sagen: Ein ist alles" (GA 55, 243). "When you have listened not to me but to the Meaning, it is wise within the same Meaning to say: *One is All*" (EGT, 59).

43. The address is intended here as happening or proceeding according to a precedence forever unable to be anticipated. Cf. also GA 55, 189.

44. Cf. the central question of the course on Heraclitus, GA 55, 219: "die Frage bleibt, wie das Gedachte ist, ob nur als Gegenstand und Objekt. . . ."

45. Cf. GA 55, 231–32.

46. That to which Heidegger at first appeared so attentive, inquiring about the "*Seinsweise*" proper to the multiplicity of regions or sectors of being, according to the multiplicity of its irreducible senses.

47. Cf. J.-F. Courtine, "Phenomenology and/or Tautology," in *Reading Heidegger: Commemorations*, ed. John Sallis (Bloomington, IN: Indiana University Press, 1993), 241–57.

48. In this sense, the destruction of logic includes the destruction of metaphysics (GA 55, 253 and 257), following the essential connection of the "*Rückgang*" and the "*Überwindung*" already well established at the time of the *Einführung in die Metaphysik*.

49. We must recall that Heidegger himself refers to this course in his "Aus einem Gespräch von der Sprache," in US, 93: "Im Sommersemester des Jahres 1934 hielt ich eine Vorlesung unter dem Titel: 'Logik'. Es war jedoch eine Besinnung auf den λόγος, worin ich das Wesen der Sprache suchte." "In the summer semester of 1934, I offered a lecture series under the title 'Logic'. In fact, however, it was a reflection on the λόγος, in which I was trying to find the nature of language" (OWL, 8).

50. "Wir haben Gründe für die Behauptung, daß gerade 'die Logik' die Wesensentfaltung des λόγος nicht nur gehemmt, sondern verwehrt hat und noch verwehrt" (GA 55, 232).

51. "Gemäß dem Geschick, nach dem der λόγος in der abendländischen Geschichte und in der Weltgeschichte überhaupt sein Wesen entfaltet und nicht entfaltet, bildet sich die 'Logik' und ihre Geschichte" (GA 55, 218). Cf. also Einführung in die Metaphysik: "Die Philosophie der Griechen gelangt zur abendländischen Herrschaft nicht aus ihrem ursprünglichen Anfang, sondern aus dem anfänglichen Ende, das in Hegel groß und endgültig zur Vollendung gestaltet wird..." (EM, 144). "The philosophy of the Greeks conquered the Western world not in its original beginning but in the incipient end, which in Hegel assumed great and definitive form . . . " (IM, 189).

52. "The word's rule springs to light as that which makes the thing be a thing. [. . . .] The oldest word for the rule of the word thus thought, for Saying, is λόγος: Saying which, in showing, lets beings appear in their 'it is'" (OWL, 155).

53. Cf. Einführung in die Metaphysik: "Die Griechen haben nicht erst an den Naturvorgängen erfahren, was φύσις ist, sondern umgekehrt: aufgrund einer dichtend-denkenden Grunderfahrung des Seins erschloß sich ihnen das, was sie φύσις nennen mußten" (EM, 11). "The Greeks did not learn what φύσις is through natural phenomena, but the other way around: it was through a fundamental poetic and intellectual experience of being that they discovered what they had to call φύσις" (IM, 14).

54. "But . . . let us skip over this whole process of deformation and decay and attempt to regain the unimpaired strength of words; for words and language are not wrappings in which things are packed for the commerce of those who write and speak. It is in words and language that things first come into being and are" (IM, 13). The problematic of language is itself historially-destinally overdetermined, as is also the question of being, of its forgetting or of its "abandoning": "Auch sind nur die Wenigsten noch imstande, dieses Miß- und Unverhältnis des heutigen Daseins zur Sprache in seiner ganzen Tragweite auszudenken. Nur die Lehre des Wortes 'Sein' . . . ist nicht ein bloßer Einzelfall der allgemeinen Sprachvernutzung, sondern—der zerstörte Bezug zum Sein als solchem ist der eigentliche Grund für unser gesamtes Mißverhältnis zur Sprache. [. . . .] Weil das Schicksal der Sprache in dem jeweiligen Bezug eines Volkes zum Sein gegründet ist, deschalb wird sich uns die Frage nach dem Sein zuinnerst mit der Frage nach der Sprache verschlingen" (EM, 39). "And only a very few are capable of thinking through the full implications of this misrelation and unrelation of present-day being-there to language. But the emptiness of the word 'being' . . . is not merely a particular instance of the general exhaustion of language; rather, the destroyed relation to being as such is the actual reason for the general misrelation to language. [. . . .] Because the destiny of language is grounded in a nation's relation to

being, the question of being will involve us deeply in the question of language" (IM, 51).

55. "[D]ie 'Seinsfrage' im Sinne der metaphysischen Frage nach dem Seinenden als solchem *frägt* gerade *nicht* thematisch nach dem Sein. Dieses bliebt vergessen. Doch entsprechend zweideutig wie der Titel 'Seinsfrage' ist die Rede von der 'Seinsvergessenheit'" (EM, 14). "[T]he 'question of being' in the sense of the metaphysical question regarding beings as such does *not* inquire thematically into being. In this way of asking, being remains forgotten. But just as ambiguous as the 'question of being' referred to in the title is what is said about 'forgetfulness of being'" (IM, 18).

56. "Is 'being' a mere word and its meaning a vapor or is it the spiritual destiny of the Western world? [. . . .] To ask 'How does it stand with being?' means nothing less than to recapture, to repeat, the beginning of our historical–spiritual existence, in order to transform it into a new beginning" (IM, 37, 39).

57. GA 51, *Grundbegriffe*, 15–16; BC, 12–13.

58. "The beginning is not the past, but, having decided everything in advance," what awaits us.

59. GA 45, *Grundfragen der Philosophie, Ausgewählt 'Probleme' der 'Logik'*, 124. *Basic Questions of Philosophy: Selected 'Problems' of 'Logic'*: "We are standing before the decision between the end (and its running out, which may still take centuries) and another beginning . . ." (BQ, 108).

60. GA 34, 324: "dieser Wandel des Wesens der Wahrheit ist die Umwälzung des ganzen menschlichen Seins, an deren Beginn wir stehen. Das Ausmaß und die Unerbittlichkeit dieser Umwälzung des Seins des Menschen und der Welt vermögen zwar nur wenige heute schon zu ahnen und abzuschätzen; aber das beweist ja nicht, daß dieser Wandel *nicht* geschieht, daß wir nicht mit jeder Stunde und jedem Tag in eine völlige neue Geschichte menschlichen Daseins hineinrollen. Ein solch innerster Wandel aber ist keine bloße Ablösung vom Bisherigen, sondern ist schärfste und weiteste Auseinandersetzung der Daseinskräfte und der Mächte des Seins. [. . . .] Die Seinsfrage ist zweideutig. Das erste, was not ist, ist der Eingang in die Überwindung der Metaphysik, deren *Vollendung* zuvor erfahren sein Muß,— dieses aber als das, was jetzt und zunächst 'ist'."

61. GA 34, 14

62. GA 45, 114–115: "Wir müssen uns deshalb darauf besinnen, ob dieses Geschehnis, daß die Griechen zwar das Wesen der Wahrheit als Unverborgenheit erfuhren und in Anspruch nahmen und stets bereit hatten, aber nicht eigens zur Frage machten und nicht ergründeten, ob dieses Geschehnis ein Versäumnis und die Folge einer Unkraft zum Fragen war, oder ob darin gerade die eigentliche Größe des griechischen Denkens besteht und sich

vollzieht. Die Entscheidung hierüber ist nicht der Erklärungs- und Rettungsversuch eines vergangenen Vorgangs . . . , wohl aber die Umgrenzung der Art und Weise, wie *wir* zur Wahrheit und in der Wahrheit stehen. Denn was im Anfang der Geschichte der Wesensgründung der Wahrheit geschah, steht *für* uns immer *vor* uns zur Entscheidung—als Entscheidung darüber, was uns und den Künftigen zum Wahren werden und das Wahre sein kann." "We must therefore reflect on this occurrence, that the Greeks did indeed experience the essence of truth as unconcealedness, took it up, and always had it available to them, but did not question it explicitly and did not fathom it. Was this event mere neglect and the result of an incapacity of questioning, or does the genuine greatness of Greek thought consist precisely in this and accomplish itself in it? The decision here is not an attempt to explain and rescue a past incident . . . but is instead the delimitation of the way *we* take a stand toward truth and stand in the truth. For what came to pass at the beginning of the history of the essential foundation of truth always remains for us still to be decided—a decision about what for us and for the future can become true and can be true" (BQ, 100–101). "*Versäumnis*" is, in return, the term regularly employed by Heidegger, being in question from Husserl or from Descartes (GA 20, *Prolegomena zur Geschichte des Zeitsbegriff*, §§ 12 and 13).

63. "[F]or the Greeks, ἀλήθεια remained inceptional and unquestionable. . . . For Greek Dasein, ἀλήθεια remained the most powerful and at the same time the most hidden" (BQ, 175).

64. "Logos (Heraclitus, Fragment B 50)," in EGT, 78. "Einmal jedoch, im Beginn des abendländischen Denkens, blitzte das Wesen der Sprache im Lichte des Seins auf. . . . Aber der Blitz verlosch jäh" (VA, 221).

65. "Moira (Parmenides VIII)": "jenes erste Aufleuchten der Sprachwesens als Sage alsbald in eine Verhüllung entschwindet . . ." (VA, 237).

66. *Das Ereignis 1941/1942* as quoted by Otto Pöggeler in *Der Denkweg M. Heideggers* (Stuttgart: Neske, 1963), 218. Cf. *Martin Heidegger's Path of Thinking*, trans. D. Magurshak and S. Barber (Atlantic Highlands, NJ: Humanities Press), 1989, 176: "In the moment of throwing off the last metaphysical misinterpretations, that is, in the moment of the first, most extreme questionability of Being itself and of its truth (lecture on truth 1929–30), Hölderlin's word, already previously known like that of other poets, became a destiny."

67. GA 39, 33.

68. Ibid. 30 sq. Cf. also the commentary on "Wie wenn am Feiertage," in *Erläuterungen zu Hölderlins Dichtung*, GA 4, 71 sq.

69. "Der Dichter zwingt und bannt die Blitze des Gottes ins Wort und stellt dieses blitzgeladene Wort in die Sprache seines Volkes . . . sondern steht 'unter Gottes Gewittern'—'mit entblösstem Haupte,' schutzlos preis- und von sich weggegeben. Dasein *ist* nichts anderes als die *Ausgesetztheit in die Übermacht des Seyns*" (GA 39, 30–31)

70. GA 39, 31.

71. "Die erste Strophe unseres Gedichtes und dieses selbst ist keine Naturschilderung, kein Vergleich. Es wird hier überhaupt nicht etwas über etwas anderes gesagt. Das Sagen dieser Dichtung ist in sich der Jubel des Seyns. [. . . .] Diese Sagen ist nicht eine Worthülle für einen Sinn und Hintersinn, sondern es selbst, so wie es gesagt ist, ist das Walten des Seyns" (GA 39, 255–6).

72. "Wir sind ein Gespräch. Wie stehen Gespräch und Sprache zueinander? Im Gespräch geschieht die Sprache, und dieses Geschehen ist eigentlich ihr Seyn. Wir sind—ein Sprachgeschehnis, und dieses Geschehen ist zeitlich, aber nicht nur in dem äußerlichen Sinne, daß es in der Zeit abläuft, nach Beginn, Dauer und Aufhören jeweils zeitlich meßbar ist, sondern das Sprachgeschehnis ist der Anfang und Grund der eigentlichen geschichtlichen Zeit des Menschen. [. . . .] Unser Seyn geschieht als Gespräch, im Geschehen dessen, daß die Götter uns ansprechen, uns unter ihren Anspruch stellen, *uns zur Sprache bringen*, ob und wie wir sind, wie wir antworten. [. . . .] Nur wo Sprache geschieht, eröffnen sich Sein und Nichtsein" (GA 39, 69-70)

73. *Aus der Erfahrung des Denkens*, GA 13, 84. Cf. also "Der Spruch des Anaximander": "Das Denken sagt das Diktat der Wahrheit des Seins. [. . . .] Das Denken ist das ursprüngliche *dictare*. Das Denken ist die Urdichtung" (GA 5, 328).

74. "Sprechen, das die Sprache durch den Menschen spricht" (WHD, 87). "Language speaks through the mouth of man" (WCT, 128).

Two

The Place of the Presocratics in Heidegger's
Beiträge zur Philosophie

Parvis Emad

So ist der Mensch; wenn da ist
das Gut, und es sorget mit Gaben
Selber ein Gott für ihn, kennet
und sieht er es nicht.
Tragen muss er, zuvor; nun aber
nennt er sein Liebstes,
Nun, nun müssen dafür Worte, wie
Blumen, entstehen.

Hölderlin, "Brot und Wein"[1]

To the extent that Heidegger's works, on the early Greek thinkers after the turn (*die Kehre*) have been published or are scheduled to appear in the *Gesamtausgabe*, they begin with his lecture course of the summer semester 1932, *Der Anfang der abendländischen Philosophie: Anaximander und Parmenides* (*The Beginning of Western Philosophy: Anaximander and Parmenides*) and end with *Heraklit* of 1966/67.

Thus, in the span of almost four decades, Heidegger produces an incomparably large body of work devoted to the early Greek thinkers. At the risk of oversimplification, it could be said that this body of work accomplishes two closely interrelated goals. First, in his published works on Parmenides (1942–1943) and Heraclitus (1944), he totally undoes the assumption—that for almost two millennia predetermined the understanding of Heraclitus and Parmenides—that Heraclitus is the thinker of change, while Parmenides is the thinker of permanence. Jean Beaufret clearly presents this long-held assumption thus:

55

It is customary to oppose Heraclitus and Parmenides, like two gladiators, sword in hand, facing each other in the beginning of thought—a custom which goes back to antiquity, as we find it already well-established in Plato.[2]

A significant consequence of undoing this assumption is the need for a new reading of Plato, which Heidegger accomplishes in several works devoted to this philosopher.

Secondly, with his works on these and other early Greek thinkers, Heidegger opens up a hitherto covered-over and forgotten domain, the domain of the aletheiological beginning of thinking. This opening is of such unparalleled philosophical magnitude that, at the end of his life and in retrospect, Heidegger can say: "In a certain way ἀλήθεια is manifest and always already experienced." ('Αλήθεια ist in gewisser Weise offenkundig und stets erfahren [GA 1, 438].)

Now, whereas this work of undoing and dismantling the dichotomy—Heraclitus as the thinker of change and Parmenides as the thinker of permanence—as well as the opening of the domain of the aletheiological beginning of thinking (if we insist on staying with these two achievements), take place in works dedicated specifically to early Greek thinking, this work is firmly grounded in *Beiträge zur Philosophie (Vom Ereignis)*, Heidegger's second major work after *Being and Time*. This work is written between 1936–1938 and published posthumously in 1989. I take seriously the words "firmly grounded" because, while I want to suggest that Heidegger's later work is grounded in *Beiträge zur Philosophie*, I do *not* want to suggest that Heidegger has a system of thought à la Hegel that beginning with *Beiträge zur Philosophie* assimilates the whole history of philosophy, including the fragmented writings of the early Greeks.

Keeping this proviso in mind while turning to *Beiträge zur Philosophie*, we initially find ourselves confronted with a surprising omission: At the juncture where Heidegger programmatically mentions his future lecture courses on the history of philosophy (GA 65, 176), he mentions Leibniz, Kant, Hegel, Schelling, and Nietzsche but *not* the early Greek thinkers, the so-called Presocratics. As I shall try to show, it is exactly this omission that points to the place of the early Greek thinkers in *Beiträge zur Philosophie*. As the first step in this direction we must understand the structure of this major work. For it is through this structure that Heidegger enacts a new thinking of being which addresses the aletheiological beginning. This thinking is new because, unlike the thinking of fundamental ontology, it traverses the pathway of non-historiographical historicality of being (*Geschichtlichkeit des Seins*), thereby unfolding the thinking of being as the thinking of *Ereignis*.

I

As early as 1931 and as late as 1932 the plan for writing *Beiträge zur Philosophie* is already laid out.[3] Having gone down the path of thinking of being, the path of fundamental ontology, Heidegger in these years realizes the need for moving from fundamental ontology into the path of non-historiographical historicality of being. It is this move that leads him to the historicality of being itself. The external indication of this move is discussed in a letter to Elisabeth Blochmann on September 18, 1932:

> People already believe and talk about my writing *Being and Time II*. That is okay. But because *Being and Time I* was for me once a *pathway* that led me somewhere and because I can no longer traverse that pathway, and it is already overgrown, I cannot write *Being and Time II*. I do not write a book at all.

> Man denkt und redet schon darüber, daß ich nun "Sein und Zeit II" schreibe. Das ist gut so. Aber da "Sein und Zeit I" einmal für mich ein Weg war, der mich irgendwohin führte, dieser *Weg* aber jetzt nicht mehr begangen und schon verwachsen ist, kann ich "Sein und Zeit II" gar nicht mehr schreiben. Ich schreibe überhaupt kein Buch.[4]

This move from thinking of being as fundamental ontology to the non-historiographical historicality of being is not an arbitrary one. It is a full and well-rounded response to "the turning-relation-in-being" (*der kehrige Bezug des Seins*) which Heidegger experiences the moment he is engaged in the thinking of being. In other words "turning-relation-in-being" is a turning that precedes the move from the perspective of fundamental ontology to that of the non-historiographical historicality of being. Put briefly, the "turning-relation-in-being" is not the result of thinking of fundamental ontology having run its course but is exactly the motivating power that sets this thinking in motion.[5]

The realization that the thinking of the non-historiographical historicality of Dasein's world (*die Geschichtlichkeit des Daseins*) in *Being and Time* does not reach the dimension of the non-historiographical historicality of being itself is rooted in "the turning-relation-in-being" and constitutes the decisive element in the thinking of being's moving from the path of fundamental ontology into the new path of the thinking of being's historicality. It is an awareness of the philosophical magnitude of this move that gives birth to *Beiträge zu Philosophie (Vom Ereignis)*.

The move from the earlier perspective to the new one takes along and transforms the structure of Dasein as worked out in *Being and Time*.[6] I shall return to this point taking a brief look at *Beiträge zur Philosophie*, because the emergence of the transformed structure of Dasein in the new perspective of the thinking of being as *Ereignis* is of unparalleled importance for determining the place of early Greek thinking in this work.

Heidegger says that *Beiträge zur Philosophie* is not "a 'work' written according to the hitherto prevailing style" (*ein 'Werk' bisherigen Stils*) (GA 65, 3). There are at least four reasons why *Beiträge zur Philosophie* is unlike any other major work of philosophy.

The first reason pertains to the language of this work. As Heidegger puts it,

> here saying does not stand over against what is to be said. Rather saying itself *is* what is to be said, namely being's in-depth-sway.

> hier ist das Sagen nicht im Gegenüber zu dem zu Sagenden, sondern ist dieses selbst als die Wesung des Seyns (GA 65, 4).

In the language of this work, saying is no longer separate from what is said.

The second reason is that this work originates from within a grounding attunement (*Grundstimmung*) called *Verhaltenheit*, in which what is to be thought is held back and kept in reserve. This grounding attunement holds in reserve the unfolding of "being's in-depth-sway" (*die Wesung des Seyns*) named *Ereignis*.

The third reason is that the thinking that goes on in *Beiträge zur Philosophie* unabatedly receives "the ongoing enjoining of a beckoning . . . " (*das Weiterwinken eines Winkes . . .*) (GA 65, 4) from the interplay between the guiding question (*Leitfrage*) of philosophy "what is a being in its being?" (τὶ τό ὄν) *and* the root question (*Grundfrage*), that is, the question of the truth of "being's-in-depth-sway" (*Die Wahrheit der Wesung des Seyns*). Here we may think of Kant. While the *Critique of Pure Reason* is concerned with determining the condition for the possibility of the objects of experience, that is, beingness of beings—and so follows the terrain of tradition's preoccupation with ὄν—this work does not take up the root question concerning the truth of "being's-in-depth-sway" as an occurrence that is simultaneous (*gleichzeitig*) with manifestness of ὄν (GA 65, 13, 222f.).

The fourth reason is that *Beiträge zur Philosophie* is not divided into main sections and chapters by which an author progressively demonstrates and establishes a preconceived thesis. In Kant's *Critique of Pure Reason* the three main sections called "Transcendental Aesthetic," "Transcendental Logic," and "Transcendental Dialectic" progressively demonstrate and establish the thesis concerning the *a priori* elements that determine "Sensibility," "Understanding," and "Reason." In contrast, we find nothing even remotely similar to such a progressive development of a thesis in *Beiträge zur Philosophie*. Strictly speaking, the thinking that goes on in *Beiträge zur Philosophie* is "not a goal-oriented activity of an individual nor a limited calculation of a community." (. . . nicht ein bezwecktes Tun eines Einzelnen und keine beschränkte Berechnung einer Gemeinschaft ist [GA 65, 4].) This becomes more clear as we take up the structure of this work.

Instead of chapters *Beiträge zur Philosophie* is made up of six "joinings" (*Fügungen*). The six joinings of this work are: The Echo (*Der Anklang*), The Inter-Play (*Das Zuspiel*), The Leap (*Der Sprung*), The Founding (*Die Gründung*), The Future Ones (*Die Zu-künftigen*), and The Last God (*Der letzte Gott*). Each joining names a region in which being sways in depth as *Ereignis*. Heidegger takes great care to describe the relationships between the six joinings in view of precisely this regioning:

> Each of the six joinings . . . stands for itself, but only so as to make the onefold [that joins them] more penetrating in its depth. In each of the six joinings [thinking] attempts to say the same about the same, but in each joining in view of an other region wherein being's sway unfolds in its depth as *Ereignis* and as what names *Ereignis*.

> Die sechs Fügungen . . . stehen je für sich, aber nur, um die wesentliche Einheit eindringlicher zu machen. In jeder der sechs Fügungen wird über das Selbe je das Selbe zu sagen versucht, aber

jeweils aus einem anderen Wesensbereich dessen, was das Ereignis nennt (GA 65, 81-82).

The word *Wesensbereich* appropriately shows that each joining is a region wherein "being's-in-depth-sway" unfolds as *Ereignis*. It is a gross misunderstanding to render this word as "essential realm," because the word "essence" resonates in the word "essential" and misleads thinking into assuming that what occurs in each "region" is a self-same, identical process reminiscent of ἰδέα, κοινόν, and *essentia*. The truth, however, is that each region/joining manifests "being's-in-depth-sway" as *Ereignis* in a manner peculiar to that joining. A mere echo that resounds in the first joining through beings' abandonment by being (*Seinsverlassenheit des Seienden*), "being's-in-depth-sway" in the sixth "joining" manifests *Ereignis* as the occurrence that takes place before the passage (*Vorbeigang*) of the last God.

It is necessary not only to understand that each joining is a region wherein "being's-in-depth-sway" unfolds as *Ereignis* but also to realize that each joining/region involves the transformed structure of Dasein. To begin to understand this transformation we must remember that, in the thinking of being within the perspective of fundamental ontology, Dasein's structure consists of "thrownness" (*Geworfenheit*), "projection" (*Entwurf*), and "being-along-with" (*Sein-bei*). All three are intimately bound to *Rede*, that is, to the deepest unfolding of language.[7] We must also remember that this structure is not a rigid and extant structure, because it is a structure *of* and *for* being's disclosure, that is, *Erschlossenheit des Seins*.

To understand the transformation that Dasein's structure undergoes when the thinking of being takes the path of being's historicality, we must bear two things in mind. First, we must take seriously the manner in which *Beiträge zur Philosophie* explicitly acknowledges the inestimable achievement of *Being and Time*:

Da-sein never lets itself be demonstrated and described as something extant. Dasein is to be obtained only hermeneutically. And this means according to *Being and Time* that Dasein is to be obtained in thrown projection.

Da-sein lässt sich nie auf-weisen und beschreiben wie ein Vorhandenes. Nur hermeneutisch zu gewinnen, d.h. aber nach "Sein und Zeit" im geworfenem Entwurf (GA 65, 231).

But *Beiträge zur Philosophie* does not stop with acknowledging the achievement of *Being and Time* in uncovering Dasein in thrown projection. Beyond this acknowledgement—the second thing to bear in mind—this work also presents directives for understanding the transformation that thrown projection undergoes when the thinking of being takes the path of being's historicality. The following passage, which calls for careful attention, presents the directives for grasping that transformation. In its entirety the passage reads:

The leap is the enactment of projection of the truth of being in the sense of shifting into the open in such a way that one who throws forth, i.e. projects, experiences itself as thrown into, i.e. appropriated by being.

Der Sprung ist der Vollzug des Entwurfs der Wahrheit des Seyns im Sinne der Einrückung in das Offene, dergestalt daß der Werfer des Entwurfs als Geworfener sich erfährt, d.h. er-eignet durch das Seyn (GA 65, 239).

It is striking that here "projection" is linked to "the leap." It is also striking that "projection" is characterized as enactment of "the leap" through which thinking opens up the truth of being. Thus we may ask: leap into what? The response is: leap into "being's-in-depth-sway" called *Ereignis* (*Wesung des Seyns als Ereignis*, cf. GA 65, 7).

But, for the leap to be enacted, two things need to be open to each other: "projection" must be open to "being's-in-depth-sway" as *Ereignis* and "being's-in-depth-sway" as *Ereignis* must be open to "projection." It is this mutual opening that is meant by the phrase "shifting into the open." For, when projection occurs as shifting into the open, projection does not enter the domain of "being's-in-depth-sway" named *Ereignis* as if "projection" were a doing (*Handeln*) initially closed off to the openness of this domain and trapped in a closure. The phenomenologically significant point concerning projection is that projection shifts into the openness of "being's-in-depth-sway," because projection itself is open and receptive to this openness. Projection is a doing which is from the beginning open to receiving and opening up "being's-in-depth-sway" as *Ereignis*. By receiving and opening up this "sway," projection opens up "being's-in-depth-sway" and keeps it open. Were it not for the crucial openness of projection to "being's-in-depth-sway," projection would indicate the intrusion of a closure into the domain of openness, namely, "being's-in-depth-sway." Were this the case, projection would be the juncture where closure to "being's-sway" and openness of this sway come into collision. Collision between closure and openness, however, is bereft of a phenomenological relevance—it is sheer speculation.

And there lies the first directive: "Projection" in the perspective of *Beiträge zur Philosophie* is openness to "being's-in-depth-sway" as *Ereignis*. This directive leads us to the second one. By opening, that is, projecting, "being's-in-depth-sway" as *Ereignis*, one who enacts the projection in the sense of opening up "being's-in-depth-sway," experiences itself as thrown into and thus appropriated by this sway's openness. The upshot of the second directive is the concomitant transformation of "projection" and "thrownness." Projection, as the opening up of "being's-in-depth-sway" (*Ereignis*), cannot be enacted unless one who projects this "sway" experiences itself as being thrown into and appropriated by "being's-in-depth-sway" (*Ereignis*).

Pulling together these two directives, we arrive at the transformed structure of Dasein. Accordingly, thrownness manifests Dasein as being thrown into "being's-in-depth-sway"; in throwing forth in this way, the "throw" is an appropriating of Dasein. However, in appropriating Dasein, being indicates not only Dasein's thrownness forth into being's appropriating throw (*ereignender Zuwurf*), but also the need of this "throw" to be projected, that is, opened up and kept open by the appropriated projection (*ereigneter Entwurf*). Thus, we sum up the transformed structure of Dasein by saying that thrownness means being thrown forth into being's appropriating throw and that projection indicates opening up this throw by the appropriated projection. It is this transformed structure which upholds and runs throughout the six joinings/regions of *Beiträge zur Philosophie*. Keeping this structure constantly in view, we now turn to the joining named "The Inter-Play" (*Das Zuspiel*), as the region in which early Greek thinking is at home.

II

Early Greek thinking shines in the joining "The Inter-Play" without becoming thematic in any direct way. Five directives held within the five sentences that make up the opening section of this joining help us see how early Greek thinking shines forth and is housed in this joining. To proceed with this task, it is necessary that we carefully read the opening section, both in English translation and in the original German. For the original German may become somewhat more accessible in the light of the readability of its English translation. Given the brevity of the opening section of "The Inter-Play," this reading may be accomplished fairly quickly:

> Coming to grips with the necessity of *an other* beginning, as this beginning emerges from out of the setting-up of the first beginning. The *guiding attunement* [in this process] is the joy in questioning the ongoing vibration back and forth of the beginnings. All the issues involved in differentiating the guiding-question from the root-question; responding to the guiding-question [as distinguished from] the genuine unfolding of this question [as] the passage to the root-question (*Being and Time*)—all belong here. [Likewise] all lecture courses on the "history" of philosophy belong here. [Moreover], the decision on all "ontologies" will be made here.

> Die Auseinandersetzung der Notwendigkeit des anderen Anfangs aus der ursprünglichen Setzung des ersten Anfangs. *Die Leitstimmung*: Die Lust der fragenden wechselweisen Übersteigung der Anfänge. Hierzu alles über die Unterscheidung von Leitfrage und Grundfrage; Leitfragenbeantwortung und eigentliche Leitfragenentfaltung; Übergang zur Grundfrage ("Sein und Zeit"). Alle Vorlesungen über "Geschichte" der Philosophie. Die Entscheidung über alle "Ontologien" (GA 65, 169).

I shall begin by first working out the five directives in the sequence in which they appear in this opening section and then by commenting on them. The first directive for determining the place of the Presocratics in "The Inter-Play" takes on the form of an imperative "to come to terms with *an other* beginning" as it gets set up in the first beginning. Briefly, this directive is summed up in the phrase "coming to terms with *an other* beginning."

The second directive addresses the unavoidable prerequisite for enacting that imperative. This prerequisite is not based on arguments that support a system of thought. Rather this prerequisite is an attunement, that precedes *and* happens in thinking. Briefly, the second directive reminds us that the first directive does not come from a subjective preference but originates from within an attunement that overwhelms thinking prior to its entrapment in subjectivity. The third directive puts forth a differentiation which is of fundamental importance for the thinking that goes on in *Beiträge zur Philosophie*, namely, the differentiation between "guiding question" and "root question." Based on this differentiation, the third directive distinguishes two ways of dealing with the "guiding question": responding to it *and* unfolding it. This distinction is of paramount importance for determining the place of the aletheiological thinking of the Presocratics. The fourth directive states that all lecture courses on the history of philosophy belong to the domain opened up by the passage from the "guiding question" to the "root question." The fifth and final directive is closely tied in with the previous one: all "ontologies" will be differentiated (*Entscheiden/ Scheiden*) in accord with the domain opened up by the questions that guide philosophy and in which thinking is grounded.

Considering these directives, we notice that the first three point to the transformed structure of Dasein. How does the first directive point to the transformation of Dasein's structure, "thrownness" and "projection"? *An other* beginning transforms this structure insofar as Dasein is *thrown forth* into this beginning's throw and opens up this throw by *projecting* it. To begin to understand "beginning's forth-throw" we draw upon the word *Anfang* (beginning). This word preserves the "activity" of *fangen* as taking, seizing, holding etc. *An other* beginning (*ein anderer Anfang*) "seizes" Dasein but, in contrast to politically and sociologically familiar modes of seizing, *an other* beginning does not seize Dasein by brute force but reticently, by way of an "enjoining beckoning." (The rendition of *Anfang* as "starting" is misleading because, aside from the mechanical connotation of this word as in "starting an engine," this word conveys the impression that, in matters pertaining to being (*Sein*), Dasein can make a start and thus be in charge—which is flatly refuted by Dasein's thrownness in being's forth-throw.)

The second directive points to the transformed structure of Dasein insofar as being's forth-throw is attuned to the joy of questioning the beginnings. This attunement hints at the "enjoining of a beckoning" that comes from the interplay between the "guiding question" and the "root question."

The third directive draws in the transformed structure of projection and is important for finding the place of the aletheiological thinking of the early Greeks in *Beiträge zur Philosophie*. It is this aletheiological thinking that needs to be projected, that is, opened up in an appropriated projection. This is clearly in keeping with what we discussed earlier about transformation of the structure called "projection." It will be recalled that "projection" is not a closure that collides with the openness of being's appropriating forth throw, because "projection" is never closed off to this openness and trapped in closure. As appropriated, "projection" opens up the aletheiological thinking of the Presocratics because "projection" is always already open to and thus appropriated by the thinking of ἀλήθεια.

The primary outcome of this projection is opening up the subtle interconnection in the first beginning between ἀλήθεια and τό ἀλήθεζ at the end of the first beginning: "Plato and Aristotle . . . always name ἀλήθεια when they name a being: ἀλήθεια και ὄν, the unconcealment, i.e., a being in its beingness (GA 45, 121–122)."[8] If the primary outcome of projecting, that is, opening the interconnection between unconcealment and an unconcealed being, not only puts in the foreground ἀλήθεια but also ἀλήθεια και ὄν, then the opening up of the aletheiological beginning is simultaneously the opening up of the question "τὶ τό ὄν" that guides the philosophies of Plato and Aristotle at the end of the first beginning. The "guiding question" τὶ τό ὄν must be carefully differentiated from the "root question." While the former guides thinking to a being, that is, ὄν, the latter is a question concerned with thinking and opening up ἀλήθεια itself. For the Presocratics name ἀλήθεια without opening it through thinking-questioning. And this means that the aletheiological beginning is ambiguous through and through.

This ambiguity comes to the fore when the "guiding question" is differentiated from the "root question," thus hinting at the place that the Presocratics occupy in *an other* beginning. This beginning assigns a place to the aletheiological thinking of the Presocratics as a thinking that names ἀλήθεια without opening and projecting it. At the same time this thinking is not identical with the ὄν-oriented thinking of Plato and Aristotle. When this thinking heeds the "enjoining beckoning" that comes from the "guiding question" τὶ τό ὄν, then it finds its place in *an other* beginning.

The fourth directive immediately follows the differentiation between the "guiding question" and the "root question." The former question is driven by an irresistible force that for the past two and a half millennia brings forth a series of responses. *Beiträge zur Philosophie* calls this process of offering responses to the "guiding question" a *Leitfragenbeantwortung*. This process steadfastly hinders the unfolding of the "guiding question," an unfolding that this work calls *Leit-fragenentfaltung*. Thus the fourth directive is concerned with the magnitude of responses to the "guiding question" and aims at the *Leit-fragenbeantwortung* as the main focus of Heidegger's later lecture courses. The later lecture courses focus on the various responses to the guiding question *in their magnitude*—for example, Hegel's response is no ordinary event!—for the sake of letting the root-unfolding (*Wesen* as distinguished from *Wesung*) of metaphysics emerge. Thus, whereas the thinking that goes on in *Beiträge zur Philosophie* takes seriously the responses to the "guiding question," this work relegates the *task* of dealing with these responses to Heidegger's later courses on the history of philosophy and attends only to the *unfolding* itself of the "guiding question."

The fifth directive follows from the fourth one. By differentiating the responses to the "guiding question" from its unfolding, the fifth directive sets the course for differentiating all ontologies beginning with the aletheiological thinking of the Presocratics.

Now, when we gather together these five directives we cannot fail to see that, in one way or another, they *all* stress the importance of the "enjoining beckoning" which comes from the crossing (*Übergang*) that spans from the "guiding question" to the "root question." By receiving this "beckoning," aletheiological thinking of the Presocratics begins to cross the domain of the first beginning toward the domain of *an other* beginning. But this crossing seems to be delayed when the fifth section of "The Inter-Play" explicitly emphasizes the first beginning. To see this, we must attend to this section of "The Inter-Play."

The title of this section is not a heading under which the text of the respective section is subsumed. Rather, this title, like all the titles of the two hundred and eighty-one sections of *Beiträge zur Philosophie*, is an integral part of the text itself. Thus, by elucidating this title I will show simultaneously the recurrence in this section of the crossing of the "guiding question" toward the "root question" and the emerging of the "enjoining beckoning."

In original German the title of the fifth section reads: "*Die ursprüngliche Zueignung des ersten Anfangs bedeutet das Fußfassen im anderen Anfang.*" In contrast to my practice so far, I postpone translating this title into English, for two closely interrelated reasons. First, translation of the word *Zueignung* is not an easy task and requires careful preparation. Second, translation of the word *Zueignung* must be *most appropriate*, for it opens the way for understanding the interplay between the "guiding question" and the "root question," the interplay which is under the mandate of the "enjoining beckoning" that comes from these questions.

What *Zueignung* says in the title of this section has nothing to do with its ordinary usage such as "dedication," as in "dedicating a book to someone." On the other hand, translating *Zueignung* with "appropriation" would eliminate the difference between *Aneignung* and *Zueignung*, the former clearly meaning appropriation. How then to translate the word *Zueignung*? I propose to take seriously the movement indicated by the prefix *zu* and look for possibilities that would bring this movement into English. After we accomplish this, we can subsequently look for a word that would convey the sense of *Eignung*.

I find the possibility for bringing the movement of *zu* into English in the prefix "en," which according to *The Concise Oxford Dictionary*, indicates bringing something into a certain condition.[9] Since German *Eignung* can readily be rendered with "owning," and since the English prefix "en" captures the movement of bringing something into a certain condition, we may combine "en" and "owning" and render the German *Zueignung* with "enowning," that is, bringing something into the condition of owning.

Now we proceed to translate the title of the fifth section of "The Inter-Play," which is also the first sentence of this section: "The original enowning of the first beginning . . . means taking root in the other beginning." (Die ursprüngliche Zueignung des ersten Anfangs . . . bedeutet das Fußfassen im anderen Anfang [GA 65, 171].) It is quite important to note that, following this title, the fifth section of "The Inter-Play" returns to the "guiding question" in its connection to the "root question," and once again places in the foreground the crossing of the one toward the other, and, by implication, highlights the "enjoining beckoning" that guides that crossing. It should be obvious that rendition of *Zueignung* with "enowning" and its differentiation from *Aneignung* (appropriation) plays a significant role in understanding the crossing and in noticing the "enjoining beckoning" that guides it. For this reason we must read the fifth section:

The original enowning of the first beginning (and that means its history) means taking root in an other beginning. Such root taking gets accomplished in crossing the *guiding question* (what is a being? as a question concerning beingness, being) toward the *root-question*, namely "what is the truth of being?"

Die ursprüngliche Zueignung des ersten Anfangs (und d.h. seiner Geschichte) bedeutet das Fußfassen im anderen Anfang. Dieses vollzieht sich im Übergang von der *Leitfrage* (was ist das Seiende? Frage nach der Seiendheit, Sein) zur *Grundfrage*: was ist die Wahrheit des Seyns? (GA 65, 171).

Recalling the opening section of "The Inter-Play" and reading the first paragraph of its fifth section, we can easily see that in both sections *Beiträge zur Philosophie* is engaged in what this work calls *Leit-fragenentfaltung*, that is, the unfolding of the "guiding question."

The unfolding of the guiding question—which is totally different from a critical debate with and an assessment of the traditional responses to this question—reveals the "root question" of the truth of being, its "in-depth-sway" as a question that is covered over by the tradition of metaphysics in the continuity of its responses to the "guiding question." Moreover, the unfolding of the "guiding question" τὶ τό ὄν is simultaneously the unfolding of ἀλήθεια as ἀλήθεια καὶ ὄν—an unfolding which directly draws in the aletheiological thinking of the Presocratics. Finally, the unfolding of the aletheiological thinking of the Presocratics along with the reverberation of this thinking in the ὄν-oriented thinking of the later Greeks (Plato and Aristotle) reveal the interplay between the first beginning and *an other* beginning. In short, this interplay is played under the mandate of the "enjoining beckoning" that is *the* guide to *an other* beginning toward which the "guiding question" is already underway.

The phrase "coming to terms with" in the opening section of "The Inter-Play" and the word "enowning" in its fifth section harbor within themselves the passage from the "guiding question" to the "root question." This passage or crossing depends entirely on the unfolding of the "guiding question" in accord with the "enjoining beckoning" that is *the* guide to *an other* beginning. Accordingly the aletheiological thinking of the Presocratics has its place in this crossing, that is, in the way the question τὶ τό ὄν plays into the question "What is the truth of being, its in-depth-sway?" For this reason the aletheiological thinking of the Presocratics should be viewed as an integral part of *an other* beginning even though *Beiträge zur Philosophie* does not explicitly indicate that this thinking belongs to that beginning.

The fact that *Beiträge zur Philosophie* neither explicitly includes the aletheiological thinking of the Presocratics in *an other* beginning nor implicitly excludes this thinking from that beginning supports the view that the aletheiological thinking of the Presocratics occupies a central place in the crossing of the first beginning toward *an other* beginning. This view is corroborated by the fact that *Beiträge zur Philosophie* explicitly omits the names of the early Greeks (such as Anaximander, Parmenides and Heraclitus) when "The Inter-Play" indicates the focal points of the future lecture courses that Heidegger plans to give *after Beiträge zur Philosophie*—lecture courses which will consider responses to the guiding question, that is, *Leitfragenbeantwortung* (cf. GA 65, 176).

However, we must not lose sight of the fact that, although "The Inter-Play" does not mention the early Greeks by name, Heidegger after *Beiträge zur Philosophie* offers a large number of courses on the early Greeks and devotes a number of treatises to them. This fact indicates that the significance of the aletheiological thinking of the Presocratics *for* the process of unfolding the question that belongs to *an other* beginning, namely, "what is the truth of being, its in-depth-sway?," is implicit in the thinking of *Beiträge zur Philosophie*.

III

I would like to conclude this presentation with a brief reflection on the language in which it is written. Although it is written in English, this language reflects Heidegger's own language. If this is the case, does not this presentation merely *repeat* what Heidegger says and, in so doing, fails to be an academically viable presentation, since repeating Heidegger does not achieve anything? By preparing such a presentation do we not ignore the "complexity of reading texts" which always amounts to "reinscribing" them?

It is my contention that, in order to deal with these questions, we need to address the relationship between being and language. If *Beiträge zur Philosophie* brings to language a radically unprecedented experience of being, then it is naive to assume that an ontologically neutral language stands ready to function as a vehicle for bringing that new experience of being into language. The upshot of the insight into the relationship of being and language is that there is no such thing as an extant ontologically neutral language. As the German language bends and twists in order to correspond to the new experience of being that sustains *Beiträge zur Philosophie*, so should English abandon the illusion of having in its treasury an ontologically neutral language for translating the language of this work. This means that a presentation such as the one attempted here takes its bearing from the relationship of being to language for the purpose of bringing to language the new experience of being that gives birth to *Beiträge zur Philosophie*.

Hence, the objection that such a presentation merely repeats Heidegger cannot be sustained because this objection is based on the assumption that there is already a consensus as to what this philosopher thinks. Such a presentation, showing as it does that this assumption is far from being true, is *itself* an attempt to take a look at those hidden "faces" of the experience of being that are turned toward us, and thus to gain access to the resources of language that correspond to those "faces."

Why did the thinking of being in the perspective of fundamental ontology take more than two decades in order to recognize the impassability of that perspective? The epigram to this essay responds to this question. Perhaps better than anyone else, Hölderlin saw the strains through which language undergoes when it gets exposed to a new experience of being:

Nun, nun müssen dafür Worte, wie Blumen, entstehen.

Now! Now words for that must come forth like flowers.

NOTES

1. Hölderlin, "Brot und Wein," in *Sämtliche Werke*, Bd. 2 (Stuttgart: Verlag W. Kohlhammer, 1955), §5.

2. Jean Beaufret, "Heraclitus and Parmenides," in Kenneth Maly and Parvis Emad, eds., *Heidegger on Heraclitus: A New Reading* (Lewiston: The Edwin Mellen Press, 1986), 70.

3. Cf. F.-W. von Herrmann, *Heideggers Philosophie der Kunst*, 2nd ed. (Frankfurt am Main, Klostermann Verlag, 1994), 2, 7, 8. Also, F.-W. von

Herrmann, *Wege ins Ereignis: Zu Heideggers "Beiträge zur Philosophie"* (Frankfurt am Main, Klostermann Verlag, 1994), 55f., 67f.

4. *Martin Heidegger—Elisabeth Blochmann Briefwechsel, 1918-1969* (Marbach am Neckar: Deutsche Schillergesellschaft, 1989), 54.

5 . I have discussed this point at great length in my essay "Heidegger I Heidegger II and *Beiträge zur Philosophie (Vom Ereignis),*" in Babette E. Babich, ed., *From Phenomenology to Thought, Errancy and Desire, Essays in Honor of William J. Richardson* (Boston: Kluwer Academic Publishers, 1995). For works related to this discussion, see Martin Heidegger, *Zollikoner Seminare*, Medard Boss, ed. (Frankfurt am Main, Klostermann Verlag, 1987), 147–73, and works by F.-W. von Herrmann mentioned in note 3 above.

6. On this point, see F.-W. von Herrmann, *Wege ins Ereignis: Zu Heideggers "Beiträge zur Philosophie"*, 30f., 55f., 70f., 331f.

7 . On the relation of "thrownness," "projection," and "being-along-with" to *Rede*, see F.-W. von Herrmann, *Subjekt und Dasein: Interpretationen zu "Sein und Zeit"*, 2nd ed. (Frankfurt am Main, Klostermann Verlag, 1985), 92–114.

8. In *Grundfragen der Philosophie: Ausgewählte "Probleme" der "Logik"* (GA 45), a lecture course text written at the same time as *Beiträge zur Philosophie*, Heidegger renders explicit the interconnection between ἀλήθεια in early Greek thinking and τό ἀλήθεζ. Considering this fact it is unwarranted to suggest that Heidegger fails "to demonstrate a certain solidarity between the Platonic dialogues and the writings of the early Greek thinkers." Cf. John Sallis, "A Wonder that One Could Never Aspire to Surpass," in Kenneth Maly, ed., *The Path of Archaic Thinking: Unfolding the Work of John Sallis* (Albany: SUNY Press, 1995), 262. The lesson we learn from reading this lecture (GA 45) is that *Platons Lehre von der Wahrheit* belongs to the broader context of the thinking that goes on in *Beiträge zur Philosophie (Vom Ereignis)*.

9. *The Concise Oxford Dictionary of Current English*, seventh ed., ed. J. B. Sykes (Oxford: Clarendon Press, 1982), 316.

to truth, with what is "easy to produce without knowledge of the truth (εἰδότι τὴν ἀλήθειαν)" (*Republic*, 599a).[2] But for the moment, I would like simply to use this scene as an emblem to illustrate that, whenever the figure of Homer arises in Heidegger's work, the relationship between concealment and revelation, falling and salvation, is always at stake. And not only concealment and revelation, falling and salvation, *in* Homer, but the concealment and revelation, the falling and salvation, *of* Homer. Whenever Homer is invoked or cited in the interest of some controversy or struggle (for example in that between Heidegger and Friedländer), one can never be sure whether it is Homer or an εἴδωλον of him that is being fought over, whether Homer is being lost or saved, lost in being saved, whether, in the end, the truth of Homer's word is being concealed by those who would take it elsewhere (to Athens, to Rome) or whether the truth of this word consists in its being concealed—to the Romans, to Aristotle and Plato, but also, perhaps, to Homer himself.

Covering the Field: An Homeric Catalogue

I shall begin by trying to give some indication of how Heidegger uses Homer throughout his work, what kind of authority is being claimed when Homer is evoked, whether Homer functions in Heidegger's corpus as a sort of sign or indication or whether the language of Homer signals the need to rethink the very nature of signs and indications. The questions posed here about language, about the relationship between philosophy and poetry, philosophy and what comes before or after philosophy, will be familiar to those who work on Heidegger, and the answers I propose will no doubt be just as familiar. The only originality or usefulness I hope to claim for this analysis, then, is that all these questions and responses will revolve around Heidegger's reading of Homer, a figure who has received relatively little attention in Heidegger scholarship. While this catalogue of the references to and uses of Homer will be by no means complete, I hope it to be somewhat representative, for while Heidegger often refers to Homer, his engagement with him is surely not as insistent or developed as is his engagement with other early Greek figures such as Heraclitus, Parmenides, or Sophocles. In the end, I will claim that, while betraying, in some sense, both the letter and the spirit of Homer's word, Heidegger tries to remain true to what is never present but is nonetheless always 'promised' in it. I will argue that Heidegger tries to keep Homer to his word in order to help us heed a certain notion of 'truth' that remains concealed and indeed must remain concealed even at the very origin of Western poetry. I will not, therefore, be trying to discredit or verify the truth of Heidegger's reading or interpretation of Homer but will be trying to think along with Heidegger what first gives or promises this truth.

First, then, to use a Heideggerian vocabulary, a few indications or pointers, beginning with the most obvious if perhaps the most deceptive. Homer is of interest to Heidegger simply because he is the first, the first poet of the West, closer than anyone else, it might thus be thought, to the origin of the Greek language and perhaps to language itself. Such an origin has, of course, been sought since the beginning of Western philosophy, and Homer has, since the beginning, been summoned to bear witness to it. Socrates asks near the beginning of *The Cratylus*, "am I wrong in imagining that I have found a clue to Homer's opinion about the correctness of names (περὶ ὀνομάτων ὀρθότητος)?" (393b)[3] Heidegger would seem to share this interest in origins and, thus, this interest in Homer. He writes in *An Introduction to Metaphysics* just before referring to Homer: "In connection with the question of the essence of language, the question of its origin has arisen time and time again" (GA 40, 180; IM, 171).

And yet the origin is not, for Heidegger, a mere chronological beginning. So it is not simply because he is the oldest that Homer turns out to be so close to the origin. In fact, "the origin of language is in essence mysterious," inaccessible, therefore, to a thinking that would wish to fix, analyze, or treat it precisely as a mere beginning. The origin of language is not some event in man's existence but coincides with his very "departure into being."

> In this departure language was being, embodied in the word: poetry. Language is the primordial poetry in which a people speaks being. Conversely, the great poetry by which a people enters into history initiates the molding of its language. The Greeks created (*geschaffen*) and experienced (*erfahren*) this poetry through Homer (GA 40, 180; IM, 171–72).[4]

Through the poetry of Homer, the Greeks would have experienced the mystery of the origin of language that coincided with their departure into being, their departure into a language in which being could be spoken. In Homer, then, we are closer to the mystery of the origin of language and so to the mystery of man's departure into being. Because "the language of Homer is," Heidegger claims, "a mixture of different dialects which preserve the earlier form of the language" (GA 40, 72; IM, 68), particular words used by Homer might be investigated so as to reveal their relation to this mystery of man's departure into language and being. Thus, in *An Introduction to Metaphysics*, Heidegger cites *The Odyssey* 24.108 "as an example of the original meaning of λέγειν as to 'gather' "(GA 40, 133; IM, 124).

But this reading of Homer as an indicator and preserver of past meaning becomes complicated when the eventual concealment of this meaning is also to be found in him, making him into an indicator of both the past and the future, of the transition between one experience of language and another. In *What is Called Thinking?*, for example, Heidegger seems to suggest that the "originary meaning" of a word such as λέγειν may be concealed to some extent even in its earliest uses, for "As early as Homer, the word (λέγειν) signifies telling a tale, and reporting. But besides, since early times and over a wide area, in all its many variants and derivations it means as much as laying" (WD, 170; WCT, 204). Λέγειν in Homer would thus seem to mean telling a tale *in addition to* laying or gathering. This could simply be read as a sign of the poetic richness and polysemy of Homer's language, but, as we will see later with ἀλήθεια, the addition of a meaning related to telling a tale and reporting, that is, to language, is not one addition among others. Indeed such an addition will threaten to restrict λέγειν to a linguistic meaning "as early as Homer," just as a certain understanding of ἀλήθεια will threaten to restrict it to the correspondence between words and things, thereby suggesting that Homer is, to put it in a single phrase, already on the way to metaphysics.

The language of Homer gives access to an origin of language, but this origin must remain essentially mysterious. It does this, however, not only for Homer but for an entire people. In the passage cited above, Heidegger speaks of "the great poetry by which a people enters into history." This poetry is not the beginning of some literary tradition with which a people might identify so as then to enter into history but is itself the very bringing of a people into history. While Homer appears to be, for Heidegger, the poet of the Greeks *par excellence*, he is mentioned in *What is Called Thinking?* along with Sappho, Pindar, and

Sophocles as having brought to language something essentially different from literature (WD, 154; WCT, 134). Each historical people has such a poetry; indeed, a people becomes historical only through such poetry. In the essay, "Hölderlin and the Essence of Poetry," Homer is mentioned along with Sophocles, Virgil, Dante, Shakespeare, Goethe, and Hölderlin as poets in whom "the essence of poetry is realized" (GA 4, 33; EB, 270).

Homer thus interests Heidegger because of his proximity to the origin of language and because the essence of poetry and the relationship of the Greeks to their own language is realized in his work. But poetry is not, for Heidegger, the same as thinking—even though one may be used to help illuminate the other. Heidegger writes: "Parmenides' language is the language of a thinking; it is that thinking itself. Therefore, it also speaks differently from the still older poetry of Homer" (WD, 114; WCT, 186). Homer will thus interest Heidegger not only because he is closer to an origin but because he may help us see how far we are from it. By returning to the pre-philosophical poetry of Homer or Sophocles, Heidegger is able to illuminate the distance between this poetry and later philosophical or metaphysical thought. In the 1966–1967 Heraclitus Seminar of Heidegger and Fink, for example, Heidegger says in response to a remark of Fink concerning χρόνος that "it is important for us that there is no theoretical conceptual determination of time as time with Homer and Hesiod. Rather, both speak of time only out of experience" (GA 15, 103; HS, 61). Similarly, in "The Anaximander Fragment" Heidegger says that "γένεσις and φθορά become conceptual terms with Plato and Aristotle and their schools. But γένεσις and φθορά are old words which even Homer knows" and "are to be thought from φύσις, and within it, as ways of luminous rising and decline" (HW, 314–15; EGT, 29–30). The non-metaphysical language of Homer thus provides a way of countering the metaphysical language of Plato and Aristotle, that is, to a certain extent, our language.[5] Homer helps Heidegger demonstrate the distance between our metaphysical thinking and the poetry of the early Greeks.

But, interestingly, Heidegger uses Homer very rarely to this end. Homer is more often used as a means of entering a pre-metaphysical thinker such as Anaximander, Heraclitus, or Parmenides. It is surely no coincidence that Homer is used throughout, and not simply cited or mentioned once or twice, in both *Early Greek Thinking* and *Parmenides*.[6] This no doubt stems in part from the fact that comparisons are often most effective when the things being compared are not too different or

distant; the above comparison between Homer's 1
and Plato's yields little more than a general obsei
is conceptual and the other is not. But Heidegger als.
order to understand or cross-over to a thinker, we someth.
proceed by means of an earlier thinker or, indeed, poet. This is .
attempt to understand a thinker by means of his influences, for, a.
Heidegger says, "Every thinker is dependent—upon the address of
Being" (HW, 340–41; EGT, 55). But in order to understand the essence
of a later thought, we must, says Heidegger, heed the earlier thought
concealed within it. For example, "in our recollecting we latecomers
must first have thought about the Anaximander fragment in order to
proceed to the thought of Parmenides and Heraclitus" (HW, 341; EGT,
55). Anaximander's thought will help us avoid simply repeating the
easy opposition between Parmenides, the thinker of being, and
Heraclitus, the thinker of becoming. And yet how are we to avoid this
if Anaximander's thought is itself understood in terms of this same
opposition? Heidegger answers by taking us even further back:

> When the Greeks say τὰ ὄντα, what comes to the fore in their
> language? Where is there, aside from the Anaximander fragment,
> a guideline which would translate (über-setzt) us there? Because
> the word in question . . . speaks everywhere throughout the lan-
> guage . . . it is necessary that we avail ourselves of an opportunity
> which in terms of its subject matter, its time, and the realm to
> which it belongs, lies outside philosophy, and which from every
> point of view precedes the pronouncements of thinking.
> In Homer we perceive such an opportunity (HW, 316; EGT,
> 31–32).

With this Heidegger begins a long commentary on five lines from the
first book of The Iliad where Homer speaks of the seer Calchas, "who
knew all that is, is to be, or once was (ὅς ᾔδη τά τ'ἐόντα τά τ'ἐσσόμενα
πρό τ'ἐόντα)." Heidegger proceeds to interpret these words in terms
of a coming into and a withdrawal from unconcealment and not as three
modes of a universal concept of presence. Through this reading of
Homer, Heidegger is able to oppose the "conceptual terms" ὄν and
ὄντα, which "appear as rootless participial endings" in Plato and
Aristotle, and the "original words ἐόν and ἐόντα" used by Homer,
Parmenides, and Heraclitus. This is important because in these

.rticipial endings "the distinction between 'to be' and 'a being' lies
.oncealed"—that is, the ontological difference itself lies concealed (HW,
317; EGT, 32–33). The stakes of understanding or translating these
original words could thus not be higher:

> We might assert in an exaggerated way, which nevertheless bears
> on the truth, that the fate of the West (*das Geschick des Abend-
> Landes*) hangs on the translation of the word ἐόν, assuming that
> the translation (*Übersetzung*) consists in *crossing over* (*Übersetzung*)
> to the truth of what comes to language in ἐόν (HW, 318; EGT, 33).

The result of this commentary on Homer is not simply a corrective of the usual way of interpreting or representing what is present
in terms of a universal concept of presence but, Heidegger claims, a
transformation or translation of our very relationship to being.

> Whither have Homer's words translated (*über-gesetzt*) us? To
> ἐόντα. . . . The word by which we translate ὄν, "being," is now
> no longer obtuse; no longer are "to be," as the translation of εἶναι,
> and the Greek word itself hastily employed ciphers for arbitrary
> and vague notions about some indeterminate universal (HW, 322;
> EGT, 36–37).

Homer thus allows us to think what is thoughtlessly uttered by philosophers who have forgotten, but whose concepts are nonetheless
determined by, the ontological difference. "In Homer's language τὰ
ἐόντα is not a conceptual philosophical term but a thoughtful and
thoughtfully uttered word" (HW, 323; EGT, 38). The language of Homer
would thus allow us to cross-over or to be translated to an understanding or experience of language that will have been concealed by later
philosophical thought, concealed by a series of transformations and
translations in and of the West.

The Case of the Fall

While Heidegger refers to Homer either to illuminate early Greek
thinking or to mark the distance between it and later metaphysical
thought, such references are often inscribed within a sort of narrative

concerning what might be called 'the fall of early Greek thought'. The opening epigraph from Heidegger's 1942–1943 lecture course on Parmenides already introduced us to this disjunction: "For the Greeks. . . . For the Romans, on the contrary. . . . " Much has been written about this fall of the Greek into or through the Latin and so all I wish to do here is simply highlight the role Homer plays in it. At issue is almost always the way certain fundamental terms are thought or translated, that is, whether they are thought in terms of an essential self-showing or self-presencing or whether they are thought in reference to human speech and perception. According to Heidegger, evidence for this transformation or fall from the self-showing of beings to the human perception of them can be found almost everywhere in later Greek and, especially, Roman thought, indeed even in the way evidence itself is thought. To illustrate this, Heidegger recalls a passage from *The Odyssey* (16.161) in which Athene appears as a young woman to Odysseus and his son Telemachus though only Odysseus can see that she is Athene, for as "the poet says . . . 'it is not to all that the gods appear ἐναργεῖς'." Odysseus and his son Telemachus both see the young woman before them but only Odysseus "apprehends the presencing of the goddess." Such presencing, according to Heidegger, is to be understood as "shining of one's own accord," "a characteristic pertaining to things themselves in their presencing." But "the Romans later translated ἐνάργεια . . . by *evidentia*; *evideri* means to become visible. Evidence is then thought in terms of human beings as those do the seeing" (BSD, 16).[7]

One could cite numerous examples of this narrative—this epic of being, truth, and language—in the work of Heidegger. While the fall or degeneration is most poignantly marked by the Latin translation of Greek terms, evidence for it can already be found in the conceptual language of Plato and Aristotle. From Plato and Aristotle to the Roman, medieval, and modern epochs we witness what appears to be a progressive fall of the Homeric/Presocratic way of thinking. In his "Alētheia" essay, for example, Heidegger analyzes a passage from *The Odyssey* in order, one might say, to recall to modern man a concealed way of thinking concealment and a forgotten way of thinking forgetting. The analysis is surely amongst the most memorable in the Heideggerian corpus relating to Homer. In an attempt to rethink the nature of ἀλήθεια in Heraclitus Fragment B16, Heidegger turns to the famous passage wherein Odysseus covers his head in the presence of the Phaeacians as he listens to the minstrel Demodocus sing of the woes of the Achaeans. Whereas the key verb ἐλάνθανε in this passage is usually understood and translated as the "transitive 'he concealed'," Heidegger wants us to hear instead "'he remained concealed'—as the one who was shedding tears" (VA, 254; EGT, 106).[8] On the basis of this reading, Heidegger is able to reinterpret the verb ἐπιλανθάνομαι, as meaning not 'I forget' (the usual rendering), but as "I am—with respect to my relation to something usually unconcealed—concealed from myself" (VA, 256; EGT, 108). By removing concealment and forgetting from the subjective, human realm and resituating them in an essential concealment from within the things themselves, Heidegger is able to recall something that we have forgotten: modern man, he says, "has forgotten the essence of forgetting." We have forgotten that forgetting and concealment belong not to us but to the essence of beings themselves, that our forgetting is the result not of "the superficiality of our contemporary way of life" but of "the essence of oblivion itself" (VA, 256; EGT, 108).

To think the transformation of the Greek world into the Roman or the modern simply in terms of a fall, then, in terms of the degeneration or forgetting of the Greek world, would thus appear to betray more than explain that fall, for it would be to forget that concealing and forgetting do not simply befall the Greek world from without but lie at the very heart of the Greek experience of beings. Such would appear to be one of the conclusions of "The End of Philosophy and the Task of Thinking," where Heidegger seems to recant or at least recast the simple, linear narrative according to which the Homeric and Presocratic understanding of ἀλήθεια as "unconcealment" (Unverborgenheit) would have been concealed and forgotten by later thought. This text, written in 1964 and published in German in 1969, would appear to be a response to Paul Friedländer's critique of Heidegger's translation of ἀλήθεια as "unconcealment" and an admission that the narrative of the fall of Greek thought is not as straightforward as first thought. It is not my intention here to retrace this complex debate between Heidegger and Friedländer, especially since it concerns a reading of Plato more than of Homer, but it will be important to underscore some of its central arguments in order to continue to analyze the role Homer plays in Heidegger's work.

Heidegger begins his seeming retraction by reiterating his oft-repeated claim that ἀλήθεια cannot be translated as "truth" understood as the "correspondence of knowledge with beings" or else as the "certainty of the knowledge of Being." These latter determinations of truth must instead be thought on the basis of ἀλήθεια, of unconcealment thought as clearing. "'Αλήθεια, unconcealment thought as the clearing of presence, is not yet truth." The unconcealment that is ἀλήθεια thus first grants the possibility of truth as *adaequatio* or *certitudo*. It might thus seem that ἀλήθεια appeared as unconcealment in Homer and the Presocratics but was then itself concealed by later conceptions of truth as correctness or correspondence or certainty. But Heidegger in 1964 seems to admit that ἀλήθεια did not mean unconcealment even for the early Greeks—indeed, not even for Homer:

> The natural concept of truth does not mean unconcealment, not in the philosophy of the Greeks either. It is often and justifiably pointed out that the word ἀληθής is already used by Homer only in the *verba dicendi*, in statements, thus in the sense of correctness and reliability, not in the sense of unconcealment. But this reference means only that neither the poets nor everyday linguistic usage, nor even philosophy, see themselves confronted with the task of asking how truth, that is, the correctness of statements, is granted only in the element of the clearing of presence (SD, 77; BW, 447).

What then about the transformation of "truth" from Homer and the Presocratics to Plato and Aristotle? Heidegger says flatly that "the assertion about the essential transformation of truth, that is, from unconcealment to correctness," is "untenable." Since "ἀλήθεια, as clearing of presence and presentation in thinking and saying, immediately comes under the perspective of ὁμοίωσις and *adaequatio*," there never was a time when it simply meant or was revealed as unconcealment. Heidegger then asks:

> Does this happen by chance? Does it happen only as a consequence of the carelessness of human thinking? Or does it happen because self-concealing, concealment, λήθη, belongs to ἀ-λήθεια, not as a mere addition, not as a shadow to light, but rather as the heart of ἀλήθεια? (SD, 78; BW, 448)

While these comments of 1964 would seem to bring to a definite close the case for a transformation or 'fall' of Homeric-Presocratic ἀ-λήθεια into metaphysical truth as correspondence or correctness, they would seem to be definitive proof of a transformation and perhaps even a fall of Heidegger's own thought, a final admission on Heidegger's part that, in David Krell's words, ἀλήθεια in "the sense of 'unconcealment' seems to have evanesced even before Homer sang."[9] Heidegger would seem to have been swayed not only by Friedländer's critique of his derivation of ἀλήθεια from ἀ-λήθεια, that is, his etymological derivation based on the alpha-privative, but, more importantly, by his claim that "from an early Greek period we have, it seems, only a single case in which ἀληθής was understood as ἀ-ληθής" and that in this single case from Hesiod what is at issue is not the concealedness of beings but the "correctness of perception."[10] While Heidegger could argue that his enterprise is not first and foremost philological and that etymology has little to do with the task of thinking, the fact that not a single example can be found in the early Greeks of ἀλήθεια as the unconcealedness of beings and not as the correctness of perception cannot simply be ignored. Moreover, says Friedländer, "in Homer, ἀλήθειη and ἀληθής, with a single exception, always occur connected with, and dependent on, verbs of assertion."[11] Heidegger's rendering of ἀλήθεια as unconcealment would thus either have to be abandoned or else his reliance upon Homer for thinking it completely foregone. Since ἀλήθεια as unconcealment is what would first give every example of truth as correspondence in Homer or Parmenides or Plato or Aristotle, no example could ever be given for it. Homer and Plato would be, so to speak, on the same side. While the thesis of a fall from the Greek to the Roman might still be maintained, Heidegger's reconciliation with Friedländer would signal the end of any real internecine conflict between the Greeks concerning the meaning of this pivotal word. But was such a reconciliation really necessary? Or better, was it really the case?

Balancing the Two Sides

Though the debate between Heidegger and Friedländer is much too complicated to enter into fully here, a couple of points concerning the matrix of words ἀλήθεια, ἀλήθης, ψεῦδος, ψευδοόμαι, etc., in Homer might be raised in order to help resituate what Friedländer himself calls the "single exception" to the rule that, "in Homer, ἀληθεία and ἀληθής . . . always occur connected with, and dependent on, verbs of assertion." Put briefly, whenever words associated with 'truth' or 'falsity' are found in Homer, it is almost always in the context not only of concealment and unconcealment but of the concealment and unconcealment of two narrative possibilities. The opposition in Homer is not so much between the true and the false as between the tale within one's breast and the tale without, between two possible narratives or fates. While one might wish to assimilate one of these tales or fates to what one knows or thinks to be true and the other to what can be fashioned to correspond or not to this, we miss a number of important details in rushing to such an equivalence. Indeed we miss the fact that ἀλήθεια, ἀλήθης, ψεῦδος, ψευδοόμαι, etc., are almost always to be found in a narrative context where certain things are revealed or concealed to certain characters in the narrative and not to others and where this difference becomes part of the narrative for the audience. In other words, the event of concealment or unconcealment is almost always revealed *as* a concealment or unconcealment and the narrative revolves around this difference. In the two passages from *The Odyssey* cited by Heidegger above, what is important is not just concealment and unconcealment but the differences established in the narrative between them: while Odysseus sees the self-presencing of the goddess Athene, Telemachus does not, and we the audience see this difference; while the Phaeacians do not see Odysseus who has become concealed as the one shedding tears, Alcinous, the king of the Phaeacians, does see him, and we the audience see this. In both cases what is revealed is the very event of concealment (to Telemachus or the Phaeacians) or unconcealment (to Odysseus or Alcinous). By focusing solely on the question of truth or falsity, on the correspondence between speech and fact, we fail to notice the role that the various relations between the characters in *The Iliad* and *The Odyssey* play in the unconcealment or concealment of the tale within, the appropriateness of this unconcealment or concealment, the relationship between not speech and thought but speech and action, and, finally, the narrative *mise en scène* of this concealment or unconcealment.

In Homer, a character is revealed to others within the narrative and to the audience without by means of their particular relationship to concealment and unconcealment. When, for example, Eumaeus in *The Odyssey* tells the disguised Odysseus how vagabonds and wanderers seeking entertainment come to Ithaca and "lie (ψεύδοντ'), and are not minded to speak the truth (οὐδ ἐθέλουσιν ἀληθέα μυθήσασθαι)" about Odysseus, what he emphasizes is just as much the character of those who tell these untruths as the fact that they are untruths (O, 14.122–27).[12] The vagabond dissembles in order to receive entertainment; indeed the role of the vagabond is determined or revealed through his relationship to dissemblance, through his tendency to conceal the tale within by means of another without.

While vagabonds conceal the truth or conceal the tale within their breast, the good or wise man usually does not. Athene encourages Telemachus in the beginning of The Odyssey to approach Nestor to learn the whereabouts of his father, saying, "do thou beseech him thyself that he may tell thee the very truth (ὅπως νημερτέα εἴπη). A lie (ψεῦδος) will he not utter, for he is wise (πεπνυμένος) indeed" (O, 3.19–20). It is clearly less a question here of Nestor lying than of him holding back or not revealing what he knows. Nestor will reveal what he knows about Odysseus to Telemachus because he is πεπνυμένος, that is, not because he is honest but because of his capacity for appropriate and judicious speech.[13] Just before the chariot race during the funeral games for Patroclus, Achilles sets as an umpire the "godlike Phoenix, his father's follower, that he might mark the running and tell the truth (ἀληθείην) thereof" (I, 23.359-61), Phoenix being chosen not so much because he will tell the truth but because he will reveal or make known what has happened in an appropriate and reliable way (see I, 24.406–408).

Revealing or concealing the tale within one's breast places one along a hierarchy of 'virtue' that runs from robbers[14] and vagabonds— often associated with the perfidity of women[15]—up to wise men, counsellors, prophets, minstrels, kings, and the gods. One thus conceals or reveals the tale within, within one's breast, depending upon who one is, who one is talking to, and the circumstances of the exchange. Indeed, it is usually inappropriate to conceal something from a family member,[16] from someone one serves,[17] or from a comrade.[18] When asked by Telemachus to tell him how he returned to Ithaca, Odysseus says, "Then verily, my child, I will tell thee all the truth (ἀληθείην καταλέξω)" (O, 16.226). Telling the truth is thus not simply the result but the very performance, the establishing or the maintenance, of a social relation.

The story of Odysseus' return is nothing other than the story of his various concealments and unconcealments; but the narrative of The Odyssey is the putting on the scene, the revelation, of these various events of concealment and unconcealment. When Odysseus arrives in

Ithaca and encounters Athene disguised as a young shepherd, he considers expressing his joy in having returned home, but, not absolutely certain to whom he is speaking (O, 13.312), he decides instead to dissemble and to say that he is from Crete: "he spoke not the truth (οὐδ' ὅ γ' ἀληθέα εἶπε), but checked the word ere it was uttered, ever revolving in his breast thoughts of great cunning" (O, 13.253–55). This capacity for concealment, for concealing the tale within at just the right moment by weaving another without, is what constitutes Odysseus's very identity. As the narrator says of Odysseus just before he reveals himself to Penelope, he made "the many falsehoods of his tale seem like the truth (ἴσκε ψεύδεα πολλὰ λέγων ἐτύμοισιν ὁμοῖα) . . ." (O, 19.203).

The difference between identities, between different narrative possibilities, lies at the heart of *The Iliad* as well. When Achilles is threatened with being overcome by the River Scamander, he blames his own mother Thetis for having "beguiled [him] with false words (ψεύδεσσιν ἔ θελγεν), saying that beneath the wall of the mail-clad Trojans [he] should perish by the swift missiles of Apollo" (I, 21.273–78). The fact that these deceptive words were uttered by Achilles's own mother is emphasized as much as the fact that they were deceptive and false. But more importantly, Achilles suggests that his own mother did not simply utter something that turned out to be false but told him a tale, reserved or promised him a fate, that will not be fulfilled. Such a promise, as John Austin has shown, is not simply a statement concerning some future action that turns out to be true or false but a speech act or performance with certain effects. To treat what is φεῦδος in Homer as merely a question of falsity is thus to miss the role speech acts such as promises and oaths play in the epic narrative. Adapting Simone Weil's famous phrase, one could say that *The Iliad* is—above all—the poem of *illocutionary* force.

In Book 19 we are told the story of how Hera beguiled or deceived Zeus into swearing an oath that resulted in Eurystheus being born king of the Argives rather than Zeus's son Heracles. Hera pressured Zeus to swear this by accusing him of uttering a false promise, that is, of abusing the formula or conventions of the promise or oath by saying something but not fulfilling or bringing it about: "But with crafty mind the queenly Hera spake unto him: 'Thou wilt play the cheat, and not bring thy word to fulfillment (ψευστήσεις, οὐδ' αὖτε τέλος μύθῳ ἐπιθήσεις). Nay, come, Olympian, swear me now a mighty oath that in very truth that man shall be lord . . . " (I, 19.106–109). Hera thus gets Zeus to make explicit the speech act that was implicit in the voicing of his wishes.

The false promise, unlike the false statement, necessarily engages human trust and brings one into an ethical order. When the Trojans break their sworn truce with the Achaeans, Agamemnon encourages his troops by reminding them that "father Zeus will be no helper of lies (ψεύδεσσι); nay, they that were the first to work violence in defiance of their oaths, their tender flesh of a surety shall vultures devour . . . " (I, 4.235–37). Antenor too predicts disaster for his fellow Trojans after they have broken the oaths of faith if they do not return Helen and the treasure Paris brought back from Sparta: "Now do we fight after proving false to our oaths of faith (νῦν δ'ὅρκια πιστὰ ψευσάμενοι μαχόμεσθα), wherefore have I no hope that aught will issue to our profit, if we do not thus" (I, 7.351–53). What characterizes the false promise or oath is just as much the telling, the speaking—and all the rites associated with it—as what is told or spoken. While a lie may have certain (perlocutionary) effects, a false promise in and of itself, as a speech act, engages certain effects. Not unlike the εἴδωλον of Aeneas, the false promise is not simply that which is at one or several removes from the truth but that which engages human activity by making a possibility appear that will not be fully realized.

But whether ἀλήθεια, ἀληθής, ψεῦδος, ψευδοόμαι, etc., are used in Homer in the context of concealing or revealing the tale within one's breast or in the context of false promises and oaths, what is significant is not only that one thing is revealed rather than another but that this revelation, this tension between concealment and unconcealment, is itself revealed or staged. This is seen most clearly when deliberation is itself represented in the Homeric narrative. For example, when in Book 10 of *The Iliad* the Achaeans wait anxiously for the return of Diomedes and Odysseus from the night raid on the Trojans, Nestor debates whether to reveal or conceal his thoughts concerning the ominous signs that he is the first to hear:

> My friends, leaders and rulers of the Argives, shall I be wrong (ψεύσομαι), or speak the truth (ἢ ἔτυμον ἐρέω)? Nay, my heart bids me speak (κέλεται δέ με θυμός). The sound of swift-footed horses strikes upon my ears (I, 10.533–35; I, 10.534 = O, 4.140).

Since Diomedes and Odysseus left on foot, Nestor fears the worst when he hears horses approaching the Achaean camp and so deliberates whether to reveal or conceal his thoughts. This line is repeated in *The Odyssey* when Helen is the first to see in Telemachus his likeness to Odysseus and so debates whether or not to reveal her thoughts (O, 4.140–41). In neither case is it a question of lying or speaking the truth, nor of saying something that turns out to be true or false, but of concealing or revealing what one is thinking, what one is saying to oneself (see I, 4.404–405, 9.115–16).

But what is perhaps more significant here is that two narrative possibilities—to conceal or to reveal—are being staged, revealed, for the audience. The audience is made privy not only to the revelations of Nestor and Helen but to the very process, the very coming to light, of these revelations. When Odysseus is looking for allies to help slay the suitors he debates whether to reveal his identity and intentions to Eumaeus and the neatherd but then concludes, "Nay, my spirit bids me tell it" (O, 21.194). And after testing them a moment, he reveals to them that he has returned with a plan to slay the suitors: "to you will I tell the truth (ἀληθείην καταλέξω), even as it shall be (ὡς ἔσεταί περ)" (O, 21.205, 212; cf. O, 18.342). The fact that the word ἀλήθεια is used here in the context of the future seems to indicate once again that it is less a question of the correspondence between speech and fact than of a revelation in speech of what will be against the backdrop of what was expected to be; it is thus more a promise or an oath than a statement.[19]

There thus always appear to be two tales, one concealed within and one revealed without, one promising or presaging good and the other one evil, one a revelation of divine desires or of fate and the other one not. Whereas we might wish to identify the desires of the gods and fate with a truth that will eventually be revealed, their structure is more akin to a promise. Because they are always revealed in speech as possibilities of what might be fulfilled or revealed, they are always open to interpretation (see I, 5.635–37), to an interpretation that is often staged as an interpretation and that often in fact changes the course of what is interpreted.[20]

Two tales are thus always competing for human attention and trust. When Hera tries to persuade Priam not to risk going to ransom Hector's body, Priam says that if anyone else, whether a seer or priest, were to have bidden this,

a false thing might we deem it (ψεῦδός κεν φαῖμεν), and turn away therefrom the more; but now—for myself I heard the voice of the goddess and looked upon her face—I will go forth, neither shall her word be vain. And if it be my fate to lie dead by the ships of the brazen-coated Achaeans, so would I have it (I, 24.220–26).

The authority of the source thus prevails, but this authority is not absolute. The word could still be false, another tale could still be told, for not even the gods know or can control fate, and the signs of the gods, the signs of their promises, must always be revealed and interpreted (see I, 2.348–53). Two tales are thus always either implicitly or explicitly being opposed in Homer; it is not a question of the one truth being opposed to all that is false but of two tales competing for the attention of the characters and/or the audience, two tales competing for the light of narrative.

Hopefully, these comments will put us in a better position to reread the famous passage from *The Iliad* wherein ἀληθής, as Friedländer himself admits, does not seem to be related to speech but would instead describe the "honest or reliable" character of a spinning woman. Friedländer mentions this exception, points out that since "this meaning of the word occurs only in this passage, it was doubted in antiquity whether Homer could have said it" and then moves on—"So much for Homer."[21] But if we look at the wider context of this line and read it in relation to the other uses of ἀλήθεια, ἀληθής, etc. in Homer, we might be able to reestablish some relation both to unconcealedness (*pace* Heidegger) *and* to speech, or at least to narrative (*pace* Friedländer). The line occurs near the middle of the epic, at a decisive turning-point in the narrative, as the rout of the Achaeans that was promised by Zeus to Thetis for her son Achilles is about to be fulfilled.

> even so [the Trojans] could not put the Achaeans to rout, but they held their ground, as a careful (ἀληθής) woman that laboureth with her hands at spinning, holdeth the balance and raiseth the weight and the wool in either scale (τάλαντα), making them equal, that she may win a meagre wage for her children; so evenly was strained their war and battle, until Zeus vouchsafed the glory of victory to Hector . . . (I, 12.432–37).

The simile seems quite clear and straightforward, the evenness of the spinning woman's scales being compared to the evenness of the battle as maintained by Zeus. But the word for scales—τάλαντα—is used throughout *The Iliad* in the context of Zeus' determination of the fates of men. In Book 8, for example, Zeus "lifted on high his golden scales (τάλαντα) and set therein two fates of grievous death . . . and down sank the day of doom of the Achaeans" (I, 8.69–70, 72; cf. 22.209 ff.). Zeus weighs two possible scenarios, two possible fates, and the scales eventually tip in one direction rather than another. It is almost as if Zeus' scales were an externalization of deliberation, of the deliberation we see Nestor or Odysseus undergo as they decide whether to reveal or conceal, as if his scales were a way of determining one narrative possibility rather than another. The spinning woman might thus be described as ἀληθής insofar as she has judiciously, reliably, or appropriately balanced her scales and has not favored one side over the other. Ἀληθής would modify not only the spinning woman's reliability but the precarious moment that immediately precedes the revelation of one tale or fate rather than another, the fulfillment of one promise and not another. In this simile, the revelation of fates would itself be revealed, the event of revelation itself unconcealed, the determination of who will live and who will die, whose eyes will once again see the light of day and whose will be enfolded into darkness.

With this simile, the debate between Heidegger and Friedländer is not so much decided as reconfigured; the scales tip not so much in one direction or another as toward the very event of their balancing and their fall. A careful reading of this entire debate would thus probably do well to maintain a balance between the two accounts—just so long as sufficient attention is paid to the event of revelation in the balance.

The Fall of the Case

Though it may seem that Heidegger in 1964 finally ceded to Friedländer's objections, first voiced in 1954 and subsequently revised, Robert Bernasconi, who has retraced the debate and taken into account Friedländer's three revisions of his critique as well as Heidegger's various responses to them, has convincingly argued that Heidegger ends up conceding the etymological and philological evidence to Friedländer "not in order to abandon the fundamental place of ἀλήθεια in his thinking, but . . . so as to maintain it the more strongly."[22] What thus looks like and has been read as a "straightforward retraction," says Bernasconi, is, in essence, a sharpening of the difference between "historical scholarship" and what Heidegger calls "remembrance." The fact that ἀλήθεια was connected from the very beginning to speech proves only that "language perhaps also resides under the sway of unconcealment," that already in Homer "the possibility to think ἀλήθεια as ἀ-λήθεια was blocked."[23] It is not a question, therefore, of returning to Homer in order to recover an understanding of ἀλήθεια that was thought and revealed in him but then lost or forgotten after but of 'remembering' at the end of metaphysics, or after metaphysics, what was unsaid before metaphysics. It is at the end of metaphysics that we must heed not what was present in Homer and then lost but the concealment that was at work already in Homer, the concealment of ἀ-λήθεια, the concealment within ἀ-λήθεια that is itself concealed when it is reduced to the relationship between things and words. It is through this concealment or forgetting—which, we now see, occurs already at the beginning—that we are to 'remember' or 'hear the echoes' of ἀ-λήθεια as un-concealment, that is, not as "the mere clearing of presence" but as "the clearing of presence concealing itself, the clearing of a self-concealing sheltering" (SD, 78; BW2, 448).

Although it may seem that Heidegger came to see only in 1964 that there was no "essential transformation of truth" from unconcealment to correctness, he had been aware for quite some time that already in Homer ἀλήθεια is connected to or under the sway of speech. Indeed, already in the *Parmenides* course some twenty years earlier, he had noted:

> . . . already with the early Greeks ἀλήθεια occurs predominantly in connection with ἔπος and εἰπεῖν, with the word and the legendary word. But the ground for this "fact" does not reside in the character of language as "expression" but in the essence of ἀλήθεια. . . . It is not because the truth is often also enunciated, but because the essence of word and legend is grounded in the essence of truth and belongs to it, that the Greek word for "true," ἀληθές, occurs already in Homer "connected" above all with "speech" (GA 54, 102; P, 69).[24]

It appears that ἀλήθεια was already experienced by Homer—and already understood early on by Heidegger—as the unconcealment of a concealment, the unconcealment of the concealing-sheltering of language.

But if there is no transformation in the nature of truth, if there is an essential unity from Homer to Aristotle, then it is difficult to see how or why Homer and the Presocratics would have any privilege in helping us to cross-over to another thinking. While the narrative of the fall of the Greek world and language into the Roman can still be maintained, the opening scene can no longer take place between Homer and Plato. Both Homer and Plato, both poetry and philosophy, would turn away from what first gives truth, that is, ἀ-λήθεια as unconcealment, as the strife between concealment and unconcealment, in order to focus on what is given or unconcealed—truth as correctness. The fall of the Greek into the Roman, the forgetting of ἀ-λήθεια, does not begin within the Greeks, that is, in Plato, but either after them, in the Romans, or else already at the beginning, with Homer. The essential unity in the Greek understanding of truth from Homer to Plato means, to put it boldly, that either all of them are saved from the fall or, more likely, that all of them are subject to it. Perhaps the Greek gods were right to save Aeneas.

Indeed in the 1969 seminar in Le Thor Heidegger seems to suggest that there is indeed a transformation in the understanding of the essence of language from the beginning of metaphysics to the end but that this transformation is less a fall than a salvation, a movement toward rather than away from the essence of poetry. Heidegger here draws all the Greeks together between the two names Homer and Aristotle.

> The Aristotelian analysis of language achieves in a certain sense the most originary comprehension of language as it already governed Homer's poetry (as *epic* poetry). In Greek, to name always already means to state (*Aussagen*); and to state is to manifest something as something. It is in this hidden comprehension that Homeric poetry moves (GA 15, 336).

There is indeed a unity in the understanding of language from Homer to Aristotle, an understanding of saying as stating that "hinders the understanding of the essence of poetry." But in Hölderlin, Heidegger emphasizes, language is thought differently, more poetically, allowing us now to see just how *unpoetic* the Greeks really were. "Since . . . for Hölderlin, on the contrary, to name is to call out (*Rufen*), one sees the deeply nonpoetic nature of the Greek comprehension of language" (GA 15, 336).[25] If there is indeed a Heideggerian narrative of the Greek fall into the Roman, the medieval, the modern, etc., then the above would perhaps be the beginning of the counter-narrative, one that would have to be told by beginning at the end, with Nietzsche and Hölderlin, in order to return to Homer or to a naming that precedes metaphysics. Such a counter-story cannot be told here. Suffice it to say that once again "the fate of the West" would hang in the balance—not as a fact that would then be recounted, but as a telling or narrative that would be part of this fate, that would, in a sense, retrospectively determine the fate that is being told. While the unity of concealedness and unconcealedness would be named and experienced by the early Greeks, it would not have been thought through by them.[26] While concealedness and unconcealedness might have been put on the scene by the Greeks, it would have been necessary to wait until the end of the circuit of philosophy, the end of the circuit of representation and of the representation of this circuit, for this unrepresentable relationship to be echoed within or at the limits of philosophy.[27] And since such an echoing could never be the object of a straightforward narrative, the very nature of a fall would need to be rethought. Heidegger writes in *Parmenides*: "Because it does not reside back in a past but lies in advance of what is to come, the beginning again and again turns out to be precisely a gift to an epoch" (GA 54, 1–2; P, 1).

The Seed of Aeneas

Five books into *The Iliad* Aeneas is saved by Greek gods, an εἴδωλον of him being set up by Apollo for the Achaeans to fight over. Five books from the end of *The Iliad*, Aeneas is saved once again by the Greek gods, saved this time specifically because of his lineage, the lineage that, according to Heidegger, will eventually come to take over and command the Greek world. This second salvation occurs as Achilles and Aeneas—these two epic heroes, these two heroes of the Greek and Roman epics—come "into the space between the two hosts" to fight each other man to man. After Aeneas recounts their respective lineages, they hurl their respective spears at one another: the shield of Achilles pierces that of Aeneas but misses Aeneas himself. Aeneas then picks up a huge stone, hoping, we are to assume—we who can still hear the echoes of Book 5—to do to Achilles what Diomedes earlier did to him, but all of a sudden the action is suspended. The poet intervenes to tell us that Aeneas *would have* hit Achilles with the stone and Achilles *would have* slain him in return had not Poseidon seen this and intervened: "for it is ordained unto him to escape, that the race of Dardanus perish not without seed (ἄσπερμος) and be seen no more (ἄφαντος)" (I, 20.302–305). And so Poseidon "shed a mist over the eyes of Achilles," drew his spear out of Aeneas' shield and set it at his feet. He then lifted Aeneas up and "swung him on high from off the ground," bringing him to the "verge (ἐσχατιὴν)" of the battle where he warns him not to face Achilles again since only he can slay him (I, 20.325–27). He then scatters the "wondrous mist" from the eyes of Achilles, who immediately recognizes this to be the work of the gods: "a great marvel (θαῦμα) is this that mine eyes behold" (I, 20.341).

And so a tale is saved and not lost, another fate, another thousand-year journey, promised and revealed. Aeneas is saved once again, his lineage preserved, his seed protected, ready now to be transplanted; lifted high off the ground he is brought back down to earth on the edge of the fray, brought back down to an earth that will never be the same because of him, because of his fall, his salvation. The founder of Rome is thus saved one last time by Greek gods, one last time, though, for Heidegger, not necessarily for good:

> For the Romans, on the contrary, the earth, *tellus*, *terra*, is the dry land, the land as distinct from the sea; this distinction differentiates that upon which construction, settlement, and installation are possible from those places where they are impossible. *Terra* becomes *territorium*, land of settlement as realm of command. In the Roman *terra* can be heard an imperial accent, completely foreign to the Greek γαῖα and γῆ (GA 54, 88–89; P, 60).

NOTES

1. My deep thanks to Will McNeill, whose superior knowledge of the Heideggerian corpus was of inestimable help in tracking down and interpreting references to Homer. As Diomedes says in *The Iliad* when choosing Odysseus to accompany him on the night raid of the Trojan camp, "When two go together, one discerneth before the other. . . . " And as in *The Iliad*, it was the one chosen to help who inevitably ended up discerning first and best. All quotations from Homer are *The Iliad* and *The Odyssey*, in the Loeb Classical Library, trans. A. T. Murray (Cambridge, MA: Harvard University Press, 1984).

2. In Homer, the word εἴδωλον does not signify that which is without truth but that which is revealed within the concealment of sleep or death. For sleep and death signify not a total concealment but a concealment from everyday modes of concealment and disclosure. What is revealed in dreams conceals the disclosure of wakefulness (see O, 4.796, 824, 835), while what is revealed in Hades conceals or dissembles what is disclosed to the living (see O, 11.83, 213–18, 475–76, 602, 20.351–57, 24.14; I, 23.103–4). Finally, there is Heracles, whose case most resembles that of Aeneas, for while Odysseus sees his εἴδωλον in Hades, it is said that Heracles "himself (αὐτὸς) among the immortal gods takes his joy in the feast" (O, 11.602–603). See Heidegger's own comments on εἴδωλον in *Platon: Sophistes* (GA 19, 425–34).

3. Plato, *Cratylus*, trans. H. N. Fowler (Loeb Classical Library, 1977).

4. Heidegger makes a similar statement in his *Hölderlins Hymnen "Germanien" und "Der Rhein"* (GA 39, 184). My thanks to Tom Davis for this reference.

5. Again in *Early Greek Thinking* Heidegger asks, "How must we understand our word 'life,' if we accept it for a faithful translation of ζῆν? [. . . .] Ζα-signifies the pure letting-rise within appearing, gazing upon, breaking in upon, and advancing, and all their ways. The verb ζῆν means rising into the light. Homer says, ζῆν καὶ ὁρᾶν φάος ἠελίοιο, 'to live, and this means to see the light of the sun'" (VA, 265–66; EGT, 116). The result of this analysis is the insight that the early Greeks thought life—or ζῆν—in a way that is totally foreign to our own zoological or biological sense.

6. Homer is cited in no less than a dozen different places in this latter volume (GA 54, 32, 34, 35, 45–46, 88, 102–103, 108, 188, 189, 190–91, 195, 202; P, 22, 23, 23, 31, 59–60, 69, 73, 127, 128, 128–29, 131, 136). One could no doubt reread the entire text by following the movement of these references.

7. Will McNeill's translation.

8. Tom Davis in an unpublished paper has a fascinating discussion of this passage in *The Odyssey*. While agreeing in essence with Heidegger's reading, Davis strengthens, I think, this reading by paying close attention to the fact that "Homer stages the *entire* scene at 8.93 to bring to our attention that Alcinous *does* notice this unnamed stranger's . . . sadness of mourning, where the others present *do* not." Davis concludes from this that "while Heidegger is right to think a subjective active voice is misplaced in translating λανθάνω, the middle-voiced event at 8.93 is more complex than he lets on." Davis thus rereads the scene in terms of a "complex interplay of atunements" that is, it seems to me, quite in line with—and more completely developed than—what is said below concerning the necessity of always reading ἀλήθεια in Homer in terms of the narrative *mise en scène* of the concealment or unconcealment.

9. Krell concludes: "There is instead an essential continuity in the history of 'truth', a tendency to regard the true as correctness of assertion or correspondence of statement and fact, without asking about the domain in

which words and things so wondrously converge," in NE 1, 251. For a beautiful analysis of Heidegger's conception of the animal in light of Homer's treatment of the horses of Achilles who mourn for Patroclus in *The Iliad*, see David Krell's "Where Deathless Horses Weep," in *Daimon Life* (Bloomington: Indiana University Press, 1992), 100–136.

10. Paul Friedländer, *Plato I: An Introduction*, trans. Hans Meyerhoff (New York: Pantheon, 1958), 222.

11. Friedländer, *Plato I: An Introduction*, 223.

12. Interestingly, the tale Odysseus proceeds to tell is one of deceit that itself involves deceit; he makes up the tale of a Phoenician who gave him "lying counsel (ψεύδεα βουλεύσας)" so as to sell him into slavery (O, 14.295–97). See O, 7.296, where Odysseus must stress that, although he is a vagabond in need, he has told Alcinous "the truth (ἀληθείην)." Indeed, Odysseus throughout *The Odyssey* at once defines and defies the role of the vagabond. See Alcinous' description of him at O, 11.363–68.

13. Nestor himself repeats the words spoken of him later in the same book when he counsels Telemachus to go to Menelaus: "do thou beseech him. . . . A lie will he not utter, for he is wise (πεπνυμένος) indeed" (O, 3.327–28). The word πεπνυμένος is used almost exclusively to describe not necessarily truthful but appropriate speech, a speech that usually comes with age and is regarded as a form of distinction. Nestor says in *The Iliad* that although Diomedes is young, he "givest prudent counsel (πεπνυμένα) to the princes of the Argives" for he "speakest according to right (κατὰ μοῖραν)" (I, 9.58-59).

14. As Priam prepares to ransom the body of Hector, he calls his remaining sons "these things of shame . . . false of tongue (ψεῦσταί), nimble of foot . . . robbers of lambs and kids from your own folk" (I, 24.261–62).

15. See I, 6.160 ff., where Anteia "made a tale of lies (ψευσαμένη)" for Proteus concerning Bellerophon. While the passage seems quite straightforward in opposing the truth within to the false tale without, the entire scene is one of secrecy and concealment.

16. When asked by Penelope what he had learned about Odysseus during his trip, Telemachus says: "Then verily, mother, I will tell thee all the truth (ἀληθείην καταλέξω)" (O, 17.108; cf. 122). But while Telemachus accurately recounts his visits to Nestor and Menelaus, he does not tell his mother that he had in fact just seen his father in Eumaeus' hut.

17. The nurse Eurycleia repeats line 16.226 when asked by Odysseus to name the servants who had betrayed Odysseus' house (O, 22.420; see also I, 7.382–83, 386).

18. When asked by Achilles in Hades how his son is faring, Odysseus responds, "I will tell thee all the truth (πᾶσαν ἀληθείην μυθήσομαι), as thou biddest me" (O, 11.507).

19. When listening to the minstrel Demodocus sing in the palace of the Phaeacians, Odysseus says, "for well and truly (κατὰ κόσμον) dost thou sing of the fate of the Achaeans" (O, 8.489). What is thus emphasized here is the concordance between the tale Odysseus knows and could himself sing and the one Demodocus has just sung. At O, 3.254–57, Nestor reveals to Telemachus what happened to Agamemnon in light of what could or would have happened had Menelaus been there to prevent it. At O, 16.61–64, Eumaeus tells Telemachus 'all the truth' about the vagabond against the backdrop of what the audience knows and Eumaeus suspects to be the truth about him. At O, 17.14–15, Telemachus says, in effect, that he will not conceal what is on his mind concerning the disguised Odysseus, all the while concealing from Eumaeus his knowledge of the stranger's identity and plans. Finally, see O, 14.361–66 and 386–89, where what is revealed is not only the difference between the tall tale Odysseus tells about himself and the one Eumaeus has himself constructed but also the difference between these tales and what the audience knows to be the case.

20. Interpretation is thus never simply correct or incorrect as measured against the truth of what is or will be. It is, rather, a making present of one narrative possibility or scenario rather than another, a wresting from unconcealment and a bringing into the open that engages human activity and brings about certain (often tragic) effects. For Homer, then, interpretation is never neutral, for with every unconcealment comes a concealment of what first gives unconcealment, that is, a concealment of the open. The false or baneful dream sent to Agamemnon by Zeus in Book 2 of The Iliad might be read in this way (see I, 2.6, 80–82). See also I, 15.159, where the dangers of misrepresentation appear inherent not only to the interpretation but to the very transmittance of the messages of the gods.

21. Friedländer, Plato I: An Introduction, 223.

22. Robert Bernasconi, The Question of Language in Heidegger's History of Being (New Jersey: Humanities Press, 1985), 21. For an excellent discussion of Heidegger's interpretation of ἀλήθεια in Plato, see Adriaan I. Peperzak's "Heidegger and Plato's Idea of the Good," in Reading Heidegger, ed. John Sallis (Bloomington, IN: Indiana University Press, 1993), 258–85.

23. Bernasconi, The Question of Language in Heidegger's History of Being, 20, 24.

24. See Heidegger's "Hegel und die Griechen" (GA 9, 443).

25. Part of this translation comes from Jean-François Courtine, "Phenomenology and/or Tautology," trans. Jeffrey S. Librett, in Reading Heidegger, 255. Interestingly, just a few lines after this citation, Heidegger speaks of the difference between εἶδος and εἴδωλον.

26. "Heidegger seems to suggest," as Adriaan Peperzak puts it, "that the word ἀλήθεια is wiser than the philosophers who pronounced it" (Peperzak," Heidegger and Plato's Idea of the Good," 266).

27. John Sallis writes in *Echoes* (Bloomington: Indiana University Press, 1990), 36, "In the regress to the clearing there sounds the echo not only of philosophy but also of another, an older voice . . . a voice which thus echoes in philosophy and in the nonphilosophy in which philosophy is completed and dissolved." See also his *Double Truth* (Albany: State University of New York Press, 1995), 72 ff. as well as Kenneth Maly's "Reading and Thinking: Heidegger and the Hinting Greeks," in *Reading Heidegger*, 229 ff.

Four

Kalypso: Homeric Concealments after Nietzsche, Heidegger, Derrida, and Lacan

David Farrell Krell

These notes on *The Iliad* and *The Odyssey*, all of them in response to the Heideggerian thought of *concealment*, are clustered about the following themes: (1) sails, veils, and verges, (2) daimons and drugs, (3) Kalypso "herself" as concealment "itself," and (4) care as heart and doom. As a whole, the notes shuttle between the isles of Aiaia and Ogygia—that is, between Kirke and Kalypso, the covert goddesses of Homer's *Odyssey*. For these two goddesses serve as the poles of the concealed tension that pervades Odysseus's adventures, just as Helen and Briseis serve to spark the events of *The Iliad*. Perhaps the most fitting devotion to these goddesses would be to trace apparitions of concealment and concealing (*Verborgenheit, Verbergen*) in Homer, on the basis of provocations from Nietzsche, Heidegger, Derrida, and Lacan.[1]

Sails, Veils, and Verges

In a note at the outset of "Plato's Pharmacy," Derrida invokes the Greek ἱστός, the verge or spindle of the loom.[2] We find it in *The Iliad* (e.g., I, 6, 491), during moments of respite from the blood and gore of battle. Yet it is only in *The Odyssey* that the other senses of ἱστός emerge, senses that remind us also of pages in Derrida's *Spurs: Nietzsche's Styles*.[3] There Derrida invokes the classic Quintillian metonymy of "sails" for ships, and the further figure of "veils," in both cases the French *voiles*. Yet what do the spurs, spars, and masts of a ship have to do with sails and veils? The relationship between spars and sails in the Homeric text is quite intimate. In fact, the words are cognate: ἱστός is not only the verge of the loom, the "large loom" of clever Penelope, who weaves by day and unravels by night, or the "grand ambrosial loom" of Kirke, who sings and weaves veils divine when she is not turning sailors into swine (O, 1, 357; 7, 110; 10, 222; 19, 139; 21, 351; 24, 129); it is also the mast of the ship, the mast to which Odysseus is securely fastened in order to resist the seductions of sirensong, the mast that is later shattered by a gust of Zeus's stormwind (O, 12, 51; 14, 311, 15, 316). Yet the ἱστοί that interest us most in Homer's text—after Nietzsche, Heidegger, Derrida, and Lacan—are those on which shimmering sails, the cognate ἱστία, are brailed. If ἱστός is the spar, ἱστία span it; if the mast thrusts upward into the sky, ἱστία nevertheless make sense of the winds.

Here are some of the passages where spurs and sails appear together: Telemachos's companions prepare to set sail, "raise the mast of pine (ἱστὸν δ' εἰλάτινον) into the air . . . and hoist the shining sails (ἱστία λευκά)" (O, 2, 424–26); his father does the same after the interview with Proteus, "loading mast and sail onto the trusty ships," ἐν δ' ἱστοὺς καὶ ἱστία (4, 578); after the year spent on Aiaia with Kirke, Odysseus sets sail for Hades, as the sorceress-goddess commands: "Raise your mast and hoist shining sails (ἱστὸν δὲ στήσας ἀνά θ' ἱστία λευκά)" (10, 506; cf. 11, 3 and 12, 402). Shimmering sails flutter like white veils against the dark mast and the brazen blue of the sky. What does Nietzsche say in section 60 of *The Gay Science*? He pictures the sailing ship drifting like a butterfly or a ghost, gliding over existence like a *Mittelwesen*, a daimon—the spurring spar, dreaming of its cognate. Nietzsche says, or writes, "*Es sind die Frauen . . .* that's it, that would be it!"[4]

We know that ἱστία comes from ἵστημι, to make stand, to erect. The parataxis of ἱστὸν δὲ στήσας and ἱστὸν στησάμενοι suggests the derivation most strongly. Setting up the mast is essential to setting sail. No spur, no sail. Yet if there were no sail, no veil, and no seabreeze, the mightiest mast would be the most useless member of the ship.

Especially when one is working in the Ionian dialect, where ἑστία appears as ἱστίη, it therefore does not seem far-fetched to wonder whether ἱστός and ἱστία have something to do with Hestia and the hearth. Are they not—as Melville (in both *Moby-Dick* and "My Chimney and I") would affirm—hearth and home to mariners, chimney and mantlepiece, stovepipe and potbelly stove? Is not the ship's mast a king of roofbeam, or the main support beam of the sailor's home? When Odysseus is engaged in his first interview with Penelope after his homecoming—or rather, in the course of his homecoming, which is not yet complete, and perhaps never complete—disguising himself as the old Cretan beggar, he says (O, 19, 304–307): "Here the flawless hearth of Odysseus (ἱστίη τ' 'Οδυσῆος) to which I draw near. . . ." Odysseus will arrive when the moon wanes but then stands again in the sky (ἱσταμένοιο). Some will say that this is fantasy, no philology, but one must wonder whether Homer entertained the connection. Could it be *she* before the mast: ἱστός, ἱστία, ἱστίη, with all the lunar attributes of Hestia? And does not Heidegger, in his book on care, say that even when the moon is at the full it remains—at least on its dark side— forever in concealment?[5]

A final note on the mighty verge of ship and loom, a note on leverage. Masts are foreign to the Cyclops, who know nothing of ships and commerce. So what is that enormous ἱστός doing in Polyphemus's cave? He plans to use it as a shepherd's crook after it has dried, even though it is the size of the mast of a twenty-oared freighter. However, after daimon wine has worked its worst on Polyphemus and he is vomiting up chunks of the men he has devoured, Odysseus sharpens one end of it and heats it in the fire of the hearth to a glowing red. It is no longer a ἱστός but a μοχλός, a lever; it will give Nobody all the leverage he needs. "Then a daimon inspired us with courage. My companions grasped the lever toward its sharpened front and plunged it right in his eye, while I braced myself upwards and turned it, like one who drills the planks of a ship. . . ; and blood streamed over the lever . . . which was like iron tempered in the juices of his eye" (9, 322, 332, 375, and 381–94). Nobody neglects to say which foot he put forward when he braced himself, the right or the left, but we can be sure that it was his best. Odysseus πολύτροπος, πολύμητις, πολύτλας, πολυμήχαν', who always knows how to get leverage—at least when he is among men.

Daimons and Drugs

Who is the daimon who breathes courage into Odysseus and his crew in Polyphemus's cave? Who or what does the word δαίμων address? Who are these middling creatures, these *Mittelwesen* who mediate between earth and sky, mortals and immortals? Heidegger refers to the daimonic as *das Übermächtige*, related in his view to anxiety, the nothing, and the holy.[6] In Heidegger's view, life itself is a daimon. The emphatic prefix ζά, cognate with διά, δύο, δίσ-, "throughout, thoroughly, very, doubly," is the root of ζάω, ζοεῖν, ζῷον, and it reflects daimonic power.[7] Whereas daimons are everywhere in Homer's texts, ζα- words are rare. The one that crops up again and again, as numberless succulent pigs and well-nourished steers wend their bloody way to the gods in sacrifice, is ζατρεφής (I, 7, 223: ταύρων ζατρεφέων; cf. ἐϋτρεφής: O, 14, 530). Proteus guards his herd of well-nourished seals, φώκας ζατρεφέας (O, 4, 450–1). And when Eumaeus, the faithful sowherd, finds he must eternally offer up the best-nourished pigs to the suitors, αἰεὶ ζατρεφέων σιάλων τὸν ἄριστον ἁπάντων (O, 14, 19), the fatness of the animals is a measure of the hybris and impending nemesis of the suitors, as it is when Odysseus's crew slaughter the Oxen of the Sun.

Curiously, ζατρεφής "well-nourished," is the very ζα- word that Heidegger (in "Aletheia" and in the Heraclitus lecture course of 1943) omits, a bizarre omission in the context of za-ology, the lore and love of life.[8] Some, following Levinas, would make much of this: it is as though Heidegger does not pay sufficient heed to the earth (and the hearth) as the site of *enjoyment*, whatever his sense of usufruct in "The Anaximander Fragment"[9] Heidegger does mention the fires of sacrifice that sear the flesh of animals. He also mentions the special mode of revealing/concealing that constitutes animal life: "But animality does belong to ζῆν in a special sense. The rising of animals into the open remains closed and sealed in itself in a strangely captivating way."[10] Yet in the end he seems determined to reserve the never-setting clearing of being for human beings and the gods, the "anyone" of τίς apparently excluding those "anythings" that happen to be animals, even if a being well-nourished pertains to humans as well as to other animals, none of which thrive on ambrosia and nectar. Human beings are particularly well nourished at feasts, where they eat sumptuously; paradoxically, it is also at feasts where they sometimes weep in secret. As we shall see in some detail in the next section, Heidegger himself is captivated by such weeping. For it shows (reveals, unveils) how "someone" can be, and, in effect, ontologically must be—in the troubling and troubled world that is the world of care.

Another ζα- word appears in Phoenix's address to the wrathful Achilles, in that song which many scholars have taken to be a later addition to the *Ur-Iliad*. No doubt Phoenix's speech does seem closer to *The Odyssey* than to the rest of *The Iliad*, and perhaps closer still to Hesiod and even to Aeschylus, with it appeals to ἁμάρτια, Ἄτε, the

Λίται, and the need to relent, repent, recant, and reconcile. It is precisely here that many critics envisage "the triumph of morality" over the heroic sense of destiny, precisely here that a Nietzschean genealogical reading of *The Iliad* would have to do its work.[11] In the great tale of vengeance that is Western "morality," which in the late 1880s Nietzsche consistently invokes under the figure of Circe the sorceress, Homer need not play second fiddle to the Bible: Achilles's revenge against Agamemnon for the latter's "rape" of Briseis (it is the concealed Briside, not Helen, who sparks the immediate events of the *Ilias* epic); Odysseus's revenge against Antinoos and the other suitors, but also against the servant-girls who consort with them, whom Odysseus will have hanged by a single rope; not to mention the revenge of one god or goddess against another, and the vengeance of Zeus Pater upon all. That is too vast (ζαμεγά!) An undertaking for these notes, to which I shall now return.

In the course of his plea to Achilles, old Phoenix says: "Thus we heard tell of earlier heroes, who, if perchance they had raged in anger (ἐπιζάφελος χόλος ἵκοι), let themselves be reconciled by gifts and words" (I, 9, 525). Another ζα- word appears in the lines Apollo addresses to Poseidon, as all the gods do battle at the river Xanthes. (After reading Derrida's *Schibboleth*, one may be tempted—again for Nietzschean genealogical reasons—to compare the two riverbank slaughters.[12]) "Why should I do battle for the sake of mere mortals!" exclaims the sun god, "mortals, who are as wretched as the leaves on the trees, flourishing at first (ἄλλοτε μέν τε ζαφλεγέες τελέθουσιν), enjoying the fruits of the earth, but then, deprived of heart, vanishing (ἄλλοτε δὲ φθινύθουσιν ἀκήριοι)" (I, 21, 464–66). Burgeoning, flourishing to the full, ζαφλεγέες τελέθουσιν, is contrasted sharply by dwindling and vanishing, φθινύθουσιν. Vanishing how? Ἀκήριοι, as those who are *entseelt*, as the German says, those who are deprived of κῆρ. And what is κῆρ? We shall come to that, if only briefly, at the end.

There are two more daimonic usages to record, not ζα- words proper, but perhaps proto-ζα. Twice the warriors confront the turbulent waters of a "Zeus-swollen river," διπετέος ποταμοῖο (I, 17, 263; 21, 326). In his lecture courses, Heidegger constantly tries to confine the daimonic and deific to the theater of theory, theory in the sense of theater, hardening the zeta and delta to the theta of θέα-, the gods being die *Hereinblickenden*.[13] Yet I wonder whether the god-swollen river is not the "earlier" appearance, the more vital and powerful epiphany, the more frightful and uncanny—that is, the more self-concealing and self-withdrawing—presencing of the daimonic? Finally, the Homeric refrain, ζείδωρα ἄρουρα, the wheat rich fields, the nourishing earth: is this not the generously giving (ζεί-δωρα) earth, and is not the ζεί somewhere between Zeus, the daimon, and life? Doubtless by way of Demeter?

But to return to that δαίμων who inspires courage in Odysseus. One of the hero's epithets is "clever," δαΐφρον (O, 1, 48; 3, 163; 7, 168; 21, 223 and 379; 22, 115, 202, and 281), certainly as clever as Penelope's ἐχέφρων and περίφρων. Odysseus is cunning, ingenious, and well versed in all tricks and turns. He is as metamorphic as Proteus, the daimon of transformations. We would say he is a clever devil. Yet he is also the man of misfortune. Athena complains to Father Zeus at the outset of The Odyssey: "But my heart is torn by Odysseus, mighty of mind, dismal of fortune," ἀλλά μοι ἀμθ' 'Οδυσῆι δαΐφρονι δαίεται ἦτορ δυσμόρῳ . . (O, 1, 48–49).

The word δαίμων appears a surprising number of times in the vocative, as one personage addresses another, always in a state of agitation or irritation. Hera has not overlooked the significance of the fact that Thetis, the mother of Achilles, has been clinging to Zeus's knee. When she confronts him with it and accuses him of conspiring with Thetis against her Achaeans, he cries, "δαιμονίη, you always know what I'm doing, nothing can be concealed from you (οὐδέ σε λήθω)" (I, 1, 561; see the discussion of Heraclitus B16, below in the next section). Listige, writes the German translator, "Oh, you cunning one!" The cunning one is the uncanny one, the one who manages to bring to the fore what ought to have remained concealed.[14] When Aphrodite tries to seduce Helen back to the bed of Paris, Paris having been helicoptered off the battlefield by the goddess of love at the moment when Menelaos is about to throttle him, Helen cries, "δαιμονίη, Oh, you cruel one, why do you try to seduce me so?" (O, 3, 399). When brother Hektor catches Paris nestled comfortably in bed, he cries, "δαιμονί', you certainly have nothing to complain about—and this is all your fault!" (O, 6, 326; cf. 521). O du Verblendeter, "Oh, you blind one," or "Oh, you guilty one," inasmuch as Verblendung is elsewhere used to translate the effects of 'Άτε. Or, in the second instance, "You fool!" Odysseus addresses the Greeks in such fashion when they show signs of weakness: "Are you out of your minds?" (I, 2, 190 and 200). Priam does the same to Hekuba when she tries to dissuade him from recovering Hektor's body: "Oh, miserable woman!" (I, 24, 194). All these emphatic apostrophes, exclaimed at moments of extreme vexation, danger, or shared suffering, suggest the overpowering power of the uncanny—the power that shows something that ought to have remained in concealment.

The Odyssey yields fewer such vocatives. Eumaeus encourages Odysseus-incognito as follows: ἔσθιε, δαιμόνιε ξείνων. "Eat, uncanny stranger" (O, 14, 443). He has already addressed him as a "frightful stranger," ἆ δειλὲ ξείνων (361). When Melantho, leader of the lubricious servant girls, mocks Odysseus in disguise, he retorts, "δαιμονίη, Wicked woman!" (O, 19, 71). And when Penelope hesitates before Odysseus, awaiting the definitive sign, they exchange strong words. Each addresses the other with δαιμονίη, Bist du ein Unhold?

"Are you a demon? What the hell kind of woman are you? "Who the devil do you think you are?" (O, 23, 166 and 174).

Reunited at last in mutual recognition, one of the pair (Odysseus) repeats the attack, but this time teasingly, as Penelope demands to hear his story, the *whole story* (264), including all the reasons for his concealed tears.

What do all these daimonic vocatives imply? Vexation in the face of a superior power; fear in the face of concealment, cunning, and cruelty; accusation in the face of the guilty one or the fool; desperation in the face of a stubborn, uncompromising woman, or perhaps simply a courageous one; astonishment in the face of a stranger. It is as though the apostrophized daimon refers to those ancient sprites, goblins, bacilli, and cobolds to which Jane Ellen Harrison refers under the name *keres*.[15]

The δαίμων itself enters on the Homeric scene either genie or beneficent power—more often the former than the latter. Here are a small handful of daimonic epiphanies, first as the helpful divinity, then as the dire demon.

The model warrior Diomedes is said to be "equal to a daimon," presumably in strength, δαίμονι ἶσος, but also in outward appearance (I, 5, 438 and 459). Well might he equal a daimon, this Diomedes, who wounds both the goddess of love and the god of war in battle (884; 336–40; 856–69). The same will be said of Achilles during the θεομαχία of Book 20 (447). Hektor hopes to engage with Ajax "until a daimon pulls us apart," thus granting victory to one people or the other (I, 7, 291–92). Nor should we forget the (good) daimon that breathes courage into Odysseus and his crew as they plunge the lever into Polyphemus's eye

(O, 9, 381). After Odysseus-incognito has spun out his little epic of lies to Eumaeus, the sowherd encourages him to tell the truth by saying, "You mournful old man (γέρον πολυπενθές), it was a divinity who brought you here to me (ἐπεί σέ μοι ἤγαγε δαίμων)" (O, 14, 386). Later he cries the same to the surly goatherd who has just given the "old man" (= Odysseus-incognito) a good swift kick: "If only Odysseus were here, if only a divinity would bring him back," ἀγάγοι δέ ἑ δαίμων, a refrain later taken up by Philoitios, Odysseus's loyal cowherd (O, 17, 243; 21, 201). Later still, Philoitios warns one of the suitors that a daimon should steal him away before Odysseus's return (O, 18, 146–47). It is surely a good daimon who "inspires" Penelope (μοι . . . ἐνέπνευσε φρεσὶ δαίμων) to sit at that large ἱστός in order to weave, ravel, and craftily procrastinate (O, 19, 138–39).

Now for the demons. In Phoenix's moralizing appeal to Achilles, it is (as one might expect) a daimon who is said to possess the hero and make him sulk. The gods themselves often relent, Achilles is told, and guilt and retribution are the order of the day, not the vengeance on which Achilles' heart is set: "Do not let a daimon drive you to it, my friend" (I, 9, 600–601). When Antinoos encourages Telemachos to send his mother to her father's house in preparation for another marriage, Telemachos replies that if he were to do so he would have two things to fear; his father, Odysseus, and the misfortunes that a daimon would invariably send (O, 2, 134–35). Nestor in Pylos recounts the parting of the ways between his and Odysseus's ships: "For I saw that a daimon planned ill for us," ὃ δὴ κακὰ μήδετο δαίμων (O, 3, 166). However laconic Menelaos's account of the matter may seem, it is surely a wicked daimon who drives Helen to the Trojan Horse and has her circle about it, tapping it and calling out the names of the Greek heroes in the voices of their respective wives, tempting them like a siren to betray themselves. "You came," says her aggrieved husband, "because a daimon commanded you, hoping in that way to enhance the fame of his Trojans" (O, 4, 274–75). Even the powerful goddess, δεινὴ θεός, cunning Kalypso herself, needs a daimon to call mortal men to her side. Neither man nor god mixes with her, Odysseus tells Alkinoos. "Yet I, poor wretch, was led by some sort of daimon to be her fireside friend (ἐφέστιον ἤγαγη δαίμων)."

Soon the daimon will conduct us as well to Kalypso's hearth. For the moment, recall Heidegger's fascination with the hearth, der Herd, especially in his lectures on Hölderlin's hymn, Der Ister.[16] Is there not something powerfully concealed, daimonically cryptic and calyptic, about the hearth and heart of any home—the uncanny unhomelike? Has not Odysseus been tasting this for months and years among the goddesses and witches of the isles?[17]

It is an *Unhold* who drives Odysseus back to Aiolia (O, 10, 64), an *Unhold* who drinks up the pool in which parched Tantalos is made to stand (O, 11, 587), an *Unhold* who puts words of mutiny of Eurylochos's mouth (even though the German translation calls this daimon *eine Gottheit*: O, 12, 295). Telemachos, dazed by the reappearance of his father, cannot trust his senses: "No, you are not Odysseus, not my father; an evil spirit enchants me," *ein Unhold berückt mich*, με δαίμων θέλγει (O, 16, 194–95). Occasionally, the word κακά appears in parataxis with δαίμων as the evil he sends; the paratactic refrain nonetheless resonates as κακὸς δαίμων, as in the phrase, τόσα γάρ μοι ἐπέσσευεν κακὰ δαίμων, *Denn alles, was es an Unheil gibt—ein Unhold schickt es in Eile* (O, 18, 256; 19, 129). Sometimes that evil appears in the form of a nightmare: αὐτὰρ ἐμοὶ καὶ ὀνείρατ' ἐπέσσευεν κακὰ δαίμων (O, 20, 87). When the Northwind stirs up the sea, a "recalcitrant daimon," χαλεπὸς δαίμων, is surely to blame (O, 19, 201). Meanwhile, Penelope is visited by daimonic cares as well: αὐτὰρ ἐμοὶ καὶ πένθος ἀμέτρητον πόρε δαίμων, "Yet a daimon (*ein Unhold*) brought me immeasurable mourning" (O, 19, 512). Finally, as Odysseus puts his father Laertes to the test, spinning out the last of his epic fables, we again hear the refrain, *Aber es trieb mich ein Unhold* (O, 24, 306). If the word *hold* in German refers to the fair and the gracious, we may take it that an *Unhold* is the ugly potency, the unpropitious power that ought to have remained in concealment but came to the fore. Yet there is always the view from the other side: one man's evil genie is another man's guardian angel. When the defunct suitor Amphimedon informs Agamemnon in Hades how he got there—in that remarkable *second* visit to the World of the Dead that opens the final song of *The Odyssey*—he tells how Odysseus found Eumaeus the sowherd: "And then there was this evil spirit (κακὸς δαίμων) who led Odysseus far out into the fields, where his sowherd dwelled" (O, 24, 149–50). That evil spirit was Pallas Athena.

In *Daimon Life*, I tried to trace the probable origins of the word δαίμων. I recorded Liddell-Scott's surmise that the word is related to δαίω, dividing up, distributing, or apportioning, as at a meal. "And after they had finished the work and prepared the meal (δαῖτα) they feasted (δαίνυντ'), and all enjoyed the meal they deserved (δαιτὸς ἐίσης)"

(I, 2, 430–31; cf. O, 7, 148 and 203). There was something distinctly noble in Eumaeus's demeanor "as he rose to distribute the meat," δαιτρεύσων, something even of the seer or the one who allots destinies; for meat is something Eumaeus "had seen," something he knows through and through, as though clairvoyant, ἤδη (O, 14, 433). Antinoos, of all people, brings the two words together when he complains about the "old man's" presence at the feast of the suitors: "What evil spirit (*Welcher Unhold*, τίς δαίμων) sent this pest to disturb our meal (δαιτός)?" (O, 17, 446).

However, a second derivation is tempting. Hera, garbed in Aphrodite's ἱμάντα, or "girdle of enchantment," brings Zeus to love and sleep. "Thus the father slept quietly on Mount Gargaron in the arms of his wife, benumbed by love and slumber." *Ganz von Liebe benommen und Schlaf*, ὕπνῳ καὶ φιλότητι δαμείς (I, 14, 535). The word *benommen* will strike any za-ologist, of course, as Heidegger's word for animal behavior—but also for the singular effect of anxiety on a Dasein that is about to become appropriate, as *Sein und Zeit* relates. A lizard sunning itself on a rock and a Dasein shocked out of its quotidian complacency are both *benommen*. *Benommenheit* is perhaps best considered a word for daimonic impact. In the face of the overpowering power of the δαιμόνιον, human existence is invaded by a kind of animal seriousness—what the Germans call *tierischer Ernst*.

A more relevant "Homeric" reason for considering δαμνάω as a source of the daimonic is the power of sleep, invoked just now, as so often in the Homeric epics: Ὕπνε, ἄναξ πάντων τε θεῶν πάντων τ' ἀνθρώπων (I, 14, 233 ff.), with Zeus alone the occasional exception. A more stunning example is the stone that Ajax sends crashing against Hektor's chest: "The dark of night veiled his eyes (ἐκάλυψε: we will soon come to such veilings), and the blow still dazed his senses (θυμὸν ἐδάμνα)" (439). Patroklos's death deals just such a blow to Achilles. Somewhere between mourning (πένθος) and raging vengeance (χόλος), Achilles remembers that even Herakles could not flee his fate: "Rather, the μοῖρα compelled (ἐδάμασσε) him" (I, 18, 119). When he makes peace with Agamemnon, Achilles says, "Let the heart in our breasts be tamed, obedient to necessity (δαμάσαντες ἀνάγκη)" (I, 19, 66). Achilles' own immortal horses warn him of his lot—a god and a mortal will bring him to submission: θεῷτε καὶ ἀνέρι ἶφι δαμῆναι (I, 19, 417).

The same word, δαμνάω, δαμῆναι, rears its daimonic head in *The Odyssey*. Nestor recounts Agamemnon's ignominious fate: "But then a sending of the gods (μοῖρα θεῶν) took him to perdition," ἐπέδησε δαμῆναι (O, 3, 269). The word is once again brought into the proximity of gods and mortals in a sententious remark by Menelaos: "It is painful for a god to have to submit (δαμῆναι) to a mortal man" (O, 4, 397). The word is again associated with "blows" when Odysseus prepares to face, in a boxing match, Iros-Airos, the Universal Bum, for the prize of a blood sausage: "Now I shall have to submit to blows (πληλῆσι δαμείω)," whines the old man, (O, 18, 54). He asks the hooting and jeering suitors not to join in the fracas, to withhold their blows (πλήξῃ), so that he does not suffer defeat at the hands of them all (57: τούτῳ . . . δαμάσσῃ).

The daimonic thus has to do with both allotments and damaging disclosures—with sendings, deliveries, blows, and submissions. It perhaps also has to do with what Heidegger calls the double *Schlag* of sexuality—the initial inexplicable dispersion of Dasein into at least two sexes, and between them, alongside the plague (πλήλη) of discord, the promise of a gentler twofold.[18] These *coups* of a dual coinage dominate Derrida's reflections on *Geschlecht*, three parts of which have been published; an unpublished and unfinished third manuscript measures these strokes of mortal sexuality in Heidegger's Trakl essay.[19] For some Homeric uses of πλήλη, see I, 3, 31, where Paris, espying on the battlefield the hero he has cuckolded, "was struck down in his innermost heart," κατεπλήλη φίλον ἦτορ; when Athena and Hera rebel against Zeus in order to help the Achaeans, he threatens to blast their chariot with a lightning-bolt, πληλέντε κεραυνῷ (I, 8, 455); later he threatens Hera with fists, σε πληγῇσιν ἱμάσσω (I, 15, 17); Patroklos's death is due to both the blow delivered by Apollo and the lances hurled by Euphorbos and Hektor, πληλλῇ καὶ δουρι δαμασθείς (I, 16, 816); Odysseus, contemplating the death of the suitors and their women, beats his breast in anger, στῆθος δὲ πλήξας (O, 20, 13); and, of course, there are dozens upon dozens of blows that fall in *The Iliad* and *The Odyssey* that I have not recorded here.

One final note on δαίμων. Its place in the poetic line is virtually always at the very end of the line—not, as far as I can see, for metrical reasons (dozens of other words would fill the rhythmic bill), but presumably because of its uncanny semantic power. It is as though the poetic line in Homer is delimited (as Charles Olson says it ought to be) by the breath; and there is invariably a catch in the breath, a caesura, in every invocation of the daimon.

Kalypso's Concealments

Is Kalypso—who, as we heard, needs a mediating daimon to call mortal men to her side—herself a mere daimon? Surely not. Odysseus calls her a powerful and uncanny goddess, δεινὴ θεός (O, 7, 246). When Hermes comes to Ogygia she recognizes him straightaway: "She knew him as soon as she saw him, Kalypso, goddess divine (78, 85, 180, 246; cf. 9, 29: δῖα θεάων), for the gods, altogether deathless, are not unknown to each other (οὐ γάρ τ᾽ ἀγνῶτες θεοὶ ἀλλήλοισι πέλονται ἀθάνατοι)" (5, 79–80). She and Hermes alike feed on ambrosia and nectar in her dining hall. And when she poses a question to Hermes, he replies, "You question me, goddess, the god who comes to you (θεὰ θεόν)" (5, 96). Yet when Hermes communicates Zeus's will to her, which is that she send Odysseus on his way, Odysseus being the lover she has nursed for seven years ("I won him over to love, I nurtured him (ἔτρεθον: cf. ζατρεφής, discussed above), I told him many times I would make him ageless and deathless all his days," 135–36; cf. 218), Kalypso suddenly dissociates herself from the gods. Ogygia seems to her—and to us—as remote as possible from Olympus. "You are hard-hearted, you gods, more jealous than all the rest," she complains. Indeed, the Olympians are particularly hard when a goddess elects a mortal for her lover. "You gods," she chides them, "whose life flows on like water," θεοὶ ῥεῖα ζώοντες (122). A goddess who abjures the gods, Kalypso is also called a nymph (5, 14, 30, 57 et passim; cf. 149: πότνια νύμφη): "Homecoming! was his cry; but the nymph was opposed" (154). To be sure, however much Odysseus weeps during the daylight hours, he spends his nights in her spacious grotto, seven years of nights. "He was compelled to do so, unwilling, by her who did the willing," ἀνάγκῃ .. παρ᾽ οὐκ ἐθέλων ἐθελούσῃ(154–55).

Precisely how unwilling is the hero? Where are the eyes that will plumb this unwillingness, this submission to external compulsion? Who will taste the flavor of these tears of his? These matters are concealed. They are, if one can say so, concealment itself.

Who is Kalypso? What are her effects? Hers is perhaps the most perfect of songs—The Odyssey, Book 5, which begins with Dawn rising from the arms of her lover Tithonos in order to show herself and bring light to immortals and human beings alike, and ends with Odysseus burying himself under dry leaves on the Phaeacian shores (where Nausicaa will find him), concealing himself as one conceals coals under heaps of ashes (5, 488: κρύπτεσθαι) in order to preserve the seed of fire (σπέρμα πυρὸς σῴζων, 490). There on the shore, as perhaps later on the Sandymount Strand of Joyce's "Nausicaa," Athena veils her hero's beloved lids in sleep, φίλα βλέφαρ' ἀμφικαλύψας (494), these being the song's final, fading words. Καλύψατο (491) is Odysseus himself, ἐνέκρυψε (487) is the glowing seed of fire, and ἀμφικαλύψας are the hero's eyelids in sleep.

> ⎮ Kalypso, Καλυψώ, κάλυψω: "And I shall veil."
> "I"? Who am "I"? "She that veils."
> Veils with what? In the first place, with night and death.

In earlier days, in the bolder days of Troy, Odysseus threatens Thersites, "the Ugliest Man," in the following way: "Watch I don't rip every shred of clothing from your body, everything that veils your shame," τά τ' αἴδω ἀμφικαλύπτει (I, 2, 263). Each time a god or goddess wants to rescue a favorite from an especially parlous situation on the battlefront, he or she veils him in a cloud and snatches him from the melee. Thus Aphrodite plucks Paris from Menelaos's vengeful grip, "concealing him in a heavy mist," ἐκάλυψε δ' ἄρ' ἠέρι παλλῇ (I, 3, 381). Once Paris is ensconced in his chambers, silver-veiled Helen comes to him, accompanied by Aphrodite. The impact is immediate, and it too has to do with parergonal veils: "Never has love so veiled my senses," ἔρως φρένας ἀμφεκαλύψεν (442), is the plaint of Paris.[20] As the tiresome Nestor—surely the prototype of Shakespeare's Polonius—recounts his exploits back in the olden days when men were men, he tells of the two who got away: the sons of Aktor, whom Poseidon snatched from the battlefield (ἐκ πολέμου ἐσάωσε, "wrapped in veils of mist," καλύψας ἠέρι πολλῇ, I, 11, 752). Others are less lucky. Earlier I mentioned Hektor, dazed by Ajax's rock: τὼ δέ οἱ ὄσσε νὺξ ἐκάλυψε μέλαινα, "Black night veiled his eyes" (I, 14, 438–9). The Trojan prince Hyperenor is lanced, his ψυχή flies from the gaping wound, and "darkness veils his eyes," σκότος ὄσσε κάλυψε (I, 14, 519). "Apollo has killed me, and cruel fate!" cries Patroklos, stripped of his armor, dismantled like Lemuel Pitkin, and "veiled in his deathly demise," τέλος θανάτοιο κάλυψε (I, 16, 855). News of Patroklos's death has almost the same effect on Achilles: ἄχεος νεθέλη ἐκάλυψε μέλαινα, "a black cloud of horror wrapped him round" (I, 18, 22; cf. Laertes' grief over his son Odysseus, presumed lost: 24, 315). When Andromache sees Hektor dragged across the plain outside the city walls, she collapses: "Gloomy night veiled her and covered her eyes," κατ' ὀφθαλμῶν ἐρεβεννὴ νὺξ ἐκάλυψεν (I, 22, 466; cf. 20, 86). Such clouds of mist sometimes conceal more than a single warrior, and they often conceal not in order to protect but to offer a foretaste of doom. Cloud-gatherer Zeus unleashes a hurricane after the Oxen of the Sun have been slaughtered. "In foggy mist he veils land and sea (κάλυψε γαῖαν . . . καὶ πόντον), and night drops down from the sky" (O, 12, 314–15). And yet there are also very different sorts of veilings.

Veiling themselves with veils, goddesses cover their faces. No, they do not cover them—they hide them in order better to show them. Sails never simply cover or cleave to the mast. Whether ἱστία, κρηδέμνοι, or καλύπτραι, veils are *parerga*. Veilings of the second order, as it were, they are supplemental *showings*. The Lakedaimonian women are "beautifully veiled," καλλικρήδεμνοι (O, 4, 623), as will be Penelope when she goes down to meet the hated suitors (18, 210; 21, 65). Κρήδεμνος is one word for evil, καλύπτρη another. Both do a great deal of revealing work in The Odyssey, especially in Books 5 and 10, those featuring Kalypso of Ogygia and Kirke of Aiaia.[21]

An ambrosial bath, unguents immortal, perfumes that permeate heaven and earth, her loveliest robes, pearl earrings, and golden brooches: Hera is on her familiar way to seduce her consort again. The final touch is a veil, κρηδέμνῳ καλύψατο, a veil shining like the sun, λευκός δ' ἦν ἠέλιος ὥς (I, 14, 185), a smaller version of the ἱστία λευκά. As if that were not enough, Hera now goes to fetch Aphrodite's girdle. "Give me now the forces of love and longing (φιλότητα καὶ ἵμερον), by which you bring all to submission (ᾧ τε σὺ πάντας δαμνᾷ—shades of the daimon!), immortals as well as mortal men" (198–9). Aphrodite undoes her girdle of enchantment, "of love, longing, and lascivious whispers that becloud the mind (ἔκλεψε νόον) even of the wisest ones" (216–17), including Zeus. Zeus eclipsed is Zeus benumbed. Yet also including the mortals, and, among them, the well-versed Odysseus.

In "Aletheia," Heidegger is occupied with λανθάνομαι, concealing. Yet his most trenchant example of concealment ostensibly reveals nothing about λήθη. (There are numerous examples of λανθάνομαι and λήθη as concealment and oblivion in Homer's poems—I, 9, 537; O, 9, 97 and 102; O, 19, 91 and 151, etc.; however, there is no need to report on them here.) Heidegger relates how Odysseus conceals himself as he weeps at Alkinoos's court—Telemachos did precisely the same at the court of Menelaos (4, 114–16)—by pulling a purple cloth over his eyes, porphyry being the color of death and mourning, "and concealing his magnificent face," κάλυψε δέ καλὰ πρόσωπα (8, 85). Prosopokalypsis, presumably out of shame, but also in the vain endeavor to conceal himself. Vain, inasmuch as King Alkinoos recognizes Odysseus's concealment for the self-showing it is.

If one searches for the antithesis of concealing, however, one finds it precisely where Heidegger found it, namely, in all the forms of φαίνεσθαι that grace the Homeric epics. "Athena takes Achilles by the hair," recalls William Butler Yeats, in "The Phases of the Moon," and as she does so she *reveals herself* to him alone, οἴῳ φαινομένη, while remaining invisible to all the others, τῶν δ᾽ ἄλλων οὔ τις ὁρᾶτο (I, 1, 198). When, years later, Odysseus prays to Athena, she hears and heeds him, but does not show herself: οὐ πω φαίνετ᾽ (O, 6, 329), partly because she fears Poseion, but also because, as Hera says, "Gods are recalcitrant when they appear in person," χαλεποὶ δὲ θεοὶ φαίνεαθαι ἐναργεῖς (I, 20, 131).

Perhaps the most familiar of such revelations, to repeat, is the invocation of Dawn: "Now, when Dawn showed herself (*sich zeigte*: φάνη), her fingers all roses . . ." (O, 2, 1; cf. 5, 2; 9, 152; and 17, 1); "Dawn found him as soon as she shone (ἠὼς φαινομένη) on strand and sea" (I, 24, 12– 13); "Helios rose . . . to bring light to the immortals (ἀθανάτοισι φαείνοι) . . ." (O, 3, 2). Helios is one of Heidegger's favorite figures, especially in the form of φάος ἠελίοιο, "the light of day." To see the light of day is to be born, to live, as Priam tells Achilles: τε ζώειν καὶ ὁρᾶν φάος ἠελίοιο (I, 24, 558; cf. 5, 120). Sometimes the light goes out: when Menelaos learns of his brother's murder he sinks into the dust and weeps: "I didn't have the heart to go on living, to go on seeing the light of day," οὐδέ νύ μοι κῆρ ἤθελ᾽ ἔτι ζώειν καὶ ὁρᾶν φάος ἠελίοιο (O, 4, 539–40). This is precisely the phrase Odysseus uses when Kirke tells him that there is one more diversion on his homeward route—he must go to hell, where daylight never penetrates (O, 10, 497–98).

There is even a moment when it seems the sun of life will never set. That is one of the themes of Heraclitus's "never-setting sun," discussed by Heidegger in "Aletheia," which we will take up once again in a moment. Odysseus's moment comes on the last leg of his journey homeward, after he has been to Hades, during that last long day at Alkinoos's court: "Again and again Adysseus turned his head sunward (πρὸς ἠέλιον . . . παμφανόωντα), that the sun might finally set (δῦναι ἐπειγόμενος)" (O, 13, 29–30; cf. 33 and 35, φάος ἠελίοιο). However, Zeus does not wish the sun to set, at least not forever: when Helios threatens to go to hell and shine on the dead (ἐν νεκύεσσι φαείνω) unless those who poached his herd are punished, Zeus commands him to shine on gods and mortals rather than shades: 'Ηέλι', . . . φάεινε (O, 12, 383 and 385).

The light of day is not the only thing that surges upward in radiance. To espy a Cyclops against the sky is like seeing "a wooded crag towering (φαίνεται) in high mountains" (O, 9, 192). And sometimes self-showing is descensional, as when Poseidon shakes the earth until it threatens to gape and expose (φανείη) the hateful domain of Hades to mortals and gods (I, 20, 64). Sometimes self-showing is deadly, as when Hektor inadvertently allows himself to shine through (φαίνετο) his armor, which is hollow at the base of his throat, at the supersternal notch (I, 22, 324). And sometimes it is deadly for another, as it is for Iros Airos, the Universal Bum, when the "old man" disrobes for the boxing match: "Large, well-formed thighs showed themselves (φαίνε), and broad shoulders appeared (φάνεν)" (O, 18, 67–68).

More often than not, however, a self-showing has to veil itself, as when Penelope, cloaked in glittering veils, shows herself to the despicable suitors, μνηστήρεσσι φανῆναι (O, 18, 160 and 165). Back, then, to veils and concealings. Back to Ogygia, and on to Aiaia—the poles of the Odyssean itinerary on the way to Ithaka—Ogygia and Aiaia being names for the uncanny homecoming that transpires in secret prior to the homecoming proper, names for the always antecedent, always anachronistic nostalgia for something other than domesticity. Ogygia and Aiaia are names—or cries—of desire and adventure. For Odysseus *did* go off to war, *did* abandon Penelope and their son, for something that elsewhere the Briside and Helen inspired. And on his way home he *was* waylaid. Or so the story goes.

Kalypso's island would charm a god—Hermes, for example, who stops to contemplate it in astonishment on his way to end the seven years of Odysseus's confinement. On that last night (or were there four or five nights attached to the four or five days during which Odysseus builds his raft?) Odysseus confines himself again to Kalypso's grotto, apparently without undue constraint, regardless of what we will have heard concerning the hero's "unwillingness": "Once again they betake themselves to her spacious grotto,/Joyously in a corner of the cave they huddle in love," τερπέσθην φιλότητι, παρ' ἀλλήλοισι μένοντες (O, 5, 227). The next morning, when Dawn shows herself (φάνη 'Ηώς),

Kalypso veils herself (καλύπτρην) from head to toe (230–32). She shows Odysseus the trees for his raft, and when the raft is finished she outfits it with food, wine, and water. She even inspires its fluttering ἱστία with wind. On the eighteenth day at sea, as Odysseus nears Phaeacia, Poseidon veils land and sea—and κάλυψις reappears, as it were. The raft's ἱστός is smashed by a sudden gust of wind. Tossed overboard, Odysseus is dragged down by the rich robes given him in parting by Kalypso (321). When after a struggle he regains his raft, or what is left of it, Ino, the Shining Goddess (Λευκοθέη, the goddess of shimmering ἱστία, one might say), commands him to abandon both raft and clothing, and to swim for it. She gives him now an ambrosial veil (κρήδεμνος ἄμβροτος) to wear about his chest until he reaches shore. Then she dives back into the sea—as the recollection of Kalypso that she is. A black wave envelopes her, μελαν δέ έ κῦμ᾽ ἐκάλυψεν (353). Odysseus wonders whether the Shining Goddess has contrived yet another trap for him, ὑφαίνησιν δόλον, but after one more blast of wind from Poseidon, he tears off Kalypso's himatia, ties the immortal κρήδεμνον around his breast, and hurtles headlong into the sea. For two days and nights he swims through the storm-tossed brine. He welcomes the eventual calm the way children welcome the recovery of their father (394: φανήη φαίνεσθαι), the father whom a wicked daimon has struck down with illness (396–67). (Must not Nietzsche have loved this image of shining—the welcome recovery of a stricken father!) Yet no safe exit onto the shore shows itself (410: οὔ πη φαίνεθ᾽). Perhaps yet another δαίμων (421) will send a monstrous fish to make a meal of him? In the mouth of a river, Odysseus at long last finds refuge, returns the immortal veil to its aqueous domain, and with Ino's help struggles ashore. Under old leaves he conceals his seed of fire, and when Athena sends sleep—φίλα βλέφαρ᾽ ἀμφικαλύψας.

These cryptic, calyptic concealments, concealments that somehow *show themselves*, reveal (Heidegger would insist) the mysterious dimension of every showing. Heidegger's entire effort in "Aletheia" is designed to frustrate all oppositional or dialectical thinking when it comes to revealing/concealing. He shies from no paradoxon or oxymoron when it is a matter of such thinking. There are so many surprises in this essay—let us look at a few of them, if they agree to show themselves to our reading.

It is a matter of engaging in a thoughtful dialogue with Heraclitus, of trying to approach Fragment B16: τὸ μὴ δῦνόν ποτε πῶς ἄν τις λάθοι;

"In the face of that which never sets, how can one hide oneself?" Concealment in the face of what never goes into concealment—that is the question. The Lethe that flows through all Aletheia—that is the mystery. And, somewhat surprisingly, inasmuch as the critics tell us that human beings mattered little to Heidegger, it always involves a τίς rather than a τί, a *who* rather than a *what*. At the end of the essay Heidegger insists that the *who* is a question of human beings and gods; earlier in his career he often called it the realm of the daimonic, τὸ δαιμόνιον.

Heidegger's first *who* is neither Heraclitus nor Clement of Alexandria (who cites Heraclitus in his Paidagogos), neither Hegel nor Nietzsche nor Plato—but Odysseus. Odysseus weeping. Odysseus concealing himself as he weeps and sighs, thus revealing who he is to all who have eyes to weep or ears to hear. Heidegger goes to some length to set the scene for Odysseus's concealed revelation, and so should we. I therefore cite "Aletheia" at length:

> Homer (*Odyssey*, 8, 83 ff.) tells how Odysseus, in the Phaeacian king's palace, covered his head each time at the minstrel Demodocus's song, whether happy or sad, and thus hidden from those present, wept. Verse 93 runs: ἔνθ᾽ ἄλλους μὲν πάντας ἐλάνθανε δάκρυα λείβων. Consistent with the spirit of our own language, we translate: "*[A]lsdann vergoß er Tränen, ohne daß alle anderen es merkten* (Then he shed tears, without all the others noticing it)." The German translation by Voss comes closer to what the Greek says, since it carries the important verb ἐλάνθανε over into the German formulation: "*Allen übrigen Gästen verbarg er die stürzende Träne* (He concealed his flowing tears from all the other guests)." Ἐλάνθανε, however, does not mean the transitive "he concealed," but "he remained concealed"—as the one who was shedding tears. "Remaining concealed" is the key word in the Greek. The German, on the other hand, says: he wept, without the others noticing it. Correspondingly, we translate the well-known Epicurean admonition λάθε βιώσας as "Live in hiding." Thought from a Greek perspective, this saying means: "As the one who leads one's life, remain concealed (therein)." Concealment here defines the way in which a human being should be present among others. By the manner of its saying, the Greek announces that concealing—and therefore at the same time remaining uncon-

cealed—exercises a commanding preeminence over every other way in which what is present comes to presence. The fundamental trait of presencing itself is determined by remaining concealed and unconcealed. One need not begin with a seemingly capricious etymology ἀλήθεσία in order to experience how universally the presencing of what is present comes to language only in shining, self-manifesting, lying-before, arising, bringing-itself-before, and in assuming an outward appearance.

All this, in its undisturbed harmony, would be unthinkable within Greek existence and language if remaining concealed/remaining unconcealed did not hold sway as that which really has no need to bring itself expressly to language, since this language itself arises from it.

Accordingly, the Greek experience in the case of Odysseus does not proceed from the premise that the guests present are represented as subjects who in their subjective behavior fail to apprehend the weeping Odysseus as an object of their perception. On the contrary, what governs the Greek experience is a concealment surrounding the one in tears, a concealment that isolates him from the others. Homer does not say: Odysseus concealed his tears. Nor does the poet say: Odysseus concealed himself as one weeping. Rather, he says: Odysseus remained concealed. We must ponder this matter ever more strenuously, even at the risk of becoming diffuse and fastidious. A lack of sufficient insight into this matter will mean, for us, that Plato's interpretation of presencing as ἰδέα remains either arbitrary or accidental.

To be sure, a few verses before the one we have cited, Homer says (86): αἴδετο γὰρ φαίηκας ὑπ' ὀφρύσι δάκρυα λείβων. In keeping with idiomatic German, Voss translates: (Odysseus covered his head) "daß die Phäaken nicht die tränenden Wimpern erblickten (so that the Phaeacians could not see his wet lashes)." Voss in fact leaves the key word untranslated: αἴδετο. Odysseus shied away (scheute sich)—as one shedding tears before the Phaeacians. But doesn't this quite clearly mean the same as: he hid himself before the Phaeacians out of a sense of shame (aus Scheu)? Or must we also think αἰδώς, on the basis of remaining concealed, as awe (Scheu), granted that we are striving to get closer to its essence as the

Greeks experienced it? Then "to shy away" would mean to be safeguarded and to remain concealed in restraint (*im Verhoffen*), in keeping to oneself (*im an-sich-Halten*).

Typically Greek, this poetic vision of Odysseus weeping beneath his cloak makes clear how the poet feels the governance of presencing—a meaning of being which, though still unthought, has already become destiny. Presencing is luminous self-concealing. Awe corresponds to it. It is a reserved remaining-concealed before the closeness of what is present. It is the sheltering of what is present within the intangible nearness of what in each case remains in coming—that coming which is an increasing self-veiling. Thus awe, and all the elevated matters related to it, must be thought in the light of remaining concealed.[22]

At the risk of becoming diffuse and fastidious, let us sit at the feet of the weeping Odysseus. The polytropic hero is weeping because the words of a song, sometimes happy, sometimes sad, have touched him. Can his invisible tears—but also his audible sighs—touch us? Homer seems to give adequate grounds for those tears, shed over the memories of the graves of so many heroes during ten long years of war. We know that Odysseus wept also on the isle of Ogygia, during the days that he sat on the shore gazing toward Ithaka. Odysseus weeps in mourning and in nostalgia. He deplores the bloodshed, and he implores the goddess to send him home.

Can one also imagine Odysseus weeping over less heroic and less homelike matters? Can one imagine him weeping in memory of seven years of nights? Seven years of awe-inspiring nights? Can one imagine him echoing the sobs of a goddess—Kalypso, for example? Perhaps he sat at her feet, as we now sit at his, or Demodocus's, or Homer's. Perhaps he kissed them on the night she hid her face upon her raised knees and wept. For Hermes had come that very day with orders, and her need to obey them left her without a sense of who she was.

"You are a goddess," Odysseus said quietly.

"How could a goddess be so unhappy?" Kalypso replied.

For a long time the mortal said nothing. Finally, he gathered up his courage and spoke.

"For seven years' of nights I have tasted the divinity of your loins and trembled before your daimonic beauty. I am a mortal, but listen to me, for this much I know: you are a goddess."

Kalypso raised her head slowly and looked long, looked longingly, into the mortal's eyes.

"If I were divine, would I need you to tell me of my divinity? And how could a goddess be so unhappy?"

Again she lowered her head to her knees, which received the streams of her tears. Odysseus could see nothing, say nothing, feel nothing but the numbness of his heart and limbs. He could not even weep, had to shy from weeping, because tears belonged to gods and goddesses now. Never again would he show himself weeping.

He no longer dared to speak, but thought to himself *I will weep for you, beloved goddess, when you are concealed from me, you who have granted me your bed and your body, you who forgot yourself in order to remember me; I will weep for you, yes, but even more I will weep for me, who will be lost at sea rather than in the balm of your body the unguent of your thighs the honey of your breasts. For I must head home—even if I no longer know who I am. . . .*

Or did Odysseus also weep because Nausicaa, who like Kalypso had rescued him, was too beautiful and too shy for words? In any event, Odysseus is someone who weeps in memory of someone who will not "set," will not go down in oblivion, even if she is overdetermined, even if she submerges again and again under the waves of his fantasies concerning her. What is it to remember someone? What is it to forget— or to *have* to forget? Heidegger suggests the following:

Λανθάνομαι says: I am—with respect to my relation to something otherwise unconcealed—concealed from myself. The unconcealed, for its own part, is thereby concealed—even as I am concealed from myself in relation to it. What is present subsides into concealment in such a way that I, because of this concealing, remain concealed from myself as the one from whom what is present withdraws. At the same time, this very concealing is itself thereby concealed. That is what takes place in the occurrence to which we refer when we say: I have forgotten (something). When we forget, something does not simply slip away from us. Forgetting itself slips into a concealing, and indeed in such a way that we ourselves, along with our relation to what is forgotten, fall into concealment. The Greeks, therefore, speaking in the middle voice, intensify it: ἐπιλανθάνομαι. Thus they also identify the concealment in which a human being founders by reference to its relation to the thing that is withdrawn in concealment.

Both in the way the Greek employs λανθάνειν, to remain concealed, as a basic and predominant verb, as well as in the experience of the forgetting of remaining-concealed, this much is made sufficiently clear: λανθάνω, I remain concealed, does not signify one form of human behavior among many others, but identifies the basic trait of ever stance we take toward what is present or absent—if not, indeed, the basic trait of presencing and absencing themselves.[23]

I am—with respect to my relation to some*one* who is otherwise unconcealed—concealed from myself. Precisely when she shows herself, my world occludes. I too am swallowed up in the occlusion.

For seven years they showed one another everything mortal, everything immortal, concealed nothing from one another. Concealed nothing but what had to remain concealed, which was all they ever cared about or for. He was able to tell her of his wife and son without betraying them or hurting her. Fidelity suddenly—in the sudden passage of seven years—redoubled its demands on him. *How now am I to be faithful to her? She cupped her hands under my joy, so that none of it would be lost. She began to feed me flowers, gave me rosewater to drink, as thought I were a bee. I felt a change coming over me, and I worshiped her. Now she says she does not know who she is. Now I do not know who I am. Even as she concealed her weeping from me, so my own weeping is concealed from me. We do not know who we are, except as those who are concealed from themselves and from one another, hidden behind cascades of tears.*

One of the oddest moments of Jacques Lacan's "Signification of the Phallus" comes when he introduces Αἰδώς or "shame" into his argument. For, initially, the phallic verge rises as the apparent—the appearing—in and for itself:

> The phallus is the privileged signifier of that mark where the share of the logos is wedded to the advent of desire. One might say that this signifier is chosen as what stands out as most easily seized upon in the real of sexual copulation, and also as the most symbolic in the literal (typographical) sense of the term, since it is the equivalent in that relation of the (logical) copula. One might also say that by virtue of its turgidity it is the image of the vital flow as it is transmitted in generation.[24]

Yet the verge's upsurgence into appearance is a far more cryptic affair, as the oxymoron of turgidity and flow suggests. For the phallus is an affair of calypsis, and can only be always on the verge of appearing:

> All these propositions merely veil over the fact that the phallus can play its role only as veiled, that is, as in itself the sign of the latency with which everything signifiable is struck as soon as it is raised (*aufgehoben*) to the function of the signifier.
>
> The phallus is the signifier of this *Aufhebung* itself which it inaugurates (initiates) by its own disappearance. This is why the demon of Αἰδώς (*Scham*, shame) in the ancient mysteries rises up exactly at the moment when the phallus is unveiled (cf. the famous painting of the Villa of Pompei).
>
> It then becomes the bar which, at the hands of this demon, strikes the signified, branding it as the bastard offspring of its signifying concatenation.[25]

From here it is not far to Lacan's identification of the cock-of-the-walk, the famboyant phallus, as an essentially *feminine* figure: "The fact that femininity takes refuge in this mask, because of the *Verdrängung* (repression) inherent in the phallic mark of desire, has the strange consequence that, in the human being, virile display itself appears as feminine."[26]

Was Lacan trying to think a certain fidelity to shying-away, to awe, reticence, and restraint—to an always frustrated expectation (*Verhoffen*)? Was he trying to contemplate a self-concealing remaining-concealed before the closeness of what is present? Was Lacan himself, as a translator of Heidegger's "Logos," shying away from the intangible nearness of what remains in coming—that coming which is an increasing self-veiling—which he named *desire*? And are we certain that in either Homer or Heidegger desire plays no role in the concealments of being?

> Kalypso, her brow motionless on her knees, murmured to Odysseus *My life consists of endless textures of the blackness of darkness; it is a warp and woof without relief or rescue, not even after years, not even after years' of years.* Was Odysseus now for the first time in his life blinded by the light of remaining-concealed? Did he, months later, disappear behind his cloak or porphyry in order to weep the tears of his own blindness and helplessness, before the desire that suddenly had nowhere to hide?

In all self-showing loves to hide (Heraclitus B123), does it also hide to love? Is this the "hovering intimacy of revealing and concealing" of which Heidegger speaks?[27] Is the history of being yet another love story, an awe-filled story of mourning and care?

Care as Heart (κῆρ) and Doom (κήρ)

Kirke's veilings—for we too shall sail now from Ogygia to Aiaia—are somewhat different from Kalypso's. Kirke's are induced by horrid drugs, φάρμακα λύγρα, which will cause Odysseus's men to forget their homeland, λαθοίατο πατρίδος (O, 10, 236). An unfortunate side-effect of these drugs is that the users become swine as well. Recall once again Nietzsche's designation of Western morality as *Circe*. Κίρκη πολυφάρμακα, the Mistress of Poisons, in his view is less involved in the raptures of sexuality than in the resentful prohibitions enforced by morality. In one of the aphorisms of *Beyond Good and Evil*, Nietzsche betrays one of the most open secrets of philosophy in the West: "Christianity gave Eros poison to drink: to be sure, he did not die from it, but he did degenerate to vice."[28]

A word, then, about Homer's pharmacy, at the dawn of our tradition. After extracting the bronze and iron from the heroes' wounds, doctors apply "alleviative herbs, mild anodynes," ἤπια or ὀδυνήφατα φάρμακα (I, 4, 191 and 218; 5, 401 and 900; 11, 515 and 741). Later, in *The Odyssey*, it is far more often a matter of deadly poisons, φάρμακα ἀνδροφόνα (O, 1, 261), and soul-destroying drugs, θυμοφθόρα φάρμακα

(2, 329). (Homer's text often places the adjective before the pharmaka, as though it were a pre-positional label.) Yet sometimes it is hard to tell whether a given *Mittel* is a *Heilmittel*, a *Gift*, or a *Gegengift*. Helen, for example, is as duplicitous a pharmacist as she is lover; or, if "duplicitous" is too unsympathetic a word (and it is), let us say that she is παλυτρόπη, wily, skillful, and well versed in the laboratory. Into Telemachos's wine she slips "a measure of enchantment," a φάρμακον that works as an antidepressant, νηπενθές, and an anticholeric, ἄχολός; it induces a kind of euphoria as it causes its user—like the patient given morphine or Valium or Darvon before surgery—"to forget everything bad," κακῶν ἐπίληθων ἀπάντων (O, 4, 220–21). Helen proffers λήθη in a mixing bowl, ἐπὴν κρητῆρι μιγείη, inducing an oblivion that banishes tears even in the face of the death of a mother or a father (close enough to Telemachos's case), a beloved son or a brother murdered by the sword (close enough to Menelaos's case) right before one's eyes. Helen, daughter of Zeus, is the mistress of such formidable φάρμακα, carried to her from Egypt, "where the fertile fields (ζείδωρος ἄρουρα) produce masses of drugs, the noble mixed with the deleterious," φάρμακα, παλλὰ μὲν ἐσθλὰ μεμίγμενα, παλλὰ δὲ λυγρά (222–30). All these drugs are brought to her by a woman of daimonic skill, a woman by the fascinating name of Πολύδαμνα.

Kirke's palace is surrounded by wolves and lions, savage beasts that have been enchanted by her and administered terrible poisons, κακὰ φάρμακα (O, 10, 213). They greet Odysseus's men cheerfully with wagging tails—it must have been the same euphoric drug that Helen administered to Telemachos. Kirke spins and sings within—is she a goddess or a woman, ἢ θεός ἠὲ γυνή, the crew wonders (228, 255)— at her massive ἱστός. Feigning hospitality, she welcomes the men, then administers the poison that induces oblivion and piggery. On his way to the rescue, Odysseus meets Hermes, who apparently words for both sides (330–31). "Take this poison, it will help," says Hermes, brandishing the most renowned of all the noble pharmaka in Western letters:

> Thus spoke the silvery, shimmering god, and plucked an
>   herb from the ground,
> Gave it to me, and showed me how it had come to be,
>   how it had grown.
> The root was black, the blossom white as milk: *Moly* the
>   gods call it.[29]

No man every allowed Kirke's poison to penetrate "the barrier of the teeth" and resisted enchantment. The sorceress goddess knows that the man who now confronts her must be the molyfied Odysseus, of whom Hermes has often spoken. "Sheathe your sword," she says, "and come to bed, where we can trust one another." After she has sworn an oath not to unman him, he follows her instructions, as he will follow those of Kalypso. (For, of course, Ogygia comes *after* Aiaia in the chronology of initiation and homecoming, though not in that of the narration). With her rhabdos (this too she shares with Hermes), Kirke drives the "swine" out of stall, sprinkles each one with yet another pharmakon. Remarkably, the restored sailors are taller and handsomer than they were before their *Schweinerei*. All the crew reunited now, Odysseus feasts in the palace of Kirke, day after day, week after week, through all the phases of the moon, for over a year. By now it is Odysseus who has forgotten the homeland, and it is his crew who must remind him of it. Whatever pacific oath she may swear, and however fortified the hero may be by Hermetic μῶλυ, Kirke retains her power to entrance, preserves her strong medicine. When Odysseus begs release from her, she replies that he must set sail for the House of Hades and the frightful Persephone, there to take further instruction from the blind androgynous seer, Tiresias. When Odysseus asks for a guide thither, Kirke tells him not to concern himself about how to get there: *Sorge dich nicht,* μὴ μελέσθω, "but only raise high the mast and hoist your sails," ἱστὸν δὲ στήσας ἀνά θ'ἱστία λευκά (505–506).

As Odysseus and his men go down to the ship in order to embark, lamenting all the way their impending voyage to the ends of— and under—the earth, Kirke disappears. She has left behind two sheep for the Ithacans to take on board, a white ram and a black ewe, shades of μῶλυ itself. Perhaps the sailors, not long for this life, will jestingly name them "Odysseus" and "Kirke," or "Poldy" and "Mol(l)y." The goddess herself, Kirke Polypharmaka, she of the serpentine coils of hair, the uncanny goddess with the voice of a human being (136: δεινὴ θεὸς αὐδήεσσα) has vanished like a wisp of smoke or a rivulet of water, ῥεῖα παρεξελθοῦσα: "Softly, furtively,/She had vanished" (573). Book 10 ends with a rhetorical question, as Kirke goes to rejoin Kalypso, she too of beautiful coils and human audition (12, 449): "Who could cast an eye on a god who does not wish to be seen, a god who wends every which way?" That sounds so much like Heraclitus B16 that it seems almost as if Heraclitus were paraphrasing Homer, thinking of Homer's goddesses, so that there would actually be something *lunar* about his sun that never sets.

When did Kirke decide not be be seen? When did she begin to wend every which way? Did Odysseus *ever* see her? And can we not pose the same questions with regard to Kalypso? Is her medicine weaker than Kirke's? Or is Kalypso—"I shall conceal, I shall remain concealed"—as potent a figure of mystery and every bit as fertile as Kirke when it comes to shying away, inspiring our awe as she wends every which way? If Kalypso and Kirke, sung in the fifth and tenth books of *The Odyssey*, serve as the axes or poles—the two ἱστία—of Odysseus's adventures, that is, as the two points at which the tension of his bow is most keenly felt, perhaps the relation of the "adventures" (Books 5–7) to the "homecoming" (Books 13–24) has to be rethought. Perhaps Telemachos's encounter with Helen would be the pendant in Books 1–4 to the tale I have in mind.

I cannot take up questions of νόστος here. If I were to take them up, it would be by focusing on the figures of Odysseus-in-disguise and Penelope-veiled: figures of concealment both to one another and to us. Figures of *remaining* concealed, even when the revelation is at hand, even after the famous "recognition" scene(s). It seems to me that *The Odyssey* can no longer be read (at least after Nietzsche, Heidegger, Derrida, and Lacan, and also after Joyce) as Odysseus's heroic overcoming of the shadowy erotic figures of Kalypso and Kirke. It is certainly not an overcoming of erotic concealment for the sake of a transparent Penelope, Penelope as the sunlit heart and erected hearth of the home. Such a traditional reading insults the *cunning* of Penelope and the *cares* of Odysseus, not to mention the *tears* of a goddess. In the sixth of his "Tautenburg Sketches for Lou," Nietzsche writes: "*Love*, for *men*, is something altogether different than it is for women. For most men, to be sure, love is a kind of *obsession to possess*; for the other kind of men, love is adoration of a suffering and veiled godhead."[30] He offers no explanation of either the godhead or the suffering; yet it is here that the acerbic misogynist reveals himself most unforgettably.

Who can descry a goddess or a woman who remains concealed?

Is Odysseus any less concealed to Kalypso?

How could one conceal oneself before a sun that never sets, unless that sun, which shines upon all lovers, dances with the dark side of the moon?

Whereof one cannot speak, thereof one should sing or write. Always in search of the better story, one should sing or write at the risk of discharging the sacred can(n)ons of literature. Imagine Odysseus arriving home, plotting against the suitors as before, but unstringing his bow forever. He calls Eumaeus the sowherd to him.

"These suitors are killing too many of our pigs. How many different ways to prepare bean curd do you know?"

He then calls the lubricious servant girls to him. No, not girls, women. Their leader Melantho is very fresh. She looks at him with a smirk, one eyebrow raised high; she swings slowly at the hip, toward her left, then back again. Odysseus is holding a piece of rope that his boy has given him. Telemachos wants them all hanged. But Odysseus is cutting the rope carefully into even lengths and unraveling the strands. He addresses the leader of the women, too shy to look her in the face. Or merely too hip.

"There are too many suitors. I've only got one wife, you know."

The women all look closely at him. Melantho is close enough to Odysseus to smell him. She remembers. When some of the other women start to snigger, she silences them with a look. Now they all know it is the man himself. Odysseus continues:

"To each of you who can lure a suitor or two away—and I know you can, just look at you—I will give a parcel of land on the far side of Ithaka. Here is a piece of rope, in case you want to bind your suitor to the bedpost. I know it's kinky, but you may prefer it to mass murder."

The women depart, their ropes in hand. They do their work. The far side of the island is soon swarming with clever little Ithakans.

One morning, as Odysseus sits on the wall of his palace parapet, watching the sun rise orange over the frosted olive leaves and purple figs, he looks west and quietly weeps. Silently, on her bare feet, Penelope steals upon him. She lays her left hand on his shoulder, he squeezes it between shoulder and wet cheek.

"You miss her?"

"Them."

She says nothing for a long moment. She lets him weep to an end before she speaks.

"Do you know, I've been thinking about taking a trip myself. You think I have a cold heart. Don't object: I know that's what you think. Maybe I do, I don't know. Telemachos calls me the Iron Lady. I'm thinking of a long voyage. It could take years."

If such a retelling of the Homeric tale seems to turn Ithaka into Manhattan, and Homer into Woody Allen, there is nothing to reply except that Manhattan too is an island, and that even in Manhattan murder doesn't always seem the sensible way to solve problems among lovers, unless perhaps you are a writer of plays and fictions. And even then there are other ways.

Sorge dich nicht. Don't worry, don't take it to heart, have no care. Already I will have tried my readers' patience beyond the breaking point. Yet I must record a final note on care, *Sorge*, even if Kalypso hides and Kirke reassures me, *Sorge dich nicht.* It is, I know, merely a series of phonemic accidents, and no one should pay them any mind. Yet anyone who has read Heidegger in English since the early 1960s responds to the sound of "care," *Sorge.* Heidegger explicitly relates the word *Sorge* to *cura,* especially in Augustine's vocabulary; but as far as I know he never mentions τὸ κῆρ, not even in *Was heißt Denken?* which, at least in J. Glenn Gray's wonderful English, is all about taking-to-heart.[31] There is no established etymological link between κῆρ and *cura,* and the Germanic *kar* bears no etymological relation to *cura.* It is to μελέτη and ἐπιμελεία that Heidegger directs our search for the ancient precursors of *Sorge,* or of what in the early 1920s he was calling *Bekümmerung.* Yet it is κῆρ, or the various senses of this strange word, that trouble me now, ἀχνυμένῳ κῆρ. For κῆρ could be *Kummer* as much as *Herz.*

In addition to words related to μελέτη used in the familiar senses of "to concern oneself with, to take care of" (I, 1, 523; 6, 492; O, 1, 305; 21, 352; etc.), there are the words κήδεται (κῆδω, apparently quite close in meaning to μελέτη: cf. I, 9, 342) and κήδεα (τὸ κῆδος), sufferings or troubles (O, 23, 306). The negative of the latter word appears to mean "without cares," *sanssouci.* While mortals are *bekümmert,* ἀχνυμένοις, the gods themselves are *sorglos,* ἀκηδέες (I, 24, 526; but cf. O, 17, 319, where it means failing to administer *Sorge* und *Pflege;* see also O, 20, 130 and 24, 187). How close are we here to κῆρ? How close are we to the heart, τὸ κῆρ, and to doom, ἡ κήρ?

Of the many words that one may translate as "heart," ἦτορ, θυμός, κραδίη, the word τὸ κῆρ is particularly notable. It too, like the word δαίμων, appears almost always at the end of a line of verse, which is not the case with any of the other heart-words. Some examples of τὸ κῆρ: Hektor's courageous heart (I, 12, 45; cf. O, 21, 247); Menelaos's loss of heart (cited above; cf. Apollo's words to Poseidon at I, 21, 464–66, and Odysseus, at O, 10, 497); Odysseus's heart, brooding on the suitors' end (O, 18, 344); the Phaeacians' hearty reception of Odysseus, περὶ κῆρι (19, 280, in mid-line, however); and Penelope's anxious heart, oppressed by cares (19, 516–17: κῆρ . . . μελεδῶναι). However, κῆρ is not only the heart and the concerns of the heart. It is also the oppressive care of mortality itself and "as such," if one may say so. One wonders if it is related to the ancient Sumerian word for the underworld, the abyss, and doom: *kur*. Which at least *sounds* like the simple Latin word *cur*, Why? At one point in *Ilias*, ἡ κήρ is addressed as a goddess or daimon, and portrayed as a formidable figure on Achilles' shield. Dominating one of the two cities of mortals, the city at war, are ῎Ερις, Strife, Κυδοιμός, Uproar, and ολοὴ Κήρ, "murderous Ker" (I, 18, 535).[32]

The overwhelming sense one has when reading both Homeric poems is that τὸ κῆρ and μοῖρα are the selfsame, both as collective fate and as the allotment of individual destinies. Which is to say, in the case of mortals, the dispensation of death. Zeus tosses two lots, δύο κῆρε, onto the scales, one representing the Trojans, the other the Achaeans, both spelling death, θανάτοιο (I, 8, 70). At the moment in question, the κῆρ of the Achaeans causes the scale to sink to the earth, while the lot of the Trojans climbs to high heaven. Soon, however, the scales will shift. Achilles proclaims himself ready to receive his own κῆρα now that Hektor's fate is set, inasmuch as even Herakles could not flee his κῆρα when μοῖρα compelled him (I, 18, 115–19). Once again Zeus tosses two lots onto the scales, those now of Hektor and Achilles, with the anticipated outcome (cf. δύο κῆρε: I, 22, 365). By far the most common appearance of κῆρ is as a pendant to θάνατος, and as a synonym of μοῖρα. After Thersites αἴσχιστος, the "Ugliest Man," has upbraided Agamemnon, Odysseus appeals to the prediction by Kalchas the seer of eventual victory over the Achaeans: "For we held it well in memory (ἐνὶ φρεσίν, often translated as "in our hearts"); you can testify to it, all you whom the keres of death (κῆρες θανάτοιο) have not swept away" (I, 2, 301–302). Parallel with the phrase πορφύρεος θάνατος καὶ μαῖρα κραταιή, "purple death and mighty destiny," or simply θάνατος καὶ μοῖρα, we find θάνατος καὶ κήρ (I, 17, 714; O, 12, 157; cf. O, 18, 155; 22, 14; 24, 127 and 414), or θάνατος καὶ κῆρες, in the plural (O, 2, 352; 5, 387), or, more rarely, φόνος καὶ κήρ, "murder and annihilation" (I, 3, 6; O, 17, 82; this is clearly the "black ker" that Penelope wishes on Antinoos: O, 17, 500). The sense of κήρ as allotted destiny, shifting unpredictably between singular and plural, in this way so reminiscent of the μοῖρα, is simply this: "No one can elude death and the keres" (O, 17, 547; 19, 558).

No one? No one except, surely, the immortals? However, can the gods themselves elude κήρα, even Zeus Pater, who occasionally usurps the prerogative of the Μοῖρα in order to manipulate lots? Or do the immortals inevitably join the mortals in loving and in mourning? This was Hölderlin's lightning-bolt thought, the thought for which Apollo struck him in the back. And it may be that when Heidegger, in *Beiträge zur Philosophie*, thinks of "the last god" he is pursuing that Hölderlinian thought: as the last god vanishes, as furtively as Kirke, there is in Heidegger's view a kind of signaling, a kind of greeting in going. The god comes to presence precisely as an absenting. The last god is eucalyptic.[33]

Are Kalypso and Kirke the last goddesses, the immortals who initiate us into our mortality? Are they the gods Heidegger means when he so readily couples human beings and divinities? Are not Kalypso and Kirke goddesses to whom something like care may be attributed, care as heart and doom? Are these the goddesses Schelling dreams of in *The Ages of the World* when he concedes that the eternal mirrorplay of Father and Son must yield to the less predictable play—and the wrath—of the goddess?[34] Indeed, must not God the Father alter his sex and his life in multiple ways before he learns how to beget and bear a child? Must he not, prior to that, suffer all the concealments of love? And are not the concealments of love bound up with *desire* and the *possibility of death*?

NOTES

1. In what follows I refer to the Greek/German texts published by the Heimeran Verlag, *Ilias* translated by Hans Rupé (Munich, 1961), *Odyssee* by Anton Weiher (Munich, 1974). I cite them by Book (or "Song") and line, designating the words as I or O, e.g.: I, 24, 130–31, meaning *Iliad*, Book XXIV, lines 130–131.

2. See Jacques Derrida, *La dissémination* (Paris: Seuil, 1972), 73n. 1; translated by Barbara Johnson as *Dissemination* (Chicago: University of Chicago Press, 1981), 65n. 2.

3. See Jacques Derrida, *Éperons: Les styles de Nietzsche* (Paris: Flammarion, 1978), 27–42.

4. See Nietzsche's works in the *Kritische Studienausgabe* (KSA), edited by Giorgio Colli and Mazzino Montinari, in 15 volumes (Berlin and Munich: de Gruyter and Deutscher Taschenbuch Verlag, 1980), 3: 424.

5. Martin Heidegger, SZ, 243; see also Krell, *Lunar Voices: Of Tragedy, Poetry, Fiction, and Thought* (Chicago: University of Chicago Press, 1995), xx.

6. See again that remarkable note on *Streuung* (dissemination) in Heidegger's *Metaphysische Anfangsgründe der Logik im Ausgang von Leibniz*, GA 26, 211: "(Zu bedenken bleiben: Sein und δαιμόνιον bzw. Seinsverständnis und δαιμόνιον. Sein qua Grund! Sein und Nichts—Angst.)"

7. See Krell, *Daimon Life: Heidegger and Life-Philosophy*, "Introduction to Za-ology" (Bloomington: Indiana University Press, 1992).

8. "Aletheia" appears in VA, 257–82, and is translated by D. F. Krell and F. Capuzzi, in EGT, 102–23. See the lecture course on Heraclitus in *Heraklit*, GA 55.

9. See Heidegger, HW, 338–39; in EGT, 53. On enjoyment, see Emmanuel Lévinas, *Totalité et infini: Essai sur l'extériorité* (Paris: Livre de Poche, n.d.), 127–51; translated by Alphonso Lingis as *Totality and Infinity: An Essay on Exteriority* (Pittsburgh: Duquesne University Press, 1969), 122–142.

10. VA, 274; in EGT, 116.

11. "Here," that is, at I, 9, 430–605, but in fact throughout, inasmuch as *Ilias* is all about wrath (μῆνις) and revenge (χόλος).

12. See Jacques Derrida, *Schibboleth: Pour Paul Celan* (Paris: Galilée, 1986), 44–56.

13. Martin Heidegger, *Parmenides*, GA 54, 147–82; see the discussion in Krell, *Daimon Life*, 301–305.

14. This is the definition proffered by F. W. J. Schelling, and accepted by Freud, as the essential definition of the uncanny. See the *Studienausgabe* of Freud's works (Frankfurt am Main: S. Fischer, 1982); "*Das Unheimliche*" appears at 4: 241–74.

15. See Jane Ellen Harrison, *Prolegomena to the Study of Greek Religion* (Cleveland: World Publishing Company, Meridian Books, 1966), chap. V. Note also her translation of the δαίμων as "potency" rather than as a more personalized type of deity (*Prolegomena*, 587, 624, 657).

16. See Heidegger, *Hölderlins Hymne "Der Ister"*, GA 53, 134–143. I will say nothing here of the kitchen stove, the oven out back, which serves as a

corrective to the nostalgia of all hearths. Again, see the Introduction to *Daimon Life*.

17. On the uncanny-unhomelike, allow me to refer readers to chap. 3 of Krell, *Archeticture: Ecstasies of Space, Time, and the Human Body* (Albany: State University of New York Press, 1997).

18. See the essay on Trakl, "Die Sprache im Gedicht, in Heidegger, US, 50. See also Krell, *Daimon Life*, chap. 8, and *Lunar Voices*, chap. 4.

19. See Derrida, *De l'esprit: Heidegger et la question* (Paris: Galilé, 1987), translated by Geoffrey Bennington and Rachel Bowlby (Chicago: University of Chicago Press, 1989); two of the four "Geschlecht" papers are published in *Psyché: Inventions de l'autre* (Paris: Galilée, 1987), 395–451, with English translations as follows: the first appears in *Research in Phenomenology*, 8, 1983, 65–83; the second, translated by John P. Leavey Jr., appears in *Deconstruction and Philosophy: The Texts of Jacques Derrida*, ed. John Sallis (Chicago: University of Chicago Press, 1987), 161–96. The third "Geschlecht" is not yet published. The fourth, translated by John P. Leavey Jr. has appeared in *Commemorations: Reading Heidegger: Commemorations*, ed. John Sallis (Chicago: University of Chicago Press, 1993), 163–218.

20. The plaint of Paris? Not Matthew Paris, not the Paris of plato (*sic*) and Socrates in Derrida's *Post Card*, although there too it is fundamentally a matter of what goes on behind the philosopher's back—to wit, *writing*. See Derrida, *La carte postale de Socrate à Freud et au-délà* (Paris: Aubier-Flammarion, 1980), "Envois"; translated by Alan Bass as *The Post Card* (Chicago: University of Chicago Press, 1987).

21. There is a vast literature on these veils—see, for example: R. R. Dyer, "The Use of καλύπτω in Homer," *Glotta* 42 (1964), 29 ff.; F. Dirlmeier, "Die schreckliche Kalypso," *Symposium R. Sühnel*, Berline, 1967, 20 ff.; H. Haakh, "Der Schleier der Penelope," *Gymnasium* 66 (1959) 74 ff.; R. Harder, "Odysseus und Kalypso," in *Kleine Schriften*, ed. W. Marg, Müchen, 1960, 148 ff.; R. Nickel, "Der Swang der Kalypso: Odyssee V, 151–55," *Philologicus* 116 (1972), 137 ff.; Wolfgang Bauer, "Vermutungen zur Herkunft der Kirke und Kalypso," *Festschrift für K. J. Merentitis*, Athens, 1972, 41 ff.; and, above all, Karl Reinhardt (familiar to readers of Heidegger), "Die Abenteuer der Odyssee," *Von Werken und Formen*, 1948, 52 ff., which Alfred Heubeck calls "masterful" and "decisive."

22. Heidegger, VA, 261–64; EGT, 106–108, translation modified.

23. Heidegger, VA, 264–65; EGT, 108–109, translation modified.

24. Jacques Lacan and the École Freudienne, *Feminine Sexuality*, edited by Juliet Mitchell and Jacqueline Rose (London: Macmillan Press, 1983), 82.

25. Lacan, *Feminine Sexuality*, 82.

26. Lacan, *Feminine Sexuality*, 85.

27. VA, 272; EGT, 114, translation modified.

28. KSA, 5: 102, no. 168.

29. Here too, with regard to *moly*, there are many things to read: P. Bussolino, "La lingua di Omero in rapporto alla psicologia femminile," *Rivista di Studi Classici* 10 (1962), 213 ff.; J. Clay, "The Planktai and Moly: Divine Naming and Knowing in Homer," *Hermes* 100 (1972), 127 ff.; A. Lesky, "Aia (Kirke)," *Wiener Studien* 63 (1948), 22 ff.; K. Hirvonen, *Matriarchal Survivals and Certain Trends in Homer's Female Characters*, Helsinki, 1968; William K. Freiert, "The Motifs of Confrontation with Women in Homer's *Odyssey*," Ph.D. dissertation, University of Minnesota, 1972; C. P. Segal, "Circean Temptations: Homer, Vergil, Ovid," *Transactions and Proceedings of the American Philological Association* 99 (1968), 419 ff.; R. Wildhaber, "Kirke und die Schweine," *Festschrift Meuli*, 1951, 253 ff.; H. Philipp, "Das Gift der Kirke," *Gymnasium* 66 (1959), 509 ff.; O. Touchefeu-Meynier, "Ulysse et Circé: Notes sur le chant X de l'*Odyssée*," *Revue des Études Anciennes* 63 (1961), 264 ff.; G. Beck, "Beobachtungen zur Kirke-Episode in der Odyssee," *Philologicus* 109 (1965), 1 ff.; B. Paetz, *Kirke und Odysseus: Überlieferung und Deutung von Homer bis Calderon*, Berlin, 1970.

30. KSA, 10: 37.

31. See part one of Heidegger, WD; WCT.

32. Note that the circumflex (usually) becomes an acute in the shift from "heart" to "doom" and "lot," and that while the heart is neutral, doom is feminine in gender. The words therefore cannot be conflated, nor can they be convincingly linked etymologically. Tò κῆρ appears to be a contraction of κέαρ, meaning a carpenter's axe, related to κεάζω, to pound or rub to pieces. Liddell-Scott lists "A" and "B" forms of the verb κηραίνω, to harm or destroy in the "A" sense, to be sick at heart or anxious in the "B" sense. Liddell-Scott does not speculate on an etymological connection between these two morphologically identical words, even if the semantic link seems compelling—how could one not be sick at heart or full of anxiety in the face of harm or destructive power? Jane Ellen Harrison's long and detailed exposition in *Prolegomena to the Study of Greek Religion* concerning the *keres* or sprites, those tiny winged creatures who generally mean mischief, makes no explicit reference to the *ker* of the heart. Yet she does argue that Eros himself is a form of *ker*, so that matters of the heart are not altogether excluded from her purview. She writes: "Eros is but a specialized form of the Ker; the Erotes are Keres of life, and like the Keres take the form of winged *Eidola*. In essence as in art-form, Keres and Erotes are near akin. The Keres, it has already been seen, are little winged bacilli, fructifying or death-bringing; but the Keres developed mainly on the dark side; they went downwards, deathwards; the Erotes, instinct with a new spirit, went upwards, lifewards" (631). Finally, on these questions, see D. J. N. Lee, "Homeric κῆρ and Others," *Glotta* 39 (1960–1961), 191 ff.

33. See Heidegger, *Beiträge zur Philosophie (Vom Ereignis)*, GA 65, part VII.

34. F. W. J. Schelling, *Die Weltalter Fragmente: In der Urfassungen von 1811 und 1813*, ed. Manfred Schröter (Munich: Biederstein Verlag und Leibniz Verlag, 1946), 10–53.

Five

Anaximander: A Founding Name in History

Michel Serres

Translated by Roxanne Lapidus

In his *Commentary on Aristotle's Physics*, Simplicius cites Anaximander, after Theophrastus's *The Opinions of the Physicists*, Fragment A2:

> Anaximander . . . said that the principle—that is to say the essence—of beings is the infinite . . . and that it is neither water nor any other of the so-called "elements," but a certain other infinite nature, from which are born all the heavens and the worlds within them; it is "that from which there is, for beings, generation; in it destruction also takes place, according to what must be; for beings render justice and reparation to one another, from their mutual injustice, according to the summons of Time," as he says in somewhat poetical terms.

From Justice on Earth to the World

Local Elements

Thales, whose thought flowered in the same years as Anaximander's, insisted that water was the basic element, the origin, or unique principle of all things. From it, he wrote, all was born, is born, will be born.

The British Museum houses a Babylonian tablet from the third millennium, where what we would call a map appears below a text chiselled in cuneiform characters. Now, doxographers claim that Anaximander was the first to have the audacity to inscribe the inhabited world in a similar schematic form.

The local and the global separate these two original maps: the one exalts the preponderant excellence of its own country by placing its city and river, the Euphrates, in the central position, while the other schematizes the world in its entirety—at least as it was known by the experts of the time. The Babylonian map is political, ethnocentric, propagandistic, while the Greek map already aims at the entire universe.

Both maps show the round, ring-like form of the immense ocean surrounding the globe. What Thales announces about genesis over time, the two maps, precisely, schematize in space: water dominates, even unto the outer limits. Now if from the ocean, water laps at the surrounding land, it also reigns in the middle of inhabited lands; here is the Mediterranean; the water in rivers sometimes flows from one to the other, like the Nile, whose source is fed by the aquatic ring and empties into the central lake. Surrounding, at the heart and traversing the land, as in the beginning and now, is water, from which come all things, in their unity and their diversity.

In opposition to Thales, Ionian physics later claimed, like Anaximenes, that air was the origin of all things. Later, Heraclitus opted for fire. Others, like Empedocles, even later, considered the four elements—water, air, fire and earth—to be the root of all. In all of these theories the principle is reduced to something concrete, determinable and local, as large as one wishes—drop, bubble, spark or clod.

Generalization of Conflicts

Now then, if our origins are in water, all things come from it and no doubt return to it, so that the entire earth, this fragile island surrounded by the ring of ocean, encompassed by it or immersed in it—torrential, streaming, overflowing—awaits, suspended, a destiny of shipwreck. On Anaximander's map, the Danube and the Guadalquivir flow into this watery matrix, as do the Black Sea, the Caspian, the Sea of Azov and the Red Sea, the Tigris and the Persian Gulf. One could say that as this island earth is being born from the waters, it is simultaneously disappearing beneath the waves. Overflowing rivers, floods, cave-ins, débâcle. In order for something else to remain after separating itself from the water, the water must somehow recede. What power will force it into retreat?

move in the opposite direction in the same cycle of evaporation and condensation, with each perceptible change comes an intermediate state where the substrata, freed of any limits, can call itself either gaseous or liquid, water or air, one or the other, indifferently or indefinitely, that is, each of the underlying principles chosen with unparalleled profundity by Thales or Anaximenes. There is no discernible boundary between these fundamental and original states to which the Ionian colleagues (rightly) attribute everything that exists in the universe. This is the ἄπειρων, and the origin of physics.

Is this already the space of "phases," or the first conception of the philosophy of mixtures? Or the impossibility of designating what came first, or who prevails?

The Ἄπειρων, in Sum

To express it negatively, what is it that this infinite *cannot* be? Neither water nor air no fire nor earth, nor some element of matter—thus neither elemental nor material. It cannot be seen or smelled, touched or heard; no sense can apprehend it.

It's almost as though it didn't exist. In any case, it is not there, because if it were, it would be bounded by a definition, a border or a perimeter. Neither here nor there, thus absent, and therefore present everywhere, since it is unbounded.

This unbounded, infinite principle thus designates not only an immense and limitless space or time (in quantitative or metric terms), but above all a limitless openness, local and global, indefinite, qualitatively or topologically deployed, without fold, contraction or closure. It is the two original conditions or the two primordial oceans of geometric thought—the underlying space-time at the origin of mathematics.

Immaterial, absent, beyond the senses, and, as an intermediary, explaining changes . . . existing before the immensity of space, underlying numbers or infinite time, predating topological beginnings—first of all is the abstract.

By eliminating water, Anaximander seems to have changed physics, rather than abandoning it, and without our being able to say that he ventured into metaphysics, since the latter did not come until later. Was philosophy as such being born?

What knowledge did he encounter? A pre-geometry, or what we later would have called a pre-topography. But above all, before either of these, he encountered abstraction itself.

What can always be falsified, by the integral of negations? Abstraction. It generates physics. Thus Anaximander marks forevermore the explanation of the world by the most formal thought possible—mathematics.

In general, the conditions for all abstract knowledge appear even before the topology of openings or the geometry of pure and limitless space, as a possible basis for physics.

As an abstraction, was mathematics born from a need for justice? For an equation expresses a contract of equivalence.

From the Campus to the Praetorium

Local Elements

No matter whether water or fire wins—you or I or some empire, this or that idea or enterprise, no matter what component of the world—the sole victor paints space in his color, while time immediately disappears in the stubbornness or stagnation of redundancy. A designated domain wins and maintains its sway, it perpetuates its takeover. In spreading its influence, a *same* cause or thing vitrifies space and freezes time.

Thus the thing is first of all this cause—the reason for the accusation that attacks and conquers or for the excuse, against which the defense and counter-attack will be made. Prosecution and the law thus precede the physical object, which is described by the accusative case. Notice with what rigor the grammatical *object*, the complement of our actions in general and of transitive verbs, is designated by a case whose name, rightly or wrongly, *accuses*? Can it be declared any more clearly that the object has its origin in *the cause*, violently called into question? Before phenomenology can say that the object appears, grammar has subpoenaed it to appear. Thus it harks back to the law.

So we must move from the principle (either abstract or drawn by Anaximander from beyond the material elements), towards what has been said about justice and vengeance, armed violence or temporary truce.

Generalization of Conflicts

Time cannot advance unless repetition of the same thing ceases. When separated from the victorious and global extension of this or that being, the forces of genesis and disappearance, evolution, Spring and its flower of youth, Autumn and the serene light of great age, birth, fecundity and destructive agony can all carry out their activities. But the reign of *sameness* must be suspended; either the others, together, form an orchestral mixture, or else the single other takes over, which is the beginning of exclusion or war, where vengeance will never end.

Like Bergson, Heidegger describes in topological terms (open and closed localities) what Hegel affirmed in dynamic schemas of *other* and *same*—the latter occupying the interior of the place, the former remaining outside its boundaries. In so doing, these modern philosophers all revive the fear of Hellenic polytheism that Anaximander, Thales and the Ionian physicists overcame.

In these paganisms, it is a matter of wiping out the reigning being, who only reigns because he murdered the one whose place he took; time and history flow with sacrificial blood. It's said that the Aztecs, atop their pyramids, cut the throats of virgins so that the sun would come up; plunged in the night like those legendary Europeans fascinated by the shades of the golden bough, the Aztecs too believed that dawn could not come without this abominable forfeit. Kill, to bring relief. The necessity for the continuation of time justifies not only death as such, but also so-called legal murders. Issuing from that split so very close to the entrenched being, time only advances through negative machinations—as these regressive atrocities express, in gallantly abstract terms! These philosophies can be reduced to a legitimation of putting people to death.

The Ἄπείρων, in Sum

At the dawn of this era, which was a new one because of him, Anaximander speaks of this universal injustice, of the eternal return of vengeance with its unfailingly mournful consequences. Following this seeming edict, do all the world's beings make war or peace; do they perpetuate revenge or stop it, do they continue the sacrifices whose rituals allow them to attach traditional time to themselves, or do they decide to invent a new kind of time?

to Anaximander, everything depends on the summons
fore what tribunal? Not only does a new time come
the channels of justice, but it summons itself.

Thus in the Greek dawn, Anaximander inaugurates the era from which our history begins. But no one can *conceive* the origin without *producing* it, nor without beginning a new time. Which one?

In court, at the opening of a case, the praetor or person who inaugurates the session, would announce in the language of ancient Roman law, pronounced in archaic Latin, the three primordial verbs of justice: *do, dico, addico,* I give, I say, I summon. These are the first performative acts or words of exchange, of the law, of language and of philosophy. We as talkative, economic animals brought together by legal and social contracts, no matter what language we speak—do we know any more fundamental actions than those designated by these *tria verba*?

At the dawn of our era, the first written word says—or writes— in Greek, in the first letters of the first alphabetical code, discovered at the same time and in the same place, the verbs *to say* and *to give,* along with the substantive form of *summons.* Using these as recognized or unrecognized objects of exchange, certain beings claim or render justice and reparation among themselves, for their reciprocal injustice.

Issuing from the infinite, like these beings, time, in which they are immersed, makes its summons before the tribunal where these judgments are rendered. This is what Anaximander, the proto-praetor, himself a temporal being, says in terms that the unimaginative doxographers call poetic (but without acknowledging its truth)—meaning productive or performative, on the balance-sheet underlying the law, whose origins lie here.

Local and Individual, Revisited

Do we understand the effort toward the infinite made by this man whose name appropriately designates the title of king (ἄναεξ) in a fortified enclosure (μάνδρα)—the potentate of an area with closed borders—that is, a royal entrenched being? Can we imagine a more beautiful, novel clemency than that of a thought that abandons its own law, founded on its own power, and, by opening its despotic limits, proclaims itself the son, the creation, the offspring of the limitless ἀπείρων, immersed in a time that subpoenas his place. Finally, can we imagine a local power that imposes restraint upon itself, a being that no longer perseveres in its own being, or someone who abandons all? Do we understand that he thereby opens up a new era, since he renounces the dismal repetition of the force of "me"?

Do science, thought, civilization and history begin with the dismissal, the abandonment, the renunciation, the detachment of a king? Thus the spoken word hinges on a single letter: *do, dico abdico,*—I give, I say, I abdicate. *I give*: I say that I abdicate; *I abdicate*: I say that I give.

Because by virtue of his name he is the entrenched being *par excellence*, and yet thinks the opposite of his title and name, the anonymous Anaximander melts into the infinity of things—into space and time. And since only the latter demonstrates an order, he lets it speak, do, render and give; he lets time summon his own place to the bar.

Magistrate, judge or praetor—is this what we should henceforth call Anaximander, by his common name? Or rather, immediately after his abdication, is this what we should call time itself, which is inaugural in its perpetual present and which, of itself, gives, says and summons to justice?

This is the origin, since time itself begins with this renunciation of Anaximander. And since then, have we ever repeated—desperately and without always understanding them—any other words than "I say, I give, I summon"?

Beyond saying them, do we authentically do anything else? There lies the beginning of history.

Six

Doubles of Anaximenes

John Sallis

In Empedocles' *On Nature* a decisive injunction came to be openly declared. What it enjoins is not any particular observation or action but rather the very stance constitutive of thinking as such, of what would come to be called philosophy. The relevant passage was preserved and transmitted as a quotation in a text by Sextus Empiricus,[1] which was written more than six centuries after the original passage and which set the passage in a context quite remote from that of early Greek thought. It begins: "But come, consider by all means how each thing is manifest."[2] Addressed to Empedocles' pupil Pausanias, the passage enjoins him to consider each thing in its manifestness—that is, expanding the translation of ἀθρέω, to look closely at, to observe, to ponder thoughtfully each thing in its way of being manifest. The injunction is that things in their manifestness be considered by all means (πάσῃ παλάμῃ), in a sense that does not exclude the use of artfulness, contrivance, even force or violence. Thus it is no mere passive beholding that is enjoined but a pondering that would, as it were, entice things into the open and surprise them in their very moment of manifestness. Referring to manifestness to sight, to hearing, to the tongue as well as other parts—that is, to what *later* will be gathered under the name αἴσθησις—the passage then concludes with utter directness: "Ponder each thing in the way by which it is manifest."

One could show how this injunction is in force throughout what can be recovered of Empedocles' thought. To say nothing of Plato, of the decisiveness with which his thought is bound to τὸ πρᾶγμα αὐτό (Letter 7, 341c), determining things by the very look (εἶδος) they present, that is, as each is itself manifest. In this perspective it is little wonder, then, that the young Heidegger, guided by Aristotle, could discover in Greek thinking an orientation to the self-manifestation of phenomena that proved even more originary than that accomplished

145

through the phenomenological turn to the things themselves. Yet Heidegger, writing retrospectively of his early engagement with the Greeks, does not ascribe such orientation only to Aristotle but extends it to "Greek thinking as a whole," thus concluding that "what phenomenological investigations rediscovered as the supporting attitude of thinking proves to be the fundamental trait (*Grundzug*) of Greek thinking."[3]

What about this extension? Is the bond to the things themselves in their manifestness decisively operative in Greek thinking as a whole? Does the force of the Empedoclean injunction extend back even to the beginning of Greek thought? Can a trace of it be discerned even in that remote beginning that is supposed to have been accomplished in the sixth century B.C. in the city of Miletus? What about Anaximenes, in particular? For in certain respects, especially in the view of the ancients, his thought represents the genuine achievement, even the culmination, of that initial moment[4]—not the simple beginning, of course, but the moment in which the beginning is articulated and gathered up as something sustaining, the moment of the ἀρχή of philosophy. Is it possible to discern in what remains accessible of the thought of Anaximenes a trace of the demand to consider by all means how each thing is manifest?

Of Anaximenes' life and activities virtually nothing is known aside from his having been a pupil and/or companion of Anaximander. The doxographical testimony to this connection serves to confirm the unmistakably audible echoes of Anaximander's thought in what the tradition has preserved of the words and thought of Anaximenes. Not that much remains: there is perhaps less than in the case of any other early Greek thinker accorded comparable significance in the ancient tradition. Only one short fragment has any claim to reproducing the words of Anaximenes himself, and even in this case there are, as commentators have noted, serious difficulties in substantiating the claim. For interpreting his basic thought, one has no choice but to rely on a few passages from much later authors that summarize his thought, these summaries in turn relying in most cases on still earlier reports, especially those by Aristotle's pupil, Theophrastus. Consequently, Anaximenes' thought as transmitted through these reports and summaries is cast for the most part in an Aristotelian language and conceptuality that almost certainly could not have been proper to it originally. Thus, any effort to gain access to his thought must systematically deconstruct these sources in such a way as to inhibit the otherwise natural tendency to read back into the earlier thought later conceptualities that first became possible on the basis of the earlier thought and of what came directly in its train. What remains of Anaximenes' thought are only those phantoms of it set moving along diverse lines in later texts. The question is whether, in and through the flight of these doubles, one can catch a glimpse of what one would call Anaximenes himself, his thought proper.

But in this case can one seriously suppose that a bond to things in their manifestness could have been operative? After all, Anaximenes is supposed to have theorized that everything comes from air. What could be less attached, less attentive, to things in their manifestness than such seemingly empty theorizing? And yet, in this very supposition, in the way that later reports as well as present-day commentaries formulate it, there is much that calls for suspicion and must indeed be suspended if there is to be hope of genuine access to Anaximenes' thought.

What is one to understand by *theorize* in the thought of one who preceded (and contributed to the possibility of) the determination of the sense of Θεωρία that came to be accomplished in the work of Plato and Aristotle? How, most notably, is the sense of Θεωρία to be determined prior to, independently of, the distinction between τὸ νοητόν and τὸ αἰσθητόν? How is it to be determined within the compass of a thought that, as in the case of Anaximenes, still stops short of gathering under the name αἴσθησις what will later be assumed to be thus gathered and hence opposed to νόησις?

What can it have meant for Anaximenes to say something like: everything *comes from* air? Presumably Anaximenes was setting forth air as the source or origin from which all things somehow come forth into their presence, their manifestness. But how, precisely, is one to understand ἀρχή without merely assuming for it the sense that was later to be explicitly determined for it by Aristotle?

Is it at all certain what is to be understood by *air* (ἀήρ)? Is it indeed even certain that ἀήρ is to be translated by *air*? What would be the sense of translation in this case, considering that the Anaximenean ἀήρ can be identified neither with air in the sense determined by modern physics (as a mixture of gases) nor with the element (στοιχεῖον) that comes to be designated by this name in Aristotle? In Homer and Hesiod ἀήρ frequently refers to what one would need to translate as *mist* or *haze*. For example, in *The Theogony*, one finds the expression Τάρταρά τ' ἠερόεντα (119); clearly the reference is not to the openness and transparency of what might be called air but to the darkness or mist that obscures vision in the underworld. Often ἀήρ refers to the so-called lower air, that which occurs between earth and sky, up to and including the clouds, in distinction from the αἰθήρ, the shining upper part, which is sometimes depicted also as fiery. Thus, a passage in *The Iliad* declares that "the fir-tree reached through ἀήρ to the αἰθήρ" (14:288).[5] The semantic link of ἀήρ to what would be called breath and wind forms the basis for the links that Anaximenes' thought seeks to forge between these; it is by no means assured that these links would remain unaffected even by the most discreet translation. Thus, in the case of Anaximenes especially, one will need to forgo translating certain basic words of his thought, on pain of translating the thought itself into something alien. Or rather, echoing Heideger, one will need in these cases to translate Anaximenes back into Greek.

Even the report that Aristotle gives of the basic thought of Anaximenes stops short of declaring him to have theorized that everything comes from air. What Aristotle says rather is that Anaximenes posited ἀήρ as the ἀρχή of the other simple bodies (*Metaphysics*, A3, 984a5; DK, A4). Thus, Anaximenes' basic thought is *not* that *everything* comes from ἀήρ but that the other simple bodies (ὕδωρ, in particular, is mentioned, presumably to mark the difference from Thales) come from it. Nothing at all is said of how all other bodies, those compounded from simple bodies, come to be.[6]

But how is one to understand this coming from ἀήρ that is such as to warrant naming ἀήρ the ἀρχή? What must ἀήρ be in order that it be capable of constituting the ἀρχή? Or rather—since the what (τί) already orients the question to later Greek thought—how much ἀήρ *be* in order to be the ἀρχή? Must it *be* at all in order to be the ἀρχή of all else that can be said simply to be?

One of the reports that most advances these questions comes from Theophrastus by way of Simplicius (DK, A5). Marking the link with Anaximander, the report declares that for Anaximenes, too, the underlying nature (τήν ὑποκει-μένην φύσιν) is one and unlimited (ἄπειρον). There can be little doubt but that the reference to the underlying nature—this very formulation—represents precisely an Aristotelian reinscription of the sense in which the other simple bodies are said to *come from* the one about to be named ἀήρ: within the conceptuality of

Aristotle's treatise on φύσις, the word ὑποκείμενον names that which underlies and endures throughout a process of change, that from which, in precisely this Aristotelian sense, things that come to be (something) may be said to come. If this sense is suspended, what remains is merely the declaration that that from which things come forth is one and is unlimited (ἄπειρον). To say that it is ἄπειρον, thus echoing Anaximander, is to say that it has no πέρας, no limit or extremity at which it would end or from which it could have begun. If, as most of the reports (although not this one) attest, that from which things come forth is to be called beginning (to isolate one—but only one—of the component senses of ἀρχή), then it will be a beginning that itself has no beginning.⁷

The report continues by marking a point that differentiates Anaximenes from Anaximander: Anaximenes does not consider the unlimited one (from which every-thing simple comes forth) to be indeterminate (ἀόριστος) but rather takes it to be determinate and indeed identifies it as ἀήρ. The word ἀόριστος overlaps semantically with ἄπειρον: both bespeak the privation of a certain limit, of an ὅρος and a πέρας, respectively. It is not, in general, self-evident how these two kinds of limits (and their respective privations) are to be differentiated, but in the present case the continuation of the passage specifies that having an ὅρος—or, as the text says literally: having been delimited (ὡρισμένη— from ὁρίζω)—means being delimited in such a way as to have an identity, so as in this case to be identifiable, in particular, as ἀήρ. On the other hand, to say that this one (from which everything simple comes forth and which is delimited as ἀήρ) is ἄπειρον is to say that there will be no limit or boundary beyond which or before which ἀήρ would *not be*. Wherever anything *is* (using *wherever* to denote together—or indifferently—what will be distinguished as place and time) there is also ἀήρ. In other words, wherever anything *is*, such as fire or stone, there will be, not one, but *two*: fire or stone *and* ἀήρ. Except perhaps where there is simply ἀήρ, there will always be a double. One might venture to say even that Anaximenes' basic thought is that of the doubling of being.

The remainder of the report from Simplicius is addressed precisely to this doubling. In saying that wherever anything else *is* there is also ἀήρ, it is imperative to stess the moment of unity: it is not as though other things merely have ἀήρ somewhere alongside them, but rather in the very unity of each thing (as it is delimited in its identity) there is also ἀήρ. Or, to turn the identity around: in everything else there is both ἀήρ and something different from ἀήρ, a doubling within the identity. Thus, the report from Simplicius says that ἀήρ is differentiated in its being (διαφέρειν . . . κατὰ τὰς οὐσίας). This differentiation is said to be effected by rarity and density. By becoming rarer, ἀήρ becomes fire—while *also* remaining ἀήρ, that is, it is differentiated from itself, becomes the double: ἀήρ-πῦρ. By becoming denser, more compact, ἀήρ becomes wind, then cloud, then water, then earth, then stones—while *also* remaining in each case ἀήρ.[8] In the phrase found in a parallel report from Hippolytus (DK, A7), ἀήρ appears different, shows itself as different, is differently manifest (διάφορον φαίνεσθαι). In his basic thought of ἀήρ as ἀρχή (which is explicit in the report from Hippolytus), Anaximenes is considering precisely these different manifestations and seeking to think what must *also be with* every such manifestation.

Both the reports name what are counted as simple bodies (in the Aristotelian formulation), namely, fire, wind, cloud, water, earth, and stones. Both then extend the discourse beyond these: the rest (that is, all beings other than the simple ones) come forth from these.

The two reports thus outline what one might call the full range of diverse manifestations. Most remarkably, however, the report from Hippolytus indicates that there is a discontinuity in this range, indeed a kind of zero-point of nonmanifestation: whenever ἀήρ is most equable (ὁμαλώτατος), it is not manifest (ἄδηλον) to sight. It comes to be manifest only when it is differentiated in its being, only when it appears different from itself. As long as it remains simply identical with itself (most equable: ὁμαλώτατος), it does not show itself. In other words, ἀήρ never shows itself *as itself* but only in connection with the manifestation of something different from it. Only when doubling commences is there manifestation.

Both reports link doubling, that is, what is called μεταβολή, to κίνησις. It is hardly necessary to stress the risk one would incur by merely translating κίνησις, without further ado, as movement or motion. The report from Hippolytus ascribes κίνησις preeminently to ἀήρ, and one could, following Boeder's proposal, take ἀήρ to be most capable of κίνησις precisely because of its lack of any limit that would set a limit to its κίνησις.[9] Nonetheless, it remains highly problematic what κίνησις could designate in the present case. What kind of movement—taking the word in the broadest and most open sense—could be ascribed to ἀήρ, understood as the one, unlimited ἀρχή from which all things come forth into their manifestness but which itself never becomes manifest as itself? Is its "movement" to be reduced to a complex of movements of invisible material particles by which it could become rarer or denser? Or does its κίνησις have to do with the very "movement" of manifestation in which things come forth so as, unlike ἀήρ, to be manifest to sight?

Everything depends on how the doubling is understood, on how it is that each thing manifest as fire, wind, cloud, water, earth, or stone is *also* ἀήρ. How is ἀήρ *with* such things, especially considering that it remains nonmanifest as such? Another report, this one from Aetius (DK, A10), bears on this question. Commenting on the ascription of divinity to ἀήρ, the report says that such a declaration must be taken as identifying "the powers that pervade the elements or bodies (τὰς ἐνδιηκούσας τοῖς στοιχείοις ἢ τοῖς σώμασι δυνάμεις)." But what kind of power is ἀήρ? What is it a power for? What does this δύναμις empower, enable? Is it not the power *for* precisely that *of* which it is the ἀρχή—namely, for the coming forth of things into their manifestness? Is it not the δύναμις empowering the κίνησις in which things come to presence? Is not the very openness, invisibility, and transparency of what is called ἀήρ precisely what makes it possible for things to come forth in their manifestness? Is it not ἀήρ that grants the open place of manifestation? Is it not precisely *as* such an open place that ἀήρ is *with* all things? And to the extent that the semantics of the word inclines also toward the Homeric-Hesiodic *mist* or *haze*, might one not suppose that ἀήρ also bespeaks the obscuring that doubles all manifestation, that shadows it?

In this case it would come as no surprise that, in the only passage that can be taken[10] to present the words of Anaximenes himself, there is a coupling of the soul and the cosmos: "As our soul, being ἀήρ, holds us together, so do πνεῦμα and ἀήρ enclose the whole cosmos" (DK, B2). For then Anaximenes would be saying: as ἀήρ empowers the coming of things into their manifestness, so does it, as soul, gather each of us and draw us to that manifestation in such a way that we are gifted with the power of apprehending what comes to presence. Thus it would be that in his basic thought of ἀήρ as the one, unlimited, invisible ἀρχή Anaximenes would have thought precisely that by which one can come to consider by all means how each thing is manifest.

Notes

1. *Against the Logicians*, I, 125. This text is commonly cited (e.g., by DK) as *Adversus Mathematicos*, VII.

2. In DK, this passage occurs as Fragment B3, 1. 9–12. Further references are indicated by DK followed by fragment number.

3. Martin Heidegger, "Mein Weg in die Phänomenologie," SD, 87. This text dates from 1963.

4. Burnet is insistent on this point: "It is not easy for us to realise that, in the eyes of his contemporaries, and for long after, Anaximenes was a much more important figure than Anaximander. And yet the fact is certain. We shall see that Pythagoras, though he followed Anaximander in his account of the heavenly bodies, was far more indebeted to Anaximenes for his general theory of the world. We shall see further that when, at a later date, science revived once more in Ionia, it was 'the philosophy of Anaximenes' to which it attached itself. Anaxagoras adopted many of his most characteristic views, and so did the Atomists. Diogenes of Apollonia went back to the central doctrin of Anaximenes, and made Air the primary substance." Cf. John Burnet, *Early Greek Philosophy* (New York: Meridian Books, 1957), 78f. For Hegel, too, Anaximenes represents the completion of Milesian thought, its highest moment: "In place of the undetermined matter of Anaximander, he again posits a definite natural element (the absolute in a real form)—but instead of the water of Thales, that form is air." Cf. G. W. F. Hegel, *Vorlesungen über die Geschichte der Philosophie I*, vol. 18 of *Werke* (Frankfurt a.M.: Suhrkamp, 1971), 214. Focusing on the fragment in which Anaximenes connects air with πνεῦμα (which Hegel translates as *Geist*), Hegel characterizes him as having also marked "the transition of the philosophy of nature into the philosophy of consciusness, or the surrender of the objective form of principle." *Ibid.*

5. See also G. S. Kirk and J. E. Raven, *The Presocratic Philosophers* (Cambridge: Cambridge University Press, 1962), 10; and Burnet, *Early Greek Philosophy*, 74.

6. See Heribert Boeder, *Grund und Gegenwart als Fragziel der Früh-Griechischen Philosophie* (The Hague: Martinus Nijhoff, 1962), 45f.

7. This is explicit in Aristotle's discussion of the ἄπειρον as an ἀρχή: τοῦ δὲ ἀπείρον οὐκ ἔστιν ἀρχή (*Physics* Γ 4, 203b7).

8. For all these names, perhaps most notably for πῦρ, one would need to exercise the same caution and reservation proposed above in regard to ἀήρ.

9. Boeder, *Grund und Gegenwart*, 47.

10. Though not without considerable difficulty. See Kirk and Raven, *The Presocratic Philosophers*, 158f.

itself to the strictures of the idea and the economies of metaphysics, it is not surprising that Heidegger turns to them, above all, in his efforts to find a language and manner of thinking that does not belong, however loosely and critically, to the rationalities and grammars of the onto-technological traditions of metaphysics. That is why Heidegger's interpretations of Presocratic texts need to be understood as part and parcel of his critique of the contemporary world. But it is important to note that these texts are not alone in the promise they hold. Poetic and early Greek texts share the same promise for Heidegger: both operate outside of the orbit of the concept and its specific, technological, calculus.[4] A calculus that has culminated today in the field that is known as "applied" ethics.

Nietzsche, who Heidegger called "the last philosopher of justice" and who was also captivated by early Greek texts, was among the first to raise serious questions about the general form of Western philosophical discourses on justice and ethical life, especially the relation of ethics and technique. His claim is that the tradition of philosophical reflections on justice that start with Plato inevitably resemble shopkeepers scales. In other words, he argues that, when justice is thought under the sign of the concept, it takes the form of a calculus, an economy of exchanges. What we find in philosophy, Nietzsche contends, is finally an elaborate form of double bookkeeping in which the units of measure are calibrated according to "the good" only to mask the truth that justice, or what is called justice, is really nothing but a calculus of power. Hence, contemporary philosophical narratives of justice are merely interpretations that hide the fact that there is no justice as such. So the real question for Nietzsche, as for Heidegger, is whether a philosopher can address the issue of justice today, something apart from the framework hitherto established by philosophy. Or is it the case that truly creative responses to the enigmas of ethical life, the riddle of shared life in time, are to be handed over to the province of art and actions such as the simple, yet concentrated, gesture of wrapping the German Reichstag?[5]

So it is not a sign of oblivion to the times that this turn to the Presocratics plays such a prominent role in the turbulent times of the early 1930's. One reads the *Introduction to Metaphysics*, "Origin of the Art Work," and even the notorious "Rectoral Address" and one finds crucial decisions in these texts being made with reference to Presocratic texts. During those years Heraclitus and Sophocles seem to play a special role in Heidegger's thought. Key words drawn from early Greek texts—πόλεμος, δεινόν, φύσις, τέχνη, λόγος—form an axis along which Heidegger's own work moves forward. But it is not only during these years that the Presocratics so powerfully animate his philosophical imagination. After the war, at a time in which the catastrophe of recent German history could no longer be evaded, and when his own personal crises almost led to a collapse, Heidegger chooses to devote himself to a powerful meditation on Anaximander's fragment on the relation of time and justice as a way of seeking out a new manner of reflecting upon what must be done today. So, in turning to these early Greek texts, and especially to the text on Anaximander that I want to address, Heidegger is not simply laboring as the custodian of another time, but is searching for a new mode of address to these times, to the crises of time which these times signal: "But here—in these years, that which the Greeks called ἀκμή presses into our existence."⁶ An urgency pervades Heidegger's attempts to take up these texts. It is, then, not the standards of philology that serve as the best measure for Heidegger's achievements in these texts, but the standards pertaining to the needs of these times of crisis.

In the "Letter on Humanism," a text written just a few months before the text on Anaximander, Heidegger argues that we need to break with conceptions of ethicality and justice that are wedded to images of "the human" and "humanism" if ethical life is to be renewed. There the argument is explicit: if justice is to be understood as something other than a calculative technique, then we need to understand the grounds of ethical life as greater than that which we, as human beings, define and can understand. There Heidegger suggests, contrary to every expectation and to the disbelief of many, that his thought has always been concerned with the ethical.⁷ But my contention is that this promise of an "original ethics" is first substantially answered in Heidegger's treatment of Anaximander.

It should be acknowledged at the outset that the attraction to Greece, especially to early Greek texts, is not new and does not begin with Heidegger. Hölderlin, whose poetic work Heidegger finds holding

a promise akin to that held by early Greek texts, already felt the imperative of turning to Greek literature so strongly that he described it in a
beautiful image drawn from nature, suggesting that our relation to Greece
is like the heliotropism of flowers that need to turn and face the sun. This
attraction is not a matter of some sort of nostalgia for a bygone era but
represents something more substantive. However, for Heidegger, even
more than the author of *Hyperion*, it is important to recognize that the
Greece to which we are indexed is not a geo-political designation. Rather,
it is the name for some sort of experience, some sort of knowing that
emerged out of that experience. What Heidegger tries to make clear in
his interpretations of Greek texts is just what this experience and knowing refer to, and why it is that this experience solicits thinking today. I
have already suggested the general form of an answer to this question,
namely, the promise that in these texts one finds the promise of a non-
metaphysical determination of justice. Here then it is possible to say
something about the possibility of justice without submitting that discourse to the rule of metaphysical-conceptual assumptions. That is why
I would argue that the text on Anaximander, which speaks most directly
to this possibility of a justice that resists calculation, stands as something
of a summit among Heidegger's texts on the Presocratics.

But what one might learn from Heidegger about justice is not a
simple recapitulation of early Greek thought—no thoughtful elaboration of the relation of justice to time could pretend to immunize itself
against the specificities of the times. Furthermore, because in a very real
sense Heidegger's point was never thematized in those early Greek
texts, only over time and the completion of the destiny of the Greek
metaphysical origins of philosophy could such matters become visible.
One pivotal illustration of such a point is found in a seemingly passing remark that Heidegger makes in his text on "Anaximander's Saying." In what seems to be an aside, Heidegger calls attention to a
peculiar feature of the early Greek literary imagination which helps
illuminate his own central insight into the character of justice as he
formulates it through an engagement with Anaximander's philosophical experience. The peculiarity to which I am referring is the tendency,
the necessity perhaps, of the Greek poetic imagination to regard those
who possess wisdom in matters of justice as blind. My argument is that

a more extended reflection upon the image of blindness in Greek literature than Heidegger himself provides supplies a means for eliciting a sense of precisely what he comes to say about justice today on the basis of his interpretation of Anaximander.

The almost invisible passage to what I want to call attention shows up when Heidegger turns to what he calls the "oldest" text of the West, a Greek text, namely, the very brief fragment from Anaximander, the topic of which is the relation of justice and time. It is, obviously, not the oldest text by any orthodox calendar. Rather, there is the very important question of how this text merits this designation; yet, to answer this question one ultimately needs to understand the sense of time formulated by the words themselves. The orthodox English translation of Anaximander's fragment is well known: "and the source of the coming into being of things is also that which destruction happens, 'according to necessity; for they must pay penalty and retribution to each other for their injustice according to the ordinance of time'." At the outset of his interpretation of these words, Heidegger suggests that the possibility of translation is at issue here, that language might remain the hidden bond in the question of the relation of time and justice spoken in this fragment. That suggestion, and the question of translation, haunt all that follows. But the special point that I want to develop first appears in the words that follow Anaximander's text, words which are from Theophrastus and which read "as he describes it in these rather poetical terms." I will return to the significance of this passage after some general comments about Heidegger's interpretation of Anaximander's text. These general comments will help set the context for my special concern with the question of why Theophrastus is compelled to characterize these words as "rather poetical."

The centerpiece of Heidegger's attentions in his reading of Anaximander is Anaximander's word ἀδικία, a word that is typically rendered as "injustice" in English, as "*Ungerechtigkeit*" in German. It is important to note that, without fanfare, Heidegger's discussion will quickly shift away from any concern with the privative form of the word and come instead to speak of δίκη. This move is decisive and not unproblematic since it signals a shift from a discourse on injustice to one of justice itself. Such a shift presumes a certain symmetry, some translation or perhaps simple negation, between justice and injustice. But it might be precisely this shift that needs to be called into question and may not be one that can be accomplished. A discourse about injustice might be possible, a discourse on justice might not be possible. Such a distinction might indeed be the distinction that separates Socrates and Plato, and may be precisely the move into metaphysics. In the end, it might just be the case that a non-metaphysical discourse on ethicality might need to rest content with the critique of injustice and abandon the dream of a theory of justice.

But it is this word δίκη, and the untranslatable possibility that it names, that captures Heidegger's imagination of justice and becomes the axis along which the question of a non-metaphysical determination of justice begins to be reformulated. I will forgo indications of how pervasive this word is in Heidegger—especially from 1935–1946—culminating in the Nietzsche volumes where Heidegger even argues that "the knowledge of δίκη, that is philosophy." Instead I will simply say in anticipation that δίκη becomes the word naming that wider horizon, that region of ethicality which is not defined by the human, to which Heidegger refers us in the "Letter of Humanism." If Heidegger refuses to translate the word and speak of "Gerechtigkeit" or "justice," it is because he wants to remind us that what is names here is a field wider than that which has yet been contained by those words. Clearly this word is one of the elemental words concerning ethicality at work in the Greek philosophical imagination. Clearly more is at stake in the question of its possible translation that the task of simply finding an equivalent term.

We find the word, for instance, already in Parmenides who, in writing of the fantastic adventure in which truth beyond the capture of time is revealed, suggests that the revelation of such knowledge is "destined" by δίκη. It is also the word that Homer uses as the answer to one of Odysseus' most broken-hearted entreaties in The Odyssey: Odysseus has descended into the land of the dead, where there is no light, in order to speak with the blind prophet, Teiresias, and before leaving the underworld of shadows, Odysseus sees the ghost of his mother. He had been gone a long time and had not known of her death. He said that he ached to hold her one more time and did not understand why that was not possible. His mother answers simply that such is the δίκη of mortality.[8] There is a certain intractable need indicated here, a necessity which we need respect.

When Heidegger finally wagers a translation of this word, he proposes the German word *"Fug."* When Derrida risks a translation of this translation, he suggest "joint" and explains that proposed translation by referring us to *Hamlet* and the phrase we find there saying that "time is out of joint."[9] In other words, δίκη, the word traditionally translated as "justice," is taken more as a name for the rightness that is when matters are as they should be. It is the name for the rightness, the appropriateness, the joint, the lawful necessity.

This is the point at which I must finally return to Theophrastus's passing comment on Anaximander's fragment; namely, that these are *poetical* terms in which Anaximander is thinking about this necessity of δίκη. It is Heidegger who has argued that the poetical is a manner of thinking with an integrity independent of the philosophical or conceptual such that what is said poetically has a necessity of its own and so cannot be said otherwise.

At a decisive point in his anlaysis Heidegger enlists a passage from Homer, not to dramatize an idea that could be made otherwise, but to make a point that is most appropriately made in an image. To that end, Heidegger cites a passage from the beginning of *The Iliad*. For nine days the Greeks had suffered a plague, and in an effort to comprehend their situation and to find a remedy, Achilles summons Kalchas, one who "sees into the future." When Heidegger discusses this passage he notes that this seeing into the future, this glimpse down the route of lawful necessity which is equally the time of my death, is the thread that joins time and δίκη. Of course this does not mean: for justice to be had, for things to be in joint, we must know the outcome of the present. Such a view would lead to a rather silly expression of justice as requiring a calculation of the future. If we understand such "seeing into the future" to refer to a sort of prophecy for which there are no surprises, then such a remark clearly does not illuminate the riddle of δίκη at all.

But this reference to the future as the concern of the ethical needs further attention, and, more precisely, it needs attention with respect to the poetical character in which it is presented. Here what Heidegger does not say is of central importance; namely, that Kalchas, the one who is called to end the sufferings of the Greeks, the one who sees into the future, is blind and it is precisely his blindness that is what we need to understand since it enables him to see what we do not see.

This relation of blindness and poetic insight is so basic to the Greek sensibility and such a relationship is so essential that it was necessary for the Greeks to understand their preeminent poet, Homer, as blind. As is well known, it is unclear whether there was in fact "a" Homer, but what is clear is that all the ancient legends that surround him find his blindness to be an element in his knowledge. That is even the case with his name: Ὅμηρος means "hostage" which was a synonym for the blind who needed to be led by a guide. In the final analysis, it is irrelevant whether or not there was a blind Homer. What is relevant is that the Greek imagination required the blindness of such a poet of ethical life. The relation of the blind to the λόγος is more acute. We, for instance, do not find the blindness of a Milton or a Borges essential to their poetic character, even though both of them have written powerfully about it.

In Greece, a culture of light, blindness was the ultimate form of human suffering. Consequently, but nonetheless ironically, blindness came to stand as the most visible image for the human condition as suffered. In a culture that equated light and life, blindness bore a resemblance to death, and so it is no accident that blind Teiresias is the only one who can see in the underworld of the dead—that has always been his element—and in one respect it is this symbolic relation with death that is the source of his insight about the destiny of the living. (As an aside let me simply say that the experiences of Teiresias are especially important for a fuller treatment of this thematic, most of all because the stories of the way he became blind—no matter which story one tells—introduce the crucial dimension of desire into the issue of the poetic.[10]) But for now my point is to indicate the extent to which blindness attaches itself to the Greek poetic imagination that thinks the riddle of δίκη. To that end, one could refer to the poet Demodokeos who was given the gift of song by the muse who took his eyes. One could refer to Thamyris, the blind poet who is the hero of the tragedy by Sophocles that we have lost. Or one could refer to Stesichorus, to whom Plato refers in The Phaedrus, suggesting that he was cleverer than Homer since Stesichorus knew how to recover the loss of his eyes: he simply wrote the lines—decisive in The Phaedrus—"This story is not true"[11] (it's a line that Socrates repeats with a veil on his head, covering his eyes, a veil he removes upon uttering those words). One could continue offering such illustrations, but to do so only confirms the general point to be made: namely, that in those instances where the origin of a blindness is explained, it is typically a punishment for trespassing the limits of human knowledge. One goes blind because one knows too much.

Were one to properly discuss the nature of poetic blindness, it would also be necessary to situate such characterizations of blind poets with respect to the enormous significance of the seeing eyes in Greek literature in general and Greek philosophy in particular. To provide such a context it would be necessary to range from philosophical presuppositions about the relation of sight to knowledge to mythological images about eyes (ranging from the Cyclops Odysseus blinds, to the Gorgon, the sight of which means death, up to Argus, the all-seeing guard with a hundred eyes and who, after his murder, was memorialized for his watchful service by having his eyes set in peacock tails). Here, of course, Plato is decisive since one finds in Plato a number of passages about eyes, passages such as the one in *The Phaedrus* where he speaks of "the stream of beauty, entering the eyes that brings a warmth that nourishes the wings of the soul."[12]

But, instead of trying to tackle such a wide theme, let me try to focus upon what we should be able to see in the case of perhaps the most celebrated image of blindness in Greek tragedy. I am referring of course to Oedipus, who blinds himself because, once he sees, seeing is too painful. At the moment of appearing on stage newly blinded, Oedipus is called "δεινόν"—by the chorus. The Greek words blend blindness, suffering, witnessing and human life in the most compact manner: ὦ δεινὸν ἰδεῖν πάθος ἀνθρώποις. With his entry into blindness, when Hölderlin suggests that Oedipus has "an eye too many perhaps," we come to understand that in the poetic imagination such blindness refers not to a physical condition, but to a moral condition.

What makes Oedipus' blindness especially interesting is that, unlike Teiresias, for instance, who was given insight simultaneously with his blindness, the knowledge Oedipus won through blindness comes only comes gradually. Only after he has "said the unspeakable"[13] does he begin to see what he did not see before—when he had eyes, but chose blindly. It is in *Oedipus at Colonus* that Sophocles charts the moral growth of Oedipus, who enters a blind beggar led by his daughter Antigone and dies in the most marvelous manner, recommending to his children "one word—love."[14] It is a remarkable death scene, one bathed in light and expressive of the most tender, yet difficult, affirmation. It is almost a serene moment in this trilogy of tragedies otherwise bursting with catastrophe. Set so clearly apart from the turmoils of tragedies, Oedipus' parting word of affirmation needs to be heard as the summit of the tragedy generally and the point at which the poetic expression of the knowledge of δίκη finds its most pristine expression. But it must be understood to be an exceedingly difficult expression of love, and one that should not necessarily be characterized as the perfect achievement of reconciliation such as is found in Hegel's claim that after the catastrophe "the wounds of spirit heal and leave no scars behind."[15] Its ethicality is inseparable from its own imperfection.

Heidegger's interpretation of the Anaximander fragment comes very close to suggesting that such pure, yet flawed, affirmation is the core thought of that fragment. In proposing that Anaximander's text is expressive of an affirmation beyond calculation, Heidegger focuses upon the word τίσις, which is commonly translated as "retribution" or "penalty." Struggling to understand that word, which is the word by which Anaximander names what can be given fittingly, Heidegger eventually comes to translate it as *"Schätzen"*—a word that means something like "honor," "esteem," and even "love" (it is, for instance, one of the words that Kant uses to characterize what we feel before the sublime, and it is also the German translation for Augustine's word *"diligis"*). But, to render difficult any understanding of this word—and of the last word that Oedipus utters before his death—Heidegger argues that this word of affirmation, which he proposes as a key word in the non-metaphysical ethical sensibility expressed in the Greek poetic imagination, does not name a human trait. It is not in our control, it is not first of all "ours" even if it is what we need to learn if justice is to be. We must give what we do not have—if there is to be the fittingness of δίκη.

While I want to say more about this sense of affirmation to which we are now referred, there remains one more point that must be said about the specific character of blindness that is crucial for an understanding of such affirmation. By this point it should be clear that what makes discussing images of blindness encountered in such poetic texts so problematic is that, if we read reflectively at all, we gradually come to realize that it is we who do not see. We watch as Teiresias sees into the future, but we still do not understand. But there is a clue to be found in understanding that such seers look into the future. It is the future that holds our destiny and the necessity that governs it, not the past. It is, however, a sense of the future quite distinct from any conception of the future as that for which we plan and calculate.

Here let me suggest that two further images might help us sort out this dilemma. The first is a common image rooted in the Greek language, the second comes from Walter Benjamin, and both concern our relation to the future. Whereas we, today, like to think of the future as that which is in front of us, as that which we are facing, in Greece the image of the future is of that which is behind us, defining our blind spot. The Greek word ὄπιθεν, which literally means "behind" or "hinter," refers to not the past but to the future.[16] We find a similar sense of our situatedness in time in Benjamin's text, "Theses on the Philosophy of History," where he writes the following:

> A Klee painting named "Angelus Novus" shows an angel looking as though he is about to move away from something he is fixedly contemplating. His eyes are staring, his mouth is open, his wings are spread. This is how one pictures the angel of history. His face is turned towards the past. Where we perceive a chain of events, he sees one single catastrophe which keeps piling wreckage upon wreckage and hurls it in front of his feet. The angel would like to stay, awaken the dead, and make whole what has been smashed. But a storm is blowing from Paradise; it has got caught in his wings with such violence that the angel can no longer close them. This storm irresistibly propels him into the future to which his back is turned, while the pile of debris before him grows skyward. The storm is what we call progress.[17]

The image here is powerful and disquieting in the way that it situates us in relation to a future that finds it possessing great force, but to which we are blind. Benjamin's sense of the inexorable in history, and of the messianic arrival of justice, is far closer to Heidegger's view of the relation of history and justice than is commonly acknowledged. Most of all, they are united in their mutually deep commitment to the idea that we are bound to the mysteries of futurity—mysteries that the Greeks thought under the notion of destiny—and that it is out of that mystery that the riddle of shared life in time is to be thought. But the point that such images highlight, the point that I believe one can find powerfully presented by Heidegger, is that the future is another time, a time apart from the calculations of the present. As the alterity of time itself, as strange even beyond the projections of the imagination, my relation to the future, to what I didn't see, is an ethical relation.

Now, however, it is necessary that I begin to move toward my conclusion to try to draw some of the threads of my remarks together. Most of all I want to say something more pointed about my contention that, in taking up the texts in which Heidegger turns to early Greek works, we find a truly innovative avenue for elaborating questions directed to the possibility of justice today. It is clear that Heidegger is working to redirect such questions and so undermines some of the assumptions that we might make about what would constitute and answer to the questions posed by our ethical being. In the end, each of us is finally confronted with the question of what we expect from an ethics. Let me suggest further that the sort of original ethics one finds in Heidegger is, to my mind, ultimately very non-Western, and that is one of the reasons that one finds such incredulous responses to efforts to enlist Heidegger in discussions of ethical life and to propose that his work, especially the work we find on the Presocratics, has an ethical import. Most important to realize is that Heidegger has sought to remove the question of ethics away from every sense that ethical life is a matter of someting calculable—it is, as Nietzsche argues, "beyond good and evil," and apart from the economics of discursive practices. He resists such a notion vigorously because it is precisely an awareness of the incalculable *as such* that first opens the promise of something like the ethical. It is precisely this which safeguards freedom, a radical freedom which must be acknowledged as beyond calculation, in time. But of course Heidegger knows all too well that freedom preserved leaves us open to the monstrous as well as the divine. He returns us to a knowledge that formed the abyssal grounds of Greek tragedy, namely, that those who do not understand the force of destiny must go blind in order to see. Original ethics begins when freedom is revealed as consisting in this risk of both the demonic and the divine.

Such a sense of the ethical begins and ends simultaneously; it becomes the exposure of the aporia of the ethical that, as Derrida argues, "infinitely distributes itself"—that indexes us to what cannot be seen and cannot be told. Heidegger, like the Greeks, knew that destiny arose as the future, as that which cannot be outwitted, cannot be calculated, as that which holds for me the end of time in my death. Heidegger knows that I am bound to something greater than me, something that I cannot understand, and that it is out of the knowledge that I am wedded to what I cannot know, this experience of limits, that I can find ethical experience.

But there is something that can be said here. It is, nonetheless, perfectly without reason and so all I can do is allude to its saying. If I were a poet perhaps I could say it properly. I have already indicated that there is a powerful sense of affirmation struggling to be expressed in Heidegger. It is an affirmation like that which Oedipus found before his death. But it is too easy, and far too misleading to speak of love at this point.

It would be misleading to suggest that the end of Heidegger's reflections on ethical life arrive at something like the emotion we call love. However, it does seem clear that he attempts to show us that we are bound to what we cannot calculate, that there are ineluctable limits that blind our speculative abilities, and that we can at least know and understand that to which we are bound as greater than that which we define (so that the "ethical" realm must include what we confusedly call animals and nature). All of these efforts somehow call for an affirmation of what we cannot see.

In saying this, I am trying to situate Heidegger's ethical thought, especially insofar as it is garnered out of a reading of early Greek texts, in a tradition of thinkers of the ethical, one that begins with Homer, Anaximander, and Sophocles, and moves up through Spinoza (for whom, as Deleuze has noted, "ethical joy is the correlate of speculative affirmation"[18]) through Hegel, who refers to the divinity of the "yes," and through Nietzsche who writes that "where one cannot love, there one should pass by."

In the end, it is all a matter of struggling with all one's might to extend the borders of what is known, and of exercising a vigorous critique of inequities on the basis of what we do understand. But it is equally a matter of knowing how to cope with our blindness, with what we didn't, what we don't see. And here what needs to be said is that it is, as Homer says, the δίκη of mortal life, that one can only love what one does not see. And one must understand what Odysseus learns in Hades: that in giving such affirmation of what is other than ourselves we must not wait for a reciprocal gift. In the end, ethical affirmation, the texture of δίκη, of fittingness, is not symmetrical, but a gift, of pure generosity.

We didn't see the seven mountains ahead of us. We didn't see how they are always ahead, always calling us, always reminding us that there are more things to be done, dreams to be realized, joys to be rediscovered, promises made before birth to be fulfilled, beauty to be incarnated, and love embodied.

We didn't notice how they hinted that nothing is ever finished, that struggles are never truly concluded, that sometimes we have to redream our lives, and that life can always be used to create more light.

We didn't see the mountains ahead and so we didn't sense the upheavals to come, upheavals that were in fact already in our midst, waiting to burst into flames. We didn't see the chaos growing; and when its advancing waves found us we were unprepared for its feverish narratives and wild manifestations. We were unprepared for an era twisted out of natural proportions, unprepared when our road began to speak in the bizarre languages of violence and transformations. The world broke up into unimaginable forms, and only the circling spirits of the age saw what was happening with any clarity.

This is the song of a circling spirit. This is a story for all of us who never see the seven mountains of our secret destiny, who never see that beyond the chaos there can always be a new sunlight.[19]

My argument has been that Heidegger's reading of Anaximander, and his reading of early Greek texts generally, is best interpreted as an effort to formulate the contours of a non-metaphysical sense of ethical life. It is a creative and philosophically imaginative confrontation with these texts, and is not, in the first instance, an effort to remedy inappropriate scholarship on the part of the classicists. In turning to Heidegger's work on the Presocratics, it is then, I believe, important to understand that they form a whole cloth and that they need to be read in tandem with Heidegger's work on poetic texts, and especially his texts on Greek tragedy. Taken as a whole, these texts do drive at something like an ethical sensibility. But they formulate only a beginning. Heidegger concludes his text on Anaximander by acknowledging this, saying that once thinking begins to poetize with respect to the riddle of being, it "brings what is to be thought into nearness with the earliest of what has been thought."[20]

NOTES

1. *Martin Heidegger—Elisabeth Blochmann: Briefwechsel 1918–1969*, ed. Joachim W. Storck (Marbach am Neckar: Deutsche Schillergesellschaft, 1989), 55.

2. One might think the logic of the alterity with reference to Hölderlin's celebrated Böhlendorf letter. On this see my "Lyrical and Ethical Subjects: On the Ordeal of the Foreign and Enigma of One's Own," *Philosophy Today*, vol. 40:1 (Spring 1996), 188–196.

3. EM, 152.

4. Here see my "Poetry and the Political," in *Festivals of Interpretation: Essays on Hans-Georg Gadamer's Work*, ed. K. Wright (Albany: SUNY Press, 1990).

5. This, of course, is a reference to Christo's project of covering the Reichstag with a shimmering fabric. That act, during two summer weeks in 1995, provoked a remarkably lively and intelligent debate about the nature of the parliament, the history of that building (especially its role in Nazi times) and its suitability for the parliament of a re-unified Germany. It also stimulated a number of responses to the question, "what is art?".

6. *Martin Heidegger—Elisabeth Blochmann: Briefwechsel 1918–1969*, 10 April 1932, 49.

7. W, 187.

8. See *The Odyssey*, Book 11, lines 248ff. It is this portion of *The Odyssey* that Plato seems to be explicitly re-writing in the "Myth of Er" in Book 10 of *The Republic*. That is the section of *The Republic* in which Plato speaks to "what awaits the dead," and the section in which the discussion of justice reaches a summit.

9. See Jacques Derrida, *Specters of Marx*, trans. P. Kamuf (New York: Routledge, 1994), 23.

10. On this point see Robert Graves, *The Greek Myths* (New York: Penguin Books, 1960), 98. Also, Nicole Loraux, *The Experiences of Tiresias: The Feminine and the Greek Man*, trans. Paula Wissing (Princeton: Princeton University Press, 1995), 211–226.

11. Plato, *Phaedrus*, 243a.

12. Plato, *Phaedrus*, 251b.

13. Sophocles, *Oedipus Tyrannus*, line 1283.

14. Sophocles, *Oedipus at Colonus*, line 1612.

15. G. W. F. Hegel, *Phänomenologie des Geistes* (Hamburg: Meiner, 1952), 470.

16. See Bernard Knox's discussion of this word in his *Backing into the Future: The Classical Tradition and Its Renewal* (New York: W. W. Norton, 1994).

17. Walter Benjamin, "Theses on the History of Philosophy," 9, in *Illuminations*, ed. Hannah Arendt, trans. Harry Zohn (New York: Schocken Books, 1969), 257–258.

18. Gilles Deleuze, *Spinoza: Practical Philosophy*, trans. Robert Hurley (San Francisco: City Lights Books, 1988), 29.

19. Ben Okri, *Songs of Enchantment* (New York: Doubleday, 1993), 3.

20. HW, 343.

Eight

The Last, Undelivered Lecture (XII) from Summer Semester 1952

Martin Heidegger
Translated by Will McNeill

Translator's Introduction

The following text presents for the first time a translation of the final lecture prepared by Heidegger for the second part of his 1951–1952 course *Was heißt Denken? (What is Called Thinking?)*. Although included in the original handwritten manuscript, this lecture was not delivered as part of the course, apparently because there was insufficient time at the end of the summer semester. The published version of the course likewise omits the final lecture. Heidegger did, however, read the text of lecture XII as part of a subsequent "Colloquium on Dialectic," which took place in Muggenbrunn on 15 September 1952. Both the protocol of the "Colloquium" and the lecture are published in *Hegel-Studien*, Band 25 (Bonn: Bouvier Verlag, 1990). The text of the lecture is significant not only because it belongs to the original manuscript of *Was heißt Denken?*, but also because it represents an early version of the essay that appeared in revised form under the title "Moira" in *Vorträge und Aufsätze*.

In preparing this translation I have had reference to the translation of "Moira," by Frank A. Capuzzi, which appears in *Early Greek Thinking* (New York: Harper Collins, 1984). The English reader should note that the German text—in particular the introduction—has a somewhat stilted style, and that this is reflected in the translation. The numbers in square brackets indicate the original manuscript pagination, and facilitate cross-reference to the German text.

Will McNeill
DePaul University

171

The Last, Undelivered Lecture (XII)
from Summer Semester 1952.

ταὐτὸν δ᾽ἐστὶ νοεῖν τε καὶ οὕνεκεν ἔστι νόημα. οὐ γὰρ ἄνευ
τοῦ ἐόντος, ἐν ὧι πεφατισμένον ἔστιν, εὑρήσεις τὸ νοεῖν· οὐδ᾽
ἦν γὰρ ἢ ἔστιν ἤ ἔσται ἄλλο πάρεξ τοῦ ἐόντος, ἐπεὶ τό γε
Μοῖρ᾽ ἐπέδησεν οὖλον ἀκίνητόν τ᾽ ἔμμεναι.

"Dasselbe aber ist Denken als auch weswegen ist Gedachtes.
Nicht nämlich ohne das Seiende, in dem es Gesagtes ist, wirst
du finden das Denken—nicht war nämlich oder ist oder wird
sein Anderes außer neben dem "Seiend," nachdem dies doch
Geschick fesselte ganz, unbewegbar auch, zu sein."

"The same, however, is thinking as is also therefore what is
thought. For not without beings, in which it is what is said,
will you find thinking—nor was there nor is there nor will be
there anything else outside of or besides that which is in
"being," since destiny has bound this to be whole and immov-
able too."

Parmenides, Fragment B8.34ff.

What is said in these words concerning the relationship between
νοεῖν and εἶναι, "thinking and Being"? [24]
So far as I can see, the various interpretations that have become
customary all maintain one of the following three perspectives, each
of which also finds some support in the text.
One perspective regards thinking as something that is, something
that we find before us like many other things. Such a being, like all of
its kind, must accordingly be counted as belonging among other beings and as included among or "integrated" into these beings. The
integral is a kind of sum-total arrived at by a process of adding together.
According to this perspective, thinking is identical in kind to beings.
The sum total of beings is called Being. Thinking thus proves to be identical to Being. We scarcely require any philosophy in order to arrive at
this conclusion. What it says is valid not only for thinking as something
we find before us. It is valid also for voyaging across the sea, for

building houses, for all human activity. One wonders why Parmenides explicitly draws such a conclusion precisely with regard to thinking, why he bothers to specifically ground it by adding the commonplace remark that apart from beings and besides beings as a whole there are no beings. Or more accurately, whenever one considers the issue in this way, one no longer wonders about it anymore. For what the philosophers busied themselves with in their first attempts at philosophy, namely, classifying among beings all that is, loses the character of a genuine task of thinking as philosophy progresses. And it would scarcely be worth while our considering this interpretation of the relation between Being and thinking—an interpretation that "amasses" and represents beings as the mass aggregate that is Being—were it not for the fact that it gives us the occasion to expressly point out that Parmenides nowhere explicitly speaks of thinking as also being one of the many ἐόντα, one of the manifold beings of which each one sometimes is and sometimes is not, thus being fundamentally both at once: present and absent. [25]

Another, more thoughtful approach at least finds "statements that are difficult to understand" at this point in the text. In order to facilitate our understanding, one seeks some assistance. Since, in the relationship between thinking and Being, the issue seems to be the relation of knowing to actual reality, one finds in the philosophy of modernity whatever assistance is needed. Modern philosophy has established a theory of knowledge that has passed through doubt, a theory that has become the authoritative fundamental trait of that questioning which modern philosophy pursues. Within such philosophy, which posits beings as objects of representation, we find a proposition that provides an illuminating pointer for interpreting the statement of Parmenides. It is a proposition of Berkeley's, one that rests on the fundamental Cartesian position and reads: *esse = percipi*: "Being is identical with being represented." By bringing this together with Parmenides' assertions, these assertions first attain the perspective of a distinct philosophical questioning.

Being is identical with thinking insofar as the objectivity of objects is "constituted" in representational consciousness. In the light of these determinations, Parmenides' statement proves to be an as yet unrefined and early form of the modern doctrine concerning the essence of knowledge. There can be no doubt that the modern proposition *esse = percipi* has its basis in the statement of Parmenides, irrespective of whatever historiographically ascertainable dependencies we have in view. Yet the way in which the modern proposition historically belongs together with this early Greek proposition entails an essential divergence in their meanings. If we are attentive, this divergence can already be seen from the manner in which the propositions speak. On both occasions, Parmenides names νοεῖν first and attributes it to εἶναι, and not the reverse. A formulation of the modern proposition fully corresponding to this would have to read: *percipi = esse*. The modern proposition by contrast attributes the *esse*, which is named first, to *percipi*, in keeping with the principle of the fundamental Cartesian proposition: *ens = ens verum, verum = certum*. [26] The modern proposition asserts something about "Being," whereas the early Greek proposition asserts something about "thinking." For this reason, an interpretation of this early Greek statement in terms of the perspective of modern thinking is erroneous from the outset. And yet it remains an attempt to appropriate Greek thought, an attempt that gets played out in manifold forms.

Finally, however, ancient philosophy itself already attempted to lend weight to the Parmenidean statement in its own way, namely the Platonic way. Here, the guiding perspective is taken from the Socratic-Platonic doctrine concerning the Being of beings (*das Sein des Seienden*). According to this doctrine, the "ideas," which constitute the "being" (*"seiend"*) in all beings (*Seienden*), do not belong to the realm of the sensible. They can be apprehended only in νοεῖν. Thus, as Plotinus would have the Parmenidean statement say, Being does not belong among the αἰσθητά, but is νοητόν. Being is, in essence, in the manner of "spirit." The statement that thinking is identical with Being means: both are in essence non- and supra-sensible. In the neoplatonic interpretation of the Parmenidean saying, this proposition is neither an assertion about "thinking" nor an assertion about "Being," nor even an assertion about the essence of their belonging together as divergent, but is an assertion about how both belong to the realm of the nonsensible.

Each of these three interpretations imports and attributes later ways of questioning to early Greek thinking. Presumably all later thinking that attempts to bring itself into a thoughtful dialogue with early thinking must speak from its own perspective and thus shatter the silence of the earlier thinking. Earlier thinking is thereby inevitably drawn into this later dialogue, transposed into its field of hearing and perspective, and thus robbed, as it were, of the freedom of its own telling. [27] Nevertheless, this does not of itself necessarily entail its being recast into later thinking. Everything depends on whether the dialogue initiated by this later thinking opens itself freely from the outset, and constantly, so as to let itself be addressed in an authoritative manner by the earlier thinking, or whether it closes itself off from such earlier thinking and covers it over with the opinions belonging to later schools of thought. Such closing oneself off occurs whenever later thinking fails to embark on an inquiry into that perspective of hearing and seeing which is appropriate to the earlier thinking. Such inquiry, of course, must not exhaust itself in simply seeking to note the inexplicit presuppositions underlying the earlier thinking. The inquiring must become an explicit pronouncement in which the perspectives of seeing and hearing, as well as their essential provenance, come thoughtfully to language. Unless such meditation occurs, a thoughtful dialogue remains altogether absent. Alternatively, by contrast, the early thinking can, by way of such dialogue, unfold into its own worthiness in its very questionability. Every attempt in this regard will therefore direct its attention toward the obscure parts of the text that are worthy of question, rather than immediately taking up residence solely at those places that bear the appearance of being comprehensible; for in the latter instance, the dialogue is over before it has begun.

The following remarks, however, content themselves more or less with merely noting and enumerating the obscure places in the text. Such an undertaking can prepare for a translation to occur, but does not of itself bring this about.

1.

What must be noted above all else is that the more detailed text in which the statement of Parmenides is handed down to us (Fragment B8.34ff.) speaks of the ἐόν. By the "beings" ("*Seienden*") thus named, Parmenides is by no means referring to beings in themselves as a whole, among which we could also classify thinking as being something. Yet nor does τὸ ἐόν mean εἶναι in the sense of "Being [taken] by itself" (*des "Seins für sich"*), as though it were a matter of merely delimiting the specifically nonsensible essence of Being from beings in themselves. In grammatical terms, the ἐόν is spoken as a participial and, [28] with regard to the issue at stake, is thought in a twofold respect. This twofold respect may be named in the turns of phrase "Being *of* beings" and "beings *in* their

Being." Yet such naming is far removed from thinking this twofold (*Zwiefalt*) itself *as such*, or even from raising it to something worthy of question.

This widely invoked "Being itself" as distinct from beings, however, is precisely "Being" in the sense of "*Being of* . . . beings." At the beginning of Western thinking, what is nevertheless all-important is catching sight of what is named by "Being" (Φύσις, Λόγος, Ἐν) by sighting it in an appropriate manner. The appearance thus arises that this Being of beings is merely "identical" with beings as a whole, and as such is that which most is (*das Seiendste*). It looks as though the twofold has faded away into the inessential, because thinking from then on moves within this twofold in such a way that the latter gives no occasion for thought, not even where, in accordance with the way in which the "*Being of* . . . beings" comes to receive the historical coining of its essence in each case, the twofold comes to be coined in diverse ways. At the beginning of Western thinking, this twofold *as such* has already fallen away. Yet this falling away is not nothing; for with this falling away the twofold falls into forgottenness. The essence of forgottenness, however, announces itself in Λήθη. Here we must ward off any premature views, in noting that we are not to interpret Λήθη as forgottenness from the perspective of a commonplace, though indeterminate conception of "forgetting." Rather the reverse is the case: We must enquire concerning the essence of forgottenness, and the name accorded to it, from out of Λήθη as concealment.

2.

According to Fragment B3 (earlier B5), thinking presumably belongs to Being. Yet such belonging must not, on the other hand, be prematurely interpreted as identity. Fragment B8, however, states more clearly, that is, pointing more penetratingly into what is worthy of questioning, the respect in which this belonging of thinking to Being must be heeded. The ἐόν is that, οὕνεχεν ἔστι νόημα. The ἐόν is that due to which there presences whatever has been "taken into heed." Thinking [29] is neither needed by "beings in themselves," nor necessitated by "Being [taken] by itself." That, however, which for its part demands νοεῖν and at the same time along with it λέγειν, letting-lie-before, and calls them on the way to itself, is the ἐόν, the Being *of* beings. Thinking itself *is* singularly due to this twofold, which is, nevertheless, not explicitly pronounced. Beings (as) being (*Das Seiende (als) seiend*), the appearing of that which is present in presencing, needs the jointure of λέγειν and νοεῖν, from out of which the metaphysically coined essence of Western-European thinking henceforth unfolds. This thinking subsequently brings beings forth to appear explicitly *as* beings (ὄν ᾗ ὄν, *ens qua ens*), in a way that does not yet appear to appear in the ambiguity of the ἐόν, an ambiguity that can be readily overheard. In this way thinking belongs together with this twofold. As belonging together in this way, ἐόν (εἶναι) and νοεῖν are the Same.

3.

What kind of belonging together is this? In accordance with the jointure of λέγειν τε νοεῖν τε which we have elucidated (Fragment B6), νοεῖν from the outset, and thus constantly, remains indigenous to λέγειν. Consequently the νόημα too, as νοούμενον, is a λεγόμενον. That which has been taken into heed is always already gathered as something lying before us. Taking into heed unfolds and preserves this gathering. Such λέγειν however, letting-lie-before, namely the letting-lie-before of that which is present in its presencing, determines the essence of saying experienced in a Greek way. The νοούμενον and its νοεῖν are in each and every case something said, not subsequently or arbitrarily, but essentially. Not everything said, however, is necessarily something spoken; what is said can also, and on occasion even must, remain something that is kept silent. Yet everything that is spoken is, before this, something said. Wherein does the distinction between the two consist? Why does Parmenides characterize the νοούμενον and νοεῖν as πεφατισμένον in Fragment B8? This word is translated correctly in lexical terms as "something spoken." Yet to what does this speaking refer which is here named by φάσκειν and φάσις? Does speaking here merely mean the utterance (φωνή) of the meaning of a word or statement (σήματα τῶν ὄντων)? Is speaking here merely the "phonetic" as distinct from the "semantic"? Not at all. In φάσκω there lies: to name in praise, to call forth before us, to let appear; [30] φάσμα is, for example, the appearing of the stars and of the moon in its alternating shapes, whence the "phases" of the moon. Speaking, φημί, is of the same, though not identical, essence as λέγειν: letting that which is present lie before in its presencing.

Parmenides is concerned with saying to where νοεῖν belongs. We can find it only wherever it indigenously belongs. Where do we find νοεῖν? Only wherever it shows itself. And it can show itself only wherever it has come to appear? Where, and in what way is νοεῖν something that has appeared? It is this as πεφατισμένον. Thus νοεῖν comes to appear in what is spoken. As something that has been uttered, whatever is spoken is something that can be perceived in the realm of the sensible. Linguistic expression forces and pushes and carries the meaning of what can be said—a meaning that cannot be represented in the sensible—into the sensible realm of discursive utterance and written inscription. Yet does Parmenides here speak of an intended nonsensible meaning that then comes to appear in the sensible through the sound of a word? By no means. His questioning asks solely about the relation of νοεῖν to εἶναι. In this regard, Parmenides says: τὸ νοεῖν . . . πεφατισμένον ἐν τῷ ἐόντι, taking into heed has come forth to appear "in beings." Does this mean that νοεῖν can be found before us among the other ἐόντα, in the realm of beings, to which there also belongs whatever pertains to the soul? Were we to reflect upon νοεῖν as an experience in the soul or to attempt to find it within the field of the "facts of consciousness," then we would never be able to bring into view νοεῖν in Parmenides' sense. Yet Parmenides does say: οὐκ ἄνευ τοῦ ἐόντος εὑρήσεις τὸ νοεῖν—not apart from "beings" can you find νοεῖν. Certainly. We find it only σύν, gathered together with the ἐόν. Why? Because νοεῖν as λέγειν gathers itself of its own accord and in a singular manner in the direction of the ἐόν, and only as that which thus gathers does it prevail in the manner that it prevails. Only as λεγόμενον does the νόημα come forth to appear in the ἐόν and is thus: πεφατισμένον. How are we to understand this? [31]

We can succeed in understanding it only if, rather than representing that which is "spoken" as that which has been uttered in the sensible, we think it in a Greek way as that which has appeared. This demands that we precisely do not restrict appearing and self-showing (σήματα) to that which emerges in the field of whatever can be perceived in the sensible, but think self-showing and appearing in the first instance in terms of what prevails as that which reveals itself before any distinguishing between the sensible and the nonsensible.

The πεφατισμένον is something that has appeared, but appeared ἐν τῷ ἐόντι, and that means: *neither* among those beings that are perceptible in the realm of the sensible, among those ἐόντα that can be taken up and taken on by δόξα (those that are actual "in themselves"), *nor* in the realm of εἶναι that is later named the ἰδέα, nonsensible "Being [taken] by itself." Νοεῖν shows itself only as νοεῖν, that is, as taking into heed the ἐόν ἔμμεναι in the ἐόν itself. The ἐόν itself prevails in the twofold of "beings being" (*"Seiendes seiend"*), and does so even when the twofold is not specifically named, nor even given thought as such.

Wherever that which is present shows itself *in* its presencing, wherever presencing in the sense of presencing *of* that which is present appears, there—namely "in" this twofold itself and in it alone—νοεῖν is in play and therefore comes forth to appear ἐν τῷ ἐόντι (thought participially); for νοεῖν does not apprehend just any arbitrary thing. It takes ἐόν ἔμμεναι, the being *of* beings (*das Seiend des Seienden*), into heed. Subsequent thinking says: Νοεῖν, in taking into heed the ἐόν ἦ ἐόν, does not take that which is present into heed as that which is present, and thus it pays heed to the presencing of what is present, always asking: τί τὸ ὄν, what is that which is present in respect of its presencing? In what way is Being in regard to beings, in what way are these, as beings, to be determined in terms of Being, and how is Being to be thought?

4.

Νοεῖν belongs to εἶναι. The relation of νοεῖν to εἶναι rests in the fact that, as the way in which λεγέιν τε νοεῖν τε is drawn into the ἐόν ἔμμεναι, this relation is in accordance with χρή. [32] To what is the οὕνεκεν ἔστι νόημα (B8.34) related back? Due to what does that which has been taken into heed prevail? Due to nothing other than that which, of its own accord, needs a taking into heed. And what is that? Presencing (εἶναι), namely as ἐόν, the presencing of that which is present. This, due to which the νόημα prevails, is the Same (ταὐτόν) as is taking into heed, that is, it is that with which νοεῖν belongs together: the ἐόν in its twofold.

What does this all mean? It calls upon us to think that, and to what extent, due to the twofold of presencing and that which is present, saying and that which it says is. Νοεῖν listens to εἶναι because, conjoining with λέγειν, it belongs to the twofold of the ἐόν. Saying is at home in the twofold of Being and beings. To what extent? Parmenides gives no answer, because of him the question is remote, as remote as is a discussion of the distinction between λεγόμενον and πεφατισμένον, as a remote as is a meditation on the possible way in which the two-fold essentially belongs together with the essence of language. With re-spect to this remoteness, we latecomers may conjecture and must ask: Is saying at home in the twofold of Being and beings because of the house of *Being* (which always means: of the *Being of* beings), because the house of the twofold is—the house, however, having been built from the essence of language?

Yet wherein does the essence of language reside? We said that saying is letting-lie-before and letting-appear. Language prevails in its essence where appearing prevails, where coming-forth-before is appro-priated (*sich ereignet*): arrival before us into unconcealment and forth from out of concealment. Language is insofar as unconcealment, Ἀ-Λήθεια, is appropriated.

Who or what is Ἀλήθεια? Parmenides names her. His thought-ful telling speaks from out of a listening to her address. Thought in a Greek manner, this means something other than the assurance that what Parmenides pronounces is entirely correct and not false. The fact that Ἀλήθεια speaks in the thinker's saying means rather that the concealed essence of the twofold in the ἐόν *and* the likewise veiled essence of language accompany thinking onto the path that everywhere remains a three-way path. [33]

And yet, Parmenides does not interrogate the essence of Ἀλήθεια. He no more asks concerning the essential provenance of Ἀλήθεια than does any other Greek thinker. Yet presumably they all— including their successors, and most lately Nietzsche in his unpublished essay from 1873, "On Truth and Lie in the Extramoral Sense"—think everywhere under the umbrella and protection of Ἀλήθεια in the sense of the unconcealment of that which is present in its presencing. This occurs even where the relationship of human beings to what is present is explained with the aid of the *lumen naturale*. This "light" already pre-supposes Ἀλήθεια, and was first ignited historically in and through Ἀλήθεια. The visibility granted by Ἀλήθεια lets presencing arise as presencing as "outward look" (εἶδος) and "aspect" (ἰδέα), in keeping with which our fundamental relation to the presencing of what is present comes to be determined as seeing, εἰδέναι, i.e., as knowing—

a determination that still comes to the fore most emphatically in the modern form of the essence of truth as certainty. The Augustinian and medieval theory of light is left in a complete vacuum with respect to the matter at issue—to say nothing of its Platonic heritage—if it is not thought back in the direction of Ἀλήθεια, whose essential provenance remains veiled. Within the same veiling, the essence of language withdraws for a vocation that gives thought to something other than those forms of language that appear and offer themselves to metaphysical (i.e., logical, grammatical, metrical-poetic, biological or sociological, and technological) representation. The theological explanation of the provenance of truth and language from God as first cause can never clarify the essence of what is supposed to be caused in this way, but rather always merely presupposes it; just as every question concerning the origin "of language" in general must already have brought the essence of language and the nature of its essential domain into the clear. At such a moment, however, the customary question of origin falls by the way. [34]

Both fragments (B3 and B8.34ff) think the belonging of νοεῖν to εἶναι, and do so in such a way that each time this belonging is emphatically placed at the beginning of the sentences. In keeping with the Greek text, the τὸ αὐτό and ταὐτὸν must in each case be regarded as the emphatic predicate of a sentence that grammatically speaking has νοεῖν as its "subject." *Only* in the step *back* of a thinking that is no longer Greek and that no longer thinks in an ontological or metaphiscal way at all can and must even τὸ αὐτό be read as the "subject" of such a sentence. Τὸ αὐτό then names the as yet unthought *essence* of Ἀλήθεια, inasmuch as this essence unfolds into the twofold of the ἐόν, a twofold which for its part "needs" the λέγειν τε νοεῖν τε, even though Ἀλήθεια never in itself shelters the essential provenance of the χρή (Fragment B6), since it itself arrives from out of something more concealed.

5.

Yet why, precisely with respect to the belonging together of νοεῖν with εἶναι, does Parmenides bring to the fore something apparently self-evident, namely that fact that "apart from beings" no beings can ever be found anywhere? Manifestly he does so only because νοεῖν gives rise to the appearance that it maintains itself alongside that which "is present." In which case, however, this appearance is not a mere appearance. For the λέγειν and νοεῖν let that which is present lie before in its presencing, and they lie over and against such presencing. The jointure of λέγειν and νοεῖν sets free the ἐὸν ἔμμεναι, the presencing in its appearing, and in so doing in a certain manner keeps itself removed from that which is present. Yet the jointure is able to keep itself removed in this way only insofar as the νοεῖν is a λεγόμενον and as such is something "spoken," that is, something that appears. Yet from where does νοεῖν appear, if not from the twofold itself, insofar as νοεῖν takes this twofold into heed and, from out of such taking, itself first receives the pledge that grants its [essential prevailing?]. Precisely inasmuch [35] as it gives that which is present to be free in its presencing, νοεῖν is drawn into and retained in the twofold of the ἐόν. Nothing that concerns the presencing of that which presences, and certainly not the jointure of λέγειν and νοεῖν, is outside of the twofold or alongside the ἐόν.

Parmenides says (B8.36ff.):

οὐδ' ἦν γὰρ ἢ ἔστιν ἢ ἔσται
ἄλλο πάρεξ τοῦ ἐόντος, ἐπεὶ τό γε Μοῖρ' ἐπέδησεν
οὖλον ἀκίνητόν τ' ἔμμεναι.

Destiny has bound the ἐόν, namely into the twofold. In accordance with this twofold, presencing gathers that which presences in its presencing and absencing. Presencing is a singular and unifying One that prevails as an entirety, cannot be fragmented, and above all is never first pieced together from whatever is present or absent in any particular instance. By contrast to whatever is moved in the manner of what is present or absent, arriving or departing, coming forth or passing away, the ἐόν always remains "without movement" (κίνησις); for it is that στάσις which, in remaining steadfast, itself *lets* whatever is present be *steadfast* in its presencing and absencing. Μοῖρα is the dispensation into the twofold of beings and Being. Such dispensation bestows the destining that is the twofold within which whatever is present appears in presencing. The destiny of "Being" (ἐόν) is the destining of the twofold, a destiny which, however, keeps this twofold as such in the realm of that which is concealed. Only that which is not given up is truly given as a gift whose destining is bestowed the possibilities of its unfolding.

Accordingly, the "history of Being" is never a sequence of occurrences that "Being [taken] by itself," as set off from beings, passes through—as though that history simply opened up, for a new form of historiography, more profound insights into the history of metaphysics as it has hitherto been thought. The "history of Being" is the destiny of the ἐόν in which there occurs the destining of the twofold in the event of appropriation. With this destiny, that which presences comes into unconcealment as that which is present. And the destiny itself? It can neither be explained in terms of that which is present, nor can it be represented in terms of presencing, nor even thought in terms of the twofold as something ultimate.

[36] For this twofold itself remains concealed in this destiny, and it does so precisely through the fact that only that which has become twofold is revealed, namely that which is present and presencing, and that these thereby lay claim upon thinking as representation. The twofold that is represented by way of these terms that belong to it appears in the form of the distinction between the πρότερον and ὕστερον τῇ φύσει, that which precedes and that which comes after with regard to its emergence: the *a priori* and *a posteriori*. With respect to this distinction, one can always insist with complete legitimacy that the difference which sustains all ontology has long been familiar to Western philosophy. It is so emphatically familiar that no occasion is sought or found to ever give thought to the essential provenance of this distinction as a distinction—and in so doing to become thoughtful with regard to thinking hitherto. The growing endeavors to "transform" the existing doctrine of thinking, namely logic, into logistics; the increasing calculative attempts to resituate language in general in the realm of logistical technology; the will to secure all saying (speaking on the radio) and writing as the production of ready-made literature—all these point to the fact that the consummation of metaphysics, which itself thrives from giving no thought to the twofold with respect to its essential provenance, stands only at its tentative beginning.

Nonetheless, this twofold of that which presences and presencing, withheld in its essence, announces its worthiness to be questioned already in the early period of Western thinking. It is all too easily overheard. For the authoritative path that thinking in its beginnings first has to traverse leads above all to its taking into heed the presencing of that which presences, so as to name that wherein it, presencing, shows itself (τὰ σήματα τοῦ ἐόντος). [37]

The λέγειν that lets εἶναι as Ἕν lie before νοεῖν comes to language in such an unquestioned manner that one can all too easily lose sight of the extent to which this path, too, which provides the authoritative measure for the way in which thinking properly proceeds, runs its course within what is worthy of questioning. For it is the path that it is only in its unity with the remaining two paths: the second, which cannot be traveled, and the third, which cannot be circumvented. This three-way path is determined in its unity from out of the first. This unity of the three-way path determines the manner in which early thinking sets out.

From its being guided into paying suitable heed to the three-way path there speaks the gathering of that call which, calling through the twofold, calls upon us to let lie before and to take into heed: that which is present in its presencing (*Anwesendes anwesend*). In the following the gathering of this call, Western-European thinking catches sight of the presencing of that which is present in those coinages of its appearing in accordance with which the fundamental positions of metaphysics are determined.

The dialogue with Parmenides will never come to an end, not only because there remains much that is obscure in the fragments of his "poem" that have been passed on to us, but because what is said itself remains worthy of questioning. The unending nature of the dialogue, however, is not a deficiency, but is the sign of a fullness of that which is worthy of thought, something kept open for thoughtful remembrance.

Whoever, on the other hand, expects only assurance and appease-ment from thinking is demanding the self-annihilation of thinking. Such a demand appears in an odd light when we meditate on the fact that the essence of mortals is called into a heedfulness of the gathering of that call which points them toward that which is to be thought.

Nine

The Ontological Education
of Parmenides

David C. Jacobs

In the history of philosophical reflection, Parmenides' pronouncement about the relationship between being and thinking stands as his pinnacle achievement. In his thinking, τὸ αὐτό links being and thinking in their relationship as a belonging together and not as an identity.[1] Even with this novel reading of τὸ αὐτό opened up by Heidegger and others, much still remains enigmatic about the relationship between being and thinking—and, since this relationship is the center of Parmenides' thinking, much still deserves careful attention in his thought. His Poem can be characterized as a depiction of a goddess instructing a youth on how to think τὸ ἐόν and mortal opinions. Focusing on this education on how to think τὸ ἐόν, we can see how the instruction moves or turns the youth's thought to think τὸ ἐόν in its presence with thought. However, if being and thinking belong together and *are* together in some sort of presence, which we will hold here, then a simple question arises: How are we to make sense of the fact that the Poem is an instruction that attempts to bring thought to being if being and thought always already belong together? We can think through this aporetic character of Parmenides' thought if we consider three things: first, we will examine what is said by Parmenides about the relationship between being and thinking; second, we will lay out the ontological education that Parmenides portrays as occurring between the goddess and the youth; and, third, we will re-think the relationship between being and thinking with the portrayal of the dispensation of τὸ ἐόν.

At the Center: The Belonging Together of Being and Thinking

In Fragment B5, Parmenides' goddess says to her young student, "it is common to me from where I will begin, for there I will return again"

(B5.1–2).² This beginning and the return revolve around τὸ αὐτό that is pronounced in the Poem; Parmenides' thinking begins and returns to this center, a center that allows for the announcement on how to think being. If his Poem is about the thinking of τὸ ἐόν, then τὸ αὐτό, which links being and thinking together in some way, is at the center of the matter at hand. We can place ourselves directly within the problem of τὸ αὐτό if we are cautious and make only preliminary remarks about the occurrence of this phrase in the Poem. These remarks will remain few until we have thought through both participants in their relationship.

This center (or centering) of τὸ αὐτό that links both being and thinking is pronounced twice in Parmenides' Poem. In Fragment B3, Parmenides links νοεῖν and εἶναι by τὸ αὐτό. Enigmatic and somewhat homeless within the Poem, this fragment indicates the central problem of Parmenides' thought. Similar to Fragment B5, this fragment cannot be easily placed within the Poem by philologists for two reasons: (1) there is no obvious connection to other fragments contextually or grammatically, and (2) the fragment seems to characterize Parmenides' thinking as a whole. Fragment B3 reads:

τὸ γὰρ αὐτὸ νοεῖν ἔστιν τε καὶ εἶναι

For the same is thinking and being.

Since many already assume what νοεῖν and εἶναι are prior to their reading of Parmenides, they merely connect the two by *identity* (and, thereby, they force their assumptions into this equation). By doing so, interpreters follow and continue an idealistic tradition that *equates* being and thinking, an equation that allows for the priority of thinking in idealism.³ With Fragment B3 alone, however, we could not easily exclude an idealistic reading, but what is made quite explicit is that being and thinking are linked by τὸ αὐτό.

In Heraclitus, we read a sense of τὸ αὐτό that will be instructive here; its meaning is certainly different from identity. In Fragment B88, he states that the living and the dead, the waking and the sleeping, and the young and the old are τὸ αὐτό.⁴ Here, the phrase means a belonging together and definitely not an identity. Thus, with this precedent in Heraclitus, τὸ αὐτό can also be read in Parmenides as determining the relationship between being and thinking as a belonging together.

When it comes to the difficult lacuna in the final step of the ontological education (B8.34-41), the text in Fragment B8 does not warrant any idealism. Thus, the *identity* between νοεῖν and εἶναι or τὸ ἐόν can be shown to a mere presupposition held prior to any reading. Moreover, the use of τὸ αὐτό in Fragment B8 gives us a deeper glimpse into the relationship between being and thinking. Fragment B8.34 reads:

ταὐτὸν δ'ἔστι νοεῖν τε καὶ οὕνεκεν ἔστι νόημα

The same is thinking and wherefore there is thought.

This "wherefore" (οὕνεκεν, "on account of," "because of") names τὸ ἐόν. It is how we can preliminarily think about τὸ ἐόν. It is on account of τὸ ἐόν that there is any thought (νόημα) at all, that is, that a thought comes to be.[5] The use of τὸ αὐτό here again indicates the relationship between being and thinking. However, more is exhibited here than in Fragment B3. In this line in B8, we see that in order for a thought to occur for νοεῖν, it is on account of τὸ ἐόν. Even in this pronouncement that gives priority to τὸ ἐόν, νοεῖν and τὸ ἐόν are held to be τὸ αὐτό, belonging together.

By running ahead to the center of the Poem, we can note two significant characterizations of the relationship between being and thinking: first, being and thinking belong together and are linked together by τὸ αὐτό and, second, thinking comes to be on account of τὸ ἐόν. We will shortly see that the belonging together is based on presence and that the Poem attempts to determine how thinking is to come to being in their belonging together.

The Ontological Education: The Turning of Thought

Even though thinking is on account of τὸ ἐόν, the Poem begins from the side of νοεῖν. Fragment B1 (the Proem) presents an allegorical description of what is to occur to the youth's thought. It displays how a youth is brought to the house of the goddess guided by the maidens and carried by a chariot. What has to be emphasized is the transporting of the youth. In the first nine lines of the Proem, the following verbs are used: to carry (B1.1, 3, 4), to escort (B1.2, 8), to bring (B1.2), to lead (B1.2, 5), and to pull (B1.5). This overemphasis portrays the urgency to drag the youth away from his mortal thinking and to a proper νοεῖν. The path that he will eventually follow is described by his divine instructor as "far away from the trodden path of humans" (B1.27). The allegory in Fragment B1 suggests how the youth must be forcibly removed and carried away from the "thinking" of mortals, a way of "thinking" that is "carried deaf, blind, and dazed" (B6.6–7). Thus, the Poem begins by explaining how the youth is plucked out of the realm of mortals (i.e., mortal "thinking" or opinions) and placed onto a path that leads to the house of the goddess. Reading the Proem as an allegorical overture for the rest of the Poem suggests the analogous relationship between mortal realm/divine realm and mortal thinking/ontological thinking. With the youth being forcibly removed from the mortal realm and carried to the divine realm, this allegory holds as the image for what is to come in the education: the youth is to learn how to think properly according to the divine; his thinking will be *removed* from mortal thinking and *brought* to think τὸ ἐόν properly.

At the house of goddess, *contact* between the mortal youth and the goddess is made. She takes the youth by the hand and says:

> Youth in the company of immortal charioteers, you reaching my house are carried by the horses, you are welcome, since no ill fate (μοῖρα) has sent you forth to travel this path (for indeed it is far away from the trodden path of humans), but right and justice (θέμις τε δίκη) have sent you (B1.24–28).

We note in passing that μοῖρα, δίκη, and θέμις have this early role in the education; later, we will bring our attention to the divine figures in the ontological education as a whole. Now, however, our concern is the goddess' words that follow:

> It is fitting that you will learn (πυθέσθαι) all things, both the untrembling heart of well-rounded truth and the opinions of mortals, in which there is no true trust (B1.28–30).

The project of the Poem centers on this learning, and this learning is hinged upon the relationship between being and thinking. Immediately after the Poem, the goddess begins to educate the youth on the truth (i.e., teaching him how to think τὸ ἐόν and how to think about mortal opinions), and we can see from the extant fragments that the instruction on the opinions of mortals is separated from the ontological instruc-tion explicitly by the goddess at B8.50–52. Thus, the education of the mortal opinions is executed from B8.53 through the remaining frag-ments (i.e., from the end of B8 through Fragment B19, excluding Cornford's Fragment[6]). Although the education of the opinions of mortals is crucial for the overall education, we will only think through the education of τὸ ἐόν.[7] In the instruction on τὸ ἐόν, the youth's thought, which was just removed from mortal opinion, will move toward τὸ ἐόν and in this movement he will begin to think τὸ ἐόν properly.

The youth's learning of the truth, or what I call the ontological education, has three primary stages:

1. the separation of ἔστιν and οὐκ ἔστιν ("is" and "is not") in Frag-ment B2

2. the instruction to look upon being(s) as present to thought in Fragment B4

3. the thinking of τὸ ἐόν properly, that is, as completely present with thought, by following the signs in Fragment B8

By explaining each of these stages, we can come to think the relation-ship between being and thinking in Parmenides' thought.

First Stage. In Fragment B2, the goddess begins the education of τὸ ἐόν by directing the thinking of the youth; she says, "come, I will tell you and pay heed having heard the story, the only paths (ὁδοὶ) of inquiry there are for thinking" (B2.1–2). The first path is the path (κέλευθος, a path directed toward its goal) of persuasion, for it follows truth (ἀλήθεια); this path is concerned with the thinking that is turned by ἔστιν ("is") (B2.3–4). The second path, the goddess says, is pointed out to be a path (ἀταρπός from ἀτραπός, short-cut, or literally no turn-ing = ἀ + τρέπειν) which is wholly unlearnable; this path is concerned with the thinking that is turned by οὐκ ἔστιν ("is not") (B2.5). One can-not follow this second path because mortals cannot recognize or indi-cate non-being (τὸ μὴ ἐόν, B2.7–8). How the youth is to think, i.e., how his thought is turned in its attention, becomes central. These paths of inquiry, as the goddess tells the youth, are for thinking.[8] His thought can think differently by following one of these paths; the proper path for thinking, which follows ἀλήθεια, is turned by ἔστιν. The improper path, which is wholly unlearnable, is turned by οὐκ ἔστιν. This κρίσις, which separates these two paths, is crucial, for without it the youth would continue to think like a mortal.

This mortal way of thinking constitutes a third possible path for thinking; on this path, one is "guided by the twisted thoughts" of the mortals; here, the mortals are "carried deaf, blind, dazed, [in] uncritical clans, by whom both being and non-being have been thought the same and not the same; the path (κέλευθος) of all things is backward turning (παλίντροπός)" (B6.7–9).⁹ The mortals are uncritical (ἄκριτα), for they have not executed the κρίσις between the first two paths; thus, their thought follows this third path which *conflates* the two. Their thought then thinks being and non-being the same and at other times not the same.

Parmenides here makes a decisive indication in language by which we can characterize the three paths. Although Parmenides relabels the first path and the third path as a κέλευθος, thus indicating that both proceed directly to their goal, the goal of the third path is *both* being and non-being. Hence, we can think of this third path as backward turning (παλίντροπος) or as a turning back and forth. Here, thought in its activity is *palintropic*, turning now to being and after to non-being, and even later to both as belonging together in some way, because the κρίσις between ἔστιν and οὐκ ἔστιν has not been made. In the second path, where no turning (ἀταρπός) takes place, thought is *atropic* since it does not turn toward τὸ ἐόν, or it is *apotropic* since in its turning toward non-being it is turning away from τὸ ἐόν. In the first path, thought is *protropic* for it turns toward τὸ ἐόν. The objective then of the education is to follow the first path, by following truth and by having thought turned by ἔστιν in order to think properly and in the end to think τὸ ἐόν itself.

We can ask here: Since we are concerned (on the side of νοεῖν in the belonging together with τὸ ἐόν) with determining how thought will come to τὸ ἐόν, how will ἔστιν function as the transporter or turning of thought to τὸ ἐόν? We have already noted that the Proem functions as an allegory for the education of the youth. Because of this reading, we ask: How will ἔστιν perform the roles that the maidens, horses, and chariot played in *carrying* the youth to the goddess? How will ἔστιν play this role of bringing thought to τὸ ἐόν? Philological evidence has been given of a use of ἔστιν in Homer's works that supports a "vector" or "conveyer" sense of ἔστιν.¹⁰ From a parallel usage, we can read

Parmenides' ἔστιν as beginning with no subject or predicate content, but both are "filled in" in the transportation of thought toward its goal. This evidence allows us to hold that the education which starts with ἔστιν transports or turns thought toward τὸ ἐόν. Thus, by performing the κρίσις between ἔστιν and οὐκ ἔστιν, the goddess has placed the youth on the path of ἔστιν, which will send or turn his thought to τὸ ἐόν in order to think τὸ ἐόν properly. In this way, thought can come to think and thereby belong with being.

    Second Stage. This stage of the ontological education is the instruction on how to "view" being(s) in a very general sense. In Fragment B4, the goddess says, "look upon beings which are nonetheless absent as firmly present beings with thought" (B4.1).[11] One must look upon or consider beings, which one normally holds as absent from thought, as firmly present with thought; that is, ἀπεόντα (beings that are away) should be thought as παρεόντα (beings that are with or present)—that is, beings that *are with thought.* Here, Parmenides's central positioning of presence in relation to thought is made explicit. Thinking in relation to beings is proper only when one "views" beings as present with thought.[12] The command "λεῦσσε (look upon . . .)," which has a visual emphasis, only clarifies Parmenides' concern with presence. This command by the goddess links thinking and the visual by subordinating the former to a particular aspect of the latter; namely, in seeing, what one sees must be in the presence of one's vision. One cannot see absent beings. *Thinking proper* now can be thought as a thinking that can only think beings as present with thought. *Thought* in its proper functioning *thinks beings* as *present* with thought. It is precisely the meaning of presence here that allows us to understand how we must think about thinking and being(s) in Parmenides' Poem. As we will see, it is in the relationship of thinking τὸ ἐόν as present with thought that will enact the final stage of proper thinking, and it is here in the place of presence that being and thinking properly belong. It is the παρ ("with," "along side") that functions as that which tells us how the belonging together of being and thinking *is.* That is, this "is" is determined by presence. To look upon beings otherwise allows for thought, following the path of οὐκ ἔστιν or the path of mortals, to turn away from τὸ ἐόν completely or to go back and forth between being and non-being.

    The next line of B4 appears to give justification for the first line regarding absent and present beings in relation to thought; it reads, "because it [thought, νόος] will not cut off τὸ ἐόν from holding fast to τοῦ ἐόντος" (B4.2).[13] Implicit, here, is the elimination of thinking τὸ ἐόν as a plurality which is stated in the first line of the fragment (i.e., absent beings and present beings). If the proper function of νόος is to think beings as present with itself, then it cannot cut off τὸ ἐόν from holding fast to τὸ ἐόν. There is no possibility to think a space or void between entities to demarcate different beings, for this would be allowing νόος to cut off parts of τὸ ἐόν. In order to think properly, we must think τὸ ἐόν as present with thought. However, for this to occur, our thought must be directed or turned toward τὸ ἐόν in order to think it entirely. Moreover, in the instruction to think τὸ ἐόν, all-that-is must be shown to be present with thought in order for us to think it at all, and thought must attend to all of τὸ ἐόν. Thus, τὸ ἐόν must be present not only with thought but entirely with itself for proper thinking to occur. The third stage prompts thought to think τὸ ἐόν in this manner.

Third Stage. In this stage of the ontological education, thought is completely turned toward τὸ ἐόν in order to think τὸ ἐόν properly, that is, as entirely present with thought. This final stage occurs by following certain signs (σήματα, B8.2) that prompt four "turnings" to take place.[14] All of these signs forbid νόος to think τὸ ἐόν improperly; they prohibit thought to turn away from τὸ ἐόν and toward non-being, and they disallow thought to turn back and forth between being and non-being. First, one must think τὸ ἐόν as ungenerated and indestructible (B8.3).[15] In order to think τὸ ἐόν as generated and destructible, one would need to involve non-being with τὸ ἐόν, so that one could think that τὸ ἐόν came from non-being or that τὸ ἐόν will go into non-being. Both of these latter options involve thinking τὸ ἐόν as not present with thought and hence are improper. However, thought here is turned away from these possibilities and is turned *toward* τὸ ἐόν by thinking it as ungenerated and indestructible. Hence, thought is turned toward τὸ ἐόν in its presence with thought.

Second, one must think τὸ ἐόν as holding together (συνεχές, B8.6; cf. B8.23).[16] If one were to think τὸ ἐόν as not holding together, a lack of τὸ ἐόν (i.e., a void) would need to be thought in order to separate τὸ ἐόν from τὸ ἐόν. Since thinking properly is thinking τὸ ἐόν as present with thought, to think the lack of something is tantamount to thinking it as not with thought, and this is excluded due to Parmenides' priority given to presence. In order to think this void, one must venture thought down the path away from τὸ ἐόν or the path that goes back and forth between being and non-being. By thinking τὸ ἐόν as holding together with itself, one's thought is turned toward τὸ ἐόν.

Third, one must think τὸ ἐόν as immobile (ἀκίνητον, B8.26).[17] In order to think τὸ ἐόν as mobile, moving from here to there, or as changing from this to that, one would need to think non-being as part of τὸ ἐόν. Parmenides here is exploiting the dual sense of κίνησις, movement and change. Since the first "sign" has eliminated change (i.e., as birth and death), the goddess states that genesis and perishing have been driven off (B8.27–28). For movement, that is, the change from place to place, to occur, one would have to think τὸ ἐόν as having the possibility to be *here* and then later *there*. However, since the *there* into which τὸ ἐόν will move is not (i.e., is not τὸ ἐόν and cannot be thought properly as present with thought), it is impossible to think that τὸ ἐόν will move into this void. Implicit here is the Greek sense of *place* (τόπος). A place is occupied by something, and a being resides in a place. Since there is only τὸ ἐόν, it occupies *the* only place. The goddess instructs that "abiding the same and in the same, it [τὸ ἐόν] lies by itself and abides firmly there in this way" (B8.29–30). By thinking τὸ ἐόν as immobile thought is turned toward τὸ ἐόν.

Fourth, one must think τὸ ἐόν as complete or as not incomplete (B8.32).[18] The completeness of τὸ ἐόν is thought in regards to having a lack, as having more τὸ ἐόν here and less τὸ ἐόν there. Parmenides writes that "if it were lacking it would lack everything" (B8.33). Since τὸ ἐόν is thought of as holding together completely with itself, it would be complete with no lacks at all *or* not be. Since τὸ ἐόν is and is holding together, it lacks nothing. Thus, we must think it as complete. This completeness turns our thought finally to think τὸ ἐόν as *entirely* present with our thought. Not one aspect of τὸ ἐόν is absent from our thought; *all* of τὸ ἐόν is present with our thought. Thus, the youth's education is complete in regards to thinking τὸ ἐόν properly. The thinking of τὸ ἐόν according to these "signs" turns thought toward τὸ ἐόν as complete in order to think all of τὸ ἐόν as present with thought.

Within the ontological education, the thought of the youth is brought to be with τὸ ἐόν in order to have a proper relationship with τὸ ἐόν, that is, being and thinking come to belong with each other in the complete presence of being with thought. Viewing the belonging together of being and thinking from within the side of νοεῖν shows that νοεῖν must come to τὸ ἐόν in some way in order to belong with it properly. The youth's thought is taught to think τὸ ἐόν as completely present with thought. In this way, the youth's thought and thinking come into the belonging together with τὸ ἐόν and hence are τὸ αὐτό. However, we emphasize that the belonging together of being and thinking is grounded on the priority of presence in Parmenides' thinking.

Returning to the Center: The Dispensation of Being

Since Hegel's philosophical interpretation of the history of philosophy as a *history*, philosophy has had to come to grips with viewing its activities as historical. We could certainly delve also into how Nietzsche pushed this historical or genealogical aspect of philosophizing further, but our concern is how, in Heidegger's thought, thinking about our philosophical history takes on a whole new approach and emphasis. Interpretative claims do not maintain the importance they once had. When reading another thinker the thinking that takes place within the dialogue between philosophers becomes the signature of what has occurred. However, this involves attempting to think what is unthought in another philosopher's thinking, not mere presuppositions but nascent thoughts or even the alterity of thinking that brought about the philosopher's thinking from its inception. Although in different terminology, Deleuze and Guattari articulate this new manner of philosophizing about philosophy and the consequences of such activity:

> Even the history of philosophy is completely without interest if it does not undertake to awaken a dormant concept and to play it again on a new stage, even if this comes at the price of turning it against itself.[19]

What we want to do in this last section of this essay is to probe back into the center of Parmenides' Poem and awaken what lies dormant there or what remains unthought. What lies dormant in our dialogue with Parmenides is a "thinking that is awake to the inception" (EGT, 86), that is, the inception of Parmenides' thinking or the inception of our own thinking.

We have already observed, in Parmenides' Poem, that being and thinking belong together, but that the education itself provides for a movement of thinking toward being or a turning of thought toward being to think being in its presence. An ambiguity presents itself: If there is in the reality of τὸ ἐόν no movement and being and thinking belong together, how is it that thought comes to think—or is moved and turned to think—being, if they must always already be present with each other? Many commentators have just boldly decided that Parmenides contradicts himself. However, the supposed progenitor of the excluded middle surely would have more logical sense than to posit a contradiction. Thus, another reading must be more plausible.

We will think through this enigma by re-thinking what Parmenides says about the dispensation of τὸ ἐόν, and our concern will shift to how τὸ ἐόν was given to Parmenides' thinking. We could easily say that the entire Poem is about the giving of τὸ ἐόν to thinking, but first we should look at how Parmenides explicitly describes this giving of τὸ ἐόν to thinking. Δίκη and μοῖρα, first pronounced in the Proem, come to have significant roles in the giving or dispensation of τὸ ἐόν to thinking. From the Proem, we already cited the greeting from the goddess to the youth:

> You are welcome, since no ill μοῖρα has sent you forth to travel this path (for indeed it is far away from the trodden path of humans), but right and justice (θέμις τε δίκη) have sent you (B1.26–28).[20]

No ill μοῖρα, but a μοῖρα nonetheless has sent the youth traveling to the goddess, and this is combined by her enunciation that θέμις and δίκη have sent him. We must highlight the role that these divine figures have later in the final stage of the ontological education. These three have sent him to the goddess to come to think τὸ ἐόν (and mortal opinions), and these same three are articulated as having a significant role in dispensing τὸ ἐόν. We will however concentrate on δίκη and μοῖρα because of the limited role of θέμις in Fragment B8.[21]

Δίκη and μοῖρα are indicated in language as significant as they are shown to participate in the "shackling" of τὸ ἐόν. We must stress the ontological roles of these divine figures and their early function in the Proem where both have part in sending the youth toward the goddess. In the final stage of the ontological education, where the youth is having his thought completely turned toward τὸ ἐόν in order to think it as completely present with his thought, the role of δίκη is crucial. In regard to how the youth must think τὸ ἐόν as ungenerated and indestructible, the goddess says, providing the divine justification of why one must think this way, "neither genesis nor destruction has δίκη allowed, relaxing her shackles, but she holds it [τὸ ἐόν] fast" (B8.13–15). Δίκη here has the significant role in that it is she who is in charge of how τὸ ἐόν *is*; she holds (ἔχει) τὸ ἐόν together in her shackles. It is this ἔχει that determines that τὸ ἐόν is συνεχές—holding together. Thus, we can say that the reason that the youth must think τὸ ἐόν as ungenerated/indestructible and as holding together (i.e., the first two signs of B8) is because δίκη maintains τὸ ἐόν to be in this manner. It is she who determines how τὸ ἐόν is and is to be thought here.

Δίκη appears twice in the Proem. First, the maidens escorting the youth to the goddess must persuade δίκη to open the gateway to the path of the goddess (B1.15–21). As an allegorical overture, this opening is the directing of thought toward τὸ ἐόν for the first time, not yet thinking τὸ ἐόν fully and completely but the turning of one's thoughtful attention toward τὸ ἐόν. Second, δίκη and θέμις (and, in my reading, μοῖρα) are said to have sent the youth traveling to the goddess. How are these very different roles of δίκη connected? Δίκη has the older sense of "way" or "course" as in the functioning of nature,[22] but in this context in Parmenides δίκη has the sense of the manner in which thought comes to τὸ ἐόν and the manner in which τὸ ἐόν must appear to the youth's thought—that is, the manner in which τὸ ἐόν is given to thinking. The youth allegorically travels to τὸ ἐόν to think it properly, but upon his arrival τὸ ἐόν is presented as completely immobile, and he must think τὸ ἐόν in this way. The role of δίκη in Fragment B8 is to disallow genesis and destruction by holding τὸ ἐόν in her shackles. We receive, from Parmenides, thought in its activity in coming or turning toward τὸ ἐόν and τὸ ἐόν in its state of being. Before we think through this dual role of δίκη, we first turn to the role(s) of μοῖρα.

We have already noticed that μοῖρα has a function at the start of the journey to the goddess' house. Near the end of the ontological education, μοῖρα reappears and has a significant function. In fact, her appearance is in the lacuna regarding νοεῖν and τὸ ἐόν in the last step of the final stage of the ontological education. The goddess says, "for nothing other is or will be besides τὸ ἐόν, since μοῖρα shackled it to be whole and immobile (οὖλον ἀκίνητον)" (B8.36–38). We receive here the divine justification for thinking τὸ ἐόν as whole and immobile. Just as δίκη gives the divine justification for the first two signs in the final stage of the ontological education (i.e., thinking τὸ ἐόν as ungenerated/

indestructible and holding together), μοῖρα provides the justification of the last two.[23] Both divine figures render how τὸ ἐόν is to be thought— in fact, how and what τὸ ἐόν is *to be*. Only if τὸ ἐόν is whole and immobile can thought come to think it in its presence with thought. Thus, the main characteristic of τὸ ἐόν is not the signs as many commentators have thought, but its *presence* with thought. The signs prompt thought to think τὸ ἐόν as fully present with thought by thought coming to think or follow in thinking the signs. The signs then present τὸ ἐόν in its presence with thought. That is, they give τὸ ἐόν over to thought so thought can function properly by thinking τὸ ἐόν in its presence. Nothing else is or will be besides τὸ ἐόν, since μοῖρα shackled it to be whole and immobile. Τὸ ἐόν has been determined by μοῖρα to be in this way. Thus, μοῖρα has determined how these signs will function in their presenting of τὸ ἐόν to thinking.

Both δίκη and μοῖρα (and θέμις) send the youth toward the goddess for his education on how to think τὸ ἐόν, but what remains significant and unthought are their roles in the dispensation of how τὸ ἐόν is to appear to thought. As mentioned, δίκη has the older meaning of "way" or "course" and we connected this to the manner in which thought comes to τὸ ἐόν and how τὸ ἐόν is given to thought. The older sense of μοῖρα also aids us in our reading. From the verb μείρομαι ("to receive one's portion"), μοῖρα still has this sense of giving over to others what is their share (their share of land, booty, honor, luck, and fate).[24] Μοῖρα surely is fate but is so because one's share has been given over to one. In our context, μοῖρα dispenses τὸ ἐόν as whole and immobile so that thought can think it in its presence with thought. Both δίκη and μοῖρα function by dispensing τὸ ἐόν in its presence with thought so that it can be thought in its presence.

Significant, then, is the coupling of sending the youth or thought to τὸ ἐόν and the dispensation of τὸ ἐόν to thinking in this particular manner based on presence. Parmenides articulates how τὸ ἐόν gives itself to thinking by presenting thought traveling to τὸ ἐόν, but also how τὸ ἐόν then presents itself or is presented. Parmenides brings to language the dispensation of τὸ ἐόν to thinking by using the movement toward it and by presenting the goddesses as participating in bringing the youth to τὸ ἐόν. Why, then, this strange paradox of immobility and movement? Because τὸ ἐόν presents itself in its presence with thought and Parmenides articulates this presentation, or what Heidegger would call the presencing of what is present.

Tὸ ἐόν presents itself as presence to Parmenides, and he must think τὸ ἐόν in its presence. However, what makes Parmenides an *inceptional thinker* along with Anaximander and Heraclitus, according to Heidegger, is that he not only attempts to think τὸ ἐόν but also how τὸ ἐόν has disclosed itself to thinking (GA 54, 10; P, 7–8). Heidegger writes, "these thinkers are *in-cepted* by the *in-ception* (*vom An-fang An-gefangenen*)" (GA 54, 11; P, 8). Heidegger is emphasizing the root verb latent in *Anfang*: *fangen*, "to capture," "to seize." In Heidegger's thinking, thinking itself is seized (*genommen*) by the claim of being (BW, 264). Parmenides, then, articulates this seizure of thinking by being in bringing to language how thought must be wrenched far away from the trodden path of humans (B1.27). What Parmenides enunciates, through the movement of thought toward being and through the dispensation of τὸ ἐόν, is how thinking was seized by being to think being in its presence with thought, or to think being as presence.[25]

In his Poem, then, Parmenides brings to language how thinking comes to think and how being presents itself to be. Thinking occurs on account of the dispensation of τὸ ἐόν as presence. Thinking, proper thinking for Parmenides, occurs when one thinks τὸ ἐόν in its presence with thought itself. Given the dispensation of τὸ ἐόν as presence and the fact that one must come to think τὸ ἐόν in its presence, Parmenides brings to language how thinking comes to think by depicting thought in its travel or turning toward τὸ ἐόν in order to have the proper belonging together based on presence. Parmenides' accomplishment, then, was to articulate how τὸ ἐόν is given to his thinking as presence, the belonging together of being and thinking, the coming to think, and proper thinking of τὸ ἐόν in its presence with thought.

Conclusion: What Deserves More Thought

Heidegger ends his essay, "Moira," with "the dialogue with Parmenides never comes to an end . . . because what is said there continually deserves more thought" (EGT, 100–1). Indeed, our reading of Parmenides' ontological education is merely the opening up of a space to think through the enigma at the center of his thought. Much more remains to be thought, and as Heidegger says, much more *deserves* to be thought. Here, we can end with a few questions that can prompt further inquiries. One must question the role of the signs in Fragment B8. How do the signs function in dispensing τὸ ἐόν to thinking? We have viewed the signs as turning thought toward τὸ ἐόν, but how in the end are they τὸ ἐόν itself in its dispensation to thinking? If they can be thought as τὸ ἐόν, how do they reveal and thereby conceal τὸ ἐόν in its dispensation?

One must examine the role of the goddess' μῦθος in relation to how one is to speak (λέγειν) of τὸ ἐόν. Does her μῦθος disclose τὸ ἐόν to the thinking of the youth? If so, then how is his instruction on λέγειν connected to her μῦθος? Is his λέγειν, the proper saying of τὸ ἐόν by mortals, similar to Heraclitus's ὁμολογεῖν in Fragment B50, where to be wise is to listen to the λόγος and then to say (ὁμολογεῖν) one is all?

One must consider the role that μοῖρα has in the Poem in the dispensation of τὸ ἐόν and how τὸ ἐόν in its dispensation is a historical event. When τὸ ἐόν is given to thinking as presence, how is this constitutive of the center of philosophical thinking in the West? These questions merely continue since the task of thinking does not come to an end. Also, our dialogue with Parmenides revolves again and again in the belonging together of the beginning and the end of thinking, for "it is common to me from where I will begin, for there I will return again" (B5.1–2).

NOTES

1. Reading τὸ αὐτό as a belonging together has also been pointed out by Heidegger in EGT, 87, and by T. M. Robinson, "Parmenides on Ascertainment of the Real," *Canadian Journal of Philosophy*, vol. 4, no. 4 (June 1975), 627.

2. All translations of Parmenides' Poem are my own from the Greek in DK; cf. David Gallop's translation, *Parmenides of Elea: Fragments* (Toronto: University of Toronto Press, 1987).

3. Cf. Hegel's words, based on Fragment B8.34, not Fragment B3: "Thinking produces itself and what is produced is a thought; thinking is thus identical (*identisch* for ταὐτὸν) with its being, for it is not outside of being—this great affirmation" (G. W. F. Hegel, *Lectures on the History of Philosophy*, vol. 1, trans. E. S. Haldane and F. H. Simson (Atlantic Highlands, NJ: Humanities Press, 1983), 253; *Vorlesungen über die Geschichte der Philosophie*, vol. 1, in *Sämtliche Werke*, vol. 17 (Stuttgart: Fr. Frommanns, 1959), 312). In the end, which is hidden within the beginning, we find that Absolute Spirit is this being which is coming to think/know itself. Although most commentators repeat the idealistic presupposition of the identity pronounced by τὸ αὐτό, most do not follow Hegel's overall view.

4. DK, Heraclitus, B88; cf. in *Heraclitus: Fragments*, trans. and ed. T. M. Robinson (Toronto: University of Toronto Press, 1987). In these contraries, for Heraclitus, their belonging together also has the added sense of changing into one another—a meaning that Parmenides does not have with τὸ αὐτό as the belonging together of νοεῖν and εἶναι. Also, see Robinson's essay in note 1.

5. We must note the reversal: in early Greek thought, thinking is dependent upon being; in the height of modernity with Hegel, being is dependent upon thinking (see Heidegger, EGT, 82).

6. See F. M. Cornford, "A New Fragment of Parmenides," *Classical Review*, vol. 49 (1935), 122–123.

7. I have discussed the education of the opinions of mortals in "Parmenides' Two Accounts of Mortal Contrariety and the Distinction between Being and Non-being," presented at the Metaphysical Society of America, Villanova University, March 1992, and in "Learning to Think *To Eon* in Parmenides' Poem," ch. 4 ("The Naming and Thinking of *To Eon* as Contraries"), Ph.D. Dissertation, Vanderbilt University, 1993.

8. We are reading the infinitive νοῆσαι as final, which means that the paths are there "for thinking" and should not be read as "to be thought." See Alexander P.D. Mourelatos, *The Route of Parmenides* (New Haven: Yale University Press, 1970), 55–56, note 26.

9. Parmenides uses πέλειν here not τὸ ἐόν or εἶναι, possibly, to emphasize the mortals' confusion.

10. See Alexander P. D. Mourelatos, "Determinacy and Indeterminacy, Being and Non-Being in the Fragments of Parmenides," in *New Essays on Plato and the Pre-Socratics*, eds. R. Shiner and J. King-Farlow, *Canadian Journal of Philosophy*, Supplemental, vol. 2 (1976), 45–60; and "Some Alternatives in Interpreting Parmendies," *The Monist*, vol. 62, no. 1 (January 1979), 3–14. Two of the examples from Homer that Mourelatos supplies are:

> Now there *is* a certain island, in mid-sea, rocky, midway between Ithaca and rugged Samos, Maiden Star, not large . . . (O, 4.844).

> Now there *was* among the Trojans one Dares, bountiful, blameless, priest of Hephaestus . . . (I, 5.9).

What Mourelatos argues for in Homer's use is that the subject and the predicate of these verb uses have been suppressed and the use of ἔστιν transports "thought" toward the filling in of the subject and predicate. My concern with this philological evidence is that ἔστιν transports νοεῖν toward τὸ ἐόν.

11. I translate νόος as "thought" and νοεῖν as "thinking" because Parmenides, in the way he constructs his thoughts, maintains νόος as an apparatus separate from thinking. It is νόος that thinks, but νόος can think improperly. Thus, I think that Parmenides is maintaining thought as an apparatus separate from proper thinking.

12. Thinking can be further understood as "to attend" with its multiple meanings of "to be present with," "to look after," and "to take heed of." The Latin *attendere* can help us in understanding thinking here. It is from *at-* ("toward") and *tendere* ("to stretch," "to extend," "to tend to") and has the sense of "to stretch toward," "to take heed of," and "to turn one's attention to." Its base comes from the Greek τείνειν, "to stretch by force." With these many meanings in place, we are taking thinking as an attending which is the stretching toward τὸ ἐόν as it comes to be present with it and to take heed of it.

13. This line eliminates an idealistic reading of Parmenides' thought. It shows precisely that thought and hence thinking are subordinate to being, that is, that thought and thinking do not determine what τὸ ἐόν is.

14. Most commentators on Parmenides, especially those within the Anglo-American tradition, have held that these "signs" are arguments for the qualities of τὸ ἐόν. They just might be arguments or proto-arguments, but what deserves to be thought is how they turn thought toward τὸ ἐόν.

15. Parmenides discusses the problems of generation and destruction at B8.6–21.

16. Parmenides discusses thinking τὸ ἐόν as holding together at B8.22–25.

17. Parmenides discusses the thinking of τὸ ἐόν as immobile at B8.26–31.

18. Parmenides discusses the completeness of τὸ ἐόν at B8.32–33 and at B8.42–49.

19. Gilles Deleuze and Félix Guattari, *What Is Philosophy?*, trans. H. Tomlinson and G. Burchell (New York: Columbia University Press, 1994), 83.

20. Δίκη is twice mentioned in the Proem. In the above citation and in the following words:

> There are the gates of both the paths of the night and day, and a lintel and a threshold of stone holds them apart, and the aetherial gates are filled with mighty doors; and δίκη, much-avenging, holds the keys of exchange of these. The maidens coaxing her with soft words, cunningly persuaded her so that she would push back the bolted bar for them swiftly from the gates; and these (opening wide) made from the doors a wide chasm, revolving in their sockets of the brazen door posts fastened together with bolts and bins; at once, the maidens guided the chariot and horses straight through them (B1.11–21).

Significant here is the imagery that δίκη maintains as allowing the entourage through to the divine realm, which as an allegory for the education would be the turning toward τὸ ἐόν to think it properly.

21. Although θέμις is mentioned, it is another divine figure that seems to have the responsibility of maintaining τὸ ἐόν. The goddess says, "for strong

necessity (ἀνάγκη) holds it fast in the chains of a limit, which fences it about. Wherefore it is not right (θέμις) for being to be incomplete" (B8.30–32). Thus, it appears that ἀνάγκη is the ruling factor in relation to τὸ ἐόν.

22. See F. M. Cornford, *From Religion to Philosophy* (Atlantic Highlands, NJ: Humanities Press, 1980), 172–174.

23. That is, if we take "whole" and "complete" to have the same meaning which is justified in the Poem.

24. Edmund Berry writes that it is now generally recognized that μοῖρα, which is from the verb μείρομαι ("to receive one's portion"), came to mean "fate" but thought in the sense of receiving one's lot or share in life (Edmund Grindlay Berry, "The History and Development of the Concept of THEIA MOIRA and THEIA TUCHE Down to and Including Plato" (Ph.D. Dissertation, University of Chicago, 1940), 1–2).

25. Two instances of the depiction of the seizure of thinking in Parmenides's Poem are: In the Proem, when the youth reaches the goddess' house to receive his education, Parmenides writes, "the goddess readily received me hospitably and took my right hand with her hand, and spoke these words . . . " (B1.22–23). This hospitable contact between the mortal and the divine allegorically names the goddess' friendly and pedagogical hold upon the youth in his ontological education. This contact between the youth and the goddess allegorically presents the "contact" between the belonging together of being and thinking. Also, when the youth's thought is entirely turned toward τὸ ἐόν and he thinks it in its full presence with thought, τὸ ἐόν has a complete *hold* over his thinking, for the transition into the education of mortal opinions attests to this. As the goddess stops her λόγος about truth, she comments that the opinion of mortals will now not ever overtake him (B8.61). His thinking has been seized or taken in on how to think properly, and any incorrect teaching he now hears will not affect him. Both references show that Parmenides did bring to language the seizure by τὸ ἐόν and in this way his thinking belonged to τὸ ἐόν in its dispensation to thinking as presence.

Ten

Heraclitus Studies

Hans-Georg Gadamer
Translated by Peter Warnek

Heraclitus remains a continual challenge for every thinker. Men such as Hegel, Nietzsche, and Heidegger met this challenge in fundamentally different ways. Countless philological commentaries have been carried out. What was true for antiquity seems no less true today. He remains "The Obscure." There is no reliable basic orientation that permits grasping this radiant figure standing between morality and metaphysics. Yet it strikes me that two points have not been considered adequately: the way in which Plato takes up Heraclitus and the style employed by Heraclitus in the formation of his statements.

I shall offer an account of the philosophical importance connected with every interpretation of Heraclitus, and then I shall enter into the hermeneutical problems that can often be of a philological sort. What we have of Heraclitus is limited to citations made by later authors who begin with Plato and stretch throughout the entire later antiquity. Moreover, one finds sentence-like propositions that were already renown in antiquity for their obscurity and profundity. Socrates is supposed to have said that what he understood of them he found to be excellent. He trusted that this was the case with the many others that he did not understand. To be sure, it would take a Delian diver—a master diver—to retrieve this treasure from the depths and to bring it to light.[1]

Yet, there is still another enormous difficulty continually leading us astray in all philosophical understanding of Greek thought, and this difficulty is also the case when it comes to Heraclitus. It is the continual effect of the rise of modern science, the pioneering act of which was Galilean physics, that dominates all our habits of thought. Henceforth, the concept of method was taken as constitutive for what is to be called science. [44] Connected with this is the fact that modern philosophy established its philosophical self-grounding upon the concept of self-consciousness. As a rule, one turns to Descartes's famous meditation on doubt for the revolution that is instigated with the development of the modern natural sciences. There the *"cogito ergo sum"* was distinguished as the indubitable reality of the one who thinks and doubts and as the most sure and unshakable fundament of all certainty. This was, to be sure, not yet a philosophy of reflection in the full sense of the word, which is grounded in the concept of subjectivity and which newly defines the meaning of objectivity in terms of this subjectivity. However, since Kant took up this Cartesian designation of the *"res cogitans"* in the critical demonstration of his transcendental philosophy and grounded the justification of the concepts of the understanding upon the synthesis of apperception, upon the fact that the "I think" must be able to accompany all my representations, the concept of subjectivity has been elevated to a position of centrality. Those who followed Kant, above all Fichte, programmatically developed the derivation of all justification of truth, all grounding of validity in general, from out of the principal of self-consciousness. In this way, the primacy of self-consciousness over and against "consciousness of something" became the stigma of modern thought. Even Husserl's ambitious attempt to achieve philosophy actually as an exact science for the first time remains planted in this soil, and it is from this soil that the bold thought experiments of Heidegger and Wittgenstein sought to free themselves. German Idealism had indeed at that time conceived of something that was well suited to philosophically characterizing the new place of the humanity in the world, this aggressive posture of modern science over and against the nature that surrounds us. Subjectivity, as transcendental philosophy, accompanied the victory march of modern science. Doubts concerning the certainty of self-consciousness have since then taken hold of modern thought and have kept it uneasy. Our century is determined by this in the most profound way. It began with Nietzsche. With regard to Descartes's meditation on doubt, the psychologist in Nietzsche set forth the injunction: "a more fundamental doubt is needed." This culminated in the radical shaking of naive self-certainty and led to doubts concerning the assertions of self-consciousness, doubts that arise from the most divergent perspectives, such as in historicism, in the critique of ideology or in psychoanalysis. It has since become an unavoidable task to think through again and again the central philosophical problem of self-consciousness.

With regard to this question we can be guided by the phenomenological evidence which Franz Brentano first reproduced but which by no means was missed by Aristotle, neither in his "anthropology" (*De Anima*, Γ) nor even in the grounding of his "first philosophy" upon the self-thinking *nous*. [45] Over and against the intentionality of consciousness, which is always consciousness of something, the reflexivity of self-consciousness possesses secondary importance. The primacy of self-consciousness can hold only if one attributes an absolute priority to the ideal of certainty, or, better still, to the ideal of a methodological confirmation of the validity and reality of mathematical construction, which, since Galileo, has made up the essence of modern natural science.

Even though the god of Aristotelian ontotheology is indeed the highest being (as the *"primum movens"* and as constant self-presence), it has in no way the function of grounding or securing human knowledge. The structure of selfhood points to other contexts than the *"fundamentum inconcussum"* by which self-consciousness maintains itself against all skepticism. If something can truly come to the aid of our modern concern with the riddle of self-consciousness, it is the fact that the Greeks had in their possession neither an expression for the subject or subjectivity nor an expression for consciousness and the concept of the I. Inasmuch as they surely did after all take into regard the wonder of thinking itself, by no means did they assert—and this includes Aristotle—the central position of self-consciousness.

In order to free oneself from this most modern perspective, one finds oneself referred back to the historical dimension which leads from Descartes to Augustine, and from Augustine to Plato. I would like to show now that it must be followed back further still, from Plato to Heraclitus.

The question arises whether one may view Heraclitus at all from the point of view of this problem of self-consciousness, or whether his thinking does not instead point in another direction, namely, to the place of the human in the world. Heraclitus enjoys a special fame. He owes this not only to the aphoristic obscurity that we have already mentioned, nor only to the use that was already of his name by Plato, nor, finally, only to his presence in Hegel, who said at the end of the entire movement of thought of Western metaphysics that there was not a single proposition of Heraclitus that he was not able to take up into his logic. Heraclitus's thinking exerts an utterly peculiar attraction upon the radical extremism of Nietzsche and upon Heidegger's insight into the end and the beginning of metaphysics. Anyone who visited Heidegger's hut up in the Black Forest even once saw the Heraclitean statement, "Lightning steers all things,"[2] carved into a piece of bark above the entrance—a strange and deeply troubling statement, an obvious paradox. Instead of the calm hand [46] that guides the ship through the waves, there is the lightning bolt that suddenly erupts and is then extinguished. One can puzzle over the meaning of this sentence, but the dominant interpretation until now which sees the lightning as an attribute of the all-governing godhead fails to take heed of the paradox in Heraclitus which certainly must not be ignored. The particular fascination that Heraclitus engenders does not ultimately have to do with the paradoxical and dialectical structure of such statements. The speculative tension of his thinking leads him repeatedly to the most extremely sharpened formulations. They are all like the statement on the eternal flowing river into which one can never step into again as the same—and from out of which the souls rise as vapors (Fragment B12).

Now, admittedly, as modern researchers educated in historical critique, we cannot allow ourselves to become entangled straight off with naive determinations of what such sentences might mean. We have to concentrate upon the particular conditions of the tradition which grant us access to the texts we are reading as fragmented pieces. Meanwhile, we know all to well what citations are, what can be done with citations, how they can be misused, and how their meaning can be covered over to the point of indecipherability. Investigation into Heraclitus presents therefore a special hermeneutic task. One must continually be asking oneself: How is it possible to uncover or strip away the prior understanding that has been transmitted to us through the authors who offer these citations? By what means can we arrive at a historically appropriate yet philosophically expressive understanding of Heraclitus and his statements?

A certain priority, I believe, can be granted in advance to our most ancient witness—and this is Plato. His writings are the very first philosophical texts that we possess in their entirety. Everything earlier is fragmentary, that is, quotations or collections of quotations from later writers who were still familiar with Heraclitus's "book" but who, at the same time, appropriated it for their own purposes. Plato, of course, did this as well; he furthered his own thinking through his references to Heraclitus. However, he is still our most ancient witness.

The Platonic dialogues yield a peculiarly ambiguous and conflicting picture of Heraclitus. On the one hand, Heraclitus is brought forward as the originator and symbol of a view of the world which knows nothing of the abiding sameness of the essence of things, the "εἶδος," but which instead sees all things in change and in flux. In a well known elaboration in *The Theaetetus*, Plato designates all previous thinkers, from Homer to Protagoras (with the single exception of Parmenides), as Heracliteans (*Theaetetus*, 152e). For someone familiar with the manner of Plato, Heraclitus is caricatured here into a type that does not necessarily correspond to what Plato himself saw in Heraclitus—or even what Heraclitus actually said and intended. It is amazing what Plato summarizes here as Heraclitean. Heraclitus here stands for merely a kind of counter-type. What is offered under his name [47] is in Plato's view intended to emphasize the one exception to what the great Eleatic represents, as the precursor to Plato's own thought of the εἶδος.

If we attend to the other references to Heraclitus in Plato's work, the matter suddenly seems completely different. In a famous passage in *The Sophist*, to which we must turn for the origin of all our acquired familiarity with Presocratic doctrines (*Sophist*, 242c ff.), it is said that, with regard to Plato's predecessors, some taught the many as true being, while others, against this, taught only the one as true being. The Ionic and Sicilian muses, however, hold it to be more clever to weave the one and the many together. "Ionic muses" means here without doubt Heraclitus. Of these Ionic muses who speak through Heraclitus, it is then said that they had thought more precisely than the Sicilian muses, in that they had not taught only the alternation of multiplicity and unity, and of world-periods of dissolution and reconstitution into unity, as had the doctrinal poems of Empedocles in the eyes of Plato. The more precise thesis is the simultaneity of the one and the many, the simultaneity of self-dispersion and self-unification. This is attributed here to Heraclitus: the one and the many do not alternate but rather, together, are the whole truth of being. In this context, Plato has the Eleatic stranger invoke a statement of Heraclitus. This statement is found one other time in Plato and is there cited by the physician Eryximachus (*Symposium*, 187a). The exact formulation of the statement is uncertain, as is the case with most Greek citations. It belongs to the elegance of writing that, as much as possible, one does not introduce a literal citation, but rather builds it into one's own movement of thought. One of the major challenges Greek texts place upon us is to hazard where a citation actually begins and to what extent it is being fitted into the current movement of thought.[3] The statement legitimated by Plato runs: διαφερόμενον ἀεὶ συμφέρεται (Sophist, 242e). To this corresponds: τὸ ἕν γάρ φησι διαφερόμενον αὐτὸ αὑτῷ συμφέρεσθαι ὥσπερ ἁρμονίαν τόξου τε καὶ λύρας (Symposium, 187a; cf. Fragments B51 and B8). Translated, this means: "The one that in itself places itself over and against itself always joins together with itself."

This is a most paradoxical dialectical formulation. Heraclitus is fond of giving examples for such paradoxes. So he continues in The Symposium, it is "like the harmony of bow and lyre." And similarly: "The barely drink that is not stirred separates."[4] Heraclitus has illustrated his own genuine wisdom, his σόφον, in many such examples. The same phrase which is found in The Sophist (242e) is placed in the mouth of the physician Eryximachus in The Symposium (187a). This is significant, because [48] his lack of understanding for the speculative unity of that which is opposed is caricatured in the manner in which the physician directs a haughty critique at Heraclitus. The passage in The Sophist shows unambiguously that Plato himself understood quite well that Heraclitus did not, like Eryximachus, mean the unity as the finally emerging result (ἔπειτα ὕστερον ὁμολογησάντων, Symposium, 187b1). On the contrary, what is decisive is the simultaneity (cf. Fragment B8: τὸ ἀντίξουν συμφέρον). Thus, we have here a secure starting-point which, moreover, is corroborated through countless variations on the same point. The question is how we are to bring together the Heraclitism of the things being constantly in flux and the tense dialectical unity which is compressed, as it were, into such statements.

Let us proceed from the phenomena that Heraclitus had in view. Here is the river into which all things in constant change flow. However, it is the same river.[5] In the end the river, too, is an example for the unity of opposites of which Heraclitus speaks in countless ways: war and peace, hunger and satiety, mortal and immortal, gods and humans, etc. He gives an abundance of extreme oppositions, and he maintains that all of them are one. The example of the river is the best one to introduce here, since it invokes the unity of the course of the river and the restlessness of its flowing. The mysterious problem that shows itself behind all these oppositions becomes manifest: what is the same shows itself as an other *without transition*. In all these examples, what appears is what the Greeks called μεταβολή, change. It is distinguished by its abrupt suddenness. The fundamental experience of thinking here appears to be that of the essential unreliability of everything which shows itself first one way and then otherwise. In the next moment, it can again present itself in a different way, no longer as before. This insight into the unreliability of all things, which is indeed also already at the basis of Eleatic thought, without a doubt, inspired Plato's thinking of the "εἶδος." The ironic artificiality with which the Heracliteans are introduced in *The Theaetetus* suggests that Plato first of all built up the opposing notion of this universal flux, in order, I believe, to proliferate his thought of the εἶδος. Also, perhaps in Cratylus or in other "genuine" Heracliteans, he had already encountered such a doctrine. This seems to me to follow indirectly from the manner in which the Eleatic thematic is set aside in *The Theaetetus*. In this text, there is not only the intriguing intimation that Eleatic thinking and *The Sophist* in particular are being referred to. The reason given for Socrates leaving aside the teaching of Parmenides, in my opinion, speaks much more clearly: "because without that for which our conversation is underway, [49] the essence of knowledge would remain uninvestigated"[6]—as if to say that knowledge would be comprehensible only without Eleatic thought. Clearly, this is indeed the very lesson that Theaetetus must draw from the dialogue with Socrates. And, for this reason, the Eleatic stranger takes over the conversation on the next day. In this dialogue concerning the sophists, Theaetetus first learns what knowledge is: not immediate evidence, but rather λόγος. However, would Heraclitus himself also have had to learn this? This process theory that Socrates in *The Theaetetus* develops from out of the doctrine of the flux has its strongest support in the statement of Heraclitus concerning the continually renewed waters that flow through the same streams. This appears, however, to take a completely different direction: "The souls too rise from the vapors" (Fragment B12)—and still the λόγος of these appears unfathomable (Fragment B45). That appears to be Heraclitus's profound meaning, and this is precisely the concern that modernity especially takes upon itself. The structure of self-consciousness appears to be implicit here—and the λόγος is indeed thought as a world principle. Hegel *ante diem*.

How does this fit with the rest of the tradition? This is decisively determined by Aristotle, as is well known. He is the main source for our knowledge concerning the Presocratics in general. However, in Aristotle, things do not look good for Heraclitus. Aristotle tells us, apparently on account of Heraclitus's paradoxical formulations, that some assert that Heraclitus did not hold the basic principle of all knowledge, the principle of contradiction, to be valid (*Metaphysics*, Γ3, 1005b24). This could come as no recommendation in the eyes of Aristotle, even if he himself obviously does not take this polemical assertion completely seriously. More weight must be given to the fact that his own main concern (i.e., physics) is extraordinarily difficult to connect with Heraclitus. This has yet to be considered carefully. The guiding perspective of Aristotle, which he sees confirmed in his review of the Presocratics and which he asserts against the Pythagoreanism of Plato, is not so much the joining of the all according to counting and proportions as it is the constitution of the being of "nature" (φύσις), that is, a self-movement from out of itself: the insight into the nature of the all teaches that it maintains itself, moves and orders itself, that in itself it is in balance. Thus, in his eyes, Greek cosmology was developed as the basic truth of the cosmogonies of the most ancient thinkers, cosmogonies which originally were religious but which gradually gained support through disciplined observation. The world is not in need of any Atlas to carry it. It maintains itself and holds itself in order. (This is also the case in *The Phaedo*, cf. 99b–c.) [50]

What we know of Heraclitus does not fit in especially well with this. That beings at bottom are fire is a position not especially well-suited to gaining an understanding of either the stable order of the world totality or an account of its emergence. No limits can prevent the all-consuming-fire from devouring everything. It does not lend itself to a proper accord with the other "elements." Plato's *Timaeus* offers us a portrayal of how in the ordering of the universe, by means of calculation and the doctrine of proportions, not only earth and fire are artfully kept distinct from each other but also, by means of air, water and fire (*Timaeus*, 31b ff.). When Anaximander, one of the greatest Ionic researchers prior to Heraclitus, is supposed to have explained the role of the heavenly body and its shape, he seems to be in a great predicament. The sun, the moon (in case one does not know that its light is only borrowed), and the stars are indeed fire. However, how can fire have such a clear shape and boundary, always lighting in the same way? At this point, Anaximander comes upon the idea of the holes or openings in the great vault of the heavens through which the concealed raging fire shines for us as a peaceful luminescence. This much at least is relayed to us by the doxography (DK 12 A11).

Now, there is certainly another way to think the mysterious essence of fire as a cosmic principle, and this is to think its presence in everything that is warm. There is something significant about the fact that the origin of life depends on warmth. One only has to think of the doxography on Anaximander in order to illustrate this (DK 12 A30). However, a material interpretation of fire as an element of things is not thereby given. The evidence for this is not exactly favorable. In fact, in *The Cratylus* (413c3), Plato mentions an interpretation of fire as "the warm itself" (αὐτὸ τὸ θερμόν) within fire, but in a context that is not only extremely playful and which also does not at all fit into a cosmogonical perspective. *The Cratylus* (413b4, c1) is instead alluding to Heraclitus's image of the sun which constantly ignites anew (νέος ἐφ᾽ ἡμέρῃ Fragment B6), or possibly the sun which never sets (τὸ μὴ δῦνόν ποτε, Fragment B16). The allusion to the sun of Heraclitus in *The Republic* (VI, 498a) also documents that this Heraclitean teaching was indeed known, but not especially renowned for its cosmological progressiveness. In other passages in Plato's work, where fire and warmth appear as almost the same,[7] nothing, in any case, hearkens back to Heraclitus. Aristotle hardly mentions Heraclitus in his introductions to *The Physics* and *The Metaphysics*. Simplicius (*Physics*, 24, 1 ff.) brings forth a pure construct which seems to have its origin in Theophrastus and which has a good understanding of its own awkwardness.[8] [51]

Even if we assume that fire is in everything warm and thereby everything living, which we might if we perhaps relied on Plato,[9] the cosmological problem of fire remains difficult. It does not easily let itself be taken as an element, that is, as a constitutive part. Aristotle is really at a loss with this problem. It is in fact not easy to see how one might build up a cosmology on the basis of the original phenomenon of fire. However, did Heraclitus present a cosmology at all?

We have reasons to doubt this. To begin with, there is an ancient tradition which, in my opinion, has not been taken seriously enough. It seems that the impact of Aristotle and Theophrastus was so powerful that the Presocratics in general were all seen as cosmologists. However, we take this from a stoic in the Ciceronian period, Diodotos, who still knew Heraclitus's text; he maintained that the text did not at all deal with nature but with the "πολιτεία," the state. When nature was discussed, this was meant only as a way to give illustrative examples.[10] One has to ask oneself whether this really was just a moralistic stoic reinterpretation—as in without doubt suggested by the alleged title (*A More Accurate Compass for the Course of Life*[11])—or whether there is not some truth to it. If we review the bulk of the citations of Heraclitus, we find in any case a large number of overt and provocative political and moral statements. There is, for example, again and again a bitter criticism of political naiveté and the superficial sensibility of the people of his own land. We also have other sentences which belong entirely to the dimension of the moral and political. Semantic details point in this same direction. The word "φρόνησις" is in Greek usage primarily "practical rationality" and thus does not really mean the theoretical use of reason.[12] Thus, there is a whole host of indications advising us to take seriously what the stoic said.[13] One has to ask oneself whether Heraclitus was a rival of the Ionic cosmologists at all or whether he did not instead work as one of their critics—in the way that Parmenides, too, without doubt had brought about a critique. [52]

How is one supposed to decide such a question, when the tradition not only offers no help but actually promotes errancy? It is not only the agenda of the meta-physician Aristotle that takes us in this direction. However, the moralistic exposition of the alleged cosmologists through the later stoics and Church fathers also imports something foreign, namely, the world "conflagration." For the Church fathers, this was to be conceived of as the fire of hell. They were able to impute that Heraclitus already knew something about this. This was the manner in which they took the fire doctrine. They were also aware that the stoics had taught the conflagration of the world, the ἐκπύρωσις. With the Christian theologians, the conflagration of the world becomes the judgment of the world. However, does the Heraclitean statement, to which all of this seems to be traceable, actually say that everything will go up in fire? It is Fragment B66: πάντα γάρ, φησί, τὸ πῦρ ἐπελθὸν κρινεῖ καὶ καταλήψεται.

What is the correct translation? As a rule, one understands the two Greek verbs as "to condemn" and as "to take hold of" or "to put under arrest." These are words that are indeed known as legal expressions and to this extent fit the image of the last judgment. Thus, in this manner, Hippolytus also enthusiastically cites this sentence. However, κρίνειν also means first of all "to cut, to differentiate, to separate." The sentence could therefore very likely mean that fire separates everything.[14] All is consumed in the heat of the fire, until it turns to cinders. Likewise, καταλαμβάνειν is a far cry from always meaning "to put under arrest" but at first simply means "to take hold of," "to grasp." This is indeed what fire is; it can place all things into the burning embers, such that the stones themselves (the coals) become fiery as they glow in the blaze—a beautiful and vivid example of the way the earth, too, "becomes fire."[15] In fact, the magma of the volcano is a good illustration of this. Thus, the sentence in Heraclitus that is summoned up for the ἐκπύρωσις could have had a completely different meaning than the one that as a rule is laid upon it. However, who knows? That the sentence had *primarily* the sense which has been outlined here—and at most only allowed the latent "moralistic" meaning to resonate slightly—this must still be weighed carefully. It is of course only a hypothesis which can present no self-reliant evidence. Still, there is, after all, a good bit of supporting evidence for this sentence and its interpretation, above all in the play upon etymology in *The Cratylus* (412d ff.). There fire is named, in addition to ἥλιος and Anaxagorian νοῦς, as "the warm itself" within fire (413c3) which permeates all appearances and which is linked to the just (the δίκαιον). [53] This is in fact "Heraclitean," in the sense given in *The Cratylus*, to the extent that this swiftest and finest (τάχιστον καὶ λεπτότατον, 412d5), through its relative velocity, lets everything else appear as being (ὥστε χρῆσθαι ὥσπερ ἐστῶσι τοῖς ἄλλοις, 412d7)—just as the theory of movement in *The Theaetetus* (156c ff.) interprets "being." At any rate, the play in *The Cratylus* best reflects the manner in which, through the fire which is all pervasive, the right (the δίκαιον) is replenished, as it were, with materiality.[16]

Let us ask ourselves, in the midst of this uncertainty inherited from the tradition, how we might proceed further. In my opinion, there is only one method of access: the *morphological*. The structure of unambiguous sentences which can belong only to Heraclitus can be established because they resemble each other as if they were members of the same family. This is not to claim that we could distinguish with certainty the imitations or reinterpretations from the genuine words of Heraclitus in each individual case. Family resemblance, too, has no original image which might provide a standard for what is similar. (Wittgenstein's metaphor considered family resemblance in this way in his critique of nominalist prejudices.) It thus speaks in no way against the guiding thought of a morphological inquiry—that is, that it can produce no strict criterion. Moreover, even where something is being imitated, the structure of thought that is imitated may not be completely unrecognizable. And if this is so, then the imitation offers instruction. For example, by following the path of a morphologically determined reduction, I have reclaimed a fragment that up until now has been lacking from the collections, although it is handed down to us expressly as Heraclitean by a most reliable source, the list of Hippolytus citations.[17] Things are presented, however, in Hippolytus in a way that is so strange to what is Christian Trinitarian that one takes it to be a mere falsification. However, it can be reconstructed by means of morphology. The result reads as follows: "The father is the son of himself." This means to say: When the father produces a son, he makes himself into a father. This seems to me to be a genuine Heraclitean sentence, in the terse style of a paradox, for which reason the later critics of style claimed that he was melancholic and that he always said his sentences only halfway. This is nevertheless something instructive for us as a reasonable guiding principle: where things proceed concisely, concentrated, paradoxically, here we have Heraclitus.

Accordingly, one of the artistic methods that plays a dominant role in Heraclitus corresponds to this paradoxical style: word-play. Word-play relies upon a sudden shift in sense and understanding from an orientation that has already been established toward one that is a completely different one. [54] There is a well-known example for this in Heraclitus: "The name of the bow is life; its work is death."[18] This relies upon the unison of the word *"bios"* for both life (βίος) and the bow (βιός). Within the word, there is already the unity of opposites. That is surely the reason why Heraclitus particularly loves word-play. It allows him to capture his own truth in the utterance of the word and to stir up, as it were, the leveled off, thoughtless usage of language. Another example that plays with words in this way in order to enhance the truth that is concealed within them is Fragment B114, where the play on words occurs in the unison between "common" (ξυνόν) and "with reason" (ξὺν νῷ), whereby something is said.[19] Reason is not only common to all, but rather everything that is common rests on reason. Something else would be for us unrecognizable. Thus, I suspect, on the basis of the citations in Aristotle[20] and the word-plays of Pausanias and Eryximachus in *The Symposium*—and considering the precedent set by Hesiod (*Works and Days*, 20 ff.)—Heraclitus made similar word-plays with ἔρως and ἔρις—with a view toward the "loving strife" to which Aristotle appears to be alluding.[21]

It has been shown by a number of researchers, by Hermann Fraenkel in particular, that other methodological techniques have this same orientation—for example, the paradoxical sentence, the parable, proportion, and also the non-symmetrical analogy. It thus becomes necessary to open up the paradoxical insights of Heraclitus through morphology.

I shall begin with a well-known sentence that offers the occasion to display the difficulty that inheres in the preconceptions operating in the citations. The sentence comes to us from Plotinus (and others), and this is, moreover, valuable for the interpretation. This platonist of the era of the Caesars is one for whom the new dimensions of inwardness have opened up. In this way, it is obvious that his understanding of the book of Heraclitus with which he was still familiar strikes out in directions that are completely different from the ones that we may assume for Heraclitus himself. And, moreover, these directions are also completely different from those of the doctrinal books rooted in the Aristotelian-Theophrastian tradition. The sentence that I have in mind is one of the most simple sentences that one can think: "The way up and the way down is one and the same" (or, "the way there and back is one and the same").[22] Already in antiquity this was understood variously in terms of the perspective of the Aristotelian [55] determined cosmology. One saw here a portrayal of the cycle of the elements, as it describes the great cyclical movement of the elements, from below to above and from above below, from the fire of the heavens to water and to air, if not the reverse, and from there to earth.[23] Yet the text found in Plotinus and elsewhere does not point to this context. Only later reappropriations developed cosmological interpretations. In Plotinus, it is the living attunement to transcendence, the mood or sensibility of the early Christian centuries, that determines the horizontal understanding of the author. Thus, he takes the statement to be concerned with the soul, which descends into the body, and with the soul's return, its ascent to the one and the true. This is for Plotinus the way up and the way down that Heraclitus is supposed to have meant. Certainly, today no one would follow this interpretation of the sentence of Heraclitus. One becomes thoroughly convinced of this when one reads how Plotinus especially praises Heraclitus for this, because Heraclitus has taught us to inquire into our souls, into our true selves.

Nevertheless, the statements in Heraclitus to which Plotinus appeals in this way still have something in them that seduces us. Here we read, for example: "I have sought myself."[24] For the biography of antiquity this meant he had no teacher, but had found everything himself. For us this sounds like an early intimation of Christian inwardness, as it is to be heard for the first time in Socratic questioning. Or even when we read: "The limits of the soul cannot be measured, no matter how far one advances, so deep is its ground."[25] Again, this hearkens to Socrates and Plato, these *"anima naturaliter christiana,"* who, at the heart of the shrine of Silenus, recognized what is truly beautiful and thus pointed toward the Christian future.[26] And yet here one should also be suspicious of this powerful resonance with our own history of the soul. In any case, whatever is addressed in this sentence ("the way up and the way down is one and the same"), it is certainly more correct to recognize in it an utterly simple observation. It is the same path which, during the ascent, seems so difficult and, during the descent, so easy (or, the same path which seems long, on the way hither, but which, upon return, appears short). In my opinion, it is a simple example of how something that is one and the same can look completely different, indeed, even opposed.

We have inherited a whole collection of sentences bearing the name of Heraclitus which demonstrate, in a similar fashion, how something can change its aspect utterly. [56] There is manifest a correspondence between the structure of the thought and the formal structure of such sentences. Evidently, Heraclitus is saying—against the basic experience of something being distinguished and opposed from and to something else—that we should see that what might present itself in this way, as differentiated, also harbors a kind of identity in the opposition itself. Heraclitus sees through the obviousness of differences and oppositions and discovers everywhere the one. This does not have to preclude that in this sentence concerning the way up and the way down still other morally nuanced usages are not supposed to be heard, or that precisely this was the proper intent. However, his λόγος is one. He attends to this in such diverse phenomena as in the flow of things, in the sudden change from fire to water, from sleep to waking; he discovers in all the same riddle, in the flame that consumes itself and is extinguished, in the movement which commences from out of itself and ceases by itself. Everywhere he sees the wonder of life, the riddle of being conscious (i.e., being awake) and the mystery of death.

What must be shown is that this is one of the points by which Plato takes up and by which he took over the heritage of Heraclitean thought in a positive manner. In any case, the usage Plotinus makes of the sentence shows how little one is obliged to apply the sentence cosmologically. On the contrary, the justification for our simplistic understanding of the sentence can be found by proceeding in a way that Heraclitus himself establishes and in fact at the very beginning of his writing.[27] By a stroke of good fortune, this beginning has been reliably handed down to us. Aristotle remarks, namely, that with regard to the first sentence of the writing of Heraclitus, we have before us a problem of interpretation. "This λόγος, which always is, over and against which humans remain always without comprehension."[28] Aristotle wonders where the "always" belongs. Contemporary philologists are also divided on this point. In this λόγος always, or does it always remain without comprehension? Presumably, this is a true case of what the grammarians call ἀπὸ κοινοῦ. Taken by itself, this is the utterly predictable and pedantic excuse of school teachers, and yet in the context of hearing this sentence such a category comes to life again. One must recall that Aristotle was a lecturer (even if he also read aloud naturally). This text was most certainly intended to be read to an audience. The speaker was thus able to express himself in such a way that the word "always" could offer light on both sides, adding color to the adjacent words.[29] Yet I am addressing this much discussed [57] and overly paradoxical sentence here in order to put a paradox into relief which seems to me to have not been properly considered and which supposedly presents a kind of guideline for the entire interpretation. Heraclitus describes his project in the following manner: κατὰ φύσιν διαιρέων ἕκαστον καὶ φράζων ὅκως ἔχει. This sounds completely conventional, like an announcement in the style of an encompassing ἱστορίη. Heraclitus promises "to lay everything out as it is." How does such laying out in truth look? The reader of the book sees it, the one who heeds the λόγος hears it. It is not exactly differentiation, but perceiving the one in all that is differentiated: that is the Heraclitean message. What others take as different, in the way Hesiod takes day and night, is in fact truly one and the same. Heraclitean teaching is continually formulated in this way: ἕν τὸ σοφόν.[30] I take this to be the authentic and original principle that seems to be variously repeated in his book. It can be extended in different ways according to this formula, ἕν τὸ σοφόν: "it does and does not want to be called by the name Zeus" (Fragment B32), or "that is the insight" (γνώμη, Fragment B41). Our formula, "one is the wise," is also hiding somehow in Fragment B50.[31]

The significance of the neuter that appears here as "the wise" is very diverse. The possession of the neuter represents one of the ingenious advantages of the Greek language for the abstractness of thinking.

Reinhardt and Snell have taught us to see this well. We are acquainted with a similar use of the neuter from German poetry, above all since Goethe and Hölderlin, who use *"das Göttliche"* or *"das Rettende"* in their poetry. When something like this is encountered in poetry, it is not to be understood as a particular being.[32] Instead, it is a presence of being that proceeds from such a neuter, a presence that fills the entire expanse. *"Das Unheimliche,"* like *"das Rettende,"* *"das Göttliche,"* or *"das Heilige,"* or whatever it is, is the fullest presence, without thereby naming a particular and determinate being. Also, in this manner, "the wise" is not in such a way that it is next to many others—it is "separate" from everything (πάντων κεχωρισμένον, Fragment B108). Over and against [58] the appearance of changing differences, it is that which authentically is. This is how Heraclitus evidently meant his λόγος, a truth which speaks from out of all things, yet which no one wants to take as true.

At any rate, the hermeneutic task of understanding the introductory sentence should not, in my opinion, be interpreted in advance in terms of the doctrine that is to come later. The announcement instead ought to awaken an expectation and it relies upon the style of the ἱστορίη. Yet this announcement steadfastly interrupts the expectation in the most paradoxical manner.[33] The Proem, moreover, does not announce that the author has a teaching that is better than the teachings of others. Heraclitus claims much more. This teaching is supposed to be better than the viewpoints of all humans as such. Heraclitus is as radical as is Parmenides when the goddess he introduces speaks of the opinions of mortals (Fragments B1.30 and B6). It should be clear finally that this is not a reference to his colleagues. Unfortunately, it is not so rigorously observed that these "viewpoints" (δόξαι) of mortals always appear in the plural and not at all in the Platonic singular.[34]

I want to insist that the Proem tells us nothing about the content of the doctrine. Nevertheless, there is at its beginning a genuine Heraclitean comparison which gives an initial indication of what Heraclitus wants to say on the whole. Here, again, there remains the opposition between the one knower and the many who do not know: "It remains hidden from humans what they do while awake, just as they forget what they do while asleep."[35] This means evidently that they learn nothing from the abundance of their experiences.[36] [59] That is what is distinctive about what we do in sleep. When we awaken, we forget. We bring into our lived actuality nothing from the dream experiences that we have undergone. The actions of dreams are inconsequential. Neither is one capable, once awakened to the wakefulness of the day, of continuing to play the game of the dream, nor does one integrate it into one's experience. This is what is meant in the introductory sentence. Hence, it is not a matter of the extent to which dreams were understood in antiquity in terms of their foreboding. Heraclitus sees with a cold and clear vision that dreaming is not being awake. That humans undergo experiences without becoming wise means that they live like dreamers. Their experiences have no consequences. And thus it literally means: ἀπείροισιν ἐοίκασιν πειρώμενοι, "they are the same as the inexperienced despite all experience." In this way, the beginning of the book offers guidance, not only in order to grasp the poetizing of the Heraclitean sentence, but also in order to seek the "one," the wise, behind the most everyday experience.

The metaphor in this violent introductory sentence is suspenseful enough. The incomprehension that humans have over and against the truth is not to be posited simply as an unalterable fact. One can wake someone from sleep. The provocation of the first sentence rests upon this. However, there is more to it; at the same time, it is an assertion that, so to speak, turns upon itself. It is a true paradox here that announces itself as the teaching of Heraclitus. This teaching leads to insight and, at the same time, teaches the chasm that yawns between the one truth and the incapacity for learning of those entangled in the manifold of human fancy and dreams. The parable of waking and sleeping not only provides an example, but it belongs at the same time to the content of Heraclitus's teaching.

We thus confront this parable repeatedly (even if perhaps not always in Heraclitean wording, as when the word κόσμος is used for "world"). The dream is for Heraclitus the symbol of the universal lack of understanding. A sentence like the following belongs here: "For the wakeful there is only one and one common world, while the sleeping turn away each into his own."[37] In this sense, Fragment B75 names those who on account of their dreaming are sleeping, ἐργτάτας (that is, a worker: a builder of an entire private world).[38] What is constantly in view is the humans who [60] while awake behave as if they were asleep. Fragment B73 expresses this directly: "One should not act and speak like those who sleep."[39] This formulation is admittedly so banal that one might well have to assume with Kirk and here Marcus Aurelius is only articulating the moral quintessence of the concluding sentence of Fragment B1.[40]

Repeatedly one finds a proposition formed between waking and sleeping on one side and living and being dead on the other side. That comparisons, analogies, and proportions were an archaic way of thought has been shown above all by Hermann Fraenkel.[41] The Heraclitean use of this manner of thinking has, however, its own character. We can observe how Heraclitus does not simply construe such proportions and comparisons, but rather loves to embellish his sentences in a paradoxical manner such that they take on a provocative and paranetic sharpness. Thus, we do not read in Fragment B21, as we might expect, a correspondence between sleep and dream images on the one side and being awake and the waking world (or life) on the other side. Instead, it reads surprisingly and provocatively: "Death is what we see while awake (and not life), and what we see as slumberers is sleep."[42] The subtlety of this surprising proportion lies in the fact that the end part of the proportion reads ὕπνος and not ἐνύπνιον, "sleep" and not "dream." The entire state of being asleep, within which dream images are encountered, is thereby attributed to those who are sleeping as what they see. The precision of this finely chiseled sentence thus becomes unmistakable. Death and sleep form the two basic terms, the correspondence of which speaks for itself. What is provocative about the sentence is its surprising beginning. In the first clause, the word "life" would be an acceptable way to proceed, and there one finds "death." What is seen in wakefulness is itself attributed as a whole, along with its apparent wakefulness, not to life and vitality but instead to being dead.[43]

The family resemblance of Heraclitean sentences calls for a very careful rhythmic analysis of what has been handed down to us. In this regard, in Charles Kahn's commentary, I already find very fine observations. At times, because I am looking in the same direction, I would like to go still further and produce through emendation and condensation the original Heraclitean sentence from out of sentences that are not well formed. Precisely, in the best formed [61] Heraclitean sentences I believe I recognize a true family resemblance. Thus, I would like to pose the question to Kahn's analysis of the tonal structure of Fragment B25 whether in the end λαγχάνουσι ("they attain") is not dispensable.[44] It is due perhaps to the ancient style of making a citation in which one at the same time explicates. The sentence could have read simply: μόροι μέζονες μέζονες μοῖραι (or, μέζονας μοίρας). The undeniable word play speaks for itself and demands consideration.

Conversely, one feels assured that one has the correct wording when a sentence reveals unmistakable basic terms as is the case in Fragment B21 in the correspondence between θάνατος and ὕπνος ("death" and "sleep"). Also, Fragment B20 reveals basic determinations of this kind with γενόμενοι and γενέσθαι.[45] In this last case I wonder whether the bond that is formed through the basic determinations in such a long sentence would not be more effective if one were to take things further by contrasting μόρους τ᾽ ἔχειν with μόρους γενέσθαι. Indeed, it is clear that the ἐθέλουσι may not be entirely separated form its object ζώειν; it is in fact established through the τε—καὶ. However, why should Heraclitus have followed the ambiguous gravitation of words only in his introductory sentence and not also have taken advantage elsewhere of their duplicitous reference? Even here the ἐθέλουσι would be heard doubled, just as this happens in Fragment B1 with "always": γενόμενοι ζώειν ἐθέλουσι μόρους τε ἔχειν καὶ [παῖδας καταλείπουσι] μόρους γενέσθαι. It is from this style that I discern placing the ἔχειν and the γενέσθαι in opposition.[46]

In this same way, the fragment that I reconstructed, πατὴρ υἱὸς ἑαυτοῦ, appears to me to be conclusive, as well as some others. In Fragment B21, dream and sleep stand for the confusion that lies in the inability to discern one and the same essence in everything different that we encounter. Heraclitus does not weary of teaching in countless variations the inseparability of opposites that signifies unity. The introductory sentence discussed above is to be included here. When the multiplicity is announced in it—the "words and deeds" as they are encountered by all—one must keep in view precisely the one that alone is the true. The sentence shows all humans to be in error in the same way, taking what is opposed as separate beings, instead of recognizing the true unity. This is the paradox: he wants "to open up the confrontation *(auseinandersetzen)*" of this being-one; and this is the λόγος to which it is proper to listen. He not only means what everyone knows— the sequence of things, the necessary dissolution of one thing into another, like day and night, summer and winter, youth and old age— but instead, above and beyond this, he means that kind of being-in-each-other that Plato [62] emphasizes in the passage in *The Sophist* from which we took our point of departure. The tension of these Ionic muses consists expressly in the fact that it is the same that holds itself together in its separation from itself (Fragment B51), like the mixed drink that would separate if one did not stir it (Fragment B125), or like Fragment

B10 with its συνᾷδον-διᾷδον ("to be in accord—to be out of accord"), or Fragment B8 with its ἀντίξουν-συμφέρον ("striving against—assisting"). In Aristotle, it becomes completely clear how this is to be understood: the high and low note must both be there if there is to be harmony.[47] The separation into opposites therefore is not the result of a process of ἔκκρισις, as Aristotle maintains that it is in Anaximander (DK 12 A16), and as it well could be behind the deepened doctrine of opposites that the goddess reveals to Parmenides. Aristotle in fact nowhere has a speculative understanding of the contradictory assertions of Heraclitus.[48] This becomes apparent in a passage in *The Physics* (A4, 187a20 ff.) that mentions, with the exception of Anaximander, only Empedocles and Anaxagoras—and precisely through the similar differentiation between "periodically" and "once only"—as among those who take up the one and the many at the same time. Here, ἔκκρισις is discussed with Heraclitus being mentioned, although given the reliance on the passage in *The Sophist* (242b) one might have expected it. Likewise, in *The Metaphysics* (A8, 989a13), Heraclitus is not named when Aristotle substitutes what is between fire and air, of which he speaks in *The Physics* (187a14), with what is between air and water. Instead of classifying Heraclitus's fire doctrine as a case of ἔκκρισις and fitting this into the principle of his doctrine of elements here, he passes Heraclitus over. Apparently, in his eyes, this could not be unified with the Heraclitean text.

One must in any case judge things this way, if one takes seriously the Platonic contrast between the Heraclitean Ionic muses and the Sicilian muses of Empedocles. A whole series of unmistakably Heraclitean fragments supports this: the image of the river, the harmony in the relation between bow and lyre, harmony as such, the barley drink. In all these cases, a unity based on mere temporal succession or on the mere suddenness of transition is no longer the issue. In any event, if what one has in mind is the suddenness of transition, one could gather the examples together without the simultaneity that belongs to the speculative unity of temporal succession.

[63] How do the stronger conceptual assertions look now? Fragment B10 does indeed lead toward a prior separation, and yet it also clearly intends the at-once, since the Platonic συμφερόμενον-διαφερόμενον appears in the series.[49] Likewise, one can understand the ὅλα καὶ οὐχ ὅλα only as the logical inseparability of the whole and parts. And it is the same with the consonance and dissonance that is secured through the

analogy of harmony (συνᾇδον-διᾇδον). This, however, firmly grounds the "out of all one" in the sense in which Plato speaks of it. If one examines the announcement of the string of citations in Hippolytus, Fragment B51,[50] it becomes possible to question whether in some cases they illustrate genuine speculative unity. All the same, my analysis of the father-son paradox cited above has strengthened the expressive power of the string of citations. Thus, on the whole, where Hippolytus expressly introduces oppositions, as in Fragment B67,[51] the one must be understood in the Platonic sense. In the case of day and night, this is confirmed by the polemic with Hesiod in Fragment B57. Likewise, death (θάνατος) and its opposition to life is confirmed by Fragment B76, which refers back to Fragment B62.[52] In contrast, other assertions seem to express only change as such and not the speculative unity inherent in change. That holds for the continuation of Fragment B67, where the different aspects of the god or of fire come to be through the admixture of different incense.[53] Nonetheless "the god" here also stands for the one. Fragment B88, the reading of which is uncertain enough, without doubt lays the emphasis on change, on the succession that is nevertheless described as sudden transformation (μεταπεσόντα). To be sure, every change in Heraclitus's eyes implies an at-once.[54] This seems to me to hold for the cosmology of Fragment B31, which we will take up shortly.

The separation into opposites, therefore, testifies generally to the unitary essence of things and their true being. They do not exist without each other, whether it is the case that they follow each other necessarily or whether they directly [64] harmonize and form the unity of a melodic joining. Regardless, one must come to the insight that the other is always already there. The best indication of this is precisely that the opposite breaks forth suddenly and immediately. All at once, what is changes its aspect utterly and the opposite emerges. This demonstrates that it was there already beforehand. In this way, I think, Heraclitus wants at bottom to assert the same for all that is, the being one of the different. And this is the reason he names the one "distinct from all." The opposites that are explicitly named are clearly given under the particular perspective that they seem to exclude each other completely. And yet, nevertheless, they allow themselves to be recognized as one and the same.

Among the oppositions of which Fragment B67 speaks, the opposition between lack and satiety appears to offer especially clear evidence. Independently of all cosmological applications and interpretations, we all know this experience. The allure of food presupposes hunger and appetite and disappears with surprising suddenness when one is sated. The opposition between war and peace is just as illuminating. The one is the total non-being of the other. The outbreak of war is a full transformation of all things. Waking and sleep, too, belong in this group. What is so astounding about the opposition between being awake and asleep is just the suddenness with which the entire condition becomes another. Whoever falls or sinks into sleep appears to be completely other and is yet the same as the one seen in wakefulness. In this way, the oppositional pairs are to be understood simply according to the model of waking and sleep (Fragment B88).

Now, admittedly among the oppositions, we also confront in Fragment B88 the "lively and dead" and moreover "young and old." What is reciprocal change to mean here? "Young and old" can perhaps be explained to a certain extent as the exchange of perspectives, insofar as "old" and "young" are things that are very relative. One can suddenly be young, and this does not only mean that one feels rejuvenated. One actually is young. Likewise, one can suddenly appear old. In this way, the Platonic formula would prove to quite right, that it is the same thing that is at once one and another; both are in it. Only the aspect of the being changes. In Plato's *Parmenides* (141a f., 152a f.), moreover, we also confront the dialectical play of "young and old" in the series of relations.

The greatest difficulty in the evidence that supports our interpretation is presented by the opposition between life and death. It is without doubt significant that this opposition does not occur here in Heraclitus as something special, but rather in a long series of similar oppositional pairs. This is a reminder that the role of death and the corresponding understanding of it within the horizon of Christian culture to which we belong [65] is a completely unusual and extraordinary one. This extraordinary place of death still makes its presence known, even today when the religious background of the modern world has paled considerably and the Easter faith in the overcoming of death through resurrection occupies the general consciousness of culture less and less. Even if death in its complete irrevocability and incomprehensible terror is no longer understood in light of the redeeming act of the sacrificial suffering of the crucifixion through Jesus and as a whole the Christian message is no longer faithfully accepted, it still is not so easy to be sufficiently conscious of the particular role death plays in our European culture and its vital history. And this is true even as one looks to the testimony of Heraclitus.

One can look at this as a classic example of what I have called in the context of the problem of hermeneutics "the consciousness of the history of effect" *(wirkungsgeschichtliches Bewußtsein)*. Our own preconceptions are so deeply entrenched that they obstruct our understanding of other cultures and historical worlds. In order to arrive at a better understanding, one must try to become conscious of one's own preconceptions. In the case of Heraclitus, this is difficult enough, since the influence of late antiquity and early Christianity upon the Heraclitean tradition, primarily through Hippolytus and Clement, obtrudes directly upon our own preconceptions and to this extent leads us astray. On the other hand, we have to remain conscious of our own preconceptions, even when we guard ourselves against making premature identifications. Greater difficulties do arise, of course, where we meet up with completely foreign cultural horizons and traditions. Once only has to consider the distortion of the Vedanta carried out by the Kantian Schopenhauer.

Human concern has everywhere ascribed great importance to the experience of death. This certainly holds also for native Greek religion, for example in the representation of Hades and the river of forgetting which cuts the living off from the dead, as depicted by the Homeric epic. And similarly, the drama of the gods that Aeschylus brought to the stage with his novel interpretation of the myth of Prometheus shows that death is a kind of question of life for humanity. At bottom all religions are answers to the riddle of death, whether this answer if found in the cult of death or in the cult of foreknowledge, or in other forms of belief in the soul or in immortality. Even the representation of Hades remains an answer to the incomprehensible riddle of death. Some myths associated with the name Orpheus and Eurydice or in a certain sense also with the figure of Büsser's Sisyphus appear to lessen the irrevocability of death. However, these myths, too, tell precisely how the overcoming of death comes to failure. To be sure, native Greek religion, with its representation of Hades and the isle of the blessed has in mind the lasting presence of the departed [66] and, in the Nekyia, even the reunification with them. And even today we are moved still by the breathtaking sorrow of Greek burial paintings. Plato himself, in his *Phaedo*, speaks of the child in man, whose anxiety before death can never be totally calmed.

However, in Heraclitus, something else is at issue: the sudden transformation from death to life is coordinated with the sudden change from life to death. Nothing like this lies hidden in the belief in Hades. The Orphean and Pythagorean belief in the transmigration of the souls and the reincarnation of the souls of the dead into new lifeless beings might make a kind of reciprocal exchange between death and life intelligible. However, in the end, this depends exclusively upon the question of whether the one who is newly incarnated in this way gains remembrance of his prior life. Although this may have been promised to the initiates of such a cult, in such religious movements in late Greece no less than in Homer there was no actual corresponding counterpart to the overcoming of death in the sense that is posited by Christian faith in the death and resurrection of Jesus Christ. One has to understand the Greek cult of death on the whole as a kind of holding fast to life, as is the case with other religions. The peculiarity of the Christian religion consists in the fact that it does not lessen but rather completely accepts the terror of death in its faith in the resurrection as the salvation from death through the sacrificial suffering of Jesus. "Christ is my life and death my gain." In this way, the pre-Christian world and thus the Greek world as a whole is separated from Christianity by an insurmountable boundary. This boundary has been described by Novalis in his "Hymns to the Night."

One also becomes aware of the foreignness of the Christian religious experience of death when one reads the first proof for the immortality of the soul that Plato in *The Phaedo* (70d ff.) puts into the mouth of Socrates.[55] It is difficult for the modern reader to understand that from out of the general cycle of natural life one is able to infer the balance between death and life, between dying and rebirth as such. The rhythm of natural life appears to be simply inappropriate to the life history of human being. Even in *The Phaedo*, Plato gives an indication of this, when Cebes only hesitantly concedes the exchange from death to life (φαίνεται, 71e). In the end, there is something astonishing in this for us, when from out of the argumentation of *The Phaedo* it is to be concluded that the souls of the dead not only continue to exist (εἶναι, 72e) but rather, as the text states, [67] that the good who have died will have a better existence than the bad (72e). To infer this is so absurd that modern philology has crossed out this additional determination as inauthentic, although the text has been handed down to us intact. However, just how is one to understand that this follows from the rhythm of natural life? Here it is easier to grasp that *The Phaedo* continues with a further proof by means of which the periodicy of natural processes is fitted into the well-known Socratic argument of ἀνάμνησις. However, here, too, one wonders how this proof is to supplement the first. The soul in the first argument is indeed something completely different from the soul that recalls itself. In any case, one might consider here how in Plato, in particular in the conversation between Socrates and the two Pythagoreans, the entire mediated horizon of the transmigration of the soul continues to echo. What is decisive is to make clear that this has nothing to do with Heraclitus.

In Heraclitus, the issue can have nothing to do with the transmigration of the soul, whereas in Plato the realm of the Greek soul common to both natural life and thinking being becomes recognizable. On the contrary, Heraclitus with his bold oppositional pairs aims entirely at the paradox of sudden change. The thought of Heraclitus is therefore much more radical. For him, there is not, as it appears to be in Plato, a determinate being, a soul, that maintains itself as inalterable even in its transformed modes of appearance and in its changed residence in the body or in Hades.

At this point, recalling an important little scene in the Platonic *Phaedo* is helpful. At 103a ff., an anonymous person interrupts the Socratic argumentation which has introduced the exclusion of the opposition between life and death to prove the immortality of the soul—an obvious clue receiving thereby extraordinary emphasis. The unknown person recalls that the transition from one to another, of opposites into each other, was asserted at an earlier point in the dialogue (namely, 70d ff.). Socrates takes this opportunity also to make clear to his friend Cebes that, when one thinks the opposites as such and has them in view in terms of their oppositional exclusion, the thought of opposites has here another sense than when one says of some such thing, a πρᾶγμα, for example the soul, that this something moves from an opposite toward another. This truly presupposes the pure thought, opposition as such, of its being an idea. It means that the opposites are distinguished from that in which they appear. In Aristotle, this is later named ὑποκείμενον; the early oppositional thinking of the Ionics and the Pythagoreans was not conceptually aware of this at all. Plato illustrates this later as the inadequacy of the earlier thinkers, when in *The Philebus* (23d, 26d) he explicitly introduces the third kind, that of the measured (in addition to that of the measure).

[68] Recalling Plato can help us to surmise Heraclitus's proper question. Neither the Aristotelian analysis of the movedness *(Bewegtheit)* of nature, nor even the representations relayed through Homer and Hesiod or the hero-cult or the mystery-religion correspond to the true intention of Heraclitus. For him, the issue is the paradox of sudden change and thereby the unity of being. What is life and what is death? What is the genesis of life and the dissolution of life? That is the riddle upon which Heraclitus meditates. He seeks in all oppositions the one, and in the one he finds opposition, in fire the flame, in the λόγος of the soul, in the one, the true (ἕν τὸ σοφόν). Plato will portray the great Parmenides leading the flustered young Socrates into the bold games that the one is in all things and that also the ideas, the oppositonal ideas themselves, go over into each other and are one. In this way, Plato is able to take up Heraclitus.

I am thus coming to the conclusion that here one ought not make reference to certain modes of representation. What is at issue in the thesis of identity is something else. It is the suddenness with which the aspect of things is altered. This is most evident in the opposition between life and death. One has to interpret the entire teaching with regard to this point. Every attenuation of opposition between death and life stands in contradiction to the overall tenor of the teaching of opposition. The thought is much more radical. Not a determinate being, the soul is to be found in everything that lives, as the unchangeable behind the altering aspect. It is the mystery of the nature of being itself, the one wise, the true divine, which makes itself manifest in the sudden exchange between death and life. Death itself is like an abrupt change in the appearance of being.

Thus, one ought to attempt once again to follow the program of the Proem and to discern in familiar experiences the unrecognized truth. If in Fragment B62 the issue is that the gods "live our death," that could mean that their being first emerges through our death. Their being articulates itself as what it is with respect to our finality (and certainly not because they stand by as spectators as Fink suggests[56]). Correspondingly, one could understand that in living we die their death, which means that the immortals do not emerge for us as what they are as long as the security and certainty of life holds us back. However, once again the truth would be that through their exchange both aspects prove their nullity and confirm the one, the wise alone, as the true.

In this way, the identity of numerous assertions concerning the changing aspect of things comes to light, the meaning of which is indisputable. [69] Thus, for example: "The ass prefers chaff to gold" (Fragment B9). Or: "Seawater is for fish drinkable and necessary for their life, for humans it is repulsive and deadly" (Fragment B61). Or: "The most beautiful ape is ugly compared to the race of humans" (Fragment B82). Or: "The wisest of humans, compared to the god, behaves like an ape" (Fragment B83). Even statements such as Fragments B84a and B84b, "change rests" or "always to be challenged and pressured by the same is tiresome" should be detached from all dissatisfactory mythical applications of the kind proposed by Plotinus. They do not deserve credibility. He himself says explicitly: ἀμελήσας σαφῆ ἡμῖν ποιῆσαι τὸν λόγον.[57] These all are negative counterparts to the identity of the different, and in their difference they allow the identical to be discerned.

Fragments B24, B25, and B27 can also be interpreted in a similar fashion. They hardly indicate any sort of particular Heraclitean teaching concerning the dead and their future fate, or a mystery-wisdom which would be closed off to those who are uninitiated but which Heraclitus would have in common with all the initiated. Rather, what is being dealt with here is also something lying there in the open, known to all, yet which none discern in its true significance. One example of something known to all is the elevating of the one who has fallen in war, "in the field of honor" (ἀρηιφάτους, Fragment B24). He is like one suddenly transformed. All honor him, and all see him otherwise, as exemplary and as transfigured. This is Heraclitus's insight and has nothing to do with any partaking of the cult of the hero. This would have been for him at most an example of the suddenness of such a change that is taken from the cult.

Similarly, a secret intimation of unforeseen experiences in the beyond cannot be the meaning of Fragment B27. Rather, the meaning is precisely that humans after their death are present otherwise, elevated, in a way that would have been thought impossible during the time of life.[58] Fragment B18 seems to express the same experience from out of the human world, "when one does not hope, one also will not find what is unhoped for."[59] It is because of hope that what enters presents itself as completely otherwise than one was able to anticipate, precisely because it was unforeseeable and appeared out of reach. Since there can be surprise, there can be fulfillment. Only those who hope can meet up with the unhoped for.

That such an interpretation gets at the meaning of the Heraclitean sentences is at the very least confirmed also by Fragment B53. There what is addressed is war, the father of all things; "it proves some to be gods, others humans." Impotence and power of the human emerge from this. From one side it emerges [70] that they are cowardly slaves, from the others that they are truly free.[60] This again means that what is already implicit in each thing does make itself apparent. War, the true god, does not only lie at the basis of the most extreme oppositions but it itself unleashes the alteration of aspect. It is common to all discord, the genuine λόγος behind the different in which things seem to show themselves. Thus, Fragment B80 states that war is in fact common to all, from which one can withdraw and which befalls all in the same measure.[61] Thus, in Heraclitus it can be said that: "Dike," what is apportioned the same to all, and "Eris," strife, are one (I prefer to read καὶ δίκην καὶ ἔριν). The community of right and community of strife encompass all things. What is common to all is in truth one and the same. The continuation that is indeed produced correctly by Diels goes along with this.[62] The immortals are also in this way a particularization and do not exist without mortals (Fragment B62). By immortals Heraclitus evidently does not mean the god of Fragment B67, the one in the multiplicity of appearances. It looks rather as if Heraclitus in bold enlightenment thought, anticipating Plato, places the traditional world of the gods in a reciprocal relationship with the world of human experience. As war makes manifest the power and impotence of humans, so does the power of the gods emerge in the failure of humans, and their barrenness in their own affluence. It is possibly all the more paradoxical that the immortality acquired by those who have fallen comes to them through death!

At this point, I would like to pose the general question of whether all the sentences concerning fame and immortality, like Fragments B24, B25, and perhaps even B27, do not aim at the transformation of the dead. Fragment B29 seems to me also to confirm this: "The noble choose the one instead of all others." This is supposed to say that their nobility consists in that in their life they actually follow what according to Heraclitus is the one true *(das Eine Wahre)*. However much these interpretations may remain individually questionable, and however much the resonance of conventional religious representations may nonetheless play a role here—the attempt fails which until now has met with general acceptance, that is, to make Heraclitus into a logical interpreter of the wisdom of the mysteries on account of his mystical tone. [71] It fails because Heraclitus demands the thinking of the one and expects thereby wisdom not from the initiated but from all humans.

However, how is all of this to be reconciled with the cosmology of fire? With regard to this question one not only has to keep in view Heraclitus's style and Plato's characterization of Heraclitus but one must also take into account the polemical references made to the Milesian teaching. Indeed, the claim to paradoxical enlightenment which the Proem puts forward has been constantly related to the comportment of humans as a whole. And yet it looks here as though the matter takes a peculiar turn. This new science too, as a consequence, must be subordinated to a certain kind of enlightenment. If we have thus far followed the general guidance of the Proem and not assumed anything that everyday human experience is not supposed to teach and in truth does not teach, we must now ask ourselves how Heraclitus criticizes in its entirety the new enlightenment which was being promoted by the Milesians, but also by the Pythagoreans and men like Xenophon, and how he thereby inserts his own insights.

This does not at all mean abandoning our basic principle. For it is not special knowledge which is thematized but rather the new way of seeing the world, to think λόγῳ The meteorological process is as plain as day to all observation. One has to ask oneself to what extent the demythologizing of the mythical world picture and the reception of the cosmogonical schema make such questions unavoidable, like the question concerning the beginning; and one has to ask whether such processes of the becoming of the world cannot continually and everywhere begin anew. The later theory of corpuscles and then finally the atomists thought in this way, and so it was thought at bottom in a manner intelligible for every thinking consciousness. I mean, therefore, that Heraclitus may not at all be seen as one who continues the Ionian cosmogony and leads this cosmogony into cosmology. In this regard, however, he frequently makes overly naive observations or applications that can mean only that the reference to cosmological matters is for him of secondary importance. When Heraclitus appeals to the cosmogonical knowledge of his Ionic neighbors, his intention does not seem to be to enter into competition with the great researchers and discoverers of Miletus. He is not claiming to introduce new knowledge from all over but rather to bring to light the truth that is concealed in all that is evident and otherwise familiar. This follows from the introductory sentence that plays with the paradox of a truth that is visible to all yet everywhere mistaken. Thus, already for this reason we shall not get far with the interpretation of the fire-cosmology as a "cosmology." The tortured attempts of the later doxographers to reconcile the Heraclitean sentences handed down to us with the cosmological schema, or even with the [72] teaching of the elements introduced by Empedocles and elaborated by Plato and Aristotle, cannot be encouraging.

What is at issue is a few cosmological sentences whose form is utterly paradoxical. There is Fragment B30 which appears to be unproblematically united with the entire early tradition of cosmological thought.[63] I do not think that one can see here a reference back to Ionic cosmogony as has been newly attempted. As if the Ionians with their cosmogony would have taught anything other than precisely this—that no god and no human has established the order of the world. Heraclitus's sentence sounds in its first part more like a positive reference to the Ionic teaching of φύσις. However, something else sounds immediately Heraclitean, and that is the emphasis that this order is the same for all (or by all). If this part of the text is genuine, it reminds one of the admonishing assertion concerning the unreason of human beings, who, like dreamers, each forms his own world (cf. Fragment B89). What is essential in this sentence is evidently that the expectation for a unchanging order of the world is to be attributed precisely to the most turbulent of all the elements, fire. What otherwise holds from out of itself the great balance of the world vision of Anaximander, what holds, that is, the measure or continually brings forth the measure anew, is imposed upon what is eternally living, the always restless fire. This measure is portrayed here as the self-igniting and extinguishing of fire—a strange contrast between measured order and what is explosively abrupt. In this way, it is apparent that ignition and extinguishing symbolize precisely what is sudden, which inspired Heraclitus's vision of the world. And yet it is just as little to be doubted that Heraclitus presupposes in any case the measuredness of all events and only wants to interpret this same measuredness anew. To this extent the issue is not to resolve the presumed cosmology in terms of mere symbolism. What is at issue is to discover in Heraclitus a new answer to the experience of the being of the whole. This seems to me to be the meaning of the riddle that is offered in Fragment B30.

If we now turn to the continued text of Clement, one can hardly doubt that the subsequent sentence, Fragment B31, connects immediately to our sentence ("fire's transformations . . .").[64] Then, however, the phrase πυρὸς τροπαί bears the same unmistakable tone of the paradox which the first sentence made evident as paradox. All things are the eruption of restless fire. It thus has nothing to do with the fully harmonious Ionic [73] event of equalization, in which all oppositions pay penalties and compensation for their prevailing.

Certainly, the turning points of the course taken by the sun could also fit in here, insofar as all change—the seasonal shifting of the sun also—and all reversal have something sudden about them, as the Greek expression τροπαί suggests. However, the connection with the preceding sentence remains decisive. Hence, the continuation must be understood from that point: What happens in igniting and extinguishing? Kahn remarks correctly that in what follows the atmosphere, i.e., air, is missing,[65] that is, precisely that which was essential to the Ionic cosmic wisdom and provided its intuitive ground (in Thales and Anaximenes). Likewise, he appears to me to be right that here the most extreme opposite to fire, the sea, is named as its other. The earthly sea approaches the heavenly fire as its extreme counterpart.

The "always alive" (ἀείζωον, Fragment B30) evidently belongs together with inflaming and extinguishing. This has to form the guiding thread of the interpretation. Even if one keeps all later distinctions between fire, light, and warmth at a distance (which perhaps already approach and play into the difference between the sensible and the spiritual) from the above sentence, it already becomes clear that fire is not a visible element but rather, on the contrary, what is continually changing over and against all constancy. This is precisely its liveliness, and it nonetheless is one—as is all life. Fire, too, inflames according to measure and is extinguished according to measure—as is the case also for the life rhythm of waking and sleep.

In this way, fire presents the universal structure of all being. Fragment B90 explains this best: "All is exchangeable with fire and fire with all."[66] This is stated as fire is compared with gold. And similar to Fragment B88: all things change like fire, striking out like a flame and collapsing in being extinguished. Fire, too, "undergoes change, when it is mingled with incense" (Fragment B67).

The emphasis is continually placed upon the one, that is the true and the wise, behind all the presumed differences, whether these are now the opposites and their transformation into each other, or relatively and the sudden change of the aspects. The changeable is itself the one.

I believe the cosmological testimony concerning the transformations, the τροπαί, is explained most easily in this way. Perhaps, what is meant here is not "turning points" but actually "transformations." The issue is not whether fire is, but rather the reverse, [74] that fire lies at the bottom of all that undergoes transformation—like the sun. The interpolations made by Clement take this to be the λόγος and god![67] Thus, the initiation of the transformations with the sea (πρῶτον θάλασσα) appears to me to be understandable only if one does not see in it a first transformation of fire into water but rather simply an assertion about the beginning as it was made by Ionic cosmology. The clarification Clement makes by appending σπέρμα τῆς διακοσμήσεως is to this extent not really so false.

And in the further process, too, fire itself precisely does not appear as a phase. Only when one decides to interpret the fragment in this manner, I think, does it first become possible to understand the continuation. Clearly, it is only stated that fire provides the ground, not that fire changes into earth and so comes out half earth, or that half of fire becomes wind, if a hot wind is whipping up. Thus, it is not being said that the sea becomes half earth and half hot wind but rather that with the drying out of the land ("half-way," so to speak) the hot wind begins. That is an experience with which all of us are familiar. When a brooding heat lies on the land, it stays cooler by the sea. The continuation handed down to us fits in with this unproblematically, that in the end the sea once again swallows up all things, as it was in the beginning. When Clement wants to interpret this reconstruction as ἐκπύρωσις, one must establish that nothing in the text speaks of this. The text says only that in the end the sea once again floods over all things. Is one to suppose that Clement actually found in the text that, in the end, all things again become fire? However, then, after this, he no longer cited this due to an oversight? We trust the words of the church fathers too readily, if we here believe in a lacuna in the text because Clement says: σαφῶς διὰ τούτων δηλοῖ. The only thing in the text of Heraclitus handed down to us that could point in this direction would be the ἀναθυμίασις, the evaporation. Here, doxography tells us fantastic things. There are bright and dark clouds over land and sea. From out of the bright clouds, basins of fire of the stars fill themselves. The difference between day and night, even the solar eclipse, is supposed to be explainable through this process. This is all downright opaque. Evidently, the source of Diogenes did not find here clear representations. It appears rather that for these tiresome constructions the only actual basis was the ἀναθυμίασις. In any case, that has nothing to do with the supposed world conflagration, the "ἐκπύρωσις." Clement was evidently not able to appeal to anything in the text for his interpretation—otherwise he would have done so.

[75] The intuition that lies at the bottom of the entire text is most easily described through Simplicius's concept of the δραστικόν (the active)[68]—a kind of general answer of the Aristotelian physics to the Ionians. The first thing that can be indicated about it is eternal movedness. It is encountered both in the never-resting fire and in the never-resting primordial sea. That the emergence of land seems like "death," from here, is quite understandable. Over and against the never-resting life of the ocean, the secure land is something dead. Thus, it seems to me that Heraclitus with his doctrine of fire asked questions that went beneath the Ionic cosmogony. Not the transformations of water (Thales) or air (Anaximenes) but rather the transformations of fire is what is described here. This is expressed in the text handed down to us with provocative emphasis. If we now consider how during this period θάλασσα is almost a catchword for the liquid, the fluid, the flowing, the unresting (ὅ καλεῖ θάλασσαν, Clement says), the entire teaching of the flux is thereby connected without coercion.

From this, there is still one last step to take. It is certainly a difficult question as to how the cosmic aspect of the doctrine of fire—even if it is understood metaphorically—is connected to the Heraclitean assertions concerning the soul. It is also to be remarked that the basic testimony of the doctrine of the flux is cited only by Eusebius because of the reference to the ψυχή, which is αἰσθητικὴ ἀναθυμίασις (Fragment B12). The stoic interpretation that brings together the doctrine of the flux with that of the soul, on the basis of its own doctrine of the pneuma, appears to me to be an excessively unreliable source. Therefore, here I would also prefer to start with those texts in which direct observations are expressed that allow Heraclitus's doctrine of fire of its own accord to be connected unambiguously with the "psychical." One result, moreover, of our skepticism against the cosmological schema of doxography was that fire for Heraclitus should not so much explain and describe the experience of the world, that is, of how something comes to be from out of something else. This issue is rather the genuine riddle of thought that fire implies. Both the emergence of fire and the extinguishing of fire are, "ontologically" considered, equally riddlesome. Where does it come form and where does it go? The extinguishing may indeed visibly die away—in embers and ashes—but where does it come from? What is this sudden enflaming? I think that Heraclitus does not so much seek here an explanation as he discerns the whole mystery of the ἀείζωον. To place fire as one element next to the "other" elements is an utterly absurd paradox. It is the liveliness itself that makes itself manifest as never resting self-movement. The genuine riddle of being is not how the same order of the whole maintains itself in the exchange of what transpires but that this being in change itself takes place. Heraclitus recognized this as the one in all oppositions—the unity of the tension [76] in what is opposed. Plato's unambiguous assertion confirms this, with which he contrasts the "taut Ionic muses" with the "Sicilian." This describes at the same time the structural law of those sentences that we would like to attribute to Heraclitus on the basis of their family resemblance. Not how the one transitions into another but rather that it is also the other without transition—this is the "one wisdom" of Heraclitus. Without transition, suddenly like lightning, the riddlesome ἐξαίφνης in Plato's *Parmenides* (156d)[69] has a meaning that does not find a proper place in the Eleatic antitheses, as is also the case with the μεταπεσόντα (Fragment B88).

The spatial expression for such transitionless otherness is touching together (ἅπτεσθαι)—the key word in the profound Fragment B26: "The human kindles a light in the night, when the eyes are extinguished. Alive he touches the dead, awake he touches the sleeping."[70] The sentence poses a number of riddles. Anyone who has ever lit candles on a Christmas tree knows that there prevails a close semantic relationship between the two meanings of ἅπτειν, "to kindle" and "to touch." If one holds the igniting candle just a little off to the side, it does not light. "To ignite" means "to touch." The question is, admittedly, to what extent these two meanings play into each other—so much so that one cannot even speak here of a play on words, even if in general the middle voice, ἅπτεται, is not used transitively.

The tradition from Clement gives nonetheless a sharp clue. He speaks of the ἀπόστασις τῆς ψυχῆς which is greater in death than it is in sleep. If one takes this as one's starting-point, then one understands easily: "living he touches the dead. Awake he touches the sleeping." Is εὕδων ("when he sleeps") supposed to have been attached by Heraclitus as a solution for those who are poor at solving riddles? The style of the polarities would be perfect without this attachment and the solution—taking its departure from the last word—would be easy enough; one understands. Waking and sleep, life and death touch each other immediately. Waking is a μεταβολή, to use a concept that one does not yet find in Plato—even though in everyday Greek language it is completely ordinary, as for example when speaking of the weather (as is *"Umschlag"* in German). There is no transition between sleep and being awake. Either one is "here" or not "here," that is, either conscious or not. The phenomena that Heraclitus is considering are "total" opposites of this kind that show themselves to be one precisely through the suddenness of the change [77] from one into the other. The one who is awake and the one who sleeps is one and the same, the very one who is "alive." When he sleeps, he is present otherwise, in a way that is riddlesome, not there, like one who is dead; and we do say of one who is fast asleep that he sleeps "like the dead." There is something mysterious in the suddenness of the change, when the one who falls asleep is "gone" all at once. This also holds for the beginning of the "sleep of death," although this is a final change. Accordingly, the epigrammatically shortened text not only does not seem to me to sound Heraclitean, but also not even worthy of Heraclitus. He comprehends the one wise (ἕν σοφόν) of death and life in being awake and in sleep, in something that everyone at all times can observe without thinking anything of it (ἀπείροισιν ἐοίκασι πειρώμενοι).

Yet, what does the first clause of the fragment want to say (ἄνθρωπος ἅπτεται . . .)? Certainly, the human "mastery" over fire and the ability to produce light is one of the most ancient experiences of humanity. This is recorded in the myth of Prometheus. It is also certain that igniting or setting something on fire remains something close to a miracle. One also understands the lighting of the candles or the oil lamp to confirm the sameness of what is burning and what can burn, so that all is fire.

However, is this all that is meant, a correspondence of nature's extinguishing and igniting with sleep and awakening, death and life and the "art" of the use of fire? Clement cites the whole thing for the sake of the awakening and the waking. In general, from Christian faith, he has in view the resurrection out of the promise of Christianity. To this end, evidently, he must have modified somewhat the authentic sentence of Heraclitus that he cites, so that the clause ἄνθρωπος ἐν εὐφρόνη φάος ἅπτεται ἑαυτῷ is either to be understood with a stoic meaning or as having been forced into a Christian context by Clement with the insertion of the ἀποθανών. This allows the Christian author to recognize in εὐφρόνη (one who is "well disposed") not only a kind of semantic testimony to the possession of φρόνησις ("deliberation," *Besinnung*) but also directly a kind of semantic testimony to the faith in the resurrection.

However, how did Heraclitus himself connect the sequel, the analogy between life and death, waking and sleep, to the first clause? That "the human being" itself kindles a light in the night already points to a very particular use of fire: "the production of light." This does not fit the situation of one sleeping. It also seems to me to be misguided to relate this general assertion about "the human" to dream life, as many interpreters do with regard to the ἀποσβεσθεὶς ὄψεις. As if we have mastered our dream life in the same way that we have mastered the fire that we light! And then the emphatic "himself" (ἑαυτῷ) would be unintelligible! To be sure, Heraclitus does often oppose the world of dreams and madness to the common world of the [78] day and of reason. Yet, if it is the case that the addition ἀποσβεσθεὶς ὄψεις must actually be maintained—and it points nonetheless to the "igniting" by means of its semantic contrast with "to become extinguished"—it must make a particular point. The extinguished eyes—if this actually occurs in the sentence of Heraclitus—necessarily give the night a metaphorical meaning. The night in which we do not dream, thanks to the light that we kindle, but instead see—this is what we all do when "the human" awakens! What is actually peculiar to "the human" is not dreaming but the upsurge of this inner light that we call thinking or consciousness.[71] Whether the phrase ἀποσβεσθεὶς ὄψεις is now actually Heraclitean or added as an aid to a solution by a good puzzler of the Heraclitean riddle—it makes the point.[72]

Thus, at this point we receive unanticipated support for thinking together what ignites self-movement and the "soul." Whatever ψυχή in early Greek thought might have been, the string of assertions made here by Heraclitus about the "soul" force us to see in ψυχή more than the living thing that departs with the last draw of breath. The Socratic-Platonic resonances are unmistakable, even if Pythagoras and the way of ἀνάμνησις as the way of salvation out of the cycle of births may have already been playing a role there.

If one assumes that here what is meant is not the light of the dream but rather the brightness that we call "consciousness" (and this is indeed actual like abrupt awakening from out of sleep, a coming "to oneself," ἑαυτῷ!), then the Heraclitean λόγος first gains its full expressive power:

the πῦρ φρόνιμον that flames up when one comes "to oneself" (with some sleepers this takes awhile!) is not isolation but the way towards taking part in the common day and the common world. It is acquired in φρονεῖν and in λόγος and is also lacking in madness.

In this way, the whole of the Heraclitean teaching is connected to the profundity of these analogies and proportions, in which fire and soul, water and death are so peculiarly entangled. And yet these assertions, at the same time, break through these entanglements and thereby take on a provocative character and exhort to insight.

Admittedly, some of these exhortations barely seem to match the morphological criteria for genuine Heraclitean style which I take as my starting point. [79] However, is this not perhaps due more often to the trivializing citations? I offer an example in which the deterioration through such trivializing is carried out in two steps. Consider Fragment B46: τὴν τε οἴησιν ἱερὰν νόσον ἔλεγε καὶ τὴν ὅρασιν ψεύδεσθαι, "he called belief epileptic collapse *(Fallsucht)* and seeing he called deception." Today, it is acknowledged that one must dislodge the assertion about οἴησις from the context of a theory of knowledge in which it seems to appear here. One has to give back to the word the original moral sense that has nothing to do with Plato's δόξα.[73] There is no need in my opinion to prove that the epistemological use of the word in Plato *(Phaedo, 92a, Phaedrus, 244c)* is not original (cf. Euripides, Fragment 643). On the contrary, the pragmatic meaning in Homer of οἴογαι (to foresee) suggests an understanding of οἴησις as "madness," and mad self-certainty, blind optimism. The self emerges from this as the preferred object of mad self-certainty.

Thus, οἴησις is to be understood as self-veneration. Does Heraclitus then actually want to make heartless fun of epilepsy, when he compares it to οἴησις? More precisely, if one considers the by now "technical" expression for epilepsy, the sacred illness, one should not place too much weight upon the "collapse" as such. When it is encountered, the "sacred illness" of epileptic collapse has much more the sense that pious devotion and forbearance for the afflicted is called for. To rob or otherwise harm one who has collapsed would be nothing less than a sacred violation.

I think that Heraclitus wants to say something important here. The moment of piety and forbearance also pertains to the opinion that all humans have of themselves. A moment of madness, blind self-indulgence, lies in every human. One could call it an illness. Through self-critique and reason, with the aid of the reason common to all to go beyond such illness, one can be led to a proper and healthy sense of self-esteem. Nonetheless, this "illness"—to the extent that it is one—requires a certain forbearance or indulgence. No one can go on without regard for oneself (even a modest one). Joseph Conrad in Lord Jim has described the life tragedy of a young man who suffers with guilt the complete loss of this regard for oneself.

The paradoxical sentence is certainly not meant as a call to have forbearance before illusions about oneself. However, Heraclitus sees the power of illusions which everyone [80] has with regard to oneself—just as he correctly sees that human fate is not decided through the divine guidance of a "δαίμων" but in the way one leads one's life ("ethos"); this is also said in Fragment B119; ἦθος ἀνθρώπῳ δαίμων. Should not both the disaster of madness and the injunction of forbearance have been emphasized in Heraclitus? They could be emphasized here: ὕβριν χρὴ σβεννύναι μᾶλλον ἢ πυρκαϊήν· τὴν δὲ οἴησιν ἱερὰν νόσον ἔλεγε . . . (Fragment B43 and attached to Fragment B46).

Perhaps, it is so. Like so much else this would certainly be in accord with the profound vision of Heraclitus, the sage of the soul. His style of thought is unmistakably more akin to the fullness and sharpness of the gnomic aphoristic wisdom that to Ionic science. The critical confrontation with the latter, which comes to expression in the doctrine of fire, gives rise to amazing assertions about the "ψυχή" and its "λόγος." That the λόγος of the soul "increases itself"[74] has to be seen, in my opinion, together with all the assertions that distinguish the one hidden unity behind opposites as the "one wise." One may not presuppose here, in a manner that is post-Cartesian, the "substantial" division between the outer and the inner. One must take note of the simplest observation, that ψυχή is "life" and that the living, in contrast to everything, is a whole that increases therefore because something is added to it; it augments, develops, moves, and in the end seeks "itself." This "itself" that in all "change" hides one and the same thing places Heraclitus in opposition to the Miletian thought of opposites. The self-igniting of the fire, the self-moving of the living, the coming to itself of the waking and the self-thinking of thought are manifestations of the one λόγος that always is. The mysterious "itself" is what holds for the entire profundity of Heraclitus. In an inimitable fashion, he holds the singular middle voice that has been lost in the reflexivity of self-consciousness in the thought of modernity: ἅπτεται ἑαυτῷ It is igniting—"for itself." Or is it becoming inflamed "by itself" like the wood in the fireplace? To not know this is not to know what is "alone wise."

From here, one can understand how the Platonic question concerning the one and the many can find itself in the "taut" muses of Ionia. Heraclitus's vision encompasses—as it seems—life, consciousness and being. It was precisely this task of thinking together what is thus separated that Plato saw placed before him. The Phaedo vividly tells this story that begins with the natural principle of the "soul" that life cannot be without the cycle of circular movement. Nature therefore continually renews life in rhythmic return such that there is no death for it. However, that is only one aspect of life and soul. There [81] is also *the* life for whom death is something, because the human is something other than simply a link in the chain of the life that roles on rhythimically. Life has memory, such that it becomes more in "experience"; it increases "itself" in traversing the cyclic course of life. This is the thought enacted in *The Phaedo*. Socrates shows his friends how the principle of life and this other principle of "thought" and "ἀνάμνησις" are one and in this way inseparable as becoming and being. (Anaxagoras did not know to unify these.)

The same insight inhabits the myth in *The Phaedrus* of the ascent of the soul and its downfall. Here—as Plato stylizes and inspires his Socrates—a true master of poetic discourse and speculative irony makes his young friend who thoughtlessly followed rhetorical virtuosity conscious of the fact that ἔρως is something other than the calculus of gain and pleasure that is presented in the artful speech of Lysis. But before the flow of mythic imagination proceeds to run its overwhelming course, Socrates proposes something like a proof: "All soul is immortal"; "all this is soul concerns itself with what is without soul."[75] Note here that suddenly the "soul" becomes the principle of self-movement! The story that is then told reports that this principle that reigns throughout all that is and through which the heavens obtain their order also has its place in the soul of the individual and indeed in the unity of "loving" and "learning." To the extent that "learning" is the remembrance of the true, "ἀνάμνησις," everyone participates in the true. This is evidently the great insight that Plato points to here, which he calls at this point ἀπόδειξις (245c4). Self-movement is a true wonder. Whereas otherwise all movement occurs by virtue of something and is in movement only so long as it is moved, the living, that is, what has soul, is in movement by its own impetus and is in movement as long as it is alive. That is evident on its own. This evidence is strong enough to derive from it yet another proof for the immortality of the soul. The world, this great ordered structure of astral and earthly movements, cannot at all be connected with the thought of a state of rest. From this Socrates concludes: Therefore that which is the cause of such self-movement, the soul, must also always exist. It looks as though Plato fulfills here the expectation that can be fulfilled "only by a wise man," as it is stated in *The Charmides* (196a), namely, to show that there is a δύναμις that moves on its own and not by virtue of something else.[76] He would thereby show himself to be the Delian diver who from out of the dark depths brought something precious to light.

In this way, Plato interprets the being of the human within the great bounds of cosmic events, in which he unifies both aspects of self-movement and "λόγος" in mythical metaphors. Aristotle sought to complete this unification in the development of his concepts (κίνησις, νόησις, ἐνέργεια).[77] And Hegel, the great Aristotelian of modernity, follows him. However, is Heidegger not right when, questioning back, he discovers a Heraclitus that is behind metaphysics, yet in whom everything still plays itself out? At the same time, could he not also have found in Plato's dialectic the continuation of this play of thought?

NOTES

1. The numbers indicated for the Heraclitus citations in the text follow the numbering in Diels/Kranz, *Die Fragmente der Vorsokratiker* (Berlin: August Raabe, 1897), cited DK. Yet this should be continually compared to I. Bywater, *Heracliti Ephesii Reliquiae* (Oxford: Clarendon, 1877) and Charles H. Kahn, *The Art and Thought of Heraclitus* (Cambridge: Cambridge University Press, 1979).

2. Fragment B64: τὰ δὰ πάντα οἰακίζει Κεραυνός.

3. The stoics called this adaptation συνοικειοῦν.

4. Fragment B125: καὶ ὁ κυκεὼν διίσταται [μὴ] κινούμενος.

5. Plato (*Cratylus*, 402a): εἴη τὸν αὐτόν. . . . And with obvious emphasis, Heraclitus (Fragment B12): ποταμοῖσι τοῖσιν αὐτοῖσιν ἐμβαίνουσιν ἕτερα καὶ ἕτερα ὕδατα ἐπιρρεῖ. . . .

6. *Theaetetus*, 184a3 ff.: καὶ τὸ μέγιστον, οὗ ἕνεκα ὁ λόγος ὥρμηται, ἐπιστήμης πέρι τί ποτ᾽ ἐστίν, ἄσκεπτον γένηται.

7. For example, *Phaedo*, 103d ff.; *Philebus*, 29b f.

8. He says (in *Physics*, 203, 24–25 Diels): καὶ δέχεσθαι τὰ ἐναντία πῦρ μένον οὐ πέφυκε. τούτου δὲ αἴτιον τὸ δραστικὸν εἶναι μᾶλλον αὐτὸ καὶ εἴδει

ἀναλογεῖν, ἀλλ' οὐχὶ ὕλη. Neither the Aristotelian concept of the ὕλη nor the Empedoclean concept of the elements matches the "active" (τὸ δραστικόν).

9. For example, *Philebus*, 29c, or *Timaeus*, 79d.

10. DK 22A1: . . . (ὅς) οὔ (φησι) περὶ φύσεως εἶναι τὸ σύγγραμμα, ἀλλὰ περὶ πολιτείας, τὰ δὲ περὶ φύσεως ἐν παραδείγματος εἴδει κεῖσθαι.

11. DK 22 A1: ἀκριβὲς οἰάκισμα πρὸς βίου.

12. Werner Jaeger has made a persuasive case that, in contrast to Parmenides, the Greek word that Heraclitus uses for "thinking" is not νοεῖν and νοῦς but rather φρονεῖν and φρόνησις. See *Die Theologie der frühen griechischen Denker* (Stuttgart: W. Kohlhammer Verlag, 1953), 121 ff., including the attached note. See *The Theology of the Early Greek Philosophers* (Oxford: Clarendon Press, 1947), 103.

13. Charles Kahn (*The Art and Thought of Heraclitus*, 21), in the meantime, does just this, as I note. I am in complete accord that this does not mean that Heraclitus would be conceivable without Ionic cosmology. It is present and remains in view, but in such a way that the critique of the πολυμαθίη is directed at ıt.

14. This is what is meant in Empedocles (DK 31 B62): κρινόμενον πῦρ. If this is supposed to be an unusual use of κρίνειν, it is a citation of Heraclitus!

15. At this point Bywater cites *Aetna*, v. 536: *quod si quis lapidis miratur fusile robur, cogitet obscuri verissima dicta libelli, Heraclitti, tui, nihil insuperablile ab igni, omnia quo rerum naturae semina iacta*.

16. Cf. *Cratylus*, 412d ff. and 413b ff. (βουλόμενοι ἀποπιμπλάναι με) the sequence: ἥλιος - πῦρ - θερμόν - νοῦς.

17. Cf. my study, "Vom Anfang bei Heraklit," in *Gesammelte Werke*, Band 6, in *Griechische Philosophie II* (Tübingen: J. C. B. Mohr, 1985), 236 ff.

18. Fragment B48: τῷ οὖν τόξῳ ὄνομα βίος, ἔργον δὲ θάνατος.

19. Fragment B114: ξὺν νῷ λέγοντας ἰσχυρίζεσθαι χρὴ τῷ ξυνῷ πάντων, ὅκωσπερ νόμῳ πόλις, καὶ πολύ ἰσχυροτέρως. . . .

20. *Nicomachean Ethics*, Θ1, 1155b4; *Eudemian Ethics*, H1, 1235a25.

21. *Nicomachean Ethics*, Θ1, 1155b6: πάντα κατ' ἔριν γίνεσθαι. Cf. Heraclitus Fragment B80: . . . καὶ γινόμενα πάντα κατ' ἔριν καὶ χρεών.

22. Fragment B60: ὁδὸς ἄνω κάτω μία καὶ ὠυτή.

23. Cf. Bywater, *Heracliti Ephesii Reliquiae*, 28. Thus, Clement also understands Fragment B31 in this way. Concerning this, see my discussion below.

24. Fragment B101: ἐδιζησάμην ἐμεωυτόν.

25. Fragment B45: Ψυχῆς πείρατα ἰὼν οὐκ ἄν ἐξεύροιο, πᾶσαν ἐπιπορευόμενος ὁδον· οὕτω βαθὺν λόγον ἔχει.

26. *Symposium*, 221d–222a: Alcibiades likens Socrates to a statue of Silenus which must be opened, and in the center of which one finds images of the gods.

27. Cf. my study, "Hegel und Heraklit," in *Gesammelte Werke*, Band 7, *Plato im Dialog* (Tübingen: J. C. B. Mohr, 1991), 32–42.

28. Fragment B1: τοῦ δὲ λόγου τοῦδ' ἐόντος ἀεὶ ἀξύνετοι γίγονται ἄνθρωτοι. . . .

29. It seems to me not to be possible, as has been maintained many times, to connect the "always" only to the λόγος, in the sense of the "λόγος that is true" (ἐὼν λόγος). Such a possibility is ruled out if one considers the position of this ὄντος behind the unitary and monolithic λόγου. Aristotle does well to leave things undecided where nothing necessitates a decision. That he takes it as a problem at all seems to illustrate the transition to a primary approach to reading that is interested in punctuation as an aide in understanding. However, the truth is that the punctuation is actually less important than the persistently bivalent tone in the psalming lecture. Kahn has a similar position, except that I do not understand the ὄντος ἀεί as "forever true," but rather as "ever-present" (and thereby "true")—"present" yet "ignored." What Kahn has shown us in his radical study on the meanings of "being" not only applies to Heraclitus, but it also shows what cannot be detached from this: "present" and "true," said from the λόγος are one, even if it always (ἀεί) remains mistaken.

30. Cf. Fragment B41: εἶναι γὰρ ἓν τὸ σοφόν, ἐπίστασθαι γνώμην, ὁτέῃ κυβερνᾶται πάντα διὰ πάντων. Fragment B32: ἓν τὸ σοφὸν μοῦνον λέγεσθαι οὐκ ἐθέλει καὶ ἐθέλει Ζηνὸς ὄνομα.

31. Fragment B50: οὐκ ἐμοῦ, ἀλλὰ τοῦ λόγου ἀκούσαντας ὁμολογεῖν σοφόν ἐστιν ἓν πάντα εἶναι.

32. Cf. my study, "Sokrates' Frömmigkeit des Nichtwissens," In *Plato im Dialog*, 85.

33. A. Mourelatos would like to avoid the triviality in this text by understanding the ὅπως ἔχει as the pregnant "holding together" that is actually the wisdom of Heraclitus. (A. Mourelatos, "Heraclitus, Parmenides, and the Naive Metaphysics of Things," in *Exegesis and Argument: Studies in Greek Philosophy Presented to Gregory Vlastos*, eds. E. N. Lee, A. P. D. Mourelatos, and R. M. Rorty (Assen: Van Gorcum, 1973), 38, note 60. In my view, the fact that we are dealing here with the first sentence of the book speaks against this. This announcement is not yet the doctrine. As the announcement of something that attains its actual fulfillment in an entirely different way, the conventional character of these sentences, on the contrary, appear to me to be highly paradoxical. I will attempt to demonstrate this.

34. Concerning this passage, cf. my study, in *Plato in Dialog*, 24 ff.

35. Fragment B1: τοὺς . . . ἀνθρώπους λανθάνει ὁκόσα ἐγερθέντες ποιοῦσιν ὅκωσπερ ὁκόσα εὕδοντες ἐπιλανθάνονται.

36. Karl Reinhardt's interpretation, which he takes from Hölscher, I do not find convincing. One expects that the preceding ἀπείροισιν-πειρώμενοι will be illustrated. (Kahn also adopts this, *The Art and Thought of Heraclitus*, 99.) The sentence is emphatically symmetrical. The subtlety of the parallel between λανθάνει and ἐπιλανθάνονται lies in its variation: despite their being awake humans live in permanent oblivion (λανθάνει), just as they forget afterwards (ἐπί) their dreams (what they did while asleep) and leave them unattended (ἐπιλανθάνονται). The same variation is met in Fragment B21, where one expects ἐνύπνιον and finds ὕπνος, a complete span of time. I also cannot follow Bollack here because he neglects the clear evidence that it is the forgetting of dreams that is being alluded to.

37. Fragment B89: τοῖς ἐγρηγορόσιν ἕνα καὶ κοινὸν κόσμον εἶναι, τῶν δὲ κοιμωμένων ἕκαστον εἰς ἴδιον ἀποστρέφεσθαι.

38. Fragment B75: τοὺς καθεύδοντας . . . ἐργάτας εἶναι . . . καὶ συνεργοὺς τῶν ἐν τῷ κόσμῳ γινομένων. In my opinion, Bröcker has rightly separated here the stoic addition καὶ συνεργοὺς from the Heraclitean sentence cited by Marcus Aurelius. *Die Geschichte der Philosophie vor Sokrates* (Frankfurt am Main: Vittorio Klostermann, 1965), 35 ff

39. Fragment B73: οὐ δεῖ ὥσπερ καθεύδοντας ποιεῖν καὶ λέγειν . . . .

40. G. S. Kirk, *Heraclitus: The Cosmic Fragments* (Cambridge: University Press, 1954), 44 ff.

41. H. Fraenkel, *Wege und Formen* (Munich: Beck, 1955), 258 ff.

42. Fragment B21: Θάνατός ἐστιν ὁκόσα ἐγερθέντες ὁρέομεν, ὁκόσα δὲ εὕδοντες ὕπνος.

43. Kahn does indeed sense the asymmetry of the Heraclitean sentence, but in my opinion he seeks it in the wrong place (*The Art and Thought of Heraclitus*, 213).

44. Kahn, *The Art and Thought of Heraclitus*, 231 ff.

45. Fragment B20: γενόμενοι ζώειν ἐθέλουσι μόρους τ᾽ ἔχειν, μᾶλλον δὲ ἀναπαύεσθαι, καὶ παῖδας καταλείπουσι μόρους γενέσθαι.

46. Concerning the extinguishing of the μᾶλλον ἀναπαύεσθαι, see Reinhardt, *Hermes* (1942), 4.

47. *Eudemian Ethics*, H1, 1235a25; *Nicomachean Ethics*, Θ1, 1155b4. This has been discussed above.

48. This is shown clearly at *Metaphysics*, Γ3, 1005b23 ff.: ἀδύνατον γὰρ ὁντινοῦν ταὐτὸν ὑπολαμβάνειν εἶναι καὶ μὴ εἶναι, καθάπερ τινὲς οἴονται λέγειν Ἡράκλειτον. Likewise G7, 1012a24ff.: ἔοικε δ᾽ ὁμὲν Ἡρακλείτου λόγος. λέγων πάντα εἶναι καὶ μὴ εἶναι, ἅπαντα ἀληθῆ ποιεῖν.

49. Fragment B10 (= Pseudo - Aristotle, *De Mundo*, 5, 396b20 f.): συνάψιες (or συλλάψιες) ὅλα καὶ οὐχ ὅλα, συμφερόμενον διαφερόμενον, συνᾷδον διᾷδον καὶ ἐκ πάντων ἕν καὶ ἐξ ἑνὸς πάντα.

50. Fragment B51: οὐ ξυνιᾶσιν ὅκως διαφερόμενον ἑωυτῷ συμφέρεται· παλίντονος ἁρμονίη ὅκωσπερ τόξου καὶ λύρης.

51. Fragment B67: ὁ θεὸς ἡμέρη εὐφρόνη, χειμὼν θέρος, πόλεμος εἰρήνη, κόρος λιμός. . . . "The god is day and night, winter and summer, war and peace, satiation and hunger."

52. Fragment B62: ἀθάνατοι θνητοί, θνητοί ἀθάνατοι, ζῶντες τὸν ἐκείνων θάνατον, τὸν δὲ ἐκείνων βίον τεθνεῶτες. For an interpretation, see the discussion above.

53. Fragment B67 (cont.): ἀλλοιοῦται δὲ ὅκωσπερ πῦρ, ὁπόταν συμμιγῇ θυώμασιν, ὀνομάζεται καθ᾽ ἡδονὴν ἑκάστου.

54. Fragment B88: ταὐτό τ᾽ ἔνι ζῶν καὶ τεθνηκὸς καὶ ἐγρηγορὸς καὶ καθεῦδον καὶ νέον καὶ γηραιόν· τάδε γὰρ μεταπεσόντα ἐκεῖνά ἐστι κἀκεῖνα πάλιν μεταπεσόντα ταῦτα.

55. Cf. my study, "The Proofs of Immortality in Plato's *Phaedo*," in *Dialogue and Dialectic: Eight Hermeneutical Studies on Plato*, trans. P. Christopher Smith (New Haven: Yale University Press, 1980), 21–38. German text was originally published in *Gesammelte Werke*, Band 6, 187–200.

56. Cf. Martin Heidegger and Eugen Fink, H, 158 ff.; HS, 98.

57. *Enneads*, IV.8.6.1, 15–16.

58. Fragment B27: ἀνθρώπους μένει ἀποθανόντας ἄσσα οὐκ ἔλπονται οὐδὲ δοκέουσιν.

59. Fragment B18: ἐὰν μὴ ἔλπηται, ἀνέλπιστον οὐκ ἐξευρήσει.

60. Fragment B53: Πόλεμος πάντων μὲν πατήρ ἐστι, πάντων δὲ βασιλεύς, καὶ τοὺς μὲν θεοὺς ἔδειξε τοὺς δὲ ἀνθρώπους, τοὺς μὲν δούλους ἐποίησε τοὺς δὲ ἐλευθέρους.

61. Fragment B80: εἰδέναι δὲ χρὴ τὸν πόλεμον ἐόντα ξυνόν, καὶ δίκην ἔριν. . . .

62. Kahn has shown quite nicely how Heraclitus goes beyond the statements on war of Homer and Archilochus (*The Art and Thought of Heraclitus*, 205). He also correctly hears in this a reference to the sentence that opens the whole text. However, I do not find here a reference to the sentence of Anaximander, familiar to us only by chance. Here, it is not a matter of *Dike* appearing as violent punishment, as it is in Anaximander, but instead the issue is the way conflict comes into play as the common (ξυνόν). This is what the ignorant (ἀπείροισιν) continually miss.

63. Fragment B30: κόσμον τόνδε, τὸν αὐτὸν ἁπάντων, οὔτε τις θεῶν οὔτε ἀνθρώπων ἐποίησεν, ἀλλ᾽ ἦν ἀεὶ καὶ ἔστιν καὶ ἔσται πῦρ ἀείζωον, ἁπτόμενον μέτρα καὶ ἀποσβεννύνεμον μέτρα.

64. Fragment B31: πυρὸς τροπαὶ πρῶτον θάλασσα, θαλάσσης δὲ τὸ μὲν ἥμισυ γῆ, τὸ δὲ ἥμισυ πρηστήρ. . . .

65. Kahn, *The Art and Thought of Heraclitus*, 139 ff.

66. Fragment B90: πυρός τε ἀνταμοιβὴ τὰ πάντα καὶ πῦρ ἁπάντων ὅκωσπερ χρυσοῦ χρήματα καὶ χρημάτων χρυσός.

67. Clement, *Sstromateis*, V. 14, 104, 4: δυνάμει γὰρ λέγει, ὅτι (τὸ) πῦρ ὑπὸ τοῦ διοικοῦντος λόγου καὶ θεοῦ τὰ σύμπαντα δι' ἀέροσ τρέπεται εἰς ὑγρὸν τὸ ὡς σπέρμα τῆς διακοσμήσεως, ὅ καλεῖ θσλάσσαν, ἐκ δὲ τούτου αὖθις γίνεται γῆ καὶ οὐρανὸς καὶ τὰ ἐμπεριεχόμενα. ὅπως δὲ πάλιν ἀναλαμβάνεται καὶ ἐκπυροῦται, σαφῶς διὰ τούτων δηλοῖ....

68. See note 8.

69. Cf. my study, "Der platonische *Parmenides* und seine Nachwirkung," in *Plato im Dialog*, in *Gesammelte Werke*, Band 7, 322 ff.

70. Fragment B26: ἄνθρωπος ἐν εὐφρόνηφάος ἅπτεται ἑαυτῷ [ἀποθανών] ἀποσβεσθεὶς ὄψεὶς· ζῶν δὲ ἅπτεται τεθνεῶτος εὕδων [ἀποσβεσθεὶς ὄψεις], ἐγρηγορὼς ἅπτεται εὕδοντος.

71. Cf. Fragment B116: ἀνθρώποισι πᾶσι μέτεστι γινώσκειν ἑωυτοὺς καὶ σωφρονεῖν.

72. Hölscher moves in the same direction in his basic interpretation, but in my opinion still takes the "physics of the soul" too literally—and yet, then again, not literally enough—when he completely dissociates the literal sense of "to touch" from ἅπτειν, a sense which is indispensible in the opening clause. Uvo Hölscher, *Anfängliches Fragen* (Göttingen: Vandenhoeck & Ruprecht, 1968), 156–160.

73. Thus, the word is found in Fragment B131 understood in a manner that is to be expected here: (ἔλεγε τὴν) οἴησιν προκοπῆς ἐγκοπήν—moreover, in the most genuine gnomic style. Also, elsewhere it is attested to as "old": Joh. Damasc., Sacra par. 693e (cf. Mondolfo/Tarán, *Eraclito. Testimonianze e Imitazioni* (Florence: La nuova Italia, 1972), 221 ff.). See also, for example, Euripides Fragment 270: δόκησις, as in Heraclitus Fragment B17 δοκέουσι. This, of course, does not prove the usage of the word οἴησις. (And *Corpus Hippocrates*, IX, 230, ed. Littré, is also no actual evidence.)

74. Fragment B115: ψυχῆς ἐστι λόγος ἑαυτὸν αὔξων.

75. *Phaedrus*, 245c5: ψυχὴ πᾶσα ἀθάνατος; 24b6, ψυχὴ πᾶσα παντὸς ἐπιμελεῖται τοῦ ἀψύχου.

76. Concerning this, cf. my study, "Vorgestalten der Reflexion," in *Gesammelte Werke*, Band 6, 116–128.

77. To do this he also refers to Heraclitus: *De Anima*, A2, 405a25–28: τὸ δὲ κινούμενον κινουμένῳγινώσκεσθαι. However, at 405a5, Heraclitus is also being invoked (τισι πῦρ).

Eleven

Appearing to Remember Heraclitus

Charles E. Scott

"The Hidden Unity of Being and Appearance. . . ."
Heidegger, *An Introduction To Metaphysics*

The Appearance of "Greece"

The questions of memory and knowledge are evoked by the subject of this volume as well as by the topic of this essay. Greek thought, all of Greek culture, appear in our culture with degrees of vividness and obscurity as though "we" were living memories of "Greece." They provide direction for us, and, in our practices and values, live through us in lineages of active as well as tacit memory. That civilization *appears* originary for our ways of thinking as well as for what we think is most profound and problematic.

This "influence" is multiplied by our post-Greek forbearers who themselves gave form and substance to our present ways of knowing and living, by Origen, Proclus, Augustine, Thomas, Maimonides, Vico, and Hegel, by many who are within our canon of knowledge and by others whose names are lost to our surveys of western philosophers. In our thought and knowledge we are their heirs. As we think and perceive we are also the heirs of those who copied texts, who "corrected" and preserved them; in our thinking we are the heirs of the destroyers of the texts, of the fires that burned them, of the mold and air that consumed and desiccated them. In our lineage, people's explicit appropriations of Greek thought and practice, their dissents, omissions, limits, and inaccuracies as well as their creative use of Greek texts directly formed our own structures of recognition, our limits and abilities of sensibility, our range of reference, our memories. Greek civilization and its appropriations by our forbearers appear in inchoate and tacit dimensions of our thought and experience as well as in the explicit traditions that trace their identities in the lineages of Plato or Aristotle. One such tacit dimension is found in our sense of the difference between appearance and reality, a difference that is articulated in the "reality" of past events as distinct from their appearance in memory and narration. The "reality" of "Greece" appears to be lost in our memory of "Greece" by means of the operative sense of the difference between appearance and reality.

We know that as heirs we are able to err. The involuntary memory of the Greeks that inhabits our language and thought as well as our ways of life is not the immediacy of Greek civilization. Greek civilization is not immediate to us in our inchoate experiences of appearance and reality, of tragedy, divinity, truth, or change. We find in these experiences, when we turn our attention to them, nothing purely Greek. In them we are also of Hebraic lineages, of Celtic, Roman, Germanic, Gothic, and multiple other descents. These descents play active roles in both our present experience and our interpretations of what remains of Greek civilization. "Greece" *appears*, in our experiences and in our approaches to it, multiplied, displaced and transferred, diluted and transformed. The dilutions and fragmentations of Greek thought and life appear, whether tacitly or explicitly, as aspects of our values, disciplines, and mentation as we read the Greek texts or as we imagine ourselves in their languages and festivals. We know that "Greece" appears to us in forms of recognition, in mediated texts, in awarenesses and blindnesses that are not of Greek lives or of Greek thought. We know that nothing Greek is present to us as simple Greek presence. We know that the being of "Greece" comes to us and is lost to us in the appearances of our Greek heritage.

We also know that these opening observations about the appearance and being of Greek thought are thoroughly indebted to "Greece." We know that we belong to "Greece" in knowing that its being is lost in its appearance. Many of us find ourselves inclined to think further in the impact of this association of loss and presence. In its appearance, we are inclined to think again of Greece and of its originary importance for us.

Sublime Memory

As I approach Heidegger's encounter with Heraclitus' truth, I turn first to Nietzsche's account of the sublime dimension of dionysian memory.

This dimension of memory is not based on literal truth or accuracy. It is rather an occurrence in which "something" excessive to identity and individuation is manifest and in which the individual experiences loss of autonomy and control. As sublime, an experience opens out to "something" beyond identity.[1] In the context of dionysian experience, the sublime occurs *in* the loss of identity, in a dismembering of the structures in which one consciously exists and knows himself or herself. Standing out from oneself—ec-stasis—occurs in an event of disjoining and falling apart. In such an event, "that" which "Dionysus" signifies becomes vivid, although "it" is without an image to preserve it.

In *The Birth of Tragedy*, Nietzsche elaborates this kind of experience by reference to "primitive" participation in dionysian festivals. In the early festivals, both those who danced and sang dithyrambically and those who were outside of the orchestra—the place of dance—and were, in modern, language, "observers," were involved without the protection of conscious distance or judgment. They were immediately engaged, without the mediation of self-consciousness. Their passions and movements arose from the loss of themselves. They were united in the movements and sounds of disjoining from everything individual and familiar to them. Both conscious and unconscious, both with and without orientation, feeling with identity without identity or identification, standing out from themselves in the passions of commonly losing their selves, suffering without a sense of justice, un-distanced from bodies, closer to dying than to individuation, without hope or defining memory, they moved in an immediacy of life. In the immediacy of both, they found sameness in loss and in life other to identity. Their dionysian spirituality was determinate indetermination, being-coming-apart.

A similar immediacy, Nietzsche says, enveloped the occurrence of performances of tragedy. But in this event, the experience of dionysian oblivion is transferred to a staged scene, and the oblivious music and movement of the earlier festival is transferred by the disordered music and cries of the chorus to an enacted narrative. The immediacy here is one of interrupted dramatic order, of the undoing of character, reputation, honor, and intelligent direction. For the unorder of Fate—its dismemberment of personal and social standing—is removed from dances of oblivion to a scenic play that is filled with images of identity. As individuals are performed and presented in their singularity and in the erosion of their singularity, those who participate by seeing and hearing undergo the "drama" and its music with an immediacy of participatory inclusion. They no longer find themselves as observing citizens, but rather lose themselves—disidentify themselves—in the drama's occurrence. They do not shudder in a sense of distance. They are in the play's life as though they were enmeshed and shuddering in a vivid dream.

In the tragedy, at its artistic finest, the enacted images give participation in an ecstatic loss of individuation by means of individualized images that, with dithyrambic music, remember dionysian dismemberment and its ecstatic release of conscious singularity. These images come with immediate vividness. They re-mind one of the sublime limit of identity and formation.

Vivid memory in this context may be described as dreamlike. In contrast to what I call to memory by imaginative and conscious action, a vivid memory is like the coming of a dream. It interrupts the state to which it occurs, for example, dreamless sleep. "Something" comes to image without explanation or voluntary effort. "I" see it or hear it or feel it without intending it. A vivid memory occurs *to* me. In its occurrence it is not like an object that I find. It is also not the same as its retention; it is held or kept only in its loss and remains. In its coming it displaces a person's personal stance and active self-consciousness. It marks a loss of autonomous activity.

Hence, even the coming of such vivid images has a dionysian aspect just as naming and preserving imagelessness by such an image as "Dionysus" has an apollonian aspect.

Our emphasis falls on re-membering in both the images and their vivid presentation the occurrences of ecstatic dismemberment that open to no image or identity. In Nietzsche's account of dionysian memory in classical Greek tragedy, we find an instance of memory *in* the coming of images, in the oblivion that the arrival of images carries. It is an immediate memory in tragic happening, "something" said in the occurrence that exceeds what the images explicitly articulate and what the images "really" are. It is a memory that happens as the images bring with them an indeterminate beginning and end that is pervasive of their "reality" or appearances.

Heraclitus' Memory According to Heidegger

Heraclitus, according to Heidegger, "says" the self-concealing of φύσις as φύσις presents itself in the coming to pass of thought: φύσις, which names the coming to presence of things, conceals itself in its self-presentation, and Heraclitus' thought remembers in its own occurrence the intimacy of self-revealing and self-concealing.[2] Heidegger writes: "Heraclitus is called 'the Obscure.' But he is the Lucid for he says the lighting whose shining he attempts to call forth into the light of thinking. . . . Lighting bestows the shining, opens what shines to an appearance" (EGT, 103). Heraclitus' lucidity is found in his bringing to language the process of coming to appear (not simply giving expression to what appears). But "coming to appear"—φύσις—does not occur only as the shining or appearing of things. It also "hides" or fails to appear or happens as other to its own appearing. Heraclitus is both obscure and lucid in not overlooking this concealing-appearing atonceness in the shining of things. "Obscure lucidity" names what happens *in* his thinking as he thinks things in their concealing-appearing occurrence.

The concealing of the coming to presence of things is given a strange vividness. It—the concealing—is not forgotten. That means that Heraclitus "thinks" a concealing dimension of things in their appearing by a reserve, a refusal to give disclosive presence dominance in his thought. His "lucidity" occurs in an obscurity that, as he thinks, is not lost in the interest of completion, explanation, or something approximate to what *we* might call clarity. On Heidegger's account, Heraclitus is most clear because he gives thought to a hiddenness and obscurity in the presencing—the φύσις or coming to life or coming to pass or coming to appear—of things.

I emphasized in the previous sections that non-voluntary memory can happen in the coming of images as well as in the occurrences of language, conceptual structure, perception of problems, recognition of things, and order of importance and insignificance. The emphasis also falls on the happening of experiences and thought more than on what is experienced and thought. Memorial transfer seems to occur *in* the coming and going of images. Memory is imbedded in both the occurrences and the structures of language, thought, knowledge, experience, and perception. We now notice that, in Heidegger's reading, "something" as unsubject to image and identity as "the dionysian" in Nietzsche's account of tragedy is found in the occurrence of Heraclitus' thought. In order to follow this interpretive claim by Heidegger, we shall consider the function of the middle voice to say—to voice—the occurrence of presencing and concealing. Through the middle voice

254 ❖ APPEARING TO REMEMBER HERACLITUS

function of language, we will find the performative expression of the thought and occurrence of concealing—something like a remembering of concealing—that exceeds the expressive capacity of active and passive formations and the images of presence. We will find concealment in the φύσις—the coming to presence—of thought, a process for the expression of which the middle voice is especially suited. In this process, we shall also find a different way of thinking what we usually call the distinction between appearance and reality; we shall find a different memory of the appearance of being from the memories that we are accustomed to identifying. These different memories are imbedded in the thought of being and appearance and in the language in which we think and say being and appearance.

Memory, as I bring the word to bear in the context of Heidegger's discussion of Heraclitus, means not forgetting, in Heraclitus' thought, the self-concealing/self-showing *Wesen* (essence or coming to pass) of appearing. This awkward language—awkward to *us* given our sense of proper clarity—means that what we ordinarily call the essence of things occurs as the coming to appear of things. Coming to appear also means coming to pass, that is, it means the "essential" happening of life. This happening, according to Heraclitus, is both (self)-showing and (self)-concealing. The essence of life is self-showing and self-concealing in the coming to pass of things. The occurrence of "essence" is neither an activity on the part of a subject nor the consequence or recipient of an action. It is self-enactment, the grammatical expression of which was the middle voice in Sanskrit and Greek. Perhaps our memory of the self-enactment of appearing/not appearing as the essence of what appears depends on recall of an intransitive middle voice meaning that is embedded in reflexive constructions.

Consider the middle voice verb, ἐπιλανθάνεσθαι.[3] The word not only means "to forget." It has also a nonmiddle voice sense of "remaining concealed": "what" remains concealed occurs (we would say, reflexively occurs) as self-concealed. Or we could say that concealing occurs as concealing (itself), as distinct from appearing. Heidegger takes a further step. The "dimension" of appearing that conceals (itself) and does not appear *happens* as not appearing. Concealing occurs in excess to appearing. This is close to the strange dionysian insight that "what" does not and cannot be an image of any kind happens as un-imageable, as with image but at once as other to image. Heidegger says that in forgetting, as "the Greeks" experienced it, the forgotten—the concealed—*happens* in concealment. We could say that concealing conceals in accompaniment with appearing.

Further, "what takes place in such indifference comes from the *Wesen* (the essence, the coming to pass) of oblivion itself. It is inherent in it to withdraw itself and to founder in the wake of its own concealment" (EGT, 108). Rather than coming to appear, concealment happens as concealing (something like the occurrence of Hades or, at times, Persephone). It does not *appear* as concealment. Rather it "is" a self-enactment of concealing. It is not subject to appearance, although it occurs with appearance.

In this intransitive middle voice, we thus find expression of something other to appearance that "occurs" (i.e., self-conceals) with appearance. From one way of looking at it, we could say that we have a distinction between the self-enactment of appearing and something other to appearing that of itself "enacts" concealment. Heraclitus finds in the appearing of things "something" quite other to appearance. Although we could not call this other to appearance "reality" or "being" in the post-platonic senses of these words, we could assume that Heraclitus finds in appearing/concealing a strangeness of life that considerably exceeds the intelligence of distinctions and "clear" appearance. We might contend as well that the middle voice can "say" the *Wesen* of things, the self-enactment of their occurrence. The word *Wesen*, as Heidegger is using it in this context, has a middle voice sense of self-enactment that is not determined primarily by formation or deformation, by identity or chaos, by being or non-being; the sense of the word, *Wesen*, is determined by the happening of coming-to-appear-withdrawing-from-appearing. Something like self-concealment and forgetting is thus "remembered" in the self-enactment of concealing that accompanies or "belongs to" appearances.

Λανθάνομαι: A middle voice verb that says, "I am—with respect to something usually concealed—concealed from myself" (EGT, 108). I occur in self-concealment as I appear with the appearing/concealing occurrence of things. Heidegger is showing by this turn in his discussion that, according to Heraclitus, the one who exists in and with the appearing-concealing of things is not removed from concealment but lives in the occurrence of self-concealment. A concealment and forgetfulness of the appearing of the "self" accompanies the appearing "self." As the dionysian appears in withdrawal from images in relation to which "it" is other, so concealment withdrawal from the appearing of whatever is manifest. This withdrawal is like forgetting. "Forgetting itself slips into a concealing, and indeed in such a way that we ourselves, along with our relation to what is forgotten, fall into concealment. The Greeks, therefore, speaking in the middle voice, intensify it: ἐπιλανθάνομαι. Thus they also identify the concealment into which man falls by reference to its relation to what is withdrawn from him by concealment" (EGT, 108–109). An individual exists in the withdrawal of appearance as well as in the disclosiveness of appearance, and both self-remembrance and self-forgetfulness occur in the withdrawal and disclosiveness of appearance.

A thorough incompleteness of not only what appears, but also of appearing itself could lead to hopelessness in the sense that one knows that nothing is simply as it appears. Its "essence" is in a "process" of withdrawal and removal from appearance. It is not only a matter of knowing that all things are passing away as they come to be, that the disaster of not being present accompanies the marvel of being present. It is also a matter of losing touch with both what one experiences and the experience of presence as such. Happening—life—is not found in presencing alone but in depresencing as well. High reputation, justice, honor, and excellent character are not only as they appear. They do not give appearance to a steady presence-for-goodness. Identity as such carries its own loss. It (identity) is a self-enactment of withdrawal from identity. Life as coming to manifest presence is at once a compound forgetfulness of no appearing whatsoever. Nothing is simply true, believable, or good. Nothing is simply alive. Nothing simply is. To remember is to forget. And, absurdly, to forget is to remember. We are the self-enactment of such darkness in our occurrence as alert and enlightened. "I remain concealed" in my best appearance and knowledge. Even now, remembering my forgetting, I am self-concealed beyond presence and remembrance.

In relation to what do I remain concealed? Heidegger says that Heraclitus' preoccupation is not with concealment but with that in relation to which concealment happens: the never-setting, the τὸ μὴ δῦνον ποτε (EGT, 109). That is, the issue is the self-enactment of φύσις, the arising and coming to be (appear) of all things. The thought is that φύσις cannot be appropriately remembered and thought if concealment in its own self-enactment is not remembered. And we have seen that for Heraclitus such "memory" is not the same as focused recollection, but is the occurrence of self-forgetting in the very φύσις of thought and language. In thought and language things appear, rise to thoughtful and expressed life. And in that "phusical" happening concealment occurs with the process of appearing as other to the process of appearing. So in Heraclitus' preoccupation with the never-setting—the always arising—he is also attentive to concealing which never occurs as arising or appearing, but which nonetheless belongs to arising and appearing. He remembers that forgetting and concealing pervade and intimately border remembering and appearing, and his thought is thus in (a middle voiced) remembrance of concealment and its enigmatic, incomplete, and obscure preoccupation with the never-setting.

Κρύπθεσθαι: A middle voice word that means, hiding hides (itself). It means self-concealment. Heraclitus says that "φύσις κρύπθεσθαι φιλεῖ" Heidegger interprets these words to mean, "rising (out of self-concealing) bestows favor on self-concealing" (EGT, 113–114). He thinks of φιλεῖ as "giving favor to," as "being inclined to": the arising of things into appearance gives favor to the self-concealing of that very event; φύσις gives favor to its own withdrawal from appearing. This coming-to-appear-withdrawing-from-appearing is the event or essence—the *Wesen*—of life. In the appearing of things, self-appearing and self-concealing "*west*": they eventuate in mutuality. They are of each other, and in that sense they are one in difference.

Hence, for Heraclitus, self-concealing does not mean the disaster of nothing at all. It means the always-arising, never-setting of the "process" of coming to appear. It means φύσις, the on-going of the emergence of appearance. This claim is not exactly the claim that Nietzsche makes for tragedy—that tragedy provides a sublime, life-affirming occurrence of the dionysian. But it is a similar claim in the sense that, in Heraclitus' thought, the dark and threatening obscurity of self-concealing means the never-setting of the coming of appearances. In his thinking, according to Heidegger, forgetfulness of self-concealment is remembered as the thought of φύσις appears. One emphasis in this memory is on unpresence *in* presencing. The implication is that when presence dominates and organizes a process of thinking—when the forgetfulness of self-concealing is forgotten— the event of coming to presence is also forgotten in the structures and appearances to which the event gives rise. In the "metaphysical comfort" of an image of complete, grounding presence, the shining life of coming-to-presence is made obscure—unlucid—and unremembered.

Heidegger's Appearing to Remember Heraclitus

Underlying this discussion is a distinction among: memory that comes with practice or habit or effort, for example, one's knowing how something in the past happened or knowing that fire burns when touched; memory in the sense of one's undergoing the emergence of vivid images or events in which something past—no longer present—comes again with renewed, if different, presence; and memory in the sense of bearing in mind the occurrence that is taking place and passing away. Memory in the form of knowing suggests intentional action, often in the forms of association, disciplines of recovery, habitual retention, and methods for cultivating retention. Vivid memory suggests the nonvoluntary emergences of images and events that are compelling in their power to bring one into their domain of meaning and experience. They suggest a certain displacement of the individual's intentionally constituted identity and boundaries. The third kind of memory, which we have considered in the context of the middle voice, suggests awareness in an event of the occurrence of appearing and not appearing, and awareness that happens in appearance and presentation but is not in the form of representations or re-cognitions. We shall consider further the second and third kinds of memory.

The prefix *re* suggests *again* or *anew*. *Remember* means "to come or to bring to mind again," "to keep in mind," or "to bestow attention upon." In Heidegger's reading of Heraclitus' Fragment B16, the elements of *again* and of *attention* occur *in* Heraclitus' thought as distinct from occurring as an object of his thought. Yet these elements also have the vividness of something coming to mind without intentional or subjective action or habitual retention. It shares a kinship with the apollonian occurrence of the coming of a dream in the occurrence of images, and with the darkness that it interrupts and paradoxically carries with it. Heidegger, however, stresses thought and language rather than images. The presentational occurrence is not one of images of past events but the coming *again* of appearing with self-concealing: again—never-setting—in the withdrawal of appearances. The *again* seems to happen in the conjunction of self-showing *and* self-concealing. The *re* of remembering appears to have a middle voice sense of happening without an active constitution of concepts or objects. Its awareness in Heraclitus' thought seems to belong to its occurrence and to show itself in the movement and language of his thought. The *re*—the *again*—is "minded" in the way in which Heraclitus' thought comes to presence. Φύσις, ἐπιλανθάνομαι and κρύπθεσθαι are "favored" (φιλεῖ) in the way in which his thought arises and comes to language. The middle voice sense of "happening again" suggests undergoing a continuous boundary in the arising of thought. Self-showing and self-concealing are not identical. Their lack of identity, while they nevertheless belong together in the arising of thought and language, suggests continuous loss and return of the *emergence* of appearance. To be alert, mindful, aware in the continuing loss and return of appearance is to remember. Remembering happens in this instance as an alert event of the coming to pass of appearances. Remembering happens in the appearing/disappearing of what is thought and said.

What can we say, then, of Heidegger's remembering Heraclitus' thought? He believes that by entering into "a thoughtful dialogue" with the fragments that they may say far more than they can directly articulate. Such a dialogue would seem to provide a space of exchange in which the fragments say (again) the essence (*Wesen*) of their words and thoughts. Heidegger is clear that he has no adequate access to Heraclitus' intentions or to his "representational range" (EGT, 120). But the words in their own thoughtfulness provide a certain vividness of presentation that is not like an interpreter's projections when one listens to them in their own extraordinary voice. By calling into question his own philosophical training, by looking again and again, by giving favor to the otherness of Heraclitus' words, a difference in Heraclitus' voice begins to emerge that is other to Heidegger's ordinary, disciplined intelligence. He knows that he cannot "prove" the correctness of his hearing and that he cannot abstract himself from his own life-situation. But he also finds that the enactment of Heraclitus' words and thought calls him out from his operative, scholarly good sense and places in question the grounds of his certainty. Heraclitus *appears* differently in relation to the voices that Heidegger is accustomed to hearing and articulating in his ordinary, academic life.

I believe that Heidegger is advocating processes that dismantle our operative certainties in order to allow considerable differences in thought and voice to arise—to appear—and to return us, in our engagement with them, to thoughts and voices in our heritage that are forgotten—obscured—in the way our heritage carries them. These thoughts and voices are recoverable in their obscurity. We can hear them again. But only if what the thought that forgets them loses the power whereby they are silenced. And the "recovery" does not occur in the techniques of certainty and discovery that define a large segment of our disciplines and knowledge. Rather, our remembering occurs in the uncertainty and questions that come with dialogical presentations. In a sense, we have to favor (φιλεῖ) what is perhaps forgotten in our honest, established knowledge. This favoring probably will not result in newly established certainty. But it might well give rise to thinking, let thinking appear as continuing engagement with what appears and is withdrawn in our heritage.

How are we to consider this kind of remembering *in* Heidegger's thought? The *again*—the *re*, the *anew*—of his mentation takes the form of a search—a listening for—what he cannot actively call to memory by associations among the concepts and images that he knows. He certainly engages in active remembrances. He also uses all of the ordinary philosophical, scholarly, and philological resources that serve his purposes. But they are in the service of a process that lets them fall into question under the impact of something that is vivid in its occurrence and that does not fit the rubrics, assumptions, and methods that helped Heidegger along his way. The *re*—the *again*—happens in the vividness of the different thinking and language that speak themselves in the dialogue's middle voice aspect. That thinking and speaking occur in the listening, in the mentation of Heidegger's engagement.

Is this vivid appearing exactly, empirically, really Heraclitus' voice? Who could know? Is it an appearance that is at once emerging and slipping away, something coming to pass in the dialogue and yet not fully retainable by reportage and repetition? It would seem so. Is this process of remembering and forgetting the same (of the same *Wesen*) as the one that Heidegger finds taking place in Fragment B16? Again, it would seem so. It would seem that Heidegger's remembering Heraclitus occurs in the appearing of Heraclitus' words and thought in a dialogue of questioning uncertainty. If that is so, then the dialogue and its minding of remembering and forgetting, and of self-showing and self-concealing in their middle voices, engages (again) the thinking of Heraclitus. He appears vividly in the oblivion of his pastness, and we recall him in his presence only in the loss of his presence. Like other appearances that distracted him, showed him far more than what they seemed to be, and gave rise in their strangeness to his thought, so Heraclitus appears in question in Heidegger's encounter with the fragment and gives rise to thought that is (perhaps) like his in its determinant indeterminacy and in its passion less to know than to let what appears continue to appear in remembrance of its enlightened darkness.

NOTES

1. *Sublime* literally means "(coming) up to below the lintel." A lintel is something that spans an opening to carry a superstructure; it gives the space, for example, for a threshold. The word has the overtone of both reaching a limit and opening out at a limit beyond the limit. In the context of Nietzsche's *The Birth of Tragedy*, sublime, dionysian occurrences are elaborated by the intransitive verbal sense of *sublime* in a context of chemistry: to come to pass from solid to vapor state and condense back again to solid. The word can also mean, to convert something inferior to something of higher worth. The word suggests both elevation and excess, suggestions found also in the German *erhaben* and *das Erhabene*.

2. The English version, in *Early Greek Thinking*, translates *sagt* as "tells of" (EGT, 103). In Heidegger's use of *sagen*, as distinct to *sprechen* or *erzählen*, the word suggests immediacy of expression rather than narration or report.

3. The following discussion of this word is a reading of EGT, 108 ff.

Twelve

Heraclitus, Philosopher of the Sign

Walter A. Brogan

The Problem of Reading and Interpreting Heraclitus

Any interpretation of Heraclitus faces extraordinary difficulties that arise due to the very character of fragmentary writing and its peculiar relationship to narrative exposition.[1] Most of the fragments are given to us already enmeshed in the later metaphysical tradition. The very words attributed to Heraclitus are already encoded for us by Plato and Aristotle who often preserve a saying of Heraclitus as a point of contrast to their own philosophical positions. Thus the task of creating a text of Heraclitus such as the one put together by Diels and Kranz requires that these sayings be torn away from the foreign (often Platonic or Aristotelian) contexts in which they are embedded. This fact not only creates complications for our attempt to read Heraclitus as an early Greek thinker, an originary pre-metaphysical philosopher, but it also bypasses the opportunity to consider the disruptive effect of these sayings and their removal on the texts from which they are sundered.

Most commentators attempt to gather and link together the fragments according to a certain overall understanding of what Heraclitean philosophy stands for. All-important to such endeavors is the choice of which fragment to put first, for from this often follows a certain prioritizing of other fragments according to an advance conviction as to what Heraclitus most wants to emphasize.[2] Interpreters give themselves the task of weaving a narrative exposition to justify the coherence of interpretative decisions. This task itself raises hermeneutical questions with regard to any strategy for reading the fragments, especially in that many commentators aspire to an exposition of Heraclitus that finds him to be a philosopher of difference. The attempt to cover over the fragmentary character of Heraclitus's thought by organizing his sayings in a systematic fashion would seem counterproductive to a reading of Heraclitus that holds him to be a philosopher of strife and discord.

The problem of language and expository writing is not only a difficulty that arises due to the historical accident that only partial texts of Heraclitus remain extant. It is a problem that inhabits every philosophy which, like that of Heraclitus, attempts to address the notion of difference. From this perspective, the fragmentary character of the sayings of Heraclitus should not be too readily ignored or covered over by commentary.³ Inasmuch as Heraclitus is a thinker of difference and change and strife, it is important to appreciate the positive contribution of his fragmentary, disruptive style as providing a λόγος befitting the matter to be thought.

In this essay, I, too, am employing a narrative style and weaving together Heraclitean sayings in an attempt to demonstrate a certain thesis, namely, that Heraclitean thought posits at the beginning a twofold λόγος and a double movement, and thus is able, in response to Parmenides, to think unity within multiplicity. This reading also depends on a decision to trace a connecting link and narrative thread through several fragments. It does so while at the same time attempting to deconstruct a one-sided reading of Heraclitus that organizes the fragments in such a way as to contrast Heraclitus's philosophy of becoming with Parmenides's philosophy of being. I argue that what is most radical in the thought of Heraclitus will be missed if we merely view his thinking as an inversion of typical philosophical priorities. Heraclitus is not simply to be admired as one who talks about becoming instead of being, or about change instead of permanence, or about opposition instead of harmony. The preponderance of evidence indicates that Heraclitus is not merely the philosopher of flux.⁴ Rather, Heraclitus is the one who thinks *being* as becoming and who recognizes that essence is change.

The difficulty of thinking identity and difference together in this way further corroborates our initial concern about the problem of interpreting fragmentary writing. But Heraclitus himself suggests the path to follow to avoid arbitrary impositions of order. So many of his fragments call for a listening to the sayings themselves and being guided by the matter for thought uncovered in the fragments. This posture of listening offsets the tendency to impose oneself upon the texts. It tries to let the fragments speak for themselves and follows the labyrinthine (παλίντροπος) and backstretching (παλίντονος, Fragment

B51) circuit of Heraclitus's difficult thought. The criteria for selection must be appropriate to the matter and the fragmentary style of writing under consideration. In this case, the task would still be to select and gather the fragments into a certain way of laying out the thought; but one would do so by listening to the fragments themselves and, guided by the sayings, allowing to be disclosed what was hidden in the discourse of Heraclitus.[5]

This strategy of listening stretches back and forth in appreciation of the tension in the thought of Heraclitus. Like the relationship of the bow to the lyre, it discovers harmony in this tension (Fragment B51). This is of course in keeping with the recommendation of Heraclitus himself who warns in Fragment B19: "Not knowing how to listen, neither can they speak." Nevertheless, we remain suspicious of any strategy that would listen in order to take the obscurity of Heraclitus and try to expose and clarify it, as we remain suspicious also of the apparent aim of making present and available the true meaning of Heraclitus's words.[6] Is this listening-reporting approach appropriate to the insight that all unconcealment remains in relationship to concealment and vice versa? Is there a more appropriate strategy and language that would not seemingly destroy Heraclitus by privileging unconcealment over concealment? At the heart of things in Heraclitus's thought is the unity of veiling and unveiling. Heraclitus tries to think the accord and, that is, the opposition between what shows itself and what does not. The opposition of revealing and concealing plays at the center of the Heraclitean cosmos. The Heraclitean commitment to a language that remains faithful to the double movement of revealing and concealing is evident in Fragment B93, where he calls such a way of speaking divine: "The Lord whose oracle is in Delphi neither speaks (λέγει) nor conceals (κρύπτει) but gives a sign (σημαίνει)." The divine language of the sign, non-metaphysically understood, would seem to locate a way in which the transitional language of difference can be expressed. One might call such an originary speaking a signing, but a peculiar sign in that it comes before, not after, and brings forth what it points out and represents.

The interpretation of this fragment as speaking of a peculiar signature that exceeds the dichotomization of revealing and concealing and speaks in a kind of middle-voice[7] of what neither can be (fully) revealed nor can be entirely hidden is warranted by other fragments such as Fragment B54: "The hidden harmony [that does not appear] is stronger than the visible," and Fragment B123: "φύσις (the emerging) loves to hide." That is, that which in its essence means revealing, emerging, coming forth into the open (φύσις) never gives itself over to be revealed, never abandons its friendship with the dark and hidden sources of revelation. Φύσις, unlike the utterly exposed products of human fabrication, never abandons its relationship to the underworld and the night, but always comes forth in a movement of returning into hiddenness. So, the harmony of φύσις pays heed to the shattering force out of which it has come forth. In imparting itself and giving expression to its being, the λόγος of φύσις attends to the secret that is held in reserve and yet makes communication possible, the secret that is signed but erased, fundamentally unable to be communicated because it is a sharing that cannot be shared. There is within φύσις itself and within λογός as such a tendency towards and need for concealment. If we understand φύσις as etymologically related to light (φάος) and appearance (φαίνω),[8] then Heraclitus is saying something peculiar: emerging, appearing, lighting are also intrinsically related to concealing. In Fragment B30, Heraclitus speaks of the everliving fire (πῦρ ἀείζωον), as a name for cosmic order. But this hidden intensity loves to withdraw and hide its raging force so as to allow what is to stand in its light. Fire is the clarity that conceals itself in shadows, the bright flame that preserves the shadow of the night.[9]

It is this double character of being as withdrawing and revealing that makes human knowledge so elusive and difficult. Thus in Fragment B34: "Not understanding, they are like the deaf, present yet absent." And in Fragment B56: "People are deceived over the recognition of visible things. What we saw and grasped (the visible), we leave behind; but what we did not see and grasp, that we bring." The aporia of thinking about being, the difficulty and impossibility of understanding in regard to such matters, is not only due to human error and lack of focus. It is intrinsic to the matter in question.

Remembering that Heraclitus, who is called the "Obscure," is also the speaker of signs,[10] we can postulate that ambiguity, a hidden intensity, a transformation, is at the heart of things. But to see this hidden power in the visible requires a doubling of vision beyond what is ordinarily seen. It is necessary to think this originary doubling in order to see that ambiguity, intensity and transformation *are* the φύσις, the fire that lights up what appears by flaming up and dying out with measure.

The Double Logos of Listening and Speaking

Fragment B1[11] says that when we in our ordinary activities use words and do things, there is no heeding of the φύσις of the things with which we are dealing. But it is nevertheless on the basis of this "nature" that such words and deeds are possible. Thus, to most people, what they are doing remains hidden to them. They do not see or comprehend *the* λόγος. This special λόγος guides and governs the ordinary words and deeds of people, but they speak and act under its guidance without being aware of its guiding force. So all human λόγος and activity depends on this other λόγος, and human awareness, perception, and involvement with things, stem from this association with the λόγος.

It is this disposition to listen and to speak in a way in which one's words are not merely full of oneself but in communication with what is other than oneself that Heraclitus refers to in Fragment B112 where he names it σωφροσύνη, "σωφρονεῖν ἀρετὴ μεγίστη: Healthful thinking is the greatest virtue." Heraclitus defines this other-directed virtue as "speaking the truth, that is, bringing forth (ποιεῖν) according to nature by listening." Σωφροσύνη puts together λόγος, ἀληθέα, and φύσις. For Heraclitus, originary λόγος and φύσις are the same. It is not only a matter of recognizing that *our* peculiar way of being is made possible by this other than human λόγος. Heraclitus also says that all coming into being, all beings are κατὰ τὸν λὸγον — they are what they are in relation to λόγος. How is it that, according to Fragment B1, when we are led from the multiplicity of ordinary speaking to the singular λόγος, we discover the whole of what is? The movement from the multiple to the singular paradoxically opens up again the question of the manifold.

Fragment B2 says: "It is necessary to follow what is common (ξυνός). But although the λόγος is common, the many live as though they had a private understanding." When Heraclitus announces that the hidden λόγος is common, does he mean that all particular beings belong to it? Is it the whole of beings, the φύσις? Λόγος would then mean the community of all things, their being-together as a whole, the totality. In thinking the unity of φύσις and λόγος, Heraclitus is not thinking out of the division of human being and nature or human being and spirit. And yet his complaint is that this split has already occurred. Thus Heraclitus calls us back from the splitting apart of λόγος and φύσις in Fragment B50: "Attuning yourself not to my λόγος, but to λόγος, it is wise to say the same, that is, to say ἕν πάντα." So what is required is a kind of listening, a turning away from one kind of listening to attend to another. There are a number of other fragments where Heraclitus mentions this need to listen. In Fragment B19, for example, Heraclitus complains that people do not know how to listen and to speak. So many of the fragments speak of listening, we might do well to entitle Heraclitus the philosopher of sound who recalls for us the ringing of being. Human speaking requires listening and attending to the φύσις/λόγος, to the light that is common to all and that unifies all beings. Thus Heraclitus points out that many people try their hand at acting and using words, but unlike these false attempts to speak truly, when he does this, he distinguishes things according to φύσις and determines how they have their being on the basis of φύσις.

Thus the *common* λόγος is not separable from what is and is available to be seen and/or heard, even by the masses. The point is not that they need turn away to another, separate realm. Rather, it is a matter of getting beyond the narrow logic of self-expression to a logic of listening that is open to being as such and able to reveal what is in this light. In Fragment B34, when Heraclitus says that people are like the deaf, he does not mean that it is essentially impossible for them to hear. Deaf people are by nature hearers. And in Fragment B72, he says of λόγος: "Though most close, yet we are separate from it; though encountered daily, it is most strange." Heraclitus often plays with this theme of nearness and farness. Perhaps there is a problem with too much familiarity that blocks us from what is essential for thinking. Overfamiliarity makes what is revealed obscured in its essence, taken for granted and forgotten. Thus in Fragment B73, Heraclitus says we are related to things as if asleep and thus know nothing of them. And in Fragment B89, Heraclitus says that those awake see the one ordered cosmos common to all, while those asleep turn away to their own. In Heraclitus, then, there is a call for a kind of reawakening, a recollection of the hidden, common λόγος, a recollection that attends to the oneness of the many, the ἕν πάντα. Elsewhere Heraclitus calls this oneness a self-differentiating harmony. That is, he hears a polemic harmony in this λόγος and at the heart of what it reveals.

The Polemic Nature of the Common Logos

Aristotle tells the story of Heraclitus warming his bottom by the hearth when a disgruntled admirer expressed his disappointment at the thinker's engagement in such a mundane activity. Heraclitus is reputed to have said, "Here too the gods dwell." No doubt this story reminds us of Heraclitus's predilection for fire. Plutarch reports that Heraclitus held the all (τὰ πάντα) to be an exchange of fire (Fragment B90). On the basis of this and a host of other fragments, Heraclitus is rightfully considered the first thinker to see instability at the heart of things. He is the philosopher for whom the all is μεταβολή, change, in the sense of exchange and immediate transition, an exchange that is more primordial than the polarities that undergo change. Fire is for Heraclitus the elementary force that says how the one/all occurs, as strife and conflagration.

In Fragment B80, Heraclitus says: "One should know that πόλεμος is common and δίκη is ἔρις and everything occurs by way of strife (being in tension with) and necessity (κατ᾽ ἔριν καὶ χρεών). The λόγος that in other fragments is identified with the common is here called πόλεμος. Every gathering is a gleaning, selecting, and struggling into expression. The common λόγος is here also called δίκη. Δίκη opens up in advance the space in which beings are in their separateness. Thus the δίκη that "steers all things" is also spoken of in Fragment B53: "Πόλεμος is both king and father of all; some it reveals as gods, others as humans; some it makes free, others slaves." Gathering is separating. Λόγος is πόλεμος. Here πόλεμος is a word for Zeus, Zeus who allows beings to appear as they are, in their place and limit. In Fragment B64, this is made explicit: "Zeus's lightening bolt steers all things (τὰ πάντα)."

Heraclitus's understanding of the λόγος that is other than his own as a disruptive, conflictual λόγος indicates how he thinks the relationship of the two kinds of λόγος. Heraclitus calls for a listening to λόγος that turns away from λόγος in the everyday sense. Nevertheless there is no evidence to support the claim that Heraclitus is a dualist. What is required of us is to be able to think the λόγος in such a way as to recognize how it is both different from and the same as ordinary λόγος. In Fragment B72, Heraclitus says of λόγος: although most close, we are separate from it; and while encountered daily, it is most strange. The unusual double status of Heraclitean λόγος leads us to call Heraclitus the philosopher of the sign, that is, a philosopher of language who understands language ambiguously as both saying and not saying, so that in the saying we are to hear also what is not said, or hidden from the saying. Such an approach to λόγος, such an ability to double the λόγος, is especially necessary for one who would interpret and speak of φύσις, since "φύσις loves to hide itself." Heraclitus's philosophy calls for a λόγος that gives heed to φύσις, a joining of λόγος and φύσις. The sameness of λόγος and φύσις, of course, cannot be appreciated within a framework that divides the subject and object. In trying to give expression to this peculiar λόγος, we recognize an element of non-subjectivity, a dis-owning of the proper λόγος that I would call my own. Heraclitean λόγος tries to speak in a voice that is non-appropriative and that gives resonance to what does not come from itself. It is the difficulty of this language that has led to the frustration of the tradition over the obscurity of Heraclitus's philosophy.

Ἐν Πάντα: The Kinship of Heraclitus and Parmenides

This effort in Heraclitus to understand the sameness of λόγος and φύσις, of thinking and being leads to accusations that he is a philosopher of darkness.[12] Yet, for Parmenides, this same effort brings him accolades for the clarity of his logic and the brilliance of his light. This disparity in the reception by the tradition of these two thinkers may not, however, be accidental. Parmenides prohibits the thinker from gazing into the dark and impossible place wherein the difference emerges. This prohibition against con-fusing being and non-being, as well as the one and the many, cannot be found in the thought of Heraclitus. In fact, his own thinking arises out of the limits of Parmenides's thought. The contribution of Parmenides was to make it possible for us to secure the one and to think identity. Heraclitus transgresses the limits of Parmenidean thought, not in order to go beyond it and to further bifurcate the matter for thought. What interests Heraclitus is the dis-junction and prohibition upon which the one is established. What he discovers is that this disjunction and its contradictory strife both ini-tiates and belongs to the one. Although Heraclitus addresses the unity of λόγος and φύσις, he does so while recognizing that λόγος and φύσις have already split apart (Fragment B1). In this sense, Heraclitus accepts the wisdom of Parmenides who says the realm of the one and that of the many are bifurcated. But for Heraclitus, this λόγος of separation goes astray and cannot be properly understood apart from a λόγος that speaks about this difference κατὰ φύσιν. The wisdom to say ἕν πάντα is achieved by way of a recovery from a sleepful condition where we have forgotten how to listen and how to speak according to φύσις, that is, according to what is common to all.

We might agree for this reason with several contemporary scholars who argue that Heraclitus philosophizes after and in response to
Parmenides.[13] Heraclitus agrees with Parmenides that the task of philosophy is to follow the divine path and to think the one, but holds that
this oneness is hidden and not readily available. Moreover, Parmenides
was wrong, according to Heraclitus, in bifurcating the path of the one
and that of the many. The path of becoming already discloses the path
of being, even though most do not pay heed to it. The one is not other
than the many. The one is the many. This contradictory unity you
missed, because you did not see that the λόγος that is common, the
λόγος that is φύσις, is war, πόλεμος. Discord lies at the heart of what
is. The singular path of what is is doubled. In fact, its singularity is only
first achieved and disclosed in this doubling. Thus, it is not accidental
that the unity of what is gets missed and covered over in our ordinary
ways of dealing with what is. The unity is itself this granting of difference, of disunity. So Heraclitus is speaking to Parmenides when he
says in Fragment B80: "One should know that πόλεμος is common and
δίκη is ἔρις and everything occurs by way of strife and necessity."
Heraclitus thinks Parmenidean necessity as strife. The bifurcated paths
of the one and the many come together in this thought of strife and
the elementary transformative power of fire that Heraclitus names
πόλεμος. One might imagine Parmenides's confusion when Heraclitus
insists that pure being, that which is in harmony, differentiates itself
and is in and of itself divisive, as Heraclitus says in Fragment B51.
Parmenides might become troubled and counter that in that case the
two paths, the path of being and that of becoming, would be the same.
And Heraclitus would respond that indeed "the way up and the way
down are the same" (Fragment B60).

In certain fragments, Heraclitus clearly establishes his kinship with
Parmenides. For example, in Fragment B114, he says, "If we speak with
intelligence (νοῦς), we must base our strength on what is common to
all . . . [and be] nourished by the one, which is divine." And in Fragment B40, we find: "learning many things does not teach one to possess intelligence (νοῦς)." Then there is Fragment B114: "If we speak with
νοῦς, we must base our strength on that which is common to all (ἕν
πάντα)." Yet in Fragment B35, Heraclitus says, "Those who love wisdom [philosophers of the one] must be inquirers into the many."
Parmenides would appear to be refuted in this statement. Despite all
the emphasis on the one, Heraclitus in the end seems to remain the

philosopher of becoming. Combining Fragments B56 and B55, Heraclitus says: "Although people are deceived over the recognition of visible things, I honor most what can be seen and heard and experienced." So we can surmise that by belonging to the λόγος, we are not drawn away from what we ordinarily do. After all, Heraclitus spends his time by the hearth and playing with children and taking mud baths.

Perhaps we can reconcile the many indications that Heraclitus is a philosopher of becoming and change and multiplicity with the contrary evidence we have gathered that his essential thought is of being and oneness, if we were to discover that for Heraclitus these two domains are not irreconcilable. Opposition and difference are at the heart of unity. Unless we attend to the unifying one in this sense, then we will not truly be lovers of the visible. So in Fragment B72, he says, "Although we are constantly dealing with the λόγος, we are drawn apart from it and therefore what we daily encounter remains separate from us." Thus, it is a question of hearing the voice of the divine as always already at work in the midst of the things with which we deal. Heraclitus does say in Fragment B108 that "what is wise [the saying of the same] is set apart from all things," but it is set apart as common to all. This is the genuine basis for our ability to see, hear, and speak about things. In order to engage in these human activities authentically, we need to stand in the midst of things in such a way as to listen to the unity that is a πόλεμος, a setting apart. When we do, he says in Fragment B112, we have the wisdom to speak the truth and act according to φύσις, paying heed to it.

The Problem of Naming the One All: Heraclitus and Hesiod

Several of Heraclitus's fragments make evident that his philosophical position is hostile to the philosophical project of Hesiod, the genealogical project of naming what is. One might perhaps be tempted to object to this claim. After all, is there not some kinship between Heraclitus and Hesiod in that Hesiod tells a story of the violent event that instituted the hierarchical order of Zeus and Heraclitus tells the story of war and strife at the heart of being? But then perhaps Heraclitus would respond that we have misunderstood him. Πόλεμος is an orginary strife, a difference that comes before the splitting apart of things into different beings. Thus, Heraclitus complains, "Hesiod did not understand that day and night are one" (Fragment B57). On the basis of what we have said so far, we can surmise that Heraclitus is not faulting Hesiod for holding apart day and night and recognizing the regulation that allows each its stay in turn and never permits them to cross paths. Heraclitus only argues that a viable understanding of this difference and opposition must realize that true difference presupposes oneness and vice versa. In other words, to think Heraclitean difference requires the abandonment of dualistic thinking that would bifurcate the one and the many, and so forth.

In the genealogy of the gods, Hesiod does not think the difference as original; he rather envisions it as instituted and the result of a titanic struggle for power and domination. There is something insufficient and inadequate about the name Zeus and all names that would attempt to make apparent what is always more than anything that appears.

There is, of course, a difficulty in this Heraclitean notion of original difference. Namely, its appeal to an original, albeit recovered, oneness seems to reestablish what we have already argued is not present in the thought of Heraclitus, that is, dualism. Heraclitus would no doubt see the face of Parmenides over his shoulder and immediately insist that the original difference does not belong to a realm other than that which is differentiated. This is at least how I take Heraclitus's reservations about giving the name of Zeus to the polemic fire that steers all things. It is not that Heraclitus is unaware of the separation of day and night, but that, despite this separation, day and night are one. Heraclitus does not think according to the bifurcated logic of identity and difference; rather he requires a logic of both . . . and. Day and night are both the same and not the same. Unlike Aristotle, Heraclitus does not add the proviso, "but not at the same time."

Even though φύσις loves to hide and to reveal itself by way of concealing itself, and even though the divine oracle or λόγος never entirely reveals nor conceals itself, but signifies its presencing in the mark or trace of the word it gives, this hidden λόγος is, Heraclitus says, "a more powerful harmony than the one that appears" (Fragment B54). To listen to the λόγος requires an attunement to the intrinsic concealment that characterizes the λόγος, an attentiveness to its traces, its sudden occurrences which happen as extraordinary bursts of lightning that suddenly flash on the scene and penetrate the obscurity that harbors the λόγος and makes it difficult to see. Fragment B18 says, "If one does not expect the unexpected, one will not find it out, since there is no trail leading to it and no path."

Thus, Heraclitus is a philosopher of the sign. The obscurity attributed to his thought belongs not to his own love of darkness, but to the matter about which he thinks. The fragments of Heraclitus themselves inhabit the character of the sign, the foreshadowing, fragmentary language of ambiguity, not because they are remnants of more complete, original thoughts, but because they are listening to the hidden harmony. The warring oneness that Heraclitus discovers by listening to the other λόγος shows that Heraclitus is not a dualist who merely prefers difference to identity and flux to permanence. Rather, the discovery of Heraclitus is that there is unity at the heart of difference.

NOTES

1. For a discussion of fragmentary writing that offers a positive philosophical account see Soren Kierkegaard, *Either/Or*, Volume I, trans. H. V. and E. H. Hong (Princeton: Princeton University Press, 1987), 152ff. See also Maurice Blanchot, *The Writing of the Disaster*, trans. Ann Smock (Lincoln: University of Nebraska Press, 1986).

2. See Martin Heidegger and Eugen Fink, HS. The debate between Heidegger and Fink as to whether to begin the interpretation with the λόγος fragment or the fire fragment is an example of the importance of this decision.

3. Perhaps the worst example of such an offence is the text of G. S. Kirk, J. E. Raven, and M. Schofield, *The Presocratic Philosophers* (Cambridge: Cambridge University Press, 1983). Their commentary is so evasive that it is often difficult to find the actual sayings of Heraclitus, even though the purpose of the text is to provide an annotated version of Heraclitus with English translation.

4. See Karl Reinhardt, *Parmenides* (Frankfurt: Vittorio Klostermann Verlag, 1977), 169ff. Reinhardt argues that Plato's famous ascription to Heraclitus of the saying πάντα ρεῖ has led to a false representation of the doctrine of Heraclitus, which does not advocate a boundless flux. The etymological connection between this word for the flow and the word χώρα, place or receptacle, would seem to support his thesis. Plato's *Timaeus* might perhaps be read in part as a meditation on the primordial flux of Heraclitus.

5. Confer Martin Heidegger, "Logos (Heraclitus, Fragment B 50)" and "Aletheia (Heraclitus, Fragment B 16)," in EGT.

6. Martin Heidegger's reading of Heraclitus is guilty of this tendency to emphasize the gathering together of all of Heraclitus's thought into a clearing, despite the extraordinary contribution that his distinction between truth

as correctness and truth as unconcealment had made to an understanding of difference in Heraclitus. Confer also Martin Heidegger, *Heraklit*, GA 55.

7. I am indebted to Charles Scott for pointing out the force of the middle voice in Presocratic philosophy in his essay, "'Ἀδικία and Catastrophe: Heidegger's 'Anaximander Fragment'," *Heidegger Studies*, vol. 10 (1994), 127–42. See also his essay, "Appearing to Remember Heraclitus," in this volume.

8. See Martin Heidegger, EM, 75ff.

9. See Martin Heidegger and Eugen Fink, HS. For Heidegger, Heraclitus is *the* thinker of *Lichtung*, the clearing. As in the Black Forest, there can only be a clearing in relationship to the surrounding darkness. It is perhaps for this reason that Heidegger considers the poet most akin to Heraclitus to be Hölderlin. He says that Hölderlin hesitates to call nature the holy awakening of the light which shines only when it is concealed and thus protects what the light shines upon.

10. Diogenes Laertius reports that Socrates read Heraclitus and said: "What I understand is good; and I think that what I don't understand is good too—but it would take a Delian diver to get to the bottom of it." See Jonathan Barnes, *The Presocratic Philosophers* (New York: Routledge, 1982), 58.

11. Diels and Kranz organize the fragments alphabetically, according to the names of the authors, beginning with Aristotle, from whom we inherit the fragments. Nevertheless, the choice of this fragment as the first is not entirely arbitrary. Aristotle says that this saying came at the beginning of Heraclitus's book (*Rhetoric*, 1407b16). It is noteworthy that already with Aristotle the written tradition had become sufficiently pronounced that it was necessary to assign the production of a book-like manuscript to eminent thinkers. It is likely that Heraclitus still belonged to the oral tradition of his times, and it may well be that the aphoristic quality of his sayings is part of their original character. Confer Charles Kahn, *The Art and Thought of Heraclitus* (Cambridge: Cambridge University Press, 1979), 3–9.

12. For an influential account of the affinity of the thought of Heraclitus to that of Parmenides, see Karl Reinhardt, *Parmenides*. Hans-Georg Gadamer's essay, "Heraclitus Studies," in this volume, provides a compelling reading along these lines.

13. See Gadamer's essay, "Heraclitus Studies." Also see Karl Reinhardt, *Parmenides*, 201ff.

Thirteen

Empedocles and Tragic Thought: Heidegger, Hölderlin, Nietzsche

Véronique M. Fóti

As a "working hypothesis," Michel Haar proposes that Heidegger's analysis of the work of art in terms of an essential strife between "earth" and "world" responds to and explicates the conflictual complementarity of the Apollinian and Dionysian art energies in Nietzsche's *Birth of Tragedy*.[1] I second this hypothesis; but I also wish to suggest that, since Nietzsche himself—as Kommerell noticed and as Beissner has pointed out—responds to Hölderlin's theory of tragedy, particularly as developed in his fragmentary *The Death of Empedocles*,[2] Heidegger's engagement with Nietzsche is, in this context, indissociable from his dialogue with Hölderlin. He certainly was aware of the complex interconnections that constrained his meditation on the work of art to engage with the theory of tragedy as developed in late eighteenth- and nineteenth-century German thought.

The question of tragedy, moreover, is as such indissociable from the entire problematic of the relationship of ancient Greece to Western modernity (Hölderlin's Hesperia), so that not only Heidegger's analysis of art and artworks, but also his guiding effort to accomplish a retrieval in difference of ancient Greece, responds to it. Far from being a peripheral or specialized issue that surfaces here and there in his work, it is tied up with the key concerns of his thought.[3] The interrelation is extraordinarily complex and has not been adequately addressed in the philosophical literature.[4] The present essay sets itself the task of exploring, in a preparatory manner, Hölderlin's understanding of tragedy, as interlinking modernity with ancient Greece, in *The Death of Empedocles*, together with its import for Heidegger through the mediacy of Nietzsche.

Consummation, Transgression: Hölderlin's Empedocles

The central concern of Hölderlin's Empedocles texts is with the transgressive moment of excess in the relationship of art (and, more generally, of the human being) to nature. Tragedy is, for him, the poetic form most suited to this concern; for, unlike Hegel, who privileges drama as accomplishing a mature balance between subjectivity and objectivity,[5] he understands the tragic ode as the vehicle of the greatest intensity or "inwardness" carried to the brink of nefas.[6] To temper and contain this intensity, the poet must cast it into the alienation, so to speak, of foreign characters and remote events which nonetheless, through an inner kinship, offer a "bolder simile" of the poetic insights and render them communicable, while also protecting them against the transience and dissipation that afflict whatever remains tied to the self. The figure of Empedocles (gleaned from Diogenes Laertius) as philosopher, poet, and as a spiritual and political innovator, together with his legendary self-chosen death in the fire of Mount Aetna, is emblematic of Hölderlin's own poetic passion and intellectual aspirations. The very title of one of Empedocles's two philosophical poems, Καθαρμόι (Purifications) may here be significant (although it was probably affixed by posterity), in that it echoes the question of the κάθαρσις that is, for Aristotle, the very work of tragedy—a work that, for Hölderlin, becomes the poetic task of purifying excess. Hölderlin recognizes a form of "pure life" in which nature and art contrast "harmoniously," art drawing sustenance from nature, whereas nature is divinized by art. Hölderlin, like Schiller, discerns the achievement of this pure interrelation in certain aspects of Greek civilization; he embodies it in the figures of Diotima in Hyperion, and of Panthea in Empedocles I and II.[7] In Panthea, however, this ideal has become marked by sorrow and solitude. The limitation of a "pure life" of human beings within nature is, that, for all its beauty, it is formed only by feeling and cannot defend itself against an intellectual challenge. For it to become knowable, nature must show itself in its "aorgic," quasi-Dionysian aspect, and art (together with the human sphere which it characterizes) in its "organicism," its separative, discriminative, form-giving energy. Only through strife can nature and art reveal the extremity of their antagonism, which was masked rather than resolved in "pure life." In the intimacy of their mutual challenge and provocation, however, each takes on the essential traits of the other; aorgic nature "concentrates" and particularizes itself, whereas organic singularity generalizes itself, veers toward infinity, and tears itself away from its own center. The fruit of this dialectics of centering and eccentricity, sprung from "highest antagonism," is an exalted moment of "highest reconciliation" which Hölderlin ranks among the most meaningful experiences that human beings can attain to. The moment of reconciliation, however, does not lead on toward further syntheses on the path toward absolute realization; it is evanescent and almost illusory; for the forces that brought it into being must immediately disintegrate it:

> [T]he individuality of this moment is only a product of the highest strife, its generality only a product of the highest strife; as reconciliation appears to be there, and the organic acts again upon this moment in its own manner, and the aorgic in its [manner], the aorgically engendered individuality contained in the moment becomes again, with respect to the impressions of the organic, more aorgic, [and] with respect to the impressions of the aorgic, the organically engendered generality contained in the moment becomes again more particular, so that the unifying moment dissolves again, like a phantom. . . . [8]

The process of dissolution is, as such, oriented toward the aorgic; and a "more beautiful" reconciliation is finally attained through the aorgic relinquishment of sovereign individuality and a sober consciousness of finitude:

> Since now the union is no longer in something singular [in which it was], for that very reason, too intimate (or too inward, *innig*), since the divine no longer appears sensuously, [and] since the felicitous deception of the union ceases to the precise degree to which it was too intimate and too singular, the two extremes—of which one, the organic, must be deterred by the evanescent moment, while the aorgic, passing over into the former, must become, for the organic, an object of mere quiet contemplation—can now, together with the inwardness (*Innigkeit*) of the past moment, be set forth more generally, with more sober differentiation, and more clearly.[9]

Such relinquishment of individuality constitutes, for Hölderlin, a tragic destiny and an essential sacrifice[10] that may historically be called for to purify a union that is too intimate and in advance of its time. The notion of ὕβρις, which links nobility and transgression, is here reinterpreted in terms of an all-embracing vision, realized by a single individual, in advance of the historical process (the complex interactions of what is "ownmost" to a people with what is alien to them) that could have led up to it, and without differential articulation. An individual who makes himself, so to speak, a vessel for the containment of the infinite within the finite hybristically transgresses the measures of finitude. Hölderlin's dialectical thought, unlike Hegel's, returns to and affirms a finitude that repudiates sublation.

Empedocles is, for Hölderlin, in an exemplary sense a man of his time and native country, both marked by "the violent opposition of art to nature, in terms of which the world appeared before his eyes." In keeping with the dialectical schema just outlined, the very intimacy and mutual fascination of the contestants in the extremity of their strife engenders a fleeting semblance of reconciliation which becomes manifest, in the person of Empedocles, as an alienation of his analytical and creative powers from his subjectivity, and as a merging of subjectivity with the unconscious and "disorganic" powers of nature. This seeming fusion of opposites in an individual consciousness is both unstable and hybristic and must therefore be tragically undone.

In Hölderlin's view, the exigency of Empedocles's time, in which the powerful antagonism of art and nature strove to gain, for its resolution, a firm foothold in a singular individual, denied to him the realization of his poetic and intellectual gifts in their proper sphere, in "restraint and purity." What it demanded of him, as one so gifted, was "a sacrifice, wherein the human being, in its entirety, becomes actually that wherein the destiny of his time in its entirety appears to resolve itself," although no such resolution can in fact be "visible and individual."[11] Hölderlin, in general, understands tragic destiny as provoked by essential historical tensions, rather than by the flaws, errors, or frailty of the protagonists; and, while he agrees, in this respect, with Hegel as well as Heidegger, he places particular emphasis on the "untimely" aspects of the character of the protagonists.

The challenge for the poet is to give concrete particularity to Empedocles's transgression. On such concreteness, Hölderlin remarks, everything necessarily depends, since "that which unites must perish, because it appeared too visibly and sensuously, and this it can only do by expressing itself as to some determinate point or case."[12] The concrete understanding of the transgression is indeed the issue on which the three versions differ most markedly.

In the first version (which is the lengthiest and most complete), Empedocles, as philosopher and sage, is so transported by the joy of his union with the elemental and vital powers of nature that he proclaims himself a god, denying his finitude, while conversely he seeks to concentrate the aorgic powers of nature within his finite individuality and to announce his mastery over nature. The two aspects of his transgression are intimately conjoined:

> Sacred Nature!
> Virginal one who flees from the coarse sense!
> I have despised you and set up myself alone
> As master, an arrogant
> Barbarian...
>
> I knew it, after all, I learned it to the end,
> The life of Nature; how could it still for me
> Be holy as before? The gods had now become
> Servile to me, and I alone
> Was god; so I proclaimed in insolent pride.[13]

The fact that the transgression is contained in a mere word is puzzling to Empedocles's disciple Pausanias; but, for Hölderlin, it is appropriate, in that language is, for him, the very element of finitude, which has been betrayed.

In the second version, the focus shifts to Empedocles's relationship to his people: he is now a Promethean figure who loves mortals excessively and who, in symbolically bringing them heaven's living fire, capitulates to their limited understanding and proclaims himself the vivifier, unifier, and giver of soul, taking advantage of their credulity and debasing nature's dignity and enigma.

In the third version, Empedocles searchingly accuses himself of having (in his excessive self-identification with nature) not loved human beings "humanly" enough, thereby inviting the inhumanity of his banishment. The crux of the drama is now his conversation with his former teacher, the Egyptian priest Manes, who has come to ask him whether he is "the single one," greater than Manes himself, who alone is ennobled by self-chosen death. This Christ-like "new savior" is born

out of the antagonism of "light and night"; and, in the extremity of
"wild antagonism," he is the healer and purifier:

> The single one, however, the new savior, receives
> The rays of heaven calmly, and lovingly
> He gathers what is mortal to his breast;
> And gentle grows in him the world's strife.
> Human beings and gods he reconciles,
> And close together they live again, as before.
> And so that, when he has appeared, the son
> May not be greater than his parents, and the holy
> Spirit of life may not remain fettered,
> Forgotten on his account, the single one's,
> He derails, the idol of his time
> Breaks, he himself, so that through a pure hand
> For the pure one may come to pass what is necessary,
> His own happiness, which for him is too happy,
> And gives what he possessed back to the element
> That glorified him, chastened.[14]

Although Empedocles acknowledges that Manes knows him, he
repudiates a self-identification with the messianic figure as a tempta-
tion and provocation to raging excess (*Zorn*) that disturbs the sacred
calm of his impending death. Rather than claiming to be the destined
savior (who would, as such, be related to the heroic and tragic figures
of antiquity), he describes himself as one whom the spirit has chosen,
from his dying land, so that through him the "swan song, the last life,
may resound." His self-description emphasizes that, even in his silence
(he has not told Manes everything), he remains a poet. The poet is no
savior and no reformer; and perhaps his or her love of the people is
not "human" enough; but as a marker of epochal as well as more
ordinary limits, s/he discloses that which is limited and must perish
in its highest beauty, a beauty indissociable from mortality and finitude.

In the Hölderlinian figure of Empedocles, the passionate impulse
of Greek antiquity to contain its natal fiery element in a lucid articulation foreign to it reaches its highest and hybristic moment (a pinnacle
only approximated, Hölderlin suggests, by the heroes of the Greek
tragic stage). The inevitable destruction of such a figure is gripping
because of the nobility and beauty of the reconciliation of the aorgic

and organic elements attained as the dying image or swan song of Greek culture; but it also opens up the possibility of a reconciliation which is more sober and differential. What is now precluded is the effort to contain the infinite within the finite; the infinite retreats as the inconspicuous opening for finite configurations.

For Hölderlin, an important consequence of the priority of the finite is to understand every moment of dialectical synthesis in relation to social and political concerns. Not only the Empedocles texts, but also the earlier *Hyperion* and the later fragmentary and cryptic "Annotations" to Sophoclean drama express "republican" and emancipatory political ideals.[15] These must be respected and considered in their own right as well as in terms of Hölderlin's relationship to the French Revolution; but they do not offer a master key to the texts; for Hölderlin's guiding preoccupation is not the politics of the day but the deflection of dialectics and essential history toward finitude.

Empedocles in the Perspectives of Hölderlin and Nietzsche

Although Hölderlin draws inspiration at least as much from Empedocles's legendary biography as from his philosophical, scientific, and religious doctrines,[16] the three versions of the tragedy and its "Ground" reveal a deep engagement with certain aspects of Empedocles's thought. Of key importance for Hölderlin is the Empedoclean opposition of the cosmic principles of Love (the quasi-organic power of unification) and Strife (the quasi-aorgic power of differentiation leading to dissolution), which are in unstable resolution at certain phases of the cosmic cycle, insofar as unification amidst differentiation (rather than the undifferentiated sphere that is "blameless Love's" consummate achievement, or the whirling elemental particles of consummate Strife) allows for the genesis of a phenomenal world.[17] The pantheism and panpsychism suggested by certain Empedoclean fragments (such as B133, B134, or B110), and perhaps also by the divine names of Zeus, Hera, Aidoneus, and Nestis that he gives to the four "roots" or elements, have profound resonances in Hölderlin's thought—resonances that reverberate beyond the fragmentary tragedy. Finally, Empedocles's "cosmic cycle" outlined in his poem, "On Nature," as well as his doctrine of the fall and redemption of spirits (δαίμονες) set forth in "Purifications," articulate an order that is at once temporal and elemental, and that is reflected in

Hölderlin's schema of the relationship between Oriental Greek antiquity (linked to the element of fire) and Occidental modernity (linked to the element of earth). This schema is lucidly outlined by Jean-François Marquet:

> Greek consciousness is born from out of the Oriental (or Asian) blaze of Ether, in an ecstatic state, from which it distances itself in order to acquire a *culture* of its own. At the end of this cultural process, it returns, with Empedocles, to its fiery source, and there is consumed, but not without having received, like Semele, a fecundation which it transmits by burying it in the *earth* of Occidental consciousness. The latter is at first disoriented (or rendered eccentric) by this foreign content, but in the end returns to itself by giving it a definite form. The Greek as well as the Hesperian consciousness are each constrained to act against its own "element," its nature, its god as yet unknown to it.[18]

For Marquet, this historical schema is represented by the figure of in finite interconnection, ∞, which differs from the figure of Empedocles's bi-polar cosmic cycle, ⊃, by its central chiasm. Ancient Greece, on Marquet's interpretation, is situated at the chiasmatic juncture, the place of the mediating powers "of light, of beauty, of love."[19]

This place of juncture is not truly a locus of tragedy. In Hölderlin's third version of *The Death of Empedocles*, the entire structure of tragedy has disappeared. All action is in the past; and Empedocles rejoices in his destiny, advising Pausanias (for whom, as for Manes, a like destiny is "forbidden fruit") to go forth fearlessly, aware that "everything returns" (*es kehret alles wieder*), and that whatever will come to pass is already accomplished.[20] As is evident, Hölderlin here foreshadows (in a text that was significant to Nietzsche) Nietzsche's thought of the Eternal Return.

Hölderlin's inability to complete the tragedy may not be due, as Prignitz thinks, to his main character's weakening position in relation to his priestly opponents[21] (who are, especially in the first version, drawn in a proto-Nietzschean manner), but to the resorption of Empedocles's individual destiny, in which the order of time "concentrated" itself, into a trans-historical schema designated by the serene figure of infinity. In his dialogue with Pausanias, Hölderlin's Empedocles of the third version voices this new understanding:

Whatever a single thing is, breaks asunder;
Love does not die in its bud;
And everywhere, in free joy,
Life's lofty tree dispenses itself.[22]

Unlike Hölderlin, Nietzsche is strangely reticent concerning Empedocles. As Gadamer points out, he initiates the privileging—consummated by Heidegger—of Anaximander, Heraclitus, and Parmenides as the unsurpassable beginning of Western thought.[23] His notes and fragments of 1872 mention Empedocles now and then in his dual aspect of *rhetor* and compassionate reformer, treating him generally as a liminal figure; but *Philosophy in the Tragic Age of the Greeks*, for which the notes are preparatory, breaks off at the very point where the discussion must turn to Empedocles.[24]

The thought of Empedocles nevertheless haunts Nietzsche; for the Dionysian and Apollinian creative energies, as presented in *The Birth of Tragedy*, and in the 1870 lectures, "The Dionysian World View" and "The Birth of Tragic Thought," reveal both an Empedoclean and a Hölderlinian inspiration.[25] The pure Dionysian impulse, symbolized by orgiastic transport and intoxication (which Dionysian art does not indulge in but rather "plays" with), linked to licentious Asiatic nature cults and characterized, not only by the collapse of individuation and social structure, but ultimately by a simultaneity of ecstasy and terror, bears more evidently the traits of Hölderlin's aorgic principle than the features of Aphrodite, who symbolizes Empedoclean Love. Nevertheless, in tension with this Hölderlinian aspect, the Dionysian energy also expresses itself in a quasi-Empedoclean reconciliation and universal harmonization:

The festivals of Dionysos not only confirm the alliance between man and man; they also reconcile man and nature. Freely earth proffers its gifts; the most ferocious animals approach ready for peace: the flower-garlanded chariot of Dionysos is drawn by panthers and tigers.[26]

In the Apollinian impulse, the separative energy of Empedoclean Strife is doubly refined, in keeping with Hölderlin's organic principle governing lucid articulation, sobriety, and measure, as well as in keeping with the plastic energy of art as the creation of radiant semblance (*schöner Schein*):

The god of beautiful semblance must at the same time be the god of true cognition. However, the delicate limit which the dream-image must not overstep, lest it act in a pathological manner, where semblance does not merely delude, but deceives, must not be lacking in Apollo's nature—that measured limitation, that freedom from wild impulses, that wisdom and calm of the sculptor god.[27]

Although Apollo is the artist-god, Nietzsche does not restage the Hölderlinian opposition of art to nature, nor does he return to Empedocles's elaboration of a philosophy of "nature" (φύσις). Rather, his Apollinian and Dionysian impulses are art energies that surge out of nature. This is not to say that his thought remains at the level of the Hölderlinian "pure life" as the harmonious interrelation of art and nature, but rather that, for him (as for Hegel), the crucial relationship is no longer that of art to nature, but of art to truth.

The initial incursion of the Dionysian impulse into pre-Homeric Greek culture (an incursion which Nietzsche, echoing Hölderlin's geo-history, traces to Oriental sources) instigated a conflict between truth and beauty since, through the Dionysian cults, nature's hidden truth was revealed "with terrifying clarity" to a people who, in an unprecedented manner, combined sensitivity with analytical reason.[28] The initial achievement of the Hellenic genius was, for Nietzsche, a κάθαρσις of the Dionysian impulse through Apollinian clarity linked, in mythical terms, to the Apollinian healing of the dismembered Dionysos. It took the form of the Olympian pantheon and of the Homeric epics, which glorified life "in the bright solar light of such divinities" with a passion that turned even laments into songs of praise—praise for a life lived in solar clarity but upon which mortals have no lasting hold. Here, Nietzsche observes, lies the reason for modernity's profound nostalgia for ancient Greece.[29]

Nietzsche himself refuses to subscribe to this nostalgia that he takes to comprise the "noblest" as well as the "most vulgar" representation; he rejects it perhaps more resolutely than does Hölderlin. The subversive energy of the Dionysian impulse cannot ultimately be contained by beautiful illusion; but rather, Dionysos is in every sense *hostis*, the potentially inimical stranger powerful enough to bring down the hospitable house.[30] Excess now reveals itself as truth, challenging the Homeric-Apollinian ideals of measure and beauty. The Greeks, however, responded to this challenge by creating "the higher μηχανή" of Attic drama with its transgressive moments of sublimity and ridicule. Nietzsche's response to Hölderlin involves his view that the higher reconciliation of opposed energies is not still withheld by history, but rather was achieved, without ὕβρις, in Greek tragedy, which awaits its rebirth in Occidental modernity. He does not draw Empedocles as a figure of Promethean or sacrificial transgression, of excess and rage (*Zorn*), but rather as foreshadowing the figure of the tragic hero as artist-philosopher and bringer of transvaluation (a figure already anticipated, for him, by Anaximander).[31]

Law, Fracture, Releasement

A crucial text for an explication of and reflection on Heidegger's engagement with Nietzsche in "The Origin of the Work of Art," and with the Nietzschean, rather than the Hölderlinian, mediation of Greek thought, is the first volume of his Nietzsche lectures of 1936–1940. A key concern of these lectures, focused on the Nietzschean problematic of the will to power, is to interpret and carry forward Nietzsche's questioning of art as a counterforce to the historical momentum of nihilism. The issue of nihilism forms the horizon over against which the questions of the philosophical import of tragedy, and of the interrelation of Hölderlin, Nietzsche, and the thought of Empedocles, must, for Heidegger, be considered.

Heidegger points out that, while Nietzsche can lay claim to originality in tracing and interpreting the Dionysian/Apollinian polarity in Greek thought (notwithstanding the influence of Jacob Burckhardt), Hölderlin had already grasped this polarity "in a deeper and nobler manner."[32] Since Heidegger traces its Hölderlinian articulation solely to the poet's letter to Böhlendorff of 4 December 1801 (which contrasts the "holy pathos" of the Greeks and the "Junonian sobriety" of Hesperia), he asserts confidently that Nietzsche (who had no access to the letter) "could have known nothing" of Hölderlin's precedence.[33] By a strange elision, the Empedoclean inspiration that interlinks the two thinkers has vanished from sight; and, notwithstanding Nietzsche's acknowledged situation at the extreme limit of "metaphysics," or his quite un-Hölderlinian preoccupation with the body as a field of forces (his "physiology," as Heidegger calls it), one is left with the impression of a fundamentally unbroken continuity between Hölderlin and Nietzsche, or perhaps a shared "unsaid" to be retrieved and consummated by Heidegger. This continuity, along with Heidegger's own position, needs to be called into question; and such questioning can he partly focused on the tragic *persona* of Empedocles.

Heidegger insightfully points out that, subsequent to *The Birth of Tragedy*, and specifically in *The Twilight of Idols*, Nietzsche no longer pits the Dionysian energy of transport or intoxication (*Rausch*) against Apollinian sobriety, but rather considers both these energies to be essential moments of transport for the self-assertion of power in its fullness.[34] Their polarity no longer disrupts the Nietzschean circle interlinking transport with beauty, artistic creation and appreciation, passion (*Lust*) and life—a circle that becomes Heidegger's own interpretive structure. On this basis, Heidegger can say that form, in its finitude, grounds the possibility of transport, or that, for Nietzsche, transport is "the brightest victory of form."[35] Excess is spontaneously— if paradoxically—reconciled with autonomous law; or again, in Heidegger's formulation, chaos and law submit to the same yoke:

> The fundamental condition [for the classical configuration], however, is the equiprimordial freedom for the most extreme opposites . . . that sovereignty that allows for the native originality of chaos, and the primordiality of law, to go toward each other in contrariety, and with equal necessity under one yoke. . . . Where the free disposition over this law is the self-forming law of coming to pass, there is great style; where great style is, art is actual in its essential plenitude.[36]

The tropology of chaos and law bound under one yoke has superseded that of trait and rent (*Riss*) that both dissevers and holds together earth and world. The shift, though subtle (and still indebted to Hölderlin's poetic language) veers from a concern for differentiation to a concern for reconciliation and integration. In the Nietzsche lectures, it is linked to a preoccupation with counteracting the discrediting of sensuous complexity that goes hand in hand with nihilism. The figure of the yoke—an artefact, a product and perhaps even symbol of τέχνη (it is prominent in the first choral ode of Sophocles's *Antigone* which extols human mastery over nature[37])—is one that calls attention to a forceful imposition of will. Like Nietzsche, Heidegger emphasizes the creative and transformative or poietic character of art which is, for him, bound up with τέχνη. Hölderlin, by contrast, stresses the markers of finitude, such as the "firm letter" and the caesura, which enable art to transmute limitation into strength. For Heidegger, as Michel Haar remarks perceptively, even a "principle of anarchy" (Reiner Schürmann's term) could not "sustain its subversive force without the support of the epoch, [and] thus of Technology. . . ."[38] Hölderlin's understanding of art, and specifically of poetry (Dichtung, in the wider sense), is eccentric, in that it bypasses any preoccupation with technology and its ὕβρις.

If one agrees with Schürmann that what tragedy brings to the fore is "the counterpull between natality and mortality" within the fracture or discordance that is being, and that it gives ascendancy to the retractive pull of mortality over any integrative force,[39] then Hölderlin, more than Heidegger, emerges as the thinker of tragedy, although he does not attempt to think its transcendental conditions in being as such. To be sure, Heidegger's law yoked to chaos is not the univocal, self-absolutizing law that, according to Schürmann, yields "hegemonic phantasms," but is perhaps more akin to the necessary and integrative violence that springs from natality. However, since it is integrative and is ultimately consummated in the "event of appropriation" (Ereignis) that, according to Haar, marks the limit at which "the History of Being . . . folds back upon the radical simplicity of the belonging together of man and being,"[40] it does not allow mortality and finitude to assert their insurpassable heterogeneity.

Neither Heidegger nor Nietzsche recognizes the force of Hölderlin's tragic κάθαρσις as an affirmation of the measures and limits of finitude through a relentless purification of the finite being's aspiration to an exalted vantage point, whether facilitated by transport and ecstasy, or by technology and art. Whereas Nietzsche understands transport as the very force of life, Hölderlin repudiates it as part and parcel of a destructive "passion for death" (Todeslust).[41] Hölderlinian κάθαρσις, however, does not seek to marginalize or discredit what it purifies; but rather, in acts of homage, it institutes a genuinely tragic recognition of what Schürmann calls "ultimate double binds." Hölderlin's ruptures or caesurae are not, in the end, inscribed in a tragic spirit, but in a spirit of serenity, as opening up the possibility of loving finite or mortal beings "humanly." Hölderlin's Empedocles of the third version, mindful of his own mortality, as well as of the disseverance of his destiny from that of his close disciple, Pausanias, remarks in the face of death:

Heaviness falls, and falls, and brightly
Life, the ethereal, blossoms above it.[42]

It is nevertheless significant that, for Heidegger, the inaugural
Greek thinker is Anaximander, whom he characterizes as standing "in
the envisagement of what presences in its unconcealedness, which at
one stroke has lighted the concealment of what absences as what
absences."[43] Anaximander's experience of beings in their being remains,
for Heidegger, essentially tragic:

> Presumably we approach the essence of the tragic when we do
> not explain it psychologically or aesthetically, but first address in
> thought its essentiality (*Wesensart*), the being of beings, in that we
> think διδόναι δίκην . . . τῆς ἀδικίας.[44]

The "injustice" (ἀδικία) of beings in their presenting is their insistence on claiming intrinsic reality, perdurance, and privilege over others; it must be assuaged, within the order of time, by the justice (δίκη)
of their relinquishment of power to others in respectful care (*Ruch*), as
they situate themselves within the limited "while" of their presenting.
Heidegger here locates the tragic within the very releasement which, for
Hölderlin, ultimately dissolves the structure of tragedy into serenity.

Rather than stressing fracture and singularization, as does
Hölderlin, Heidegger affirms an integrative justice, τάξις, or law which
fits the finite being (in the manner of *Fug*) into an articulation or topology of presenting. For him, to heed this binding and unbinding
justice or law, rather than attentiveness to finite beings in their singularity and sensuous complexity, constitutes the main antidote to nihilism. Though it is integrative, the justice or law at issue is not severe
and univocal, as is the law of Aeschylean and Sophoclean tragedy,
which mandates the escalation and final self-undoing of the prota-
gonist's initial hybristic blindness or "tragic denial." It is, rather, a law
that leads on to releasement. Heidegger ultimately rejoins Hölderlin not
only in his engagement with but also in his surpassing of the structure
of tragedy. He rejoins him, however, by a different path, a path that is
more properly that of the thinker of manifestation (being) than the
poet's path of attentiveness to the singular in its unique presenting. The
intimate conjunction of these two paths shows the belonging together
of poet and thinker. They belong together, however, in a free yet essen-

tial complementarity, rather than in keeping with Heidegger's own quasi-messianic and sometimes apocalyptic paradigms.

NOTES

1. Michel Haar, *The Song of the Earth: Heidegger and the Grounds for the History of Being*, trans. Reginald Lilly (Bloomington: Indiana University Press, 1993), 108. See Martin Heidegger, "Der Ursprung des Kunstwerkes," HW, 7–68; and Friedrich Nietzsche, *Die Geburt der Tragödie aus dem Geiste der Musik*, in *Werke: Kritische Studienausgabe* (henceforth KSA), eds. G. Colli and M. Montinari (Berlin: de Gruyter, 1980–1988), Vol. I, 9–156. For a discussion of the versions and chronology of Heidegger's text, see Jacques Taminiaux, "The Origin of 'The Origin of the Work of Art'," in *Poetics, Speculation, and Judgment*, trans. and ed. Michael Gendre (Albany: SUNY Press, 1993), 153–169.

2. Friedrich Hölderlin, *Der Tod des Empedokles* (three fragmentary versions, to be referred to as *Empedocles* I, II, and III), together with the "Frankfurter Plan" and the "Grund zum Empedokles," in *Sämtliche Werke*, "Grosse Stuttgarter Ausgabe" (henceforth SA), ed. F. Beissner, followed by A. Beck, 15 vols., (Stuttgart: Kohlhammer, 1946–1957), vol. 4, 3–168. According to Christoph Prignitz carefully worked out chronology in his *Hölderlins "Empedokles"* (Hamburg: Helmut Buske Verlag, 1985), 13, the "Frankfurter Plan" probably dates from 1787, the first and second versions from the following two years, the "Ground for Empedocles" from August or September 1799; and the third version was abandoned in 1800. For an English translation of the "Grund zum Empedokles," see Thomas Pfau, trans., ed., *Friedrich Hölderlin: Essays and Letters on Theory* (Albany: SUNY Press, 1988), 50–61.

For Kommerell's and Beissner's comments, see Max Kommerell, *Geist und Buchstabe der Dichtung*, fourth ed. (Frankfurt a. M.: Klostermann, 1956), 345, and Friedrich Beissner, "Erläuterungen," SA 4, 332, 348. Both writers point out Nietzsche's citations from and allusions to Hölderlin's Empedocles texts. For Nietzsche's outline sketch of a Hölderlin-inspired Empedocles-drama of his own, see *Nachgelassene Fragmente*, 1869–1874, KSA 7, 233-237.

3. The two key texts are Heidegger's *Einführung in die Metaphysik*, 112–126, and his lecture course on *Hölderlins Hymne "Der Ister"*, GA 53, 69–152. Both of these texts address, in part, Sophoclean tragedy; but Heidegger does not, to my knowledge, comment on Hölderlin's Empedocles texts. I discuss Heidegger's treatment of Sophoclean tragedy, together with Hölderlin's commentaries on his own Sophocles translations, in a paper scheduled to appear in James Risser, ed., *Heidegger: The Work of the 30s* (tentative title; SUNY Press, forthcoming).

4. For recent philosophically oriented scholarship on Hölderlin's theory of tragedy, see the articles in the section, "La Grèce, la tragédie," in J.-F. Courtine, ed., *L'Herne: Hölderlin* (Paris: Editions de l'Herne, 1989), and section I in

Christoph Jamme and Otto Pöggeler, eds., *Jenseits des Idealismus: Hölderlins Letzte Homburger Jahre (1804–1806)* (Bonn: Bouvier, 1908). Martha C. Nussbaum's *The Fragility of Goodness: Luck and Ethics in Greek Tragedy and Philosophy* (Cambridge: Cambridge University Press, 1986) includes some discussion of Hegel, but none, unfortunately, of Hölderlin.

5. G. W. F. Hegel, *Vorlesungen über die Aesthetik*, vol. 2, Hermann Glockner, ed., *Werke*, "Jubiläumsausgabe," 4th ed., vol. 14 (Stuttgatt-Bad Cannstatt: Friedrich Fromann Verlag, 1964), 479–544.

6. "Grund zum Empedokles," SA 4, 149–52; Pfau, *Friedrich Hölderlin*, 50–52. I have consulted Pfau's translation of the "Ground for Empedocles" but have not followed it closely. Translations from the three versions of the tragedy (not included by Pfau) are my own.

7. Hölderlin, *Hyperion*, D. E. Sattler, ed., *Samtliche Werke*, "Frankfurter Ausgabe" (Frankfurt a.M.: Roter Stern, 1982), vols. 10 and 11.

8. "Grund zum Empedokles," 154; Pfau, *Friedrich Hölderlin*, 54.

9. "Grund zum Empedokles," 154; Pfau, *Friedrich Hölderlin*, 54.

10. Heidegger takes over the notion of the essential sacrifice in "Der Ursprung des Kunstwerkes" ("The Origin of the Work of Art"); but the rather cryptic meaning he gives it is not necessarily Hölderlin's.

11. See "Grund zum Empedokles," 156f. Pfau translates Hölderlin's *Opfer* sometimes as "sacrifice" and sometimes as "victim." The latter term, in my view, does not convey Hölderlin's sense.

12. "Grund zum Empedokles," 161; Pfau, *Friedrich Hölderlin*, 60.

13. SA 4, 20.

14. SA 4, 136, Mares speaking. I have rendered *geläutert* as "chastened" but the translation does not capture the connotation of purification, clarification, or refinement by fire.

15. See Hölderlin, "Anmerkungen zum Ödipus," and "Anmerkungen zur Antigonä," SA 5, 195–202, 265–272; Pfau, *Friedrich Hölderlin*, 101–16.

16. Concerning the sources available to and probably used by Hölderlin (which include, besides Diogenes Laertius, Stobaeus, Plutarch, and certain Aristotelian texts, Henricus Stepharus, *Poesis Philosophica* [1573], and Ralph Cudworth, *Systema intellectuale huius mundi* [1680]), see Uvo Hölscher, *Empedokles und Hölderlin* (Frankfurt a.M.: Insel Verlag, 1965), ch. 1: "Hölderlins Quellen." As to the relation between the philosophical and religious aspects of Empedocles's thought, see Charles Kahn, "Religion and Philosophy in Empedocles' Doctrine of the Soul," in Alexander P. D. Mourelatos, ed., *The Pre-Socratics: A Collection of Critical Essays*, 2nd ed. (Princeton: Princeton University Press, 1993).

17. I accept and presuppose the understanding of Empedocles's "cosmic cycle" as bipolar rather than quadripolar (and involving an inverted world), following J. Bollack, U. Hölscher, F. Solmsen, and A. A. Long. See A. A. Long, "Empedocles' Cosmic Cycle in the 'Sixties," in *The Pre-Socratics*, 397–425. Mourelatos's updated bibliography lists sources since Long's article. Solmsen's "Love and Strife in Empedocles' Cosmogony," appears in R. E. Allen and D. Furley, eds., *Studies in Presocratic Philosophy* (Atlantic Highlands: Humanities Press, 1975), vol. 2, 221–64. Solmsen ascribes cosmogony to Strife and zoogony to Love—an interpretation that appears untenable, notwithstanding the merits of his basic position.

18. J.-F. Marquet, "Structure de la mythologie hölderlinienne," in *L'Herne: Hölderlin*, 352–369 (my translation).

19. Marquet, "Structure de la mythologie hölderlinienne," 361.

20. SA 4, 133.

21. Prignitz, *Hölderlins "Empedokles."*

22. SA 4, 127 (punctuation added).

23. Hans-Georg Gadamer, "The History of Philosophy," in *Heidegger's Ways*, trans. Jon W. Stanley (Albany: SUNY Press, 1994), 153–80 (158).

24. F. Nietzsche, *Die Philosophie im tragischen Zeitalter der Griechen*, KSA I, 800–72; *Philosophy in the Tragic Age of the Greeks*, trans. Marianne Cowan (Washington, D.C.: Regnery Gateway, 1987 [1962]).

25. F. Nietzsche, "Die dionysische Weltanschauung," KSA I, 553–557, and "Die Geburt des tragischen Gedankens," KSA I, 581–599.

26. KSA I, 555. Compare *The Birth of Tragedy*, §1.

27. KSA I, 554.

28. KSA I, 561.

29. KSA I, 550–562.

30. I follow Nietzsche's Greek and Latin play on *hostis*. In Greek, the term played on is ὅς τις, meaning simply "whoever (whatsoever) s/he (it) may be," but in Latin, *hostis* is "stranger and enemy," whereas *hospes* is "guest-friend," and *hostia* is "sacrificial victim."

31. See Nietzsche's discussion of Anaximander in *Philosophy in the Tragic Age of the Greeks*, §4.

32. N 1, 124.

33. N 1, 124.

34. N 1, 117.

35. N 1, 141.

36. N 1, 151.

37. Heidegger's interpretation of Sophocles, in *Einführung in die Metaphysik* as well as in *Hölderlins Hymne "Der Ister,"* is focused entirely on this ode.

38. Haar, *The Song of the Earth*, 4; see also, 157, note 6. Haar's reference is to Reiner Schürmann's *Le principe d'anarchie: Heidegger et la question de l'agir* (Paris: Seuil, 1982).

39. Reiner Schürmann, "Ultimate Double Binds," M. Brainard, D. Jacobs, and R. Lee, eds., *Heidegger and the Political, The Graduate Faculty Philosophy Journal*, vols. 14:2–15:1 (1991), 213–36.

40. Haar, *The Song of the Earth*, 3.

41. For further discussion, see my *Heidegger and the Poets: Poiēsis, Sophia, Technē* (Atlantic Highlands, NJ: Humanities Press, 1992), ch. 5.

42. SA 4, 132.

43. Heidegger, "Der Spruch des Anaximander," HW, 296–343 (320); the essay dates from 1946.

44. HW, 330.

Contributors

Walter A. Brogan, Professor of Philosophy at Villanova University, is the author of many articles on Ancient Greek philosophy and Contemporary Continental philosophy. With Peter Warnek, he co-translated Heidegger's *Aristotle, Metaphysics Theta 1–3: On the Essence and Actuality of Force* (GA 33). His research often centers on the interface of Greek philosophy with Contemporary Continental thinking. He is presently working on a book for SUNY Press on Heidegger's interpretation of Aristotle.

Jean-François Courtine is Professor at the École normale supérieure and the University of Paris-X and Director of the Husserl Archives in Paris. He is the author of *Suarez er le système de la métaphysique; Heidegger et la phénoménologie;* and *Extase de la raison: Essais sur Schelling.* He has also published several French translations of works by Heidegger and by Schelling.

Parvis Emad is Emeritus Professor of Philosophy at DePaul University and co-editor of *Heidegger Studies,* a journal he is currently editing from the University of Wisconsin—La Crosse. He is the author of *Heidegger and the "Phenomenology" of Values* and many essays on Heidegger and phenomenology. He is the co-editor of *Heidegger on Heraclitus: A New Reading;* he co-translated Heidegger's *Hegel's Phenomenology of Spirit* (GA 32), *Phenomenological Interpretation of Kant's "Critique of Pure Reason"* (GA 25), and Heinrich Wiegand Petzet's *Encounters and Dialogues with Martin Heidegger 1929–1976.* He is currently translating (with Kenneth Maly) Heidegger's *Beiträge zur Philosophie (Vom Ereignis)* (GA 65), about which he has recently contributed an article to *The Encyclopedia of Philosophy Supplement*.

Véronique M. Fóti is Associate Professor of Philosophy at Pennsylvania State University. She does research on phenomenology and existentialism, contemporary European philosophy, the history of philosophy, and Heidegger. She has authored *Heidegger and the Poets: Poiesis, Sophia, Techne* and has edited *Merleau-Ponty: Difference, Materiality, Painting*.

Hans-Georg Gadamer is Professor Emeritus at Heidelberg Universität and is the author of *Truth and Method*; *Hegel's Dialectic*; *Philosophical Apprenticeships*; *Reason in the Age of Science*; *The Relevance of the Beautiful*; *Heidegger's Ways*; *Literature and Philosophy in Dialogue*; and *On Education, Poetry and History*.

Martin Heidegger was born in Messkirch, Baden, in 1889, and he died in 1976. Prior to his philosophical studies, he studied for the priesthood at the Albert-Ludwig University in Freiburg, which he later abandoned. He received his Doctorate in Philosophy under Schneider and Rickert. In 1919, he became Husserl's assistant at the University of Freiburg. In 1923, he began teaching at the University of Marburg. With Heidegger's background in phenomenology he taught phenomenological interpretations of classical philosophy; he taught courses on the Presocratics, Plato, Aristotle, Augustine, Aquinas, Descartes, Kant, Hegel, and Husserl. From the publication of his first work, *Being and Time*, in 1927, he was propelled into philosophical celebrity. In 1928, he became Professor of Philosophy at the University of Freiburg. He became Rector of this university in 1933, under the rule of the National Socialist Party (which Heidegger joined in that year); he resigned his Rectorship in the following year. He continued teaching courses on classical philosophy and now included extended readings of Hölderlin's poetry, the problem of modern science and technology, and Nietzsche's philosophy. In addition to his teaching, Heidegger had continually published essays, from his early years onward, raising the question of being in a variety of philosophical ways, exploring our philosophical relation to the tradition of philosophy, re-thinking the modern period, questioning the metaphysical issues involved in technology, and formulating the contemporary task of thinking. Heidegger's lecture courses, seminars, and essays are now being published in his multi-volume, *Gesamtausgabe*.

David C. Jacobs is Assistant Professor of Philosophy at the University of Tennessee at Chattanooga. He co-edited "Heidegger and the Political" (*Graduate Faculty Philosophy Journal*, 1991). His research centers on ancient Greek philosophy and nineteenth and twentieth-century continental thought. He has written on Parmenides, Nietzsche, and Heidegger, and more recently his work examines the role of the human body in the history of philosophy.

David Farrell Krell is Professor of Philosophy at DePaul University in Chicago. His books include *Infectious Nietzsche; Lunar Voices: Of Tragedy, Poetry, Fiction, and Thought; Daimon Life: Heidegger and Life-Philosophy; Of Memory, Reminiscence, and Writing: On the Verge; Postponements: Woman, Sensuality, and Death in Nietzsche;* and *Intimations of Mortality: Time, Truth, and Finitude in Heidegger's Thinking of Being*. He is editor and translator of a wide range of books and articles in German and French thought and letters and the author of two novels, *Nietzsche* and *Son of Spirit*.

Michael Naas is Associate Professor of Philosophy at DePaul University in Chicago. He has written numerous articles on Ancient Greek literature and philosophy and on contemporary French thought. He is the author of *Turning: From Persuasion to Philosophy* (Humanities Press, 1995) and is the co-translator of Jacques Derrida's *The Other Heading* (Indiana University Press, 1992) and *Memoirs of the Blind* (University of Chicago Press, 1993), as well as Jean-François Lyotard's *Hyphen: The Judeo-Christian Connection* (Humanities Press, forthcoming).

John Sallis is Liberal Arts Professor of Philosophy at Pennsylvania State University. He is the author of numerous books, including, most recently, *Double Truth; Stone; Crossings: Nietzsche and the Space of Tragedy; Echoes: After Heidegger; Spacings—Of Reason and Imagination;* and *Delimitations: Phenomenology and the End of Metaphysics*.

Dennis J. Schmidt is Professor of Philosophy at Villanova University and serves as editor of the Series of Continental Philosophy at SUNY Press. He is the author of *The Ubiquity of the Finite* and *On Germans and Other Greeks* (forthcoming), the translator of Bloch's *Natural Law and Human Dignity*, and editor of *Hermeneutics and the Poetic Motion*. He has also written essays on art, literary criticism, ancient philosophy, and post-Kantian continental philosophy.

Charles E. Scott is Edwin Erle Sparks Professor of Philosophy at Pennsylvania State University. His recent books are *The Question of Ethics* and *On the Advantages and Disadvantages of Ethics and Politics.*

Michel Serres is Professor of the History of Science at the University of Paris-I (Sorbonne) and Professor of French at Stanford University, was elected to the Académie Française in 1990, and has authored nearly thirty books. He has written on classical philosophy, the origin of the natural sciences, the indeterminacies, order, and chaos within scientific investigation, the relation between the sciences and the humanities, and the relationship between science, natural conceptual frameworks, information, and power. His books include *Le Système de Leibniz et Ses Modèles Mathématiques; Hermes I* through *Hermes V; Angels: A Modern Myth; Atlas; Rome: A Book of Foundations; Les Cinq Sens; The Natural Contract;* and a book of interviews with Bruno Latour, *Conversations on Science, Culture and Time.*

Index